REMEMBERING
Horowitz

Also by David Dubal

Reflections from the Keyboard
The Art of the Piano
Conversations with Menuhin
Evenings with Horowitz

REMEMBERING
Horowitz

125 Pianists Recall a Legend

Compiled and Edited by
DAVID DUBAL

SCHIRMER BOOKS
An Imprint of Simon & Schuster Macmillan
NEW YORK

Prentice Hall International
LONDON MEXICO CITY NEW DELHI SINGAPORE SYDNEY TORONTO

Schirmer Books
An Imprint of Simon & Schuster Macmillan
866 Third Avenue, New York, N.Y. 10022

Library of Congress Catalog Card Number: 93-13630

Schirmer Books paperback edition 1995

Printed in the United States of America

printing number
1 2 3 4 5 6 7 8 9 10

Library of Congress Cataloging-in-Publication Data

Remembering Horowitz : 125 pianists recall a legend/compiled and edited by David Dubal.
p. cm.
Includes index.
ISBN 0-02-87-0676-5 (hardc)
ISBN 0-02-860269-2 (pbk)
1. Horowitz, Vladimir 1903-1989. I. Dubal, David.
ML417.H8R45 1993
786.2'092—dc20
[B]

93-13630
CIP
MN

This paper meets the requirements of ANSI/NISO Z39.48-1992 (Permanence of Paper).

For
Jack and Alice Ormut
with gratitude and love

Contents

Illustrations follow pages 114 and 226.

CD Program Information

1.	Introduction	6:13
2.	Scarlatti	4:17
3.	Clementi	2:11
4.	Beethoven; Czerny	1:37
5.	Schubert	2:06
6.	Schumann	2:03
7.	Chopin	3:55
8.	Liszt; Brahms	7:21
9.	Rachmaninoff	4:02
10.	Scriabin; Prokofiev	6:16
11.	Transcriptions	5:23
12.	Orchestral Music	1:19
13.	Spontaneity and Contrast	1:30
14.	Practice, Recording, Performing	4:26
15.	The Instrument	2:23
16.	Early Years	7:21
17.	The Debut	2:44
18.	Epilogue	0:39

Postproduction by Leszek Wojcik, Carnegie Hall Recording Studio

Preface

When Vladimir Horowitz died in 1989, the whole pianistic world reeled. Horowitz was the yardstick of pianistic prowess for most of the twentieth century. Not since Liszt and Paderewski had any pianist created such a legend. When he condescended to perform, lines formed days in advance. He sold more records than any other classical artist, and his recordings, constantly in print for more than half a century, are unique documents in the art of piano playing.

Arguably the outstanding pianist of the age, Horowitz enlarged the scope of piano playing itself. Called a sorcerer, a magician, and a trickster by his peers, he changed forever the way the piano is played, conjuring in the mind's ear the spectrum of an orchestra and the expressive beauty of the greatest singing. Pianists may not find congenial everything that Horowitz played, but, like him or not, every pianist in the world must come to terms with his achievement.

For this reason, I felt it would be valuable to create a record of Horowitz's artistic personality as it was and is experienced by the pianists themselves, his peers and colleagues. Such is the purpose of the present volume.

* * *

I want to thank the pianists who took their time to write essays for this book. They were invariably cooperative, and it was a labor of love for them. Talking to them, I understood how important Horowitz had loomed in their lives. The book is not only a homage to Horowitz, but it shows the goodwill of the pianistic community.

As I had limited time, I could not ask every important member of the pianistic profession to contribute. But it was my intention to present a wide overview of the piano world, including well-known teacher-performers. I asked many that I knew would contribute good essays. In all, I contacted around 175 pianists. These artists are among the busiest people in the world, and about twenty of them simply did not have the time and energy, or were in poor health. Several that I expected would love to write essays never answered. In the case of some pianists, I wrote, faxed, or phoned up to a dozen times, taking the risk of being a nuisance—but with no answer. In the case of a few who were Horowitz admirers I was surprised that they declined. A few others simply were not Horowitz fans; one famous virtuoso wrote saying he did not write about cults, and another even more celebrated pianist wrote that he did not deal in mythologies, forgetting that mystery and legend are not a negligible aspect of the performing art. The majority of refusals came from those who said they were literally incapable of putting into words what the phenomenon of Horowitz meant to them.

It has been my privilege to know Vladimir Horowitz, and to show him to others in a light that might not otherwise have been shed. I venture to hope that, in this collection of essays, those who have contributed will help to illuminate not only Horowitz's artistry but also their own.

Acknowledgments

I want to thank my agent, Richard Curtis, who asked if there was another Horowitz book in me besides my *Evenings with Horowitz.* I emphatically said, "No. But there is a book of essays by other pianists about Horowitz." The idea was quickly appreciated by the editor-in-chief of Schirmer books, Maribeth Anderson Payne, who acquired the project for Schirmer, and who has encouraged me throughout the task. Her professional skills are of the highest, and she gave me much valuable guidance. I wish to thank Schirmer's editor, Jonathan Wiener, who has helped in many directions beyond the call of duty. His sensitivity to the book is deeply appreciated. Also my thanks at Schirmer's to their fine production supervisor Jane Andrassi as well as to Scott Hoerle, David Schulenberg, Elizabeth Halleron, Ellen Greenberg, and Soo Mee Kwon.

Thanks also go to Marco Praderio, Ju-Ying Song, Stella Simakova, and Agnes Bruneau for their help in translating several of the pieces.

Others who contributed help are Richard Probst, Richard Cionco, Giselle Guibord, Philicia Gilbert, Constance Schuman, Judith Kurz, Josephine Hemsing, Dan Cameron, Patricia Kelly, Lola Cantor, Susan Tilley, Christian Steiner, Julian Kreeger, Pavel Berman, Brenda Brilliant, Barbara Wing, Daniel Gorgoglione, Maxim Gershunoff, Jay K. Hoffman, Joanne Rile, Patrich Widhalm, Hans Boon, Michael Davis, Thomas Thompson, Claudette Sorel, Cynthia Herbst, Shirley Kirshbaum, Kingsly Day, Sarah Davies, and Shawn Randall.

A special thank you to Peter Goodrich at Steinway & Sons for many favors, including the use of photographs of Horowitz.

I am indebted to Leszek Wojcik for his superb editing in creating the CD of some of my conversations with Horowitz.

ACKNOWLEDGMENTS

For permission to reprint Vladimir Feltsman's essay, I am grateful to James Rohner, publisher of *Clavier* magazine.

Above all, my gratitude goes to Eri Ikezi, whose organizational and editorial skills are considerable. It was her fortitude that made the volume possible.

Introduction

Horowitz was called the "last Romantic" so frequently that this appellation became a cliché. But what does the phrase mean? Was Horowitz a musical anachronism, appealing nostalgically to music lovers who now receive a different kind of music making? Are we living in a culture that differs from the world Horowitz was born to?

Horowitz lived part of his long life during the final years of the so-called Golden Age of Pianists, a period of about one hundred years, beginning around 1830 when the finishing touches were being made on the "modern" piano. During this time, the virtuoso pianist was glorified, and the piano was the major medium of musical literacy—the most widely disseminated musical instrument in history. Countless people played the piano; a house was not a home without its piano in the parlor.

The piano's literature from Beethoven to Debussy was more or less composed during this brief period, and most of the composers were themselves pianists, playing their highly colored music with great freedom. Major differences in interpretation between pianists were expected. When Liszt played Schumann's Fantasy for the composer, Schumann thrilled to the unexpected aspects of the work that Liszt brought forth. Chopin asserted, "I should like to rob Liszt of the way he plays my own etudes." Connoisseurs of piano playing proudly boasted that they could tell their favorite pianists even if blindfolded, merely by hearing a phrase or two. Anton Rubinstein said, "I miss enough notes in a recital to make another recital." Those wrong notes did not occur because of a lack of technique, but because his playing, as James Huneker wrote, was "volcanic. He was as torrid as midday in the tropics." Rubinstein's wrong notes were "inspired." They sprang from an overflow of temperament, from taking chances. Today, when most of our listening to music is through recordings, we cringe at the repeated hearing of any imperfections. Liszt, Chopin, Clara Schumann, Tausig, von Bülow, Friedheim, Scharwenka, Sauer, Sofie Menter, Teresa Carreño, and dozens of others were tumultuous virtuosi, each with a highly charged personality.

In the 1870s alone—a generation before Horowitz—Godowsky, Scriabin, Lhévinne, Bauer, Dohnányi, Rachmaninoff, Gabrilowitsch, Cortot, Landowska, Viñes, Hofmann and a host of others were born. It was to this tradition of creative pianism that Horowitz belonged. But during the last four decades of his life, the performance of music became much more standardized and far less creative in the hands of many interpreters attempting to be faithful to the composers' wishes. This respectful attitude, combined with the aridity of recording, made piano playing much less variable, less reckless. This type of music making was applauded by many music lovers who felt that the excesses in which Romantic pianists indulged had exceeded legitimate stylistic limits. Horowitz's blazing temperament, his reliance on the instinctive, his lack of respect for certain textual matters divided him against his more conservative colleagues. However, Horowitz's greatness was universally acknowledged, and the public adored him extravagantly. He continued to flaunt his individuality, playing as a law unto himself. If individuality and fierce personal convictions about each work spell "Romantic," then Horowitz was indeed the "last Romantic." At one of his recitals, a piano teacher said to me, "With such eccentric and bizarre playing, Horowitz would not get past the first round in a piano competition, and he misses notes, too." Such is our age. It is significant that Horowitz states in his last will and testament that there is never to be a piano competition in his name.

When reading the essays in this book, one is struck by how many of these sensitive artists saw the danger of imitating Horowitz, even though he did not represent the musical values of our time. His power was indeed persuasive, and to the young often overwhelming. If imitation is the sincerest form of flattery, than not since Liszt has any pianist been so emulated. Of course, imitation is feeble and superficial. But Horowitz's imitators were not attempting just to duplicate an idol; they were unconsciously trying to re-create a past age. They failed because they were not Horowitz, and they sounded silly trying to be godlike virtuosi in a prosaic, cheerless era. Those who blatantly imitated Horowitz remained confused and were musically destroyed. How does one follow the letter of the score and still attain the dionysian rapture of a Horowitz? Their teachers taught them to be good, cautious musicians, not virtuoso-gods.

For Horowitz, there was only one worthwhile tradition, the recreation of a composition as if he was the composer himself. He laughingly resented anyone playing his repertoire; each piece he worked on became his obsession, as if he owned it or had composed it. He disliked it when anyone tried to play his transcriptions, refusing to write them down and declining any publisher's offer. Horowitz on stage possessed the white heat of creation. With such intensity, he was able to make an audience red-hot. He did this as only Liszt, Rubinstein, Rachmaninoff, Grainger, D'Albert, Hofmann, Schnabel, Paderewski, Rosenthal, and Busoni had done. Each of these giants was also a composer.

Let me examine just a few of the reasons why Horowitz in his later years was the "last Romantic." Horowitz was born in 1903, the year of the birth of flight. Liszt, perhaps the greatest executant artist in history, had died only seventeen years earlier. Anton Rubinstein, the second most celebrated pianist, had died only nine years before. Liszt had been undoubtedly the most famous person in Europe, his life the culmination of a century that had deified great artists. When Beethoven died, Vienna grieved. Nearly thirty thousand people walked in his funeral cortege. Chopin died in 1849; the Madeleine in Paris was jammed. With Wagner's death in Venice, thousands were bereft. In 1901, when Verdi passed on, he was an Italian senator and a national treasure. In 1896, Sir Charles Hallé died and thousands lined the streets to say farewell to the conductor who had created the city of Manchester's orchestra. The century was rich not only in its glorious creative fertility but in the creation of countless cultural institutions, conservatories, halls, museums, and orchestras.

When Horowitz died, the piano itself and the institution of the solo recital had started to decline. At the beginning of his life, art was still a cherished ingredient of civilized life. For many in the nineteenth century, art had replaced religion. Art was felt to be the supreme and enlightened manifestation of the human spirit, and "all art aspired to the condition of music." Concerning Wagner's operas, Alan Bloom notes in his book *The Closing of the American Mind*, "They had the Religious sense that Wagner was creating the meaning of life and that they were not merely listening to his works but experiencing that meaning." In 1911, the child Horowitz played for the great pianist-composer Alexander Scriabin, an artist who thought of himself as the Messiah, his music a catalyst to purify the world. Scriabin told Horowitz that he would certainly become a pianist, but that his mission was to become a cultured man in many ways, to delve deeply into all the arts. Horowitz never tired of telling of this meeting with Scriabin.

Horowitz grew up in Western society at a time when high culture still held immense prestige. Katherine Anne Porter wrote, "There was the unchallenged assumption that Classic culture was their birthright; the belief that knowledge of great art and great thought was a good in itself not to be missed for anything." However, the rot had already set in. In the very year of Horowitz's birth, Rachmaninoff went to play for Tolstoy, who chastised him for playing music that was too sophisticated for "the people." "Play simple music, easily understood," the great writer-prophet exhorted. The twentieth century would put Tolstoy's words into action in a way he never anticipated, harnessing the power of commercialism to the manufacture of a vast "pop culture" that comes ever closer to displacing the tradition of high art in our society. One evening, Horowitz pointed to a *New York Times* ad where his recordings were offered next to those of Elvis and Michael Jackson. He said, "I doubt there will be piano recitals in fifty or a hundred years."

Horowitz was born at the divide between two worlds: the Victorian producer–work-ethic culture, where a great many things were still made by hand and where craftsmanship was valued according to its quality; and a world of commercial consumerism, where business and economics within a technological frame created an almost entirely passive population ready to purchase anything and everything, from the newest brand of potato chip to a minor Picasso at sixty million dollars. The piano itself provides an eloquent example of this transformation, as Arthur Loesser wrote in *Men, Women and Pianos*:

> The Piano's decline was the Twentieth-Century fate of any object, or any publication, or performance, or idea that cannot be sold quickly to scores of millions of people. Pianos are made by machinery, but they cannot call forth the machine's fuller potentialities. . . . Good machines must give way to better, those that make things for a million are thrust aside for those that can produce for a hundred million, while the supplying of mere thousands becomes an act of charity or of eccentric devotion. The logic of the machine, then, colors all sense of values and all ethics of human relations. People acquire not what they might want for themselves, but what machines can most conveniently and profitably make in the largest amounts.

When Horowitz was a boy, there were many excellent piano builders flourishing in Europe and America. Horowitz was six years old in 1909, when the United States with its more than 300 piano builders manufactured over 370,000 pianos. Thousands of mothers bought new sheet music monthly, and played and sang to their children, who in turn took lessons. The decline had begun by the teens of the century, but nobody knew it. Thousands attempted Paderewski's Minuet in G. The critic James Huneker, living in Brooklyn, reported the din coming from every apartment, where Flatbush flappers happily pounded Rachmaninoff's C-sharp minor Prelude. When Paderewski appeared in his private railroad car in a small Midwestern town, a brass band would strike up his minuet. The mayor would make a speech. The lion-pianist had arrived, bringing culture. The men were awed, the women agog. Mystery and romance lurked in his noble feline gestures. Paderewski, soon to become the first president of his downtrodden Poland, played Chopin and people wept.

Amateur piano playing was still very much alive. People went to hear their favorite pianists and returned home to ape their betters, attempting some of the works the masters played. But the machines would soon devaluate the concept of playing music for oneself. Record players and player pianos were becoming forces that would help dethrone home music making. The idea of hard work and laborious practicing was undermined. A consumer culture rather than a producing culture would relentlessly triumph. Amateur music making was greatly weakened, and music performance became an increasingly professional matter. The band master and "March King," John Philip Sousa, predicted as early as 1906 that "canned music" would destroy amateurism and would produce a marked deterioration in musical taste.

Already by 1914, more than 500,000 phonographs were being produced annually in the United States, as compared to 323,000 pianos made that year. An advertisement in 1913 for Victor talking machines described the phonograph as a musical instrument, like a piano, "more than a piano, it is orchestra if you want it; band if you want it, piano if you want it; voice if you want it. And it plays itself. It is not like an idle piano standing around with nobody to play it."

An ad for the pianola, a reproducing mechanism, read, "The amount of practice necessarily required to become a finished artistic pianist is discouraging. The pianola is a substitute for the human fingers." What a contrast to the great pianist Hans von Bülow, who said, "I crucify, like a good Christ, the flesh of my fingers, in order to make them obedient, submissive machines to the mind, as a pianist must."

Naturally, pianists were quickly persuaded to cash in through recordings. Many were skeptical of entrusting their art to a machine. After all, the essence of a Romantic musician was spontaneity, the adventure of the moment. Many were terrified that they would lose their individuality, although the lure of immortalizing their art was powerful. However, by the 1920s, with radio and electrical recording introduced in 1925, making recordings was becoming an important adjunct to a career. The institution of recorded music would irrevocably transform the relationship between performer and audience that made it possible for a virtuoso like Horowitz to exist. Yet, in the first year Horowitz came to the United States, he, too, traveled to the RCA studio in Camden, New Jersey, to make records.

In 1925, Horowitz escaped from Soviet Russia. The 1917 revolution stunted his education and destroyed his ambition to be a composer. His family dropped into poverty and he became the main support of a demoralized household. He performed continuously from around 1919, and during 1925–28 he conquered the European audience. At the end of three years of concertizing he was still poor. He felt his only hope was the American dollar. Dozens of European pianists had made America their home. The impresario Arthur Judson signed Horowitz for an American tour early in 1928.

The success of Horowitz's orchestral and solo debuts at Carnegie Hall was overwhelming. After New York, he toured the rest of the country to great acclaim. America and Horowitz clicked. He liked the young country's brash materialism and its simplistic, optimistic view of life. In return, American audiences were struck by the unbridled passion of Horowitz's Third Concerto of Rachmaninoff and his Tchaikovsky Concerto. These two works were his inseparable musical baggage. In 1980, when I interviewed Horowitz, he discussed his arrival in his future home. "When I had my success here," Horowitz said, "it was wonderful! Everybody here was playing to sold-out houses: Rachmaninoff, Paderewski, Hofmann, Iturbi, Novaes, Schnabel, Lhévinne, Myra Hess, Gieseking, Friedman, Backhaus. It was an amazing time, and they were all there at my debut. They liked me right away."

After hearing his debut in January 1928, a veteran pianist in the audience prophesied, "Our careers will never be the same." And he was right. The following year, the Great Depression hit, and Horowitz was one of the few performers who maintained a good portion of their former fees for the next several years. During the 1930s, Horowitz played in the United States and Europe until he was incapacitated by exhaustion and depression. In 1936, he took the first of his retirements; this one lasted two and a half years. Early that year, he played a concert on February 27 to a rave review by the difficult critic of the *Manchester Guardian*, Neville Cardus. Horowitz was soloist with the Hallé Orchestra under Malcolm Sargent. That evening, he played not only the Tchaikovsky Concerto, his war horse, but the Brahms D minor Concerto.

Cardus wrote:

> The playing in the Tchaikovsky Concerto was exquisite. . . . There are passages in the music of rapid figuration so delicately performed as they were by Horowitz they seem born of the purest fantasy. . . . Cascades of notes fell from the heights to the depths of the keyboard, and the orchestra tried in vain to match the pianist's ravishments.
>
> Horowitz is deepening in expression—musical expression—every day. His Brahms at this concert was not teuton, but by no means small. There was eloquence without effect and without the obvious classical attitude.

Horowitz was thirty-three years old, and had been playing nonstop for fifteen years. He had to recuperate. His health was precarious. He was a husband and father in 1934. He had married Wanda Toscanini, the daughter of the great conductor. In 1939 he returned to the concert stage, but when World War II made life impossible in Europe the family moved to New York.

During the war years, Horowitz barnstormed the United States, playing an endless succession of triumphant concerts as audiences stamped and screamed for his arrangement of *The Stars and Stripes Forever*. In those years he raised an enormous amount of money at War Bond Concerts. Horowitz seemed to tailor his playing to the American scene—sleek, skyscraper playing. He was often described during those years as an "Age of Steel" pianist. He started feeling alienated from his Romantic roots. Romantic piano playing seemed dead, and his colleagues were dying off: Lhévinne, Godowsky, de Pachmann, Rosenthal, Levitzki, Barère, Friedman, and Paderewski. When Rachmaninoff passed away in 1943, he felt desperate. Musical performance had acquired a new set of ideals. Toscanini said, "I don't want this crescendo, Beethoven wants it." When an orchestra player said that a Beethoven symphony was metaphysical, Toscanini retorted, "No, it's Allegro con brio."

Horowitz was again exhausted and ill; colitis and depression tortured him. It was an increasingly ugly society—atomic bombs, genocide, and television. In 1948, the long-playing record caused a revolution in music consumption. Like chewing gum, music became one more consumer item. In 1953, after fourteen years of steady concertizing, Horowitz could continue no longer. He quit. He was just forty-nine years old. In the following years, he rested, indulged himself, and lived the life of a recluse in his luxurious town house, surrounded by the paintings he had bought in the 1940s. During this period of revival, he started exploring a whole range of music that he had never had time for. He recorded a pioneering album of Clementi sonatas and, more important, he had the leisure to study the sum of Scriabin's piano music. Scriabin, who had practically disappeared from the repertoire, became his daily bread. The Horowitz-Scriabin symbiosis is one of the great chapters in the history of piano playing. Horowitz's recordings of Scriabin possess a devastating immediacy. Horowitz was in the grip of a powerful obsession. Scriabin and Horowitz, two mercurial playmates, their sexuality burning! Horowitz's Scriabin playing is eroticism at its most smoldering.

As the lonely years passed, the Horowitz mystique developed into a legend. A whole generation of postwar pianists had not heard him. For them, Horowitz was a beacon, a throwback to the halcyon days when a pianist was a Romantic hero; when a Paderewski could sign a peace treaty at Versailles for his nation; when Liszt, hearing the dreaded Czar Nicholas I talking while he played, had the courage to stop, saying, "Music herself should be silent when Nicholas speaks"; or when the Princess Metternich asked Liszt, "You gave concerts in Italy—did you do good business?" and Liszt replied, "Princess, I make music, not business," and left the room. To the young, Horowitz was their culture hero. He thumbed his nose at the world and did as he pleased. The young yearned to hear him play again. He had the aura of a superman.

Practically every pianist in the last half century had literally grown up on Horowitz's recordings. It is the most listened-to discography of any artist in history. Horowitz had an instinct for recording, and he understood how to deal with the impersonality of the medium. The recording process did not interfere with his sound as drastically as it did with that of some artists, and he was never afraid to record. There is little doubt that hearing Horowitz "live" went far beyond hearing his recordings. Yet his essence is clearly and vitally heard on records, unlike that of, say, Arthur Rubinstein, who made many fine recordings that do not compare to the inspiration of his recitals. Rubinstein, like Myra Hess and many others, was somewhat intimidated by recording.

Horowitz's recordings from the thirties and forties have survived despite their inferior sound. One can mention from this period his Czerny Variations on *La Ricordanza*, which displays dazzling finger control and a ravishing sense of early Romantic style. There are Tchaikovsky's Dumka and Dohnányi's F minor Caprice. The recording of the Sonata in E-flat by Haydn is a classic, and one must not miss his recordings of early Schumann, such as the *Traümeswirren* and especially the Presto passionato. His Liszt Sonata from 1932 is immortal and is much-discussed in these essays, as is the 1930 recording of the Rachmaninoff Third Concerto. Perhaps the most controversial of his recordings is the Mussorgsky *Pictures at an Exhibition*, which Horowitz substantially amplified in order to bring out what he felt Mussorgsky really wanted to say pianistically. Purists persist in hating it, and some have sarcastically commented that Horowitz put graffiti on the score. But this pianism is awesome in its impact—a force of nature—and is so perfectly Horowitzian in manner that it must be judged an extraordinary oddity, a pure melding of intention and realization.

From the thirties and forties there is a batch of Chopin, including feather-light elegance in the Fourth Scherzo. His Liszt Rhapsodies, with his own emendations, are supreme. His octaves in the Sixth Rhapsody are the octave playing that all others aspire to. Other great Liszt performances of that period include the piquant *Valse oubliée* No. 1; the *Sonetto 104 del Petrarca*, played with a burning passion; the cool and fragrant *Au bord d'une source;* and, most of all, Liszt's grief-stricken *Funérailles*. The range of nuance, the subtlety of his timing, the massive build-up of his left-hand octaves have made this work Horowitz's own. Other indispensable performances are Debussy's *Pour les arpèges composés*, the Poulenc Toccata, the Saint-Saëns *Danse macabre*, his bewitching *Carmen* Variations, and the transcription of Sousa's *Stars and Stripes Forever*, where Horowitz was called a one-man band. During the forties he recorded the Prokofiev Toccata and the Seventh Sonata. Hearing the recording of the sonata, Prokofiev sent Horowitz a copy of the score inscribed: "To the miraculous pianist from the composer." Other excursions into 1940s modernism are the wonderful recordings of Kabalevsky's Third

Sonata and the landmark performance of Samuel Barber's Sonata, of which he gave the world premiere.

These and other recordings make a formidable list, especially when one considers the thousands of electrical recordings on 78s made from 1930 through 1950 by dozens of pianists of whom very little has survived. Connoisseurs know something of Friedman, Hofmann, Lhévinne, Cortot, and Fischer, as well as the entire output of Rachmaninoff, Schnabel's historic Beethoven sonata cycle of the 1930s, and Lipatti's few recordings.

The Horowitz legend had grown to mythic proportions. Finally, on May 9, 1965, he played at Carnegie Hall his first recital in twelve years. Several pianists in this volume write about this concert and what it meant to them. Joseph Kalichstein describes it as "like Zeus coming down from Mount Olympus, performing miracles on Fifty-Seventh Street." Horowitz was 62 when he returned to the concert stage. He was to live for another quarter century, but never again would he undergo the constant stress and strain of endless performance and travel. He would ration his appearances self-protectively. Every concert was a major event, each town blessed by his appearance. Horowitz knew how to remain a legend, and his tantalized public remained fearful that each concert would be the last. Waiting through the night in long lines for the box office to open, they hoped not to miss the great artist. He had become the symbol of the piano; only Arthur Rubinstein could count on drawing full houses, while Glenn Gould had retired, Richter remained in Russia, and Michelangeli always cancelled. Rudolf Serkin and Claudio Arrau, Horowitz's great contemporaries also born in 1903, continued to perform. But the Horowitz glamour was invincible.

In 1969 he retired once again, this time for five years. He returned in November 1974 with the first piano recital ever given at the Metropolitan Opera House at Lincoln Center. The legend could now demand the highest fee in history for his recitals. In 1986 he startled everyone by announcing he would return to play in Russia. He had often said that he would never again see the land of his birth. His appearances in Moscow and Leningrad crowned his career. The Moscow recital was televised and heard by millions. The concert had a deep impact upon many. In his presence and performance, people seemed to feel a sense of loss. The world wanted to hold on to this old man. An old trouper, as he called himself, a troubadour still singing his songs to an unhappy world. But it was a moving moment in world history. Horowitz had returned at the beginning of the downfall of the hideous political system that he had fled sixty-three years before. He said he felt like an ambassador of peace. "Maybe people won't kill each other any more," he said. In Moscow he paid homage to Scriabin, dead since 1915, by playing at the Scriabin Museum. There the composer's daughter, still alive, heard the great pianist play on her father's piano.

Horowitz had long been an idol to Soviet pianists locked away from the world. His playing of Russian music was their yardstick of achievement. It is touching to read the essays by Slobodyanik, Berman, Viardo, Alexeev, Yablonskaya, and Feltsman. His short visit was like a sunburst. Vladimir Viardo writes, "The sense of freedom and communication was overwhelming. . . . I thought that we Russians were rigid in our mentality. Horowitz sort of exuberantly spread the seeds of a new approach to art."

After leaving Russia, he played to ovations in other capitals of Europe as well as in Tokyo. He was showered with ribbons and medals, and received the Presidential Medal of Freedom upon his return home. Back in New York, Horowitz resumed his passionate love affair with Mozart, and prepared for his Mozart concerto recording in the spring of 1987 in Milan. On December 14, 1986, his last concert in the United States took place at the Metropolitan Opera House. In 1987 he performed in Berlin, Hamburg, and Amsterdam, and gave his first concert in Vienna in fifty-three years. It was the last concert of his life. His technique was still miraculous. He lived another two years and had finished making a recording days before he died. The piano and its literature remained for him a never-ending adventure. The piano was all he wanted, all he needed.

Horowitz brought a sense of occasion to the concert stage. He was a master program-builder, and provided something special for everyone. He was as highly aware of an audience as he was of the acoustical properties of a concert hall. He knew that people did not come to a recital to be educated. An audience wants to be enthralled, to lose themselves for two hours, to transcend their isolated body and daily routine, to dream again of things charmed, and always to be amazed by daring technical feats.

Lazar Berman writes in his essay how grateful he is that Horowitz, throughout his career, always had his own instrument at his disposal. Few pianists are fortunate enough to have with them an instrument attuned to their spirit. I remember talking to Arthur Rubinstein about one of his recitals. "Ah, yes," he said, "I played well because I had my own piano with me." In January 1991 the House of

Steinway sent Horowitz's beloved piano (Concert Department 503) on a long tour, where it was shown at Steinway dealers in seventy-five cities. Peter Goodrich, director of concert's and artists for Steinway, had asked me to create a multimedia show entitled "Steinway Salutes Horowitz," and to play on the "Horowitz Steinway" during the program. During the piano's stay in each city, the dealers made time available for local pianists and students to play on the instrument for a short period. I was delighted to see the reverence that people had for Horowitz's piano. However, most of the time when I heard it being played it was banged unmercifully. Everyone was attempting Horowitzian storms. Even good pianists fell into the trap almost immediately, and most sounded unmusical.

As I was often alone with the piano, I soon realized that this instrument was Horowitz's creation. Over the years he had worked with Steinway's head technicians, Bill Hupfer and later Franz Mohr, to create a unique springy action. The instrument's sound, with its glassy, glittering upper register and mighty bass, became the ideal for many pianists. CD 503 was marvelously suited to the largest halls. The piano's sensitivity is extraordinary; Horowitz would say of his piano, "The humidity makes me miss notes, the piano is sluggish." I thought, "Ah, yes, the devil made him miss the notes." But I now know that the instrument is highly sensitive to climatic change, and if it is too humid the humidity plays havoc with the piano mechanism as well as with the pianist's preparation. Yet Horowitz's piano was beautifully suited to his unparallelled gift for variegated touch and nuance. The instrument is a tribute to his knowledge of his own special powers.

Good "modern" pianos after 1840 have pretty much a homogenized mechanism. The piano may be mellow or brilliant, but as long as it is properly voiced and regulated there will be no surprises if one knows the instrument well. Before the dissemination of the Paris-based Erard piano, which became the model for all concert pianos, piano builders differed greatly from one another, and individual pianos had distinct qualities. The performer had a greater ability to manipulate the instrument. Chopin, the last of the small-scale salon pianists, commented, "When I am feeling ill, I play on an Erard piano, where I easily find a ready-made tone. But when I feel in good form and strong enough to find my own individual sound, then I need a Pleyel piano."

Horowitz needed an individualized instrument with which his special sonority could flood concert halls with fountains of sound, but which would also enable him to create a variety of soft timbres. The Horowitz piano is not, as so many have speculated over the years, an instrument that plays itself. On the contrary, it is a piano that is highly temperamental, much more difficult to play than other Steinways. It is a piano on which one has to create every sound, and which demands time and study. With Horowitz, every note counted, thanks to his varied inflections within a phrase.

I feel this is an important volume. It is a summing up not only of what pianists feel and think about Horowitz, but about the art of piano playing as we conclude the twentieth century. Naturally, many of the essays discuss Horowitz's playing: his technique, color range, sonority, and repertoire. It is interesting to read what one pianist loves and another dislikes. Of course, not every essay is laudatory, and criticism occurs frequently. I had made it clear when talking to the contributors that they were to write from any point of view they wished. The essays vary in length, concentration, and quality, but I find something fascinating in every one of them. Above all, there is a feeling of "authenticity." These are thoughts about a pianist by pianists, not by critics who may not even know how to read or play music, and who have not the slightest idea of what it takes to go on stage to play professionally, let alone artistically.

These pianists have studied and taught the same works as did Horowitz. They speak from a depth of understanding about their instrument, its foibles, and its possibilities. Busoni said, "Take it for granted that the piano can do anything, even when it cannot." This was in a sense Horowitz's motto.

Liszt gave the first all-solo piano concerts in 1839, even coining the term "recital." There is still reason to believe that the institution will survive. At any rate, this book is a unique document about the man who dominated the piano for more than half a century, as Liszt did in the nineteenth century. I hope the book will be a pleasure for all those who admire the art of the incomparable and legendary Vladimir Horowitz.

Van Cliburn

Born in Shreveport, Louisiana, Van Cliburn studied with his mother until he was 17, when he entered the Juilliard School to work with Rosina Lhévinne. In 1954 he won the Leventritt Award and made his New York Philharmonic debut with Dimitri Mitropoulos conducting. In 1958 he was launched to world fame as the winner of the First Tchaikovsky Competition in Moscow. Upon his return to the United States, Cliburn was given a ticker-tape parade in New York. Annual world tours followed, along with a tremendous recording schedule. His RCA recording of the Tchaikovsky Concerto, with Kyril Kondrashin, quickly became an all-time best-seller. Other recordings followed: Rachmaninoff's Concerto No. 3, Prokofiev's Concerto No. 3, the MacDowell Concerto, the Barber, Prokofiev, Chopin, and Liszt sonatas, and many others.

In 1962, Van Cliburn gave his name and energy to the establishment of the Van Cliburn International Piano Competition.

In the history of the performance of classical music Mr. Horowitz will always be an indelibly unforgettable personage—master pianist, singing instrumentalist. His art sprang from the great Russian school of pianism that gave scope to melody, breadth to sound, and vision to a narrative.

My mother, Rildia Bee O'Bryan Cliburn, was enchanted to meet him in one of his early appearances in this country. Since she was a pupil of Arthur Friedheim, who was a pupil of Liszt, she was thrilled during their brief visit to hear him tell her about his association with Siloti (also a Liszt pupil and cousin of Rachmaninoff). When asked to describe Horowitz she said he was totally unique—a great pianist and a kind and gracious gentleman.

Later, I was fortunate to know him and his lovely wife, Wanda. Our visits, though relatively few, were punctuated with the most delightful repartee and cogent remembrances of the glorious musical days in Russia, Europe, and the world. He always expressed genuine concern and interest in the continuity of great musical traditions, as well as wishing to lend his support and inspiration to the outstanding young talents of the day. His knowledge of the wide spectrum of musical literature, including opera, which he loved, gave him the ability to perceive any musical composition regardless of length as a large canvas. In his view there were no small works of music, there were only grand conceptions.

His intense quest for beauty, not only in the musical arts, but also in the visual arts, was the fabric of his being. From the beginning of my life in music my mother told me about the Liszt school, which concentrated on making the piano a lyric instrument, striving always to envelop the listener with a beautiful sound. During a very spirited conversation over dinner one night, I remember the discussion that my mother and Mr. Horowitz were having about the use of the pedal with the illusion of sound and about the fact that the piano was always treated as a lyric instrument. His intuitive insight into certain of the great works revealed a very subjective approach to everything he did. That selfsame subjectivity was to be his greatest talent, which was communicating to millions of people.

Those of us who revere his memory and treasure his friendship will always be inspired by his great recorded legacy in sight and sound.

Gaby Casadesus

Gaby Casadesus was born in Marseilles. At the Paris Conservatoire, she won the first prize in piano. She played music by Fauré, Florent Schmitt, and Ravel under their personal guidance. When she married the great pianist Robert Casadesus, she joined her career with his and performed as a duo-piano team throughout the world. Their son, Jean Casadesus, was a distinguished pianist.

Gaby Casadesus's recorded output includes music of Fauré, Debussy, Ravel, and her late husband. Throughout her career, she has taught at the Fontainebleau School. She gives master classes at the Ravel Academy, and is frequently a judge in international competitions. She has been influential in the founding and maintenance of the Robert Casadesus Competition at the Cleveland Institute of Music, and has played with major orchestras as well as with Zino Francescatti, the Guarneri Quartet, the Juilliard Quartet, and many other chamber ensembles.

It was during the summer of 1935, in Salzburg, that Robert and I had a most pleasant meeting with Horowitz. We had long heard about this brilliant and successful Russian pianist, whose talent and charm had taken Paris by storm ever since his arrival, but our paths had never crossed.

After our concert at the Mozarteum, conducted by Bruno Walter, Toscanini very kindly invited us to lunch with his wife and his daughter, who had just married Horowitz. Robert and I felt extremely pleased and privileged to be at the Maestro's table, and to meet Horowitz himself. The conversation immediately turned to music and the piano repertoire. Horowitz seemed anxious to change his programs. He felt he should play more serious works, such as by Franck and even Fauré, as well as Bach, and perform fewer flamboyant pieces. Of course, Maestro Toscanini seemed delighted with this, and was interested and approving. We said our goodbyes, full of promises for many pleasant encounters in the future.

It was not until several years later that we finally heard Horowitz at a recital in Chicago. He thrilled us with a very eclectic program where he played, among others, some Scarlatti, a Beethoven sonata, and several Romantic works. For his encore, he played his own transcription of *Carmen,* which brought the audience to their feet. His technique was dazzling and so natural that it seemed effortless. One could not help but be captivated. Our only regret was that in spite of his lovely performance of Beethoven, the public preferred, above all, the showier side of this remarkable pianist.

I would not want to share these precious memories without mentioning another meeting, this time at Steinway Hall in New York. Robert was on tour, so I took my son, who was still young at the time but a future pianist, to a private concert to hear Horowitz present the premiere of the Barber Sonata. We had the good fortune to be seated in the front row, so we were very close to the pianist. We were astonished by the ease of Horowitz's piano playing. Despite the differences in sonority and strength, he gave the impression that, physically, nothing could stop him. Everything seemed simple, which is the proof of a great artist.

Santiago Rodriguez

Born in Cardenas, Cuba, Santiago Rodriguez came to the United States in 1961 at age nine. The following year, he played Mozart's Twenty-Seventh Concerto with the New Orleans Philharmonic. He studied at the University of Texas and the Juilliard School. In 1981 he was awarded the silver medal at the Van Cliburn Competition and was given a special prize for his performance of the competition's commissioned work, Bernstein's Touches. *In 1982 he received an Avery Fisher grant, and in 1986 he was the first recipient of the Shura Cherkassky Recital Award of New York's 92nd Street Y.*

Among Rodriguez's recordings for the Elan label are Surinach's Concertino, Castelnuovo-Tedesco's Piano Concerto No. 1, the Brahms-Paganini Variations, Book 2 of Debussy's Preludes, and an all-Spanish album.

Vladimir Horowitz was the most influential pianist of the twentieth century—for better and for worse. Many composers and their music found overdue acceptance by the musical establishment through his performances and recordings: Scriabin's etudes and late sonatas; Rachmaninoff's Third Concerto, Piano Sonata No. 2, and *Etudes-Tableaux;* Schumann's *Humoreske,* Sonata No. 3, *Blumenstück,* and *Arabeske;* Prokofiev's Sonata No. 7; the Barber Piano Sonata. Clementi sonatas and even Scarlatti sonatas achieved greater visibility and interest because Horowitz played them.

It was not just the works but also his manner of performance that became fashionable, for Horowitz's recitals were all hyphenated events: Beethoven-Horowitz, Schumann-Horowitz, Chopin-Horowitz. True, he almost never changed the actual notes on the page, but one always got the feeling that one was listening to a composition very heavily filtered through Horowitz. None of this "let the music speak for itself" nonsense. He challenged you with his playing, and you either loved it or hated it. But there was no ignoring it.

I always had the feeling that Horowitz performed only those works he cared for deeply and wished that he had composed himself. For me, that was a great lesson: Learn as much as possible but only perform those works which you truly love. So hypnotic and addictive was his physical command of the piano that many pianists have destroyed themselves physically and emotionally in their hysterical pursuit of the "Horowitzian Holy Grail." Some compositions have taken quite a beating as well. The Tchaikovsky Concerto, in particular, has been subjected to more pummelling by aspiring "felines of the invories" (except Van Cliburn) who hoped to duplicate the intensity of the Horowitz-Toscanini recordings. What was under Horowitz's hands a magical experience became just a lot of banging and flailing by the impostors. However, it is unjust to blame Horowitz, as some writers have done, for this wave of dexterous narcissism. There will always be more sheep than shepherds.

I heard him four times in public and probably heard every recording he ever made. As astonished and impressed as I was by Horowitz, however, I must confess that, down deep, I felt very little affection for his playing. I truly wished at times that I would get the feeling that this incredible pianist would tell me through his music, "I am glad to be alive and damn happy to be playing for you." However, his recording of the 1953 Carnegie Hall concert, including Scriabin's Ninth Sonata and Liszt's Second Rhapsody, as well as the encore album which includes some of his own arrangements, still remain for me some of the greatest piano playing I have ever heard.

Gabriel Tacchino

Gabriel Tacchino was born in Cannes. He studied at the Paris Conservatoire and won prizes at several competitions, including the Marguerite Long and the Busoni. He has been a frequent soloist with major orchestras in Europe and America, and has performed with Leinsdorf, Monteux, von Karajan, Dohnânyi, Martinon, Prêtre, and many others. He has recorded for Erato, Vox, and EMI, and has received various prizes for his discs.

Beside his work as soloist and recitalist, he is often heard in chamber music with Mady Mesple, Gary Hoffmann, Patrice Fontanarosa, and Jean-Pierre Rampal. Gabriel Tacchino teaches at the Paris Conservatoire and has given master classes in Korea and Japan.

From my youth, the Horowitz legend was always kept bright by the two most important teachers of my life, the wonderful pianist Jacques Février and Francis Poulenc. They both became Horowitz's intimate friends, and were his guides during his visits to Paris. They became an inexhaustible source of details concerning Horowitz's flamboyant personality, his piano technique, and his playing.

Février was fascinated by Horowitz's stage presence and his ability to project subtle and highly personalized musical ideas to the far reaches of any concert hall. This great power of projection cost the pianist a great deal of tension, just as his audiences had to listen on a higher level than usual. Février told me many Horowitz anecdotes, such as the card games that lasted far into the night, his care in choosing his ties and clothes, and his love for fine automobiles. All of this awed the young pianist that I was, and brought him closer to me.

As for Poulenc, he was completely spellbound by Horowitz's pianism, and the great composer particularly admired his sense of structure as a pianist as well as the logic and perfect mastery in Horowitz's transcriptions. Poulenc told me that he hardly recognized his Toccata (dedicated to Horowitz) under Horowitz's fingers, so completely had the pianist imbued it with his own personality. Poulenc wrote for me on the Toccata's first page, "For Tacchino who will play this Toccata 'alla Volodya'." This was a perpetual encouragement for me, and I still think of it when I perform the piece in public.

Poulenc and Février were, of course, extraordinary musicians, and it fascinated me that both of them were so overwhelmed by Horowitz. Seldom did a lesson go by that Février did not utter Horowitz's name in relation to an octave or double-note passage, or how he brought out a phrase or produced a special color. Although Horowitz no longer played in Paris, I somehow felt that I was keeping in "contact" with him. Only later with more maturity did I realize completely Février and Poulenc's fascination with Horowitz. Horowitz's pianism was complex, as was his musical being. It was through him that a great part of the twentieth century could realize the meaning of what could be accomplished in the realm of technical mastery. Horowitz knew how to infuse new life into the piano. His success will be encouragement for all pianists in the future.

James Tocco

James Tocco was born in Detroit, Michigan, and began studying piano at 6. In Paris he studied with Magda Tagliaferro and in New York with Claudio Arrau. In 1973 he won the International Competition in Munich.

Tocco has been a busy recording artist in a diversified repertoire. He has recorded for Gasparo the Chopin preludes, the four piano sonatas of MacDowell, and the complete piano music of Griffes. For Pro Arte he made the world-premiere disc of Bernstein's complete solo music and a recording of Copland. Recently Deutsch Harmonica Mundi released his complete Bach–Liszt organ transcriptions. He premiered John Corigliano's Etude-Fantasy, *and has performed the Corigliano Concerto with the Louisville, Atlanta, San Diego, and Detroit Symphonies. Tocco is artist-in-residence at the University of Cincinnati Conservatory of Music, and professor of piano at the Musikhochschule in Lübeck.*

In 1953, just about the time that Vladimir Horowitz had decided to abandon the concert stage, I began to study with a Russian piano teacher in Detroit, Boris Maximovich (he was really from Ukraine, but we didn't make such distinctions then). I was all of ten years old, had been playing the piano for about six years, and taking lessons for four of those. The first thing I had to do under my new teacher was get rid of the bad habits that literally cramped my style. Maximovich was a patient and exacting pedagogue. Though the work was tedious, involving many hours of exercises, scales, Hanon, and Czerny, it paid off. I acquired a disciplined technique, and could play the piano fluently, without paralysis. (There are certain things one should never take for granted!)

My family was strictly blue-collar, with no other musicians, so we had neither the means nor the tradition of regularly subscribing to the symphony or any of the recital or chamber music series then available in the area. I relied heavily on radio performances (the Met on Saturdays, the New York Philharmonic on Sundays) and records to acquaint myself with the great artists of the time. After I started to work part-time in high school, I would spend much of my modest income on records and concert tickets. I became the proud holder of a season subscription to the Detroit Symphony Orchestra (student ticket, last row in the balcony—twenty concerts for $25!). These concerts, and the occasional recitals of visiting artists, were the mainstay of my musical life. Among the many pianists I can remember hearing then were many grand masters: Rubinstein, Richter, Arrau, Serkin, Bachauer, Casadesus, Gilels.

There was, however, one pianist conspicuously missing from the scene: Vladimir Horowitz. During my years of tutelage, Maximovich would regularly have me listen to the latest additions to his record collection, and every new batch would include a release by Horowitz. I was excited not just by the recordings themselves, but because Maximovich claimed a sort of musical parentage with Horowitz: Maximovich's teacher, Simon Barère, had studied in Odessa with Horowitz's teacher, the legendary Felix Blumenfeld. In any event, there was not a single Horowitz recording during those years that I did not hear, often repeatedly, and usually with extensive commentary—music of Chopin, Beethoven, Scriabin, Prokofiev, the premiere recording of the Barber Sonata (a revelation!), and, above all, what I still consider the single greatest piano record ever made, the twelve Scarlatti sonatas recorded for CBS in the early sixties. Horowitz to me was this great disembodied presence whose strange and wonderful sounds welled up over the fifteen-inch Electro Voice loudspeakers of my teacher's living room. The typical jacket-cover portrait of him in elegant formal attire, sitting on a Louis XVI armchair, holding a closed score, only made the alienation more intense. Somehow I could never imagine this stilted, foppish person actually sitting at an instrument and playing *that* way. When I listened to the recorded performances, a demonic and disheveled enfant terrible sprang up in my mind. I saw arms and legs flailing, a writhing torso, hair flying about (I often thought, if you took away the professorial wire-rim specs and gave him a head of hair, Rudolf Serkin in performance *looked* the way Horowitz *sounded*). In any event, my imagination painted a certain picture of Horowitz and fleshed it in, in amazing detail.

During the first years of his tenuous comeback, in the mid-sixties, I was studying in Paris. He played only a handful of performances and refused to travel abroad (his fear of flying and famous dietary foibles were cited in all the press accounts), so I had no chance to see or hear him live until my return to the States. In 1968, while I was attending the University of Wisconsin on a senior fellowship, Horowitz gave a one-hour recital on network TV. It was a watershed event, the chance at last to hear the legend live, and to see him close-up to boot. Two things hit me right off the bat: the quietness of his demeanor at the piano and the strangeness of his technique. All the assumptions I had made about Horowitz during those many years of listening to records were shattered. Here was someone who played with near total abandon, *yet scarcely moved!* Moreover, after being led to believe that I was a direct descendant of the fabled line of pianism of Barère and Horowitz, I came face to face with its living embodiment, only to find an approach to the instrument that was *the absolute negation of everything I had been taught!* He broke all the rules. Perhaps it was this visual shock that made me, for the first time, view Horowitz with a certain objectivity and come to grips with what I was hearing as well: a style of music-making that defied logic and made up its own rules, a style so willful that it related to nothing in my musical education. The experience was keenly disappointing to me. (I later found out that listening to Horowitz play on a seventeen-inch TV with a tiny monaural speaker is akin to experiencing the Atlantic Ocean in a bucket of seawater.)

With the passing of my student years, I began to concentrate more consciously on the development of my own style. My veneration of the great piano giants abated. Recordings took on much less importance to me than live concerts, and I attended these concerts with a far more critical ear than before. I studiously excised what I felt were imitative tendencies in my playing and avoided contacts that I thought would be "damaging." One day, in the mid seventies, I found myself in the Steinway basement after hours, practicing in a studio adjoining the room where the concert pianos were kept. Suddenly David Rubin, the director of Steinway's concert and artists department, came into the room to ask if I would take a break for about a quarter of an hour. Then he led me out to greet none other than Horowitz himself, in the company of his wife, Wanda, and Franz Mohr, the head technician for Steinway. He had come to check on the condition of "his" piano. I mumbled something about what an honor etc., lied that I had already finished my practicing, and fled the premises. That was to be my one and only meeting with the mother of all pianistic legends.

Not long afterward, in 1976, I finally had the chance to hear Horowitz live in recital at Carnegie Hall. I remember that the hall was electric with excitement. Looking around one could see the familiar faces of musicians who were celebrities in their own right. There was a sense that something important was about to take place. Nevertheless, I was determined to maintain my critical objectivity, and viewed the proceedings with a certain degree of skepticism. While I was perusing the specially printed, oversize program notes, a gentleman on my left leaned over to me and asked, "Did you ever in all your life read such garbage?" Since in fact I hadn't, I readily nodded my consent. "I wrote it," said my neighbor gleefully. He turned out to be Marvin Saines, then president of CBS Records. With egg on my face, I thought to myself, "Well, I really didn't want a recording contract anyway." Good thing, too, because I never got one from CBS. . . .

Finally Horowitz appeared, sat down, and, without fuss, began to play the Clementi F-sharp minor Sonata. It was like nothing I had ever heard before. From the first meltingly beautiful tones to the last excited flourish, I was held in thrall to a kaleidoscope of colors and an incredible gamut of emotions. It was as though for the very first time I was hearing what a piano was capable of. Never had I heard such dynamics. In the *Kinderscenen* of Schumann, Horowitz would at times play down to a triple piano, without losing a single note, *and still make a diminuendo!* In the Scriabin Fifth Sonata that followed, and especially in the last encore—the finale of the Rachmaninoff B-flat minor Sonata—he unleashed the Furies and drove the instrument to triple and quadruple forte, yet still managed to muster even more force for the sforzato accents. The way the sound was layered and textured, the ravishing use of the pedals, all this was a revelation. And in the Chopin group that comprised the entire second half of the program, I was taken by the freshness of Horowitz's approach, finding the most unusual and daring voice-leadings, employing a freedom of movement and liberating the music from the tyranny of the printed page, creating an intensely personal statement, even at the risk of offending or being called contrived. Horowitz did not so much defy logic as transcend it.

All of this could only really be hinted at in the many studio recordings of his retirement years or in the later recordings from his live concerts. It was certainly missing from the telecast performance

I had witnessed. That single concert I attended in Carnegie Hall remains one of the most thrilling and significant events I have ever attended; and I am convinced that to have experienced Horowitz in any way other than in the hall at a live concert is not really to have heard him at all. Sorry to say, I never had another chance. The recordings from his last years saddened me, as it seemed to me he was very much in decline. Then, with the broadcast of his moving return to Moscow, he seemed again to have found that spark and spontaneity—and mastery—of earlier days. Whether because the technical sound of this telecast was superior to the earlier one, or because I still had the aural image of the Horowitz sound from Carnegie Hall and projected it onto the TV image, the experience was most satisfying. I thought to myself, "This is the way I want to remember him." And then he was gone.

David Bar-Illan

Born in Haifa, David Bar-Illan's first major appearance on the international stage took place in his native Israel with the Israel Philharmonic conducted by Dimitri Mitropoulos, who urged Leonard Bernstein to engage him for appearances with the New York Philharmonic. Since then he has appeared with the major orchestras of the world. Bar-Illan gave the world premiere of Robert Starer's Third Piano Concerto with the Baltimore Symphony. As a recitalist, he was accorded the honor of giving the first piano recital at the John F. Kennedy Center in Washington, D.C. He was Pierre Boulez's first soloist with the New York Philharmonic. For the Audiofon label he has issued the Moszkowski Concerto, Weber's A-flat major Sonata, Schumann's G minor Sonata, and various works by Debussy, Chopin, and Schubert.

I was 12 when I first asked my father to name the greatest living pianist. It was 1942. World War II was raging, and the allies were retreating everywhere. Living in what was then the British Mandate of Palestine, later Israel, we were threatened by the Axis forces in Syria and Egypt and a hostile Arab population who had allied with the Nazis. With childish insouciance, however, I was more concerned with the trouble I was having with the presto of the Mendelssohn Fantasy, one of the pieces I was preparing for my annual recital, than with the almost daily air raids. And for reasons I cannot for the life of me reconstruct, I needed to know who the greatest pianist was. My father, an amateur pianist with an awe of Czerny and a passion for Brahms, answered in an instant. "Horowitz," he said, "Vladimir Horowitz."

It was a new name for me. Isolated from the world in those days, I knew the names of but a few international performers. Toscanini, who, with violinist Bronislaw Huberman founded the Palestine Symphony, now the Israel Philharmonic; pianist Benno Moiseiwitsch, whom I had heard in recital in an old gymnasium; and Artur Schnabel, whose 78-rpm discs of Beethoven sonatas were all we had in our record library.

Five years later, when I enrolled at the Juilliard, I found that my father's opinion was shared almost unanimously by my American colleagues. I thoroughly envied their acquaintance with Horowitz's playing in concert and on records. From then on, I heard virtually every Horowitz New York concert and every record and pirated recorded performance in existence. To say that I, too, now consider him the greatest pianist is to mock my own rejection of such titles. Artists are not athletes. They are unique, and they can neither be compared or measured. Yet that is how I would answer the question I posed to my father a half-century ago.

Perhaps I should qualify. Horowitz is not "the greatest." He is just not like any other pianist: the only virtuoso of our time who could be mentioned in the same breath with the two greatest composer-performers of the piano, Liszt and Rachmaninoff. That this is so has nothing to do with his formidable technique, nor with his legendary virtuosity, nor, as some cynics insist, with his marriage to Toscanini's daughter, nor with the elusiveness and mystery with which he surrounded himself. If by technique and virtuosity one refers to dazzle, speed, tonal beauty, and all-around mastery of the keyboard, there are pianists who can match him. And many more are better musicians. But Horowitz dwarfed them all. More than any other pianist, he embodied the concept of the performer as the center of the universe. When he played, no one thought of Chopin, Liszt, Tchaikovsky, or Scriabin. Only Horowitz mattered; it was the genius and personality of Horowitz the performer, unabashedly using the music as a vehicle, which gripped his audience. It was *his* ability to thrill, scare, move to tears, rattle soul and mind, devastate and comfort, which made him our idol.

Like an actor who with unrelieved intensity makes one forget the text, the playwright, the theater, the world, Horowitz made the composer's pristine "intentions" totally irrelevant. (Which is probably precisely what most composers really want.) He was not praying at anyone's altar, he was not anyone's humble messenger. It was he who was sitting on Mt. Olympus, no one else. He, the master magician who breathed life into sounds. He, the mesmerizer, the spellbinder. And he was probably the last of a breed. The day of the magician-pianist is gone. And many would undoubtedly say good riddance.

But I listen to pianists who faithfully convey the printed page, who play faster octaves than he did, whose tone is more ravishing, phrasing more natural, musicianship more impressive; and I remember the tear brought on by his Scarlatti, the terror of his Liszt Sonata, the palpitations induced by *Pictures,* the wrenching anguish of the Rachmaninoff Third, the other-worldliness of *Kreisleriana,* the childish joy of Moszkowski, the sheer disbelief of *Stars and Stripes* . . .

And I feel I was privileged to know a world gone forever.

Bella Davidovich

Born in Baku, Azerbaijan, Bella Davidovich entered the Moscow Conservatory, where she studied with Konstantin Igumnov and Jakob Flier. In 1949 she was awarded first prize in the Chopin Competition. During Davidovich's Russian career she was soloist with the Leningrad Philharmonic for twenty-eight consecutive seasons. In 1978 she left Russia and settled in New York; in 1988 she became the first Soviet emigré musician to receive an official invitation to perform in her native country.

Bella Davidovich has often collaborated with her son, violinist Dmitri Sitkovetsky. Recently she recorded the Grieg and Schumann concertos with the Seattle Symphony, conducted by Gerard Schwarz, for the Delos label. She has also recorded for Melodiya and Philips. In 1991 she served as judge at the Queen Elisabeth Competition in Brussels.

I regret to say I never heard Horowitz live because he left Russia before I was born and I lived in Russia until 1978. However, I heard much about him in my native Baku, whose music lovers had heard him play in Tbilisi when he was very young. These admirers of his could literally not find words to describe his playing.

In the sixties I became acquainted with Horowitz's older sister, Regina, who was also a pianist and who had accompanied David Oistrakh. She was by then elderly and taught in Kharkov. As I had performances each year in Kharkov, I made a point of visiting her each time as she and her husband, Yevsei Lieberman, seemed very simpatico. She spoke of her famous brother with great frequency. She had received his recordings, and he often called her by phone. On her piano stood a photo of Horowitz and Wanda. Regina physically resembled her brother greatly.

I also heard many recordings at the great pedagogue Jakob Flier's home, and at Jakob Zak's home. Zak had visited Horowitz in New York in 1965 and received from him a set of recordings. Zak brought home a Chopin disc, with the rarely played Introduction and Rondo in E-flat major. I had never heard it before, and Zak told me this was a work especially for me. I literally ran home and learned it under the spell of the recording. I remain forever grateful to Horowitz for this discovery.

His Mozart, Scriabin, the *Carmen* transcription and other transcriptions, his Liszt Second Rhapsody, *Stars and Stripes Forever*, Moszkowski's *Sparks* and the Rachmaninoff Second Sonata, the Chopin A-flat major Polonaise are just some works that come to mind that were matchless. Such a combination of pianism and personality will hardly appear on this earth soon again. Today, many confuse the electrically charged playing of Horowitz with playing merely fast. It was ever so much more than that. After hearing him, one felt compelled to play, carried away by the force of his inspiration.

The films on Horowitz are incomparable and a great joy to watch. I was performing in New Jersey at the time of his Moscow concert. I will never forget how moving it was to know that all over the world, we watched this great moment amidst unbelievable enthusiasm. I remain his fervant admirer forever.

Christoph Eschenbach

Christoph Eschenbach was born in Breslau (now Wrocław). During the 1960s he established himself as one of the important German pianists of his generation, performing worldwide in recital and with orchestra. He recorded many albums for Deutsche Grammophon, including the Intermezzi of Schumann, Beethoven's "Hammerklavier" Sonata and "Emperor" Concerto, Chopin's Preludes Op. 28, Schubert's posthumous Sonata in B-flat major, the complete Mozart sonatas, and the Henze Piano Concerto No. 2.

As a conductor, Eschenbach regularly conducts the major international orchestras, including the Boston, Chicago, San Francisco, Philadelphia, and Cleveland orchestras. He has been music and artistic director of the Tonhalle Orchestra of Zurich, and principal guest conductor of the London Philharmonic. A guest conductor at leading American festivals, he has appeared fifteen times at Tanglewood and at the Ravinia Festival. He is music director of the Houston Symphony.

After my first American tour in 1969, I spent two weeks in New York City without touching the piano. On my last day, Gian Carlo Menotti called me, saying, "I know how much you have wanted to meet Horowitz, and tonight, he wants to see you." My immediate answer was, "But I cannot play for him because I haven't practiced for two weeks." That night, Mr. Menotti introduced me to Horowitz, and I apologized that I could not play for him. Horowitz reacted, "I don't bite" as his face turned into that famous grin with which he could defeat and disarm everybody.

Very soon, I found myself playing Schubert's posthumous A major Sonata. It wasn't great. But I felt Horowitz's aura while he was sitting at the edge of the sofa, glasses on, watching my every move. I was more inspired than intimidated. After finishing he gave me some excellent advice in half-pedalling for the opening of the slow movement, so that the effect of the left-hand staccato notes was not ruined, while the right hand was still able to sing deliberately. Looking around, I saw books scattered, each relating to Schumann. Books by Jean Paul, E. T. A. Hoffmann, Schumann's criticism, diaries and letters—all in German. He said, "I have to record Schumann's *Kreisleriana.*" While telling the E. T. A. story of Kapellmeister Kreisler, Horowitz mimicked the amateurishness of Kreisler's conducting in the left-hand part of the last piece of *Kreisleriana.* He then began massaging the fifth finger of his right hand, complaining that he had a hangnail and it hurt. He grumbled that he had to play a recital in a week and how could he do it if the pain persisted. He seemed very involved with his finger, and rushed to the bathroom to put a Band-aid around it. He went right back to the piano, exercising it while he philosophized on how difficult it is to play only a few times a year instead of staying in the "routine."

All of a sudden, the first of the *Kreisleriana* pieces emerged, and after a wistful look, he continued playing the whole huge work. Again, he pointed out the odd rhythms of the left hand of the last piece. All at once, it seemed that the room was possessed of Kreisler, Hoffmann, Clara, and Robert. Horowitz *was* Schumann. *He* was Florestan and Eusebius of the *Davidsbündler. He* was the *zerrissene Seele,* but also the *blaue Blume* of Romanticism. The whole epoch came alive through the mystery of Horowitz's sound. Only *he* had the ability to create such communion through sound. Sound was essence and real substance in one; sound was time as time becomes space in certain moments; sound defined space: a bridge to eternity.

Although I now had heard Horowitz at home, I had never heard him in recital. That was to take place at Constitution Hall in Washington on a Sunday in 1971 at 4 P.M. I had reserved a ticket in a front row. I flew in from Paris just for this event. As I looked at my ticket, I found, to my astonishment, that it was in row 42. I almost wanted to leave and go back to Paris and listen to a recording of my beloved Horowitz. But then, as through an inverted binocular, tiny, fast, like in a Chaplin movie, the great pianist appeared, sat down, and began the first piece on the program, Schumann's *Blumenstück.*

The miracle happened with the first A-flat. As through an enormous zoom of an invisible camera, I was drawn into the second row of the hall by the "ring" of this sound, which was only a piano, not even a mezzo piano. But that ring! And throughout the whole recital (the *Arabeske*, *Concert sans orchestre*, and a Chopin second half), I stayed in this imagined seat spellbound and enchanted by that ring which shall never leave my life. Its magic has transformed everything in my conception of art.

Imagine: one A-flat! When I was a child, my favorite piece was the little minuet in A-flat from Mozart's London Sketchbook, and when I die I somehow want to hear the A-flat closing music of Wagner's *Parsifal*. But the center of my life was this A-flat in Washington. It confirmed what I had experienced two years earlier at Maestro Horowitz's home: sound = time = space = eternity.

Samuel Lipman

Samuel Lipman studied in San Francisco, California, with Lev Shorr and later at the Juilliard School with Rosina Lhévinne. In 1965 he gave the New York premiere of the Elliott Carter Piano Concerto in 1965 at Carnegie Hall. From 1972 to 1985 Lipman was a member of the Artist Faculty of the Aspen Music Festival, and from 1982 to 1988 he was a member of the National Council for the Arts.

He has been the music critic for Commentary *since 1976, and publisher of* The New Criterion *and director of the Waterloo Music Festival in New Jersey, both since 1982. He has received two ASCAP awards for music journalism. He is the author of four collections of essays, most recently* Music and More, *and the editor of a new edition of Matthew Arnold's* Culture and Anarchy.

When one observes a great artist closely over a long period of time, he becomes a part of one's own psyche. So it was for me with Vladimir Horowitz. I did not know him personally, though I did shake hands with him in his dressing room after a Constitution Hall recital in Washington, D.C., about 1975. Some years earlier, the pianist Constance Keene, then close to Horowitz, said that she had mentioned my name to him as someone gifted, and that he replied (or so I remember her story), "He must be a very nice person, because he has never asked to play for me." Thus warned about the vaunted Horowitz self-absorption, I resolved to keep my distance from such a solipsistic figure. And so when, after I started to write in the mid-1970s, I found myself preparing an article on Horowitz, I turned down an invitation (transmitted by a mutual friend) for drinks from the great man himself. What I might have learned about Horowitz through personal contact just didn't seem worth the risk of being drawn in by the charms and subtleties—and doubtless much worse—of his colossal ego.

But of course I did in fact know something about Horowitz musically. Before I was in my teens (I was born in 1934), I had heard him play several recitals in San Francisco, and had heard some of his many recordings as well. Three of his performances in this period stand out in my memory: his playing as a recital encore of his own transcription of Sousa's *Stars and Stripes Forever*, and his 78-rpm recordings for RCA of the Prokofiev Sonata No. 7 and the Tchaikowsky Concerto (the latter with his father-in-law, Arturo Toscanini). I was amazed in the Sousa at his preternatural feats of clarity, energy, and (not least of all) the imitation of the sound of band instruments. I was spellbound in the Prokofiev by both the hard-edged brilliance of his playing and the equally hard-edged beauty of the music itself. I found myself agog at the Tchaikowsky; it was the first time I had ever heard the piece, and I was astounded at the melody of the opening and the indescribable power of Horowitz's scales—scales had always been a weak point in my own pianistic armor—at the end of the third movement, just before the great octave passage and the final statement of the rondo theme.

At this time, I knew little or nothing of Horowitz's playing of other music, and in particular of his playing of Chopin and Liszt. When I changed piano teachers in 1948, my new teacher, Alexander Libermann, was a great Horowitz admirer, and indeed a one-time student of Felix Blumenfeld, one of Horowitz's teachers in Russia before the 1917 revolutions. Libermann told me to listen to as many Horowitz recordings as I could. Most of his pre–LP recordings were then easily available. Some of them, like his Mendelssohn and Liszt, were made for RCA in 1946 and 1947, and still remain the standard, both for the delicately beautiful playing of several Mendelssohn Songs Without Words and the still very much underrated *Variations sérieuses*. Included in his Mendelssohn playing too was a stunning recording (quite on a par with his *Stars and Stripes Forever*) of his own arrangement, after Liszt, of the "Wedding March"; among his Liszt was a crystalline performance of the charming *Au bord d'une source*, and a breathtaking performance of the Sixth Hungarian Rhapsody, with octaves better played than I have ever heard, or hope to hear.

At this time I also listened to Horowitz's prewar recordings of the Liszt Sonata, the Beethoven Thirty-Two Variations in C minor, and several small pieces of Chopin. I was then hard at work myself on the Liszt Sonata, and I found Horowitz's playing of it altogether arbitrary and hasty, an opinion I still hold. It was otherwise with the Beethoven and the Chopin: the difficult Beethoven variations were child's play for Horowitz, and he played them with an easy elegance no one else in my memory has attained; the Chopin, which included three etudes, the E major Scherzo, and three mazurkas, were marvels of technical wizardry in the etudes and the scherzo, and sad, nostalgic charm in the mazurkas.

About 1950, I heard Horowitz play in recital the Samuel Barber Sonata, which had just been written for him; I was stunned, and I immediately bought, and was as stunned by, his recording of this masterpiece. In fact I was so stunned that I quickly started to learn the work for myself. I was affected in the same way by Horowitz's 1947 recording of the Mussorgsky *Pictures at an Exhibition;* after I heard his superlative playing of this work, I began to try to play it. As is well known, Horowitz retired from the concert stage in 1953 but continued to make recordings for several years thereafter. I do not remember hearing very many of these later recordings; those I did hear, including some Chopin, struck me as overly perfumed and altogether too wayward. I am sorry to this day that I heard nothing till many years later of his marvelous Clementi records, made during this retirement.

By 1959 I had come to New York to study with Rosina Lhévinne at Juilliard. Though she had immense respect for Horowitz as a pianist, I think she thought little of him as a musician. What that meant was that his playing was too aggressive for her. She preferred a quieter, less bombastic virtuosity and a less attention-getting playing of lyrical passages; quite clearly, her own favorite pianist had been her brilliant but musically recessive husband, Josef. Mrs. Lhévinne's first task with me was to break me of what I had tried to appropriate from Horowitz, particularly the fast tempos and the clangorous sound, and these particularly in the Tchaikowsky Concerto. Not surprisingly, she liked the musical, even gentle, performance of her famous former student Van Cliburn; whereas Horowitz had played the Tchaikowsky as if it were a cross between Liszt and Prokofiev, Cliburn played it as if it were a cross between Schumann and Brahms.

However, I hardly gave up my preference for Horowitz, a preference which not even my real love for many of Arthur Rubinstein's 1930s HMV recordings could shake. It was at this time—about 1961—that a friend gave me the 78-rpm album of Horowitz's magnificent 1930 recording of the Rachmaninoff Third Concerto; once again I was stunned, and once again I started to learn a work that Horowitz so marvelously played. When the pianistic world was stirred by Horowitz's return to recording in 1962 for Columbia, I hastened to buy the first release, a recital including Chopin, Rachmaninoff, Schumann, and Liszt. The playing seemed wonderful, but a bit cautious; altogether, it seemed that the "new" Horowitz had substituted perfection for excitement. Put another way, for Horowitz, every musical element was in place, and there it stayed. This first Columbia recording was a smash success; some say it sold 120,000 copies the first week alone. Sadly, I remained unstirred by the releases that soon followed. Though his earlier recordings had led me to expect much, I was even unmoved by Horowitz's Scarlatti LP: such high accomplishment, I thought, such high pianistic polish, so much art expended in the service of these small pieces, and all ultimately so glacial.

It was in 1965, of course, that the real bombshell of Horowitz's career exploded. He decided to return that spring to the stage, scheduling a recital in Carnegie Hall. As was only to be expected, the demand for tickets was immense, and a long line of 1,500 Horowitz fans, piano students and music lovers alike, formed many hours before the box office opened. I no longer am sure just how my wife, the pianist and teacher Jeaneane Dowis, and I got our tickets; I think we got them through the late Jack Romann, the concert and artist manager of Baldwin, the piano we then played. The concert was recorded live, and released with some of the clinkers mended by rerecording; the resulting album is still available, now, of course, on CD.

But the clinkers were not what was important about the concert. What was important was the joy of piano playing Horowitz demonstrated, along with flashes—and much more than flashes—of his old power, fleetness, and sheer magic. His piano sang, it roared, he gambled time and time again, and time and time again he won. His playing in this concert was unlike his Columbia studio recordings; here at least, he was the old Horowitz.

As Horowitz sat there playing on the stage of Carnegie Hall, I became aware of a rising feeling in me, one that I immediately recognized the best of his playing had always produced in me: listening to Horowitz play the piano so marvelously made me want to play the piano. Some pianists of great technique and utter perfection of execution—Vladimir Ashkenazy is one example—have always made me want to quit, for I knew that such accomplishments were quite beyond me. Other pianists of high musical reputation—Emil Gilels is an example—left me so bored that I wondered just what I had ever seen in being a pianist at all. But Horowitz was different, and on this great occasion he was sublimely different. His playing seemed to me contagious; I went home to practice, and I thought that if I worked I might be able to play, if not like Horowitz, at least in his spirit.

I think I only heard Horowitz live four times after this glorious moment in 1965. As I mentioned earlier, I heard him in Washington, D.C. in the mid-1970s. Just before this concert, I had been allowed to try his preferred piano when it was being worked on at Steinway. The instrument was unbelievably brilliant, loud, and quick in mechanical response, and I instantly knew that only the greatest of virtuosi could master such a devilishly assertive instrument. In late 1977, a friendly orchestra member smuggled me into a Carnegie Hall rehearsal of the Philadelphia Orchestra in which Horowitz "tried out" the Rachmaninoff Third Concerto with Eugene Ormandy in preparation for his appearance several weeks later with Ormandy and the New York Philharmonic at Carnegie. My major memory of this occasion, aside from the incredible control Horowitz was still able to exert over the orchestra from the keyboard, was hiding myself in the uppermost reaches of the balcony to avoid the posse of staff that was trying to empty the hall of spectators. I went to the Philharmonic performance of the Rachmaninoff and found Horowitz's playing emotionally torn-apart and often technically muddy, but withal heroic. And then, about 1985, I heard him play a bit at a Deutsche Grammophon press conference; his playing still seemed commanding, though somewhat physically weakened, but what struck me most was Horowitz's by-now childish willfulness. Old age had made him all too young again, and the spectacle wasn't pleasant. The last time I saw Horowitz was just before his death in 1989, at the memorial service for John Steinway of the piano family. He was feeble, and holding on to his wife, Wanda, for dear life. He seemed to have not much longer to live. When he died, I remember thinking that with him, in a sense, piano playing had died too.

I idolized Horowitz, not as a man, but as a musician and a pianist. Why, then, did I not want to meet him, to hear his numerous post–1965 New York concerts, or to listen carefully to his many late live concert recordings? Because I loved him less, or because I loved him more? Clearly there were no practical difficulties standing in the way of my hearing Horowitz; I could easily have bought tickets, and his records were featured in every store. But there is an answer—my answer—to my questions that exists beyond the practicalities. The answer is that I did not want to lose my memories, to lose the inspiration that Horowitz had always been to me. I had my memories, and they were mine to keep as long as I did not attempt to revalidate them in the present as time passed. My memory of Horowitz is of the possibilities of the piano; my goal was to protect that memory, to keep it alive, at first in the face of his ability to manipulate those around him, and then even when age, that stern judge, supervened to enfeeble a once-mighty genius. I have succeeded in my goal: my Horowitz, at least, lives forever.

Vladimir Feltsman

Vladimir Feltsman was born in Moscow. At the Moscow Conservatory he studied with Jacob Flier. Later he was the winner of the Long/Thibaud Competition in Paris. In 1979 he asked to leave the Soviet Union. However, his request was not granted until 1987, and his musical activities were severely curtailed during this period. Later in 1987 he made his Carnegie Hall debut, and early in 1988 he performed the Brahms Second Concerto in his New York Philharmonic debut, with Zubin Mehta conducting.

Feltsman's discography includes Tchaikovsky's First and Third concertos, with Mstislav Rostropovich conducting the National Symphony; Rachmaninoff's Third Concerto and Rhapsody on a Theme of Paganini, with Zubin Mehta; an all-Liszt album; and the "live" recording of his Carnegie Hall debut.

The spring of 1986 in Russia was a very special one because a miracle happened; Vladimir Horowitz returned after sixty-one years to play concerts in Moscow and Leningrad. For musicians, music lovers, and the general public, it was something unbelievable. In our eyes, Horowitz was like a mythological hero, an Orpheus whose songs we had known and loved for many decades but whom we had never seen in person. The excitement was enormous, but it was not surprising because Horowitz generated a unique electricity wherever he played.

He gave two performances in Moscow, a public rehearsal and the concert itself. At the first performance, the stage of the grand hall of the Moscow Conservatory was filled with cameras, technicians and assistants. When the Maestro finally walked onto the stage, people literally jumped to their feet. Horowitz played his appearance brilliantly: first he acted surprised to see so many people; next he pretended not to have expected such an enthusiastic welcome; and then he ignored it all and started talking with someone on the stage. Finally, he went to the piano and greeted the public with his childish smile. He was charmingly awkward and in full command of all of us.

It is nearly impossible to describe the feeling his playing generated. Many books and articles will be written about it, and many critics will try to define the Horowitz miracle. They will never succeed, of course, nor will the many pianists who try to imitate him. What struck me most of all about his playing was his sound. Alive, vibrating, long-lasting, and floating, his sound almost transformed itself into visible light.

When the rehearsal was over, my wife and I were taken backstage to Horowitz's dressing room. After I repeated my name several times, he recognized me, and said, "Oh, of course. I know you. I have seen you on TV. You played Liszt's B minor Sonata." Then he asked me how his playing had sounded out there, and we spoke for a while. Horowitz was definitely in a good and playful mood.

A few days later, he played his recital. It was exactly the same program in the same hall, but many things came out differently. The tempos and dynamics were slightly different, as were certain small tricks. In other words, his entire program sounded fresh. Horowitz stayed at the residence of the American Ambassador, Arthur Hartman, who gave a party following the concert. Despite the large crowd there, Maestro recognized me and gestured for me to sit next to him on the big sofa.

"Well, how was it today?" he asked.

"Beautiful and very different."

"Of course, it was different. It's always different. I simply cannot play it in exactly the same way." Then he asked me specific questions about his concert. It was crystal clear that he understood and remembered exactly what he had done and why.

The next day, Donna Hartman telephoned to invite me to listen to the Maestro practice and have a cup of tea with him and Mrs. Horowitz. I got there with the speed of light, and it turned out to be one of the most special afternoons of my life. After we had spoken for a while, Horowitz said, "Do you want to play for me?" I missed my historic chance by saying, "Maestro, since we only have half an hour, would you please play yourself?" which he did. After this meeting, he and Mrs. Horowitz gave me a scarf with a keyboard design on it, which has become one of my most valued possessions.

I met Horowitz only one more time, in New York. However, even my limited experience of knowing him helps me understand him better. Horowitz was a well-read man with a wide and deep knowledge of music. He knew exactly what he was doing and why; the popular impression that he played mostly by intuition is incorrect. I am not trying to idealize him; he was a human being with his own problems, difficulties, and complication. He really does not need any idealization anyway because he was too great for it. His swan song was filled with beauty, simplicity, and a bit of sadness, and he completed his artistic development by rediscovering his favorite composer, Mozart.

Finally, the cycle of his life came to an end. I, naturally, felt sad when I learned that the Maestro had died, especially for Mrs. Horowitz. But somehow, my grief was not that strong, and after a while, I understood why. Vladimir Horowitz had accomplished what he was born to do. He died with a full life behind him and at the height of his glory. In a way, he had already become immortal during his lifetime, and his voice will always be present in this world, his song floating above us forever.

Lydia Artymiw

Born in Philadelphia, Pennsylvania, Lydia Artymiw made her debut at age eight with the Philadelphia Orchestra. Her principal teacher was Gary Graffman, with whom she studied for eleven years. She is the recipient of numerous awards, including the 1989 Andrew Wolf Chamber Award and the 1987 Avery Fisher Career Grant. She has garnered top prizes in the Leeds and Leventritt competitions.

Artymiw has appeared with over eighty orchestras in the United States, the Far East, and Europe, including the Boston Symphony, the Cleveland Orchestra, the Philadelphia Orchestra, and the New York Philharmonic. She has collaborated with the Guarneri and Vermeer quartets and with Michael Tree, Arnold Steinhardt, and Yo-Yo Ma. She is on the faculty of the University of Minnesota.

Even though Vladimir Horowitz left a substantial legacy of recordings, he was perhaps the last of the "live" pianists. One had to have heard him in a live performance in order to fully appreciate his powers as a performing artist and the impact he made on his listeners. Audiences attending a Horowitz recital came to the hall with such a feeling of anticipation and excitement. Tickets were often difficult to obtain (and were relatively costly), and there was always the lurking fear that the Maestro might cancel. These factors contributed to making each Horowitz appearance even more of a special event.

I vividly recall a recital which Horowitz played in Boston's Symphony Hall in 1976 on a Sunday afternoon at four o'clock as was his habit. The mood in the hall was supercharged, and every seat was filled, as nobody would dream of arriving late! Moments before the recital was to begin, the entire audience had their eyes glued to stage left, watching the stage door for the eagerly anticipated moment when Horowitz would make his first entrance. We all waited—no sign of the Maestro. Suddenly he was on stage, having entered from stage right, not left where everyone was watching. The entire audience gasped, then broke into chuckles. Horowitz had outfoxed us all! Even more surprising, after having heard for years the legends about his nervous breakdowns and eccentricities, was to see how relaxed he seemed, apparently delighted to be on stage and eager to perform for his many admirers (and perhaps a few curiosity seekers).

From the moment he began playing, he created a magical atmosphere through his incredible command of color, range of dynamics, and amazing technique. The most difficult passages were effortless for him—like child's play—and his projection of sound was phenomenal. He played to the hall and possessed an uncanny instinct of timing and sonority. Climaxes were perfectly scaled and judged, and he could project even his softest passages to the furthest seat in the three-thousand-seat hall. I will never forget the *sound* he produced in Liszt's D-flat major *Consolation* (this time, again in Boston, in 1978), a sound whose sheer beauty and soaring quality no recording could ever capture.

Horowitz's playing truly represented an aesthetic that predates commercial recording. Most pianists today are influenced by the microphone, whether or not they are recording. Their primary goal seems to be not only to achieve accurate execution (mistakenly referred to as "technical perfection") but also to produce a performance which could withstand multiple hearings. The Horowitz performance, on the other hand, was calculated for the moment, designed, for maximal effect, to be heard only once. This is not to say that one cannot re-listen with great pleasure to a Horowitz recording, but it is the first hearing that will always have the most telling impact. This is because each performance contained some important element of surprise. No matter that the "surprise" may have been carefully planned by a cunning Horowitz who delighted in astonishing his listeners! It was still unexpected to the audience. Obviously such gestures drew attention to the performer himself, but they also alerted us to details of the musical compositions that we may never have noticed or perhaps took for granted.

Listen, for example, to the way he played the andante from Rachmaninoff's Cello Sonata with Mstislav Rostropovich at the "Concert of the Century" celebrating the eighty-fifth anniversary of Carnegie Hall, recorded on May 18, 1976. In the coda (bars 60–61), a brief solo piano passage introduces a "new" theme, which will soon serve as accompaniment to a final statement of the movement's main melody. Horowitz turned this brief passage into a "special moment" by leaning on and lingering on the tenutos and through his inimitable "voicing" of the accompanying chords—once again, timing and sound. I have listened to this recording a number of times, but it has never had so arresting an effect as it did the first, when I wasn't expecting it. Now the anticipation weakens some of the surprise. This kind of experience makes us realize how careful we must be when we treat recordings as "documents"; the memory of the first hearing may be far more "real" as a "record" of the performance than any number of actual re-hearings. I confess that I can hardly play this passage myself without remembering what he did, and yet trying to copy him would be out of the question. It could only result in caricature and not the authentic expression that he projected.

Another striking example from a live concert comes to mind—the Chopin A minor Waltz, Op. 34, No. 2, which he played as an encore in Boston. I was startled when he began because it seemed so dry and detached—quite different from my conception of the piece. I listened, wondering what he had in mind. Soon I found out. Toward the end (starting in bar 169) the left hand begins a meandering scalar string of eighth notes that struggle up to an F before slowly relaxing and sinking down to a low E (and the key of E major), an arrival celebrated by a spacious arpeggio rising more than two octaves in the space of four beats. The change in mood was breathtaking, and I then understood that the character of the beginning had been necessary for the degree of contrast that Horowitz wished to create for this astonishing moment. But the best was yet to come, for on top of the new left-hand melody Horowitz (on behalf of Chopin) introduced the simple right-hand melody, little more than a turn in some performances, but in this context a precious gift that seemed to have fallen from heaven. The moment came and passed. The subsequent return of the opening A minor theme, which closes the waltz, has never seemed more tragic. I was convinced once again that Horowitz was an artist who possessed a profound musical intelligence.

There is no doubt that Horowitz has had a tremendous impact on my musical development, both directly from his live and recorded performances and indirectly from my lessons with Gary Graffman, himself a Horowitz student. I therefore feel proud to consider Vladimir Horowitz my "musical grandfather!"

Mieczyslaw Horszowski

Mieczyslaw Horszowski, born in 1892, died May 22, 1993. He had the longest career in the history of the performing arts. At 5, he was playing from memory and transposing Bach inventions. Soon after he studied with Theodor Leschetizky. He made his debut in Vienna at 8 and began touring Europe with ever-increasing success. In 1957, in twelve recitals at New York's Town Hall, he presented Beethoven's entire works for piano solo. In 1960 he played ten recitals of Mozart's piano music. At the invitation of President and Mrs. Kennedy he performed at the White House with Alexander Schneider and Pablo Casals. In 1978 he returned to the White House to perform an all-Chopin recital at the invitation of President and Mrs. Carter. Horszowski received many awards, including the Polish Medal of Honor and Paderewski Prize. Throughout a distinguished teaching career at the Marlboro Festival and the Curtis Institute of Music, he was an inspiring link between the great musicians of the past and the artists of our time.

From the first time that I heard Mr. Horowitz, my admiration for his art remained unchanged.

In the many occasions that I listened to him, a culminating moment was to hear Mr. Horowitz playing the *Humoreske* by Schumann. I would be happy by these few words that the extraordinary beauty of this performance is always remembered.

Tong-Il Han

Korean-born Tong-Il Han studied at the Juilliard School with Rosina Lhévinne and in London with Ilona Kabos. By the age of fifteen he had appeared with the New York Philharmonic, the Cleveland Orchestra, the Denver Symphony, and the Indianapolis Symphony. Han was the first-prize winner in the twenty-fourth International Leventritt Competition. He has concertized in over twenty-five countries, performing with Bernard Haitink, Charles Dutoit, Herbert Blomstedt, Raymond Leppard, Edo de Waart, and many others.

Han has recorded for Phillips (Korea) and the SKC label. His discography includes Chopin's twenty-four preludes, four ballades, and four scherzos. His most recent compact discs include the Brahms Sonata Op. 5 and the Schubert A major Sonata D. 959, as well as Sonatas of Beethoven. In 1973 Han was awarded Korea's Order of Civil Service Merit. He is professor of music at Boston University.

I first heard about the legendary Vladimir Horowitz in a record store in Los Angeles. Having been born and raised in economically depressed and war-torn Korea for the first twelve years of my life, I had hardly any knowledge of many of the world's great pianists. I had heard of Arthur Rubinstein, but other great artists such as Lhévinne, Rachmaninoff, Prokofiev, Hofmann, and Godowsky among many others were all new discoveries for me after I came to the United States in 1954. During the summer of 1955, I was searching for a record of Tchaikovsky's First Piano Concerto. A salesperson suggested that I buy the recording by Horowitz with Toscanini and the NBC Symphony Orchestra. My reaction on the first hearing of this incredible pianist could be summed up in four words: It blew my mind! I had never experienced such an electrifying and hair-raising performance prior to that time. And to this day, some thirty-eight years since, I have very rarely witnessed such force of magnetism.

While studying at the Juilliard School I collected several more recordings by Horowitz, such as the Brahms Second Piano Concerto, Rachmaninoff's Third Piano Concerto with Fritz Reiner and the Chicago Symphony Orchestra, and his own piano transcription of John Phillip Sousa's *Stars and Stripes Forever,* which was another mind-blowing experience. Hearing those recordings I thought Horowitz could do no wrong.

As an ardent admirer of Rubinstein, one season, I went to all of his recitals of the particular series he was giving at Carnegie Hall. At the time, I could not afford the price of the orchestra seats. But on one particular occasion, I had received two tickets from Mrs. S. Pinkney Tuck, who gave several scholarships to the Juilliard School. At the intermission of Rubinstein's recital, I casually looked in front of me and immediately froze. Sitting in front of me was Horowitz with his wife, Wanda Toscanini. It took me some time to recover and find enough courage to ask him for an autograph on Rubinstein's program. Soon the word spread that Horowitz was in the audience. Many people, mostly Juilliard students, swarmed around him. One piano student was beside himself and was blabbering, in a loud voice, praise after praise to the effect that Horowitz was the greatest of them all. While I shared much of his enthusiasm, I felt quite embarrassed in front of many of Rubinstein's fans, especially on the occasion of his supremely elegant recital. However, it was a truly exciting evening!

I met Horowitz again at Steinway & Sons on West Fifty-Seventh Street. One day I went to check on some pianos and went up to the second floor to see David Rubin, the director of the concert department at the time. In front of his desk was a couch. On that couch, there he was! Horowitz, reclining comfortably on it, was engaging in an amiable conversation with Mr. Rubin. He said to Horowitz, "Do you know Tong-Il Han?" Horowitz, smiling, jumped up from the couch and extended his "gigantic" hand. It was my turn to blabber some remarks in expression of my great admiration for him. I still recall that moment with a sense of awe. His greeting was very warm.

The announcement in the *New York Times* simply said, "Vladimir Horowitz, Pianist." This was the most eagerly awaited and almost miraculous return of the pianist to the concert stage after twelve years. The possibility of seeing and hearing the legend in person was almost unbelievable, and I was in a mild state of shock from anticipation. I went to Carnegie Hall early in the afternoon of the day before the concert. I think I was one of the first two hundred people standing in line by the box office. The vigil, lasting all day and all night in front of the hall, was an exciting event for me. Finally, the moment arrived. I was sitting in the first row of the balcony section in Carnegie Hall. Many Juilliard students were sitting around me, and we were all nervous with excitement as well as being concerned that Horowitz might change his mind and not show up. But there he came, walking briskly to the piano, and created the most spontaneous and overwhelming standing ovation. How well I remember the infinite shades of tone color that he produced in Scriabin's Poem and his Sonata No. 9, and the rest of the program made me gasp. The concert was one of the great experiences of my life, and it will remain with me always.

Although physical deterioration from aging is naturally inevitable, in his late years Horowitz produced some of the most beautiful and elegant musicianship and pianism of his career. It was a wonderful discovery to hear his Mozart Piano Concerto in A major K. 488, with Carlos Maria Giulini. The pianist said he was the oldest member of that recording team, but as the television documentary showed, he was the youngest of them all. He died at 86, but as a young man, full of youthful spirit. This is how I will always remember him.

John Browning

The American pianist John Browning is a native of Denver, Colorado. In Los Angeles, California, he worked with Lee Pattison, and at the Juilliard School he was a scholarship pupil of Rosina Lhévinne. In 1954 he won the Steinway Centennial Award, followed by the Leventritt Award in 1955. In 1956 he came in second in the Queen Elisabeth Competition. His career as a major pianist was launched when, in 1956, he made his New York Philharmonic debut with Mitropoulos. World tours quickly followed.

In 1962 Browning premiered the Barber Piano Concerto at the opening of Avery Fisher Hall at Lincoln Center. He toured the Soviet Union with George Szell and the Cleveland Orchestra. He has recorded the Chopin etudes, the Beethoven Diabelli Variations, the five Prokofiev Concertos (with Leinsdorf), and many other works of the standard literature. His recent recording of the Barber Concerto won a Grammy Award. He has received an honorary doctorate from Occidental College.

When I was a teenager in Los Angeles, Vladimir Horowitz came to play about once every two years. The artists and music teachers I knew were not of one mind about him: for some, he was incomparable; for others, little more than a circus performer unworthy of a serious musician's attention. No one was lukewarm. The purists of that period reacted to Horowitz as if he were a dangerous drug. Yes, he would give you a "high," a rush, but you should be very careful about it all, wary of his ideas and disapproving of his speed, brilliance, and extremely personal rubati. He had become, for many, an example of what young impressionable piano students should *not* do. In any event, one must never become *addicted* to Horowitz.

The 1940s must have been both exhilarating and problematic for

Horowitz. Although he was one of the new triumvirate of musical gods—Toscanini, Heifetz, and Horowitz—who were replacing the older onces like Mengelberg, Kreisler, and Schnabel, he was less comfortable than the other two in the German music dominating public taste at that time. The sound of music making was changing. Tempi were getting much faster, personal liberties and rubati were frowned upon, and the quality of sound was becoming more and more brilliant. Transcriptions of Bach organ works for the piano were absolutely taboo in New York concerts. Almost all non-German Romantic music was viewed by the new cognoscenti with some suspicion and even disdain. Horowitz was more of a romantic than either Toscanini or Heifetz. His technical wizardry and highly projected tone fitted the New Style perfectly; but his very personal approach to Romantic piano music was a throwback to an earlier period that was generally out of favor.

I think Horowitz tried to modify his musical style to fit the prevailing, rather rigid taste of the 1940s. The results were not always artistically happy for him. In addition, he was pushed into a breakneck schedule of concerts, many of them for war bond drives, which was an absolute guarantee of physical and nervous exhaustion. In the early 1950s he "retired" from the concert stage for a decade and a half. It was when I started listening seriously to the recordings he made during this retirement period—when the playing seemed to regain its early warmth and charm—that I fell in love with Horowitz's pianism and art. I became hooked. At last I had heard the message and the magic.

History will finally acknowledge, I believe, that Horowitz changed the way we hear the piano, think about the piano, and play the piano more than anyone else of the twentieth century. He even changed the way American Steinways sound. Allowing that there have always been slight differences in tone quality between New York and Hamburg Steinways, nonetheless one can hardly dispute that from Horowitz's debut in this country until the present—with his career almost exclusively centered in the United States—American Steinways have become increasingly more powerful than their European sisters. Since World War II, pianists and public alike in this country have demanded a piano that can deliver the "Horowitz sound."

Sitting in Chicago's Orchestra Hall one Sunday afternoon, waiting for Horowitz to come out on stage for a recital, I was suddenly struck by the thought that, looking at the lonely Steinway with the long low bench only Horowitz used, I was anticipating far more than a piano that afternoon. I had a mental image of the stage filled with phantom French horns, trumpets, timpani, woodwinds, cymbals, and strings which would shortly be brought to life by a PIANIST. No one else had ever given me that feeling.

I first met Horowitz during the period before my premiering Samuel Barber's Piano Concerto in 1962. One day Sam said to me, "John, I think it's time to take the concerto, or as much of it as I've written, over to Volodya to get his opinion of it, as well as any help he can give you." My heart started pounding. I became terrified at the thought of meeting, let alone playing for, the Great One. Finally the appointed day came. Sam took me, somewhat like a parent with a child on the first day of school, to the beautiful town house on the upper East Side. After playing the concerto for him and discussing many things, including tempi and some passages that I felt were unplayable the way Sam had written them at the tempi Sam wanted (Horowitz mercifully agreed with me!), we were treated to Horowitz at the keyboard for close to two hours, playing Liszt transcriptions of Beethoven symphonies, Scriabin, and Rachmaninoff. He was totally charming, polite, and immensely kind to me throughout that afternoon. When we left, both of us almost in a state of trance, Sam and I walked more than thirty blocks down Fifth Avenue. No one adored Horowitz and his playing more than Samuel Barber. He wrote his Piano Sonata for Horowitz in 1949. Yet, as if talking to himself, Sam said to me, "Volodya is so enigmatic. He can organize a rambling late Scriabin sonata so extraordinarily that it will sound perfectly constructed—yet sometimes music that *is* perfectly constructed will become almost formless under his hand."

In the final analysis, what produced that feeling of risk, of danger, of a highwire aerial act, always present at a Horowitz concert? We all have different impressions. Mine? First, the piano was voiced so brilliantly that you heard everything as if magnified; every note, every detail was enlarged, exposed. Second, Horowitz used the pedal more sparingly, other than in melodic playing, than virtually any other pianist we have heard. Entire passages performed with great speed and power were often played with little or no pedal at all. The effect was that of a highwire act performed without a safety net. Third, Horowitz, the master showman, knew how to create illusion. We can no more explain that gift than we can define "star" quality. And the voicing! For me, that was *the* Horowitz magic. No one in my listening experience has equalled him in the art of chiselling melodic lines—both primary and secondary—so intensely, so pointedly that he could surround them with a wash of harmonic texture many dynamic levels softer and filled with infinite color, and it all sounded clear, orchestral, and yet balanced. No one has ever done that with such mastery and (well, why not admit it?) sorcery.

Horowitz played with rather flat fingers. Some people have found that highly unusual. Yet those of us who were taught by Russian teachers from the old school are not surprised. My own teacher, Rosina Lhévinne, taught a flat finger, particularly for melodic playing, because it produced a less rapid, percussive approach to the key. This was a tradition she said came down from the legendary Anton Rubinstein. It was in direct conflict with the more German school of piano technique exemplified by Leschetizky and his disciples. Horowitz confessed to me once, in private conversation, that with all his technical prowess he had real problems with parallel runs—that is, scales in unison. He said he would do almost any kind of complicated reworking of the passage to avoid such runs. Most of us will probably be comforted to know Horowitz found something technically awkward. He also told me he felt that the secret to Schumann was to play it like "organized improvisation." Those words have always stuck in my memory.

Like every one of the greatest virtuosi, Horowitz stretched the boundaries of his instrument beyond anything his colleagues had imagined. Of all the pianists I have heard, he was the only one who made the piano sound truly orchestral. It is ironic that, though he sought and found timbres from *outside* the piano itself, he was so often viewed by critics as little more than just a wonderful pianist. I think Horowitz concentrated, not on the sound of his piano per se, but rather on the sounds of invisible orchestras and singers that were in his head. Rudolf Serkin once said to me, "You know, John, it really does get a little easier. The more I forget the piano and concentrate only on how I want the music to sound as I hear it in my head, oddly enough the better the piano does sound." We then spoke of Horowitz. Serkin's eyes were shining as he told me with great warmth of his early days in Europe with Horowitz—the two often vacationing together—and that he loved and idolized his playing.

To most of his colleagues, Horowitz "owned" the Liszt Sonata, Mussorgsky's *Pictures at an Exhibition,* and Rachmaninoff's Third Concerto. What does it mean to "own" a work? Very simply, it means that an artist's colleagues accept, whether with joy or envy, that his or her performance of a certain work has established the world standard for that work against which all other conceptions will be judged. In addition to those three works, the special musical moments I will always remember with joy are his recording of the Scriabin Third Sonata (the slow movement of which is as ravishingly beautiful as anything I know), the "Serenade for the Doll" by Debussy, Moszkowski's F major Etude, Several Rachmaninoff *Etudes-Tableaux*, and one particular performance of Schumann's *Traumerei*, a work Horowitz struggled all his life to play with great and simple beauty.

It is far easier to try to describe the pianism of the man than his interpretive genius. Any pianist who has attempted to interpret the works Horowitz "owned" in a fashion as successful and satisfying as Horowitz's knows all too well how supreme his musical mastery was. Perhaps, as Samuel Barber thought, his great strengths did not lie with the music of Schubert and Beethoven. Yet we all heard great Schumann from him. My own intuition is that this stupendous virtuoso had the rare gift of remaining a child in his innermost self. He was very bright and remarkably learned about many things. He was certainly not naive about the world around him. There was always in his playing a strong sexuality. Climaxes were physical and explosive. When the music called for the heat of passion, he gave you all you could hope for, like a superb lover. But, coexistant with that adult white heat, was the emotional innocence and cruelty and sweetness and selfishness and tenderness and wisdom of a precocious child. The mixture was irresistible. Above all, he had an infallible instinct for the big line, the important voices, the harmonic modulation that would unlock the passage's emotion. He could dazzle you to despair with those fabulous fingers; five seconds later, you would have tears in your eyes from a phrase turned so exquisitely, so innocently, so humanly, so movingly that you would remember that one phrase—and everything about it—for the rest of your life.

Hans Graf

Viennese-born Hans Graf entered the Musical Academy of Vienna in 1947 and studied with Bruno Seidlhofer. He was awarded prizes at several international competitions. Since then he has played in Europe, the Americas, the Near East, Japan, and Korea. In addition to his activities as a concert pianist, he has dedicated himself to teaching. He founded a school of music in Rio de Janeiro, and subsequently was invited to become a professor at the Vienna Academy of Music.

Graf has given master classes at the Mozarteum in Salzburg and at the Beethoven Festival in Bonn, and was twice a guest professor at the Indiana University School of Music in Bloomington. He has served on the juries of many prestigious piano competitions.

I first heard the name Horowitz at the end of the War, when I started listening to the available recordings. Unfortunately, I heard Vladimir Horowitz in concert on only one occasion, on May 1, 1987, at the Grosser Saal of the Musikverein in Vienna. It was his first Viennese recital in fifty-five years.

Like all arts, the interpretation of piano music has undergone changes and fashions. The first recordings for the phonograph on wax cylinders and the first gramophone records prove this and allow us to draw conclusions about the trends during Liszt's and Thalberg's lifetimes. Technical acrobatics and musical depth dominated alternately with artistic taste. For instance, many pianists living at the turn of the century played like a precise machine. Their playing was far removed from the composer's intentions, and such musical ignorance or incompetence forces us to smile at the performance.

Horowitz was one of the first pianists of his time to take into consideration the composer's musical intentions. I also admired him unconditionally for his unattainable technique and his high musical creativity. In addition, he had that certain something, a halo that surrounded him, a type of charisma that every famous artist must have.

During the last years of his life, Horowitz's approach to playing seemed to change dramatically. While watching televised broadcasts of his last concerts in London, Moscow, and Tokyo, I felt rather disappointed because I thought he had added too much of "himself" to the music, not letting the composers speak easily. I felt he showed certain insecurities and I concluded that he had not conscientiously prepared for the performance. However, these negative impressions were completely swept away by his last piano recital, in Vienna. It was a hot, early summer afternoon and the windows were open. During Schubert's Impromptu in G-flat major, the church bells of the nearby Karlskirche could be heard. One could really imagine being in heaven. Many listeners had tears in their eyes.

Normally a good teacher would say that one cannot play the piano at all with Horowitz's flat finger position. A large full tone just cannot be produced with flat fingers. Yet this was not the case with Horowitz, and there are few pianists capable of matching him in volume of sound. This tells me that the technique of playing the piano can and must be different for each pianist. A person who has his own personal hand position and finger technique from the beginning may be considered fortunate. Horowitz seemed to be one of those lucky few.

Often people unjustifiably reproached Horowitz for producing an intepretation that was merely superficial or lacking in profundity. However, in my opinion, he thought a great deal and his performances are imbued with much reflection. Everything sounded natural and convincing, and I never had the feeling that it was calculated or artificial.

One of Horowitz's exceptional qualities was his richness of tone and his use of both pedals. The softest pianissimo and the loudest fortissimo were always controlled and beautiful. This was because he used the right pedal sparingly, which gave his tone a transparent and crystal clear quality. Perhaps his use of the left pedal could be called excessive, but it played an essential part of his art. I shall never forget his playing the B-flat major Sonata K. 333 by Mozart. From a stage seat I watched his left foot. He played the whole sonata with the soft pedal and raised it only for a few single notes. The effect made a very special impression.

There is a large number of excellent pianists in the world, but Vladimir Horowitz was an exceptional phenomenon among them.

Jean-Yves Thibaudet

A native of Lyons, Jean-Yves Thibaudet began studying the piano at the age of five. At the Paris Conservatoire his principal teachers were Lucette Descaves and Aldo Ciccolini.

Thibaudet won the 1981 Young Concert Artists Auditions. For eleven seasons he has participated at the Spoleto Festival in the United States and Italy. An exclusive recording artist for London/Decca, he has recorded Liszt's two concertos, the Totentanz, *and the Hungarian Fantasy with the Montreal Symphony and Charles Dutoit. His first solo discs for London/Decca were a two-CD set of the complete solo music for piano by Ravel. During the 1992 season he performed Ravel's complete piano music in two recitals at New York's 92nd Street Y. In 1992 he made his debuts at the Tanglewood Festival and the Proms of London, as well as performing in Australia.*

One of the great regrets of my life will always be that I never heard Horowitz perform live in concert. From childhood, I used to listen to his recordings. I will never forget the first time I heard his Rachmaninoff Third Concerto, with Albert Coates conducting. It was given to me when I was nine or ten years old. I was shocked. Since then, this recording has become one of my favorites, and it remains the version I prefer of his three recordings of the concerto.

I was immediately fascinated by his electrifying approach to the piano. It was so exciting, brilliant, daring and digitally thrilling, and at the same time of great elegance. I admired the clarity of his playing; he used the pedal in such a way that each note was distinct, like a strand of pearls. This approach also reminded me a little of the digital technique of the great jazz pianists of the time, like Art Tatum or Fats Waller.

I must admit that in my youth I was not especially impressed by

Horowitz's musical qualities. I found his playing a little superficial and sometimes even affected, lacking in simplicity. But as I matured I started to appreciate all the other qualities of this giant of the piano. I realized that his greatest gift, the most unique and the most personal, was his tone. Horowitz had a luminous and *magical* sound that allowed him to create bewitching atmospheres.

What has been an extraordinary experience for me was to observe the musical evolution and development of the aging Horowitz. His music became more and more introspective and sober, and his playing became simple, for example, in his Mozart and the Wagner–Liszt *Liebestod,* recorded only a few days before his death. Another equally fascinating aspect of his career is that he gave, all in all, so few concerts in the last thirty-five years of his life. He was one of those rare artists who became a myth during his lifetime.

Horowitz will continue to live among us through his magnificent recorded output. In them, he exemplifies the great tradition of Romantic piano playing. They will remain treasures for generations to come.

Vladimir Viardo

Vladimir Viardo was trained at the Moscow Conservatory as a student of Lev Naumov. At the age of twenty-one he was awarded a top prize in the 1971 Marguerite Long Competition. Two years later he was the winner of the fourth Van Cliburn Competition. Soon after an American tour with the Moscow State Symphony, his travel visa was revoked for unexplained reasons, and for thirteen years Viardo was kept inside the Soviet Union. In 1987, with glasnost, he was permitted to accept engagements in Germany and the United States, where he was appointed artist-in-residence at the University of North Texas. Since then his concert tours have taken him around the world in recital and as soloist with leading orchestras. Viardo has also made numerous recordings for Melodiya, Pro Arte, and Nonesuch.

After winning the Van Cliburn Competition in 1973 I had many concert tours within the frame of the competition in 1974 and 1975. One day, Horowitz was to give one of his rare concerts in Carnegie Hall, but I myself had a concert the same day. Although I was well acquainted with Horowitz's records, I had never seen him perform "live" and was desperate to hear him. Somehow, a substitute was arranged for my concert.

I was most curious. Actually, I was ready not to like him. Our school taught us that Horowitz was more superficial than Vladimir Sofronitsky, Maria Yudina, and Richter. These "dionysians" were deeper and had more classical roots than the "apollonian" Horowitz. However, I was quickly surprised. Instantly I was drawn into every sound he made. I felt palpitations. My hands were icy, and my skin tingled. Everything was illogical. Horowitz did something to the music and to the audience as well. His stage presence was absolutely riveting. It is my belief that people attend concerts not only to hear music but to participate in a physical process. After all, an audience is within this process. With Horowitz, the audience was involved. He was definitely a genius of communication.

After the concert, I was brought backstage. He had obviously enjoyed the concert and was very relaxed. He was sitting in a chair and receiving only people that he knew, such as Van Cliburn. When I was introduced to him he gave me an autograph "to Volodya Viardo." He asked, "Did you really like it, did you really like it?" begging for compliments in a good humored way. I was feeling wonderful, but all of a sudden thunderstruck. I was wearing a suit, but because of my own concert and some confusion, I was wearing an ascot, as it was in fashion at the time. I had not known about Wanda Horowitz's obsession about not showing proper respect to her husband, of which not wearing a tie was the chief outward manifestation. She told everyone there, including Van Cliburn. She made a veritable scandal out of it. "No tie, no tie. This is outrageous!" she said. She didn't know that I had cancelled my own concert to come from another state to his concert. Van Cliburn said to me, "Please always keep a little tie in your pocket." So that day was a joy musically, but socially I was a failure. Nevertheless, Horowitz . . . inquired of me by calling his sister, Regina Horowitz, several times. She was a professor at Ukraine's Kharkov Conservatory at the time.

I was not to see him again so soon. After 1975 I was kept in Russia, never to be permitted out for thirteen years. I was imprisoned pianistically. One day, early in 1986, I was having dinner at Sviatoslav Richter's. During our dinner, in the middle of some conversation, Richter said, "By the way, I heard that the best pianist in the world is coming to play for us." Richter was being a little facetious. Everyone at the table jumped up saying, "Oh, no, no. We know who is the best pianist in the world," looking at Richter.

Obtaining tickets to the Horowitz Moscow recital was no simple matter. Although Horowitz might have remembered me, I could not call the embassy in those politically dangerous and bad years. Fortunately, I knew someone in the crew that was televising it. Everyone in Bureaucratic Services got tickets from the Ministry of Culture. It was an honor to hear Horowitz and they used the concert as a sort of spiritual bribe. Half of the audience there were not attracted to music at all. The students were literally hanging through the roof trying to get to the ceiling so they could listen and see him through the chandelier. It was quite awful. There was hysteria, and some students fell.

My friend Richard Probst from Steinway said, "You have tickets, but what about your son, Philip?" He was then about nine and was studying the piano. Probst knew it was impossible to get a ticket for him, but said, "Have Phillip come two hours before the concert. I'll sneak him in." So Philip came, and during that time, the TV people needed someone to play at Horowitz's piano. Philip was in good form and played a Mozart sonata. I was not there, but Richard Probst told me the crew loved him, and so my son got to play on Horowitz's Steinway CD 503.

Horowitz's concert, which was televised to the world, was unbelievable. He continuously united with some sacred spirit. I was sitting with the wife of Richter, Nina Dorliac. Richter was not there. She was the "spy" from the family. He did everything contrary to what we were taught at the Moscow Conservatory. He was playing Mozart with a freedom that we were taught not to indulge in. Nina would look at me, I would look at her. We kept glancing at each other, but suddenly, in the middle of the sonata, we stopped looking at each other. After the performance, she jumped to her feet applauding. His communicative power was so persuasive.

Horowitz in Moscow was an important concert in many ways. Horowitz had no fear of the stage. He came out, smiled, and waved to everyone. The sense of freedom and communication was overwhelming. It was something new in the concept of Russian concert life, normally strict and conservative. Even before he played there was a fresh spirit, and the atmosphere in the audience was unique. I perceived during his performance that as he had become older Horowitz had purged all bad taste. The artist's input to the process of "fertilization" of the piece performed often resembles "bad taste." People who play with so-called good taste, however, resemble artistic impotence unacceptable to a musician. Horowitz was very "fertilized" in that sense, and I respect fertilization much more than impotence.

I also think he was deeply affected by his return to Russia. There was a painful tint of nostalgia. During that concert, Horowitz was speaking to himself, but also with an amazing directness to the audience. Many of them were openly weeping. After the concert, I was fished out from the crowd along with the famous tenor Kozlovsky. Horowitz was pleasantly rude to him. He said, "You, Kozlovsky. I remember you seventy years ago in Kiev. But you got old." Kozlovsky shook his hand and said with emotion and obvious satisfaction, "You, too. You got old, too."

When I arrived backstage, the TV crew introduced me as the father of Philip. Probst took Philip to Horowitz and said, "Shake hands with Maestro Horowitz," and then, addressing Horowitz, "This is the boy who played on your piano a sonata by Mozart."

Horowitz looked at him and said in a suddenly keen voice, "You played *my* sonata?" Philip assured Horowitz that it wasn't *his* Mozart sonata but another one. Horowitz said, "Good".

Horowitz was disturbed that I said that he had such beautiful pianissimos, that his soft playing was wonderful. "But," he protested, "I can play loudly and I did. I'm not too old for that."

After the concert, there was a reception at the Spaso House, the residence of the U.S. ambassador, with the cream of Soviet society present. I was several tables away from Horowitz and could not see him. There were three good balalaika players playing popular music. Suddenly there was the clanking sound of forks and knives over expensive glasses accompanying the balalaikas. I wondered who would do such a thing at this formal affair. I asked the violinist Vladimir Spivakov who was making the commotion. Spivakov in his deep voice said, "He who has the right to make a disturbance." It was Horowitz, who was very gay and happy. It amazed me how free and uninhibited he was.

Later, the mood was broken somewhat, and I felt that Wanda was upset. She obviously had had a quarrel with the Maestro and was now sitting aside from the crowd. I felt sorry for her and afterwards came over to where she was sitting and said, "Wanda, it was a great concert and you are a great wife." Wanda proceeded to shout several times, "Did everybody hear that? I'm a great wife!" She probably needed to massage her "scandal glands" to cheer herself up. But it appeared that Horowitz needed her. They seemed to need the roles they played with each other.

When I finally left the Soviet Union, I had hoped to see Horowitz again, but I was very busy with concerts and then he died. He had great influence on me and on so many Russian pianists I grew up with. Indeed, after the Moscow recital, I was very inspired. I practiced in a completely different way. I thought that we Russians were rigid in our mentality. Horowitz sort of exuberantly spread the seeds of a new approach to art. This freedom connected with great skill is what Horowitz possessed. This freedom is the most happy condition that an artist can acquire. It cannot be achieved unless the artist believes in himself. With age, Horowitz had become greater than ever.

Even before he came to Moscow, I had learned a great lesson from him. I was always terrified of any wrong notes. I would eat my elbows out. When I practiced, the windows and doors were closed. I had to be sure that no one was going to come in. Those were my years of exile, and I could only receive small pieces of information. But someone sent me a video tape from the TV show *60 Minutes* containing an interview with Horowitz. He didn't particularly want to play for the cameras, but Wanda said, "Sit down and play, Volodya," and he would start to play, hitting wrong notes. As he hit them, he would scream out loudly something that sounded like "HA! HA!" as if with the intention to do it again. He wasn't ashamed of doing it wrong. My wife, Natasha, said, "You are going to watch this tape fifty times until you learn how to approach your own mistakes. You are not going to close yourself off in fear." I realized that it was a philosophy, much larger than just a stupid wrong note. For this I am eternally grateful to Horowitz.

Leon Fleisher

Leon Fleisher is a native of San Francisco. He studied with Artur Schnabel from the age of nine. In 1944, at 16, he made his debut with the New York Philharmonic in the Brahms D minor Concerto. At the age of twenty-four he won the Queen Elisabeth Competition, and in 1964 he gave the New York premiere of the Leon Kirchner Concerto, which had been written for him. Later that year an ailment crippled his right hand. Since then he has maintained an extensive career playing the left-hand concerti of Ravel, Prokofiev, Britten, and others, while conducting orchestras and opera.

Fleisher is currently artistic director of the Boston Symphony's Berkshire Music Center at Tanglewood. He holds three honorary doctorates and teaches at the Peabody Conservatory. His discography includes his collaboration with George Szell and the Cleveland Orchestra in Beethoven's five piano concertos.

My fondest memories of Horowitz are those of the several occasions when, in the late forties, I had the opportunity to play for him. He lived in a town house on the east side of New York, filled with wondrous paintings. I remember vividly how difficult it was to play under the sad, haunted gaze of a Rouault *Jesus*. The extraordinary as well as delightful compensation was that once I finished with my playing, he gently shoved me off the bench, seated himself, and proceeded, for the next several hours, to deliver himself of his latest and most current passions, which could range from Scarlatti or Clementi to Scriabin. What a marvelous feast it was!

However, I am not convinced that his legacy is not tinged with a touch of malignancy, both musically and technically. In an effort to reproduce his inimitable, searing brilliance of sound, many a young pianist has wound up with a case of tendinitis or worse, while his tendency to employ stylistically inappropriate Romantic devices in all music has seduced if not perhaps misguided several generations of young ears. Despite such habits and foibles, once recognized and faced, one could in full pleasure lose oneself in some of the most ferociously superb pianism, instrumental imagination, and coloristic artistry of our century.

Jose Feghali

Born in Brazil, Jose Feghali gave his first public performance at age five. In 1976 he moved to London, where he was a scholarship student at the Royal Academy and studied with Maria Curcio and Christopher Elton. In 1985 he was awarded the gold medal at the seventh Van Cliburn International Competition at Fort Worth. He made his American debut soon after at the Ambassador Auditorium in Pasadena. Since then, he has appeared in over two hundred performances with orchestras. Equally active as a recitalist, he appears regularly in the major European halls in London, Munich, Hanover, Barcelona, and Amsterdam, as well as in his native Brazil. He is currently artist-in-residence at Texas Christian University.

I was very young when I was introduced to Vladimir Horowitz through recordings my mother owned in Brazil. It was not until I moved to London in 1976 and started to acquire a record collection of my own and listen to Radio 3 on the BBC that I realized what a great artist he was. I became "Horowitz-crazy" after listening to his record of Scarlatti sonatas, as a lot of young pianists invariably become. That recording must surely figure among the ten best recordings of all time, especially since Horowitz was not renowned for his playing of the pre–Romantic literature. The clarity of the playing, the way the phrases are absolutely fluid, and, above all, the sound he coaxes out of the instrument are astonishing.

Another one that became my favorite was Rachmaninoff's Third Concerto, with Eugene Ormandy and the New York Philharmonic. I remember quite a few late nights with my friends listening to the other two recordings of the same concerto that Horowitz had previously made, arguing about the merits of each. In the end, I could not decide as to the absolute best, since each one had so much to offer in different ways. But I always had a soft spot for the last one, so much so that I ended up buying five copies of it, since I could not stand having even a single "click." My other favorites include the Prokofiev Sonata No. 7 and the best performance of Chopin's Barcarolle I have ever heard. Very few pianists have recorded so many works that are considered as the "favorites" of his fellow musicians.

Only once did I have the opportunity to see Horowitz perform in a live concert, when he came to London after a very long absence to perform two recitals at the Royal Festival Hall. I could not get tickets for the first concert, which was televised live in the presence of Prince Charles. I had saved my money for a long time to be able to afford a decent seat for the other concert, and that afternoon I ended up about ten rows from the front. Horowitz's entrance was unforgettable. I had seldom seen a unanimous standing ovation at the Royal Festival Hall, let alone *before* the concert even started! There was plenty of vintage Horowitz in those concerts, especially in the Rachmaninoff Sonata No. 2 and the Chopin Polonaise in A-flat major.

Horowitz was a master of control, with a superb balance of technical prowess and an ear for sound, line, and structure. He was able, for instance, to make passages sound faster than the actual speed he was playing, through the sheer clarity of articulation and rhythmic control. He also had one of the best pedal techniques I have heard. His musical genius was unique and has inspired much plagiarism. Of course, no one can possibly emulate Horowitz's playing, but he was and will be remembered as one of the greatest and most inspiring pianists in history.

Leon Bates

Leon Bates is a native of Philadelphia. At Temple University he studied with Natalie Hinderas. His career has taken him to Europe and Africa, and he has played with the leading orchestras in the United States. His video of the Gershwin Piano Concerto, made with the Basel Symphony, has been shown throughout Europe. Bates has also performed at various summer festivals and has appeared on television, including CBS's Sunday Morning *and NBC's* Today Show. *In 1988 he was chosen to perform at the gala celebration at Carnegie Hall for Steinway's five hundred thousandth piano.*

Bates holds an honorary doctorate of music from Washington and Lee University. He is often asked to give master classes and has taught at the University of Delaware. His recordings appear on the Orion, Performance Records, and Naxos labels.

In 1971, I was a contestant in the Levintritt Competition in New York. One of the judges was Gitta Gradova, a fine pianist and a great friend of Horowitz. She asked me if I would like to meet and play for Vladimir Horowitz. I was elated but also wary. After all, I was going to play for a living legend!

Some of the music I was playing at that time was in Horowitz's own repertoire: the *Kinderscenen* of Schumann, the G minor Ballade of Chopin, the *Etudes-Tableaux* of Rachmaninoff. I had already heard his recordings of these pieces, which had left a great impression on me. Now I was faced with the challenge of playing them as my own without being influenced by his interpretive style. I also thought that whatever I did could never rival what Horowitz could do. One part of my pleasure of playing in front of the public was in impressing them with my abilities. What would impress Vladimir Horowitz about me?

When the great day arrived, my parents drove me to Horowitz's

East Side home in New York. I will never forget the moment when he opened the door with his great smile, wearing one of those colorful bow ties. He was in good spirits and was quite warm and hospitable. I briefly met Mrs. Horowitz, who offered me some refreshments. After the preliminary conversation, Mrs. Horowitz left us alone, and Horowitz invited me to the piano. The piano had a wonderfully responsive action and a big, beautiful sound. The first piece I played for him was Schumann's Fantasy Op. 17. I felt as if I was giving a recital because he let me play the entire piece from beginning to end. I caught myself smiling a couple of times and fighting to redirect my focus as I reminded myself that this was not a dream; I was actually playing for Horowitz.

When I finished the Schumann, he was complimentary. He suggested some voicing changes in the piece, accentuating individual melodic lines in such a way that they became more vocal. I then played for him the G minor Ballade of Chopin and several of the *Etudes-Tableaux* Op. 33 of Rachmaninoff. He made more suggestions after I finished each piece. His responses were positive. He was very interested in how I had gotten involved in music and with classical music in particular. Later, he asked me if I experienced nervousness before performances. When I told him I didn't, he seemed surprised and pressed me several times about it. I caught a slight bit of annoyance when I assured him that I never experienced nerves before a concert.

After a time, Mrs. Horowitz reappeared, offering me more refreshments. I chatted with them briefly and then it was time to leave. As I prepared to say goodbye, I thought about how time had stopped while I played Vladimir Horowitz's piano. It was like I was floating in space, lost in a wonderful dream. When I woke up, so to speak, three hours had passed. I said my goodbyes and thank yous and headed out into the night.

Ian Hobson

Born in Wolverhampton, England, Ian Hobson at age seventeen was the youngest recipient of the recital diploma in the history of the Royal Academy of Music. His international career burgeoned in 1981 when he won first prize at the Leeds Competition.

As a pianist, Hobson has performed in the major capitals of the world. Recently he presented the complete cycle of thirty-two Beethoven sonatas. He regularly appears as soloist with important orchestras. In the last several years he has conducted many orchestras, as well as leading, from the keyboard, the English Chamber Orchestra in Mozart concertos on their Far East tour.

Hobson has recorded for Arabesque Records the complete piano sonatas of Hummel, the Etudes-Tableaux *by Rachmaninoff, and etudes by Chopin in Godowsky's transcriptions. He is a professor at the University of Illinois.*

Although I never had the occasion to meet Vladimir Horowitz, I was fascinated by his wizardry from my early years. As a student in London, I snatched up all the recordings even though he had not been to England since before I was born. When I anticipated my own further studies in the United States, his presence there, even if unseen, was exciting. He personified New York, and his performances mirrored the confident, sometimes abrasive, and certainly audacious nature of his adopted city.

One of my first acts upon arrival in the United States was to write down from the recording Horowitz's famous transcription of Sousa's *Stars and Stripes Forever,* in order to find out how he did it and to have the fun of playing the piece for myself. The dean of the Yale School of Music where I was studying got to hear of my manuscript and as he was trying to coax Horowitz to join the faculty, he asked whether he might send it to the Maestro. I concurred. A few weeks went by and then the dean informed me, with a smile, that Horowitz thanked me for sending the music, especially as he had no copy himself!

We tend to think of the extremes with Horowitz—the breathtaking octaves of the Sixth Rhapsody of Liszt, the spring-loaded finger work in the *Carmen* Fantasy, or the deep-toned poetry of *Traumerei*—but the fact is that everything in his limited repertoire was applied to the hilt. He never played too fast or too slowly. He dazzled on the outer limits of speed by his clarity and uncanny sense of rhythm. He beguiled us in slower music with an unprecedented ability and desire to voice with multilayered richness. The appeal of his playing was exceptional, not because he did these things so well but because he *dared* to do them in a unique and convincing way. There is not a great resemblance between his playing and that of his (and my) great idol Rachmaninoff, although he probably resembles Rachmaninoff more closely then he resembles any other pianist.

For better or worse, Horowitz probably had more influence on twentieth-century piano playing than any other pianist. I would suggest that this is at least partially as a result of another rare factor: that his recordings are as stirring and spontaneous-sounding as his live performances. This should be cause for gratitude and a source of inspiration for all pianists in the future.

Janina Fialkowska

Janina Fialkowska was born in Montreal. In 1969 she went to Paris to study with Yvonne Lefebure, and in 1970 she entered the Juilliard School, where she worked with Sascha Gorodnitzki. She won acclaim in 1974 as a prize winner at the first International Arthur Rubinstein Competition. Fialkowska has appeared as guest artist with the Concertgebouw Orchestra of Amsterdam, the Hallé Orchestra, the Israel Philharmonic, the London Philharmonic, and many others. In 1991 she performed a new concerto by Libby Larsen with the Minnesota Orchestra, and in 1992 she gave the North American premiere of the Piano Concerto by Sir Andrzej Panufnik.

Recently the CBC produced an hour-long television documentary, "The World of Janina Fialkowska." This program was awarded a Special Jury Prize at the 1992 San Francisco International Film Festival.

If someone were to ask me who I thought were the greatest pianists I had ever heard perform in concert, I would unhesitatingly reply: Arthur Rubinstein and Vladimir Horowitz. But immediately, I stumble upon a paradox because, in point of fact, there is an astonishingly high percentage of Horowitz's musical output that I frankly do not enjoy or even like. To explain this conundrum will obviously reveal not only my own peculiar musical tendencies but also the background wherein my own modest talent was developed. For it is with a little shame, I confess, that in making my first declaration of Horowitz's greatness, it is possible that I am succumbing to a bit of peer pressure that remains from my student years in Paris and New York—years of guilt at not being more entranced by his music making. Where I came from, Horowitz adulation was de rigueur.

My mother first introduced me to Horowitz recordings when I was a child. Her memories of him dated from pre–World War II

Paris. At the time, Paris was the center of the artistic world, and the young Russian from Kiev took the city and everyone in it by storm. "Never," she would repeatedly tell me, "had anyone heard a technique so sensational!" And amongst the less than perfect techniques based in Paris at that time, Cortot and Rubinstein for instance, this was not surprising. Actually, it wasn't his basic technique per se that was so much more advanced. Older pianists such as Rachmaninoff, Hofmann, Lhévinne, and Godowsky had in many ways far more all-encompassing techniques than he did, and certainly many played more difficult repertoire, all with greater ease. No. What stood out, and what still sets him apart from all others, is how he managed to bypass a pianist's natural concern for gaining the respect of his colleagues with the integrity and perfection of his playing, proceeding directly to the public forum, becoming along the way a sort of master magician, a demonic puppeteer who could, at will, manipulate audiences' emotions, whipping them into feverish frenzies by extraordinarily vivid and sometimes shocking colorings and sounds, by amazing, almost insane dynamic effects, and by diabolical turns of phrases always geared for maximum effect. This was not cold, calculated behavior, ignoring composers' wishes and the dictates of the printed score; I believe this was a true reflection of this man's musical personality—a mirror of his own soul: maniacally tense, anguished, contorted, childish, cruel, manipulative; but also producing moments of extraordinary beauty, bizzarely but so rewardingly imaginative, and, above all, generating more visceral excitement than any pianist except for perhaps the great Liszt himself.

My imperfect knowledge of Horowitz's art relies heavily on his recordings and videos, as I was only able to attend two of his recitals, both in New York in the seventies. Yes, I stood in line for most of the night to acquire tickets, but I never could honestly feel part of the pre-concert hoopla that felt so artificial to me, although to others it was almost a ritual. Going to the concerts was almost like going to a rock concert, insofar as the public was concerned; the atmosphere was "wired." And though musically they may have nothing in common, Horowitz himself was rather like a rock star in terms of the reactions he elicited from his public. One did not leave a Horowitz recital with one's heart overflowing with love and happiness and warmth. One left slightly hysterical, tingling with excitement, and with a highly accelerated pulse rate.

In his older years the great strength became almost caricature, helped along by the doctored pianos. Shades of the inhuman control were still there, but the ideas were so stilted and the phrases were so neurotically stretched in all directions as to sabotage the burning natural flow of the younger man. The spine-tingling pianissimos were now a bit precious and the exuberant, monster fortes had degenerated into mere pounding. And yet I do remember an amazingly beautiful performance of a Rachmaninoff Sonata and equally mesmerizing Scriabin. And the short virtuoso showpieces were still breathtaking. Probably the reason I am such a reluctant fan is that the repertoire that in my opinion suited him the best and in which he excelled the most was the repertoire to which I feel the least empathy. I unhappily could not bear what little of Chopin I heard him play. For me, his First Scherzo, A-flat major Polonaise, and First Ballade were bombastic travesties. In fact, the strength of his personality was such that his tortured renditions of the simplest mazurkas made me feel quite ill. Schumann labelled the Chopin mazurkas "cannons buried beneath flowers," but Horowitz approached them as sort of nuclear mutants. From all my readings of Chopin, I think he probably would have been offended by the Horowitz interpretations of his music. But as so many musicians and non-musicians have been transported or at least transfixed by the Horowitz Chopin, I personally simply cannot accept my own negative judgment so easily without qualifications, explanations, and, yes, a little guilt. But the way in which he could turn a simple child's dream (*Traumerei* of Schumann) into a work possessing the power of a psychotic's nightmare illustrated again the dichotomy of my feelings toward him: admiration for a pianist who could literally conjure up anything with his fingers, but disappointment in some of the musical choices his fingers made.

Last year I sat on the jury for an international Mozart competition. I heard endless Mozart, all sincerely and some beautifully played. Many young people trying to be so faithful to the composer's intentions, to the Mozart style in which they believed. By the end of two weeks I actively craved a dose of Horowitzian Mozart—something I had formerly so cavalierly and yet puritanically dismissed as self-indulgent, unmusical, and offensive. It was inherently distasteful to my own artistic soul maybe, but my God, it was compelling, it stirred one's emotions, never was it boring, and above all, it entertained!

In conclusion, I would like to mention that of all the many wonderful recordings he made, including the stunning Toscanini collaborations, my favorite happens to be his Brahms D minor Violin Sonata with Nathan Milstein: a performance of simplicity, great warmth, beauty, and sensitivity, in a way a rather atypical performance at least by contrast to how he has come to be perceived over the years. Perhaps it is I who is being the manipulator here, as I wish he had played that way more often; clearly it was possible for him. But I am wrong. This greatness came from his complex nature and the fact that he was capable of reflecting all of its myriad facets into his pianism, while remaining wholly true to his unique artistic vision. I shall go on admiring and respecting him with all my heart. But like him unreservedly? I am not sure.

Sahan Arzruni

The Armenian pianist Sahan Arzruni was born in Istanbul. He has achieved recognition as a pianist in a wide repertoire and as a writer, composer, and ethnomusicologist. He has appeared frequently on television and has been featured in a number of PBS specials. Arzruni has made recordings for Musical Heritage Society, Composers Recordings, Varese/Sarabande, and Philips. He has also recorded a three-record anthology of Armenian piano music and is the author of numerous scholarly articles in, for example, The Dictionary of the Middle Ages *and* The New Grove Dictionary of American Music. *He has hosted radio programs, performed frequently with Victor Borge, and propagated many contemporary works.*

"Feverish carnality" is the pervading spirit of Vladimir Horowitz's pianism, an utterance of passion and frenzy, that agitates sensitivities and disquiets sensibilities. Spawned in the chthonian world—murky, oozy, and swampy—Horowitz's art is fantastic and shapeless. His piano sound, erupting out of volcanic violence, causes delicious agony and excruciating pleasure. His music, narcotic rather than hypnotic, induces anxiety and effects stupor. Hearing Horowitz play is to experience musical priapism.

Strange as it is, I have not heard Horowitz play live, only on records and through telecasts. Particularly vivid in my memory is his interview with Mike Wallace. But I feel I know him; I feel I understand him intimately. My appreciation of Horowitz comes from my close association with Victor Borge—both, artists of genuine distinction; both, personalities of quirky character. Recently, when Lesley Stahl of *60 Minutes* asked Borge what the difference was between him and Horowitz, Borge shot back, "He is dead."

The act of transcription, a preoccupation with both Horowitz and Borge, is the key to my particular insight. The involuted workings of a transcriber's mind have always fascinated me. For the pianist-composer, transcribing is both liberating and limiting: a measure of freedom is gained by performing one's own arrangements, yet a degree of distinction is relinquished when resorting to the proven popularity of pre-existing material. Like Borge, Horowitz has spun a number of brilliant arrangements of celebrated melodies, keeping them, however, exclusively for personal use.

The art of transcription could be an exalted expression of reverence. Bach fervently argues the case of Baroque composers when he transcribes their music into a new medium; he expounds substance inherent in the original. Similarly, in arranging Bach's work for piano, Busoni acts as a great commentator; he enlarges and amplifies matter and thought implicit, for example, in Bach's Toccata, Adagio, and Fugue in C major, a composition Mr. Horowitz chose to render upon his return to Carnegie Hall.

Vladimir Horowitz's transcriptions belong to the Liszt/Rachmaninoff tradition, essentially a re-formation of musical gesture. In the hands of a truly creative power, such music possesses imaginative beauty and inexhaustible inventiveness, at times charged with dramatic energy, and at others imbued with glowing color, warmth, and charm. In Mr. Horowitz's hands, it also provides a harrowed path to his musical psyche. Therein lies a profile of his identity, insurgent and submissive all at once.

In the sphere of aesthetics, duality is of the essence: either conflicting forms competing against each other, or converging impulses complementing one another. A purging of emotions—a catharsis—is provoked when with exquisite skill these impulses are brought to a tremulous point of balance. With Mr. Horowitz, this fragile equilibrium is wanting. His lack of architectonic power, exemplified in his endless digressions and discursions, creates an impression of diffusiveness and redundancy that obscures the mystery of the whole. For Mr. Horowitz, the parts seem to be greater than the whole. He leaves me unhinged, in need of a more satisfying emotional relief, a more urgent necessity for emotional adjustment.

Vladimir Horowitz projects a passionate self-abandonment, executed with wild magnificence. His propulsion is heedless, his engine visceral. He allows himself an aesthetic license, reckless and extravagant, defiant of restraint and convention. He delivers the music with a voluptuous vigour of movement, with an animalism that wars against the concerns of the spirit—an animalism of love and hatred, both in extremes, out of center and harmony. His art craves internality, an internal core, an inner center.

In his transcriptions, Mr. Horowitz replaces technical rhetoric—the thundering octaves or the gossamer glitter—for musical outline. He is unconcerned with inspiring in the listener nebulous images. He is even less mindful of coordinating such images, since they are perfunctory, dictated by distressing fluency and vapid reiteration, robbing the music of its conviction and potency.

Had it not been for an accident of time, Vladimir Horowitz would have been among the Decadents, along with Oscar Wilde, Aubrey Beardsley, and Walter Pater, artists celebrating the erotic, macabre, and cruel expressions of human emotion. Alexander Scriabin too, with his frequent sallies into the salacious and the diabolic, should be figured among the Decadents, of whose music Horowitz arguably is the best interpreter. Owing to a sensory make-up of surpassing eccentricity, he plays with a stimulation far wider and more intense than merely cerebral excitement. Seated there, at the piano, he seems engaged in humid personal pleasure, surrounded by dancers in an ithyphallic ritual.

Leslie Howard

Leslie Howard was born in Australia. He has traveled extensively as a recitalist and has played with many of the world's finest orchestras. He has made numerous recordings of worthy and forgotten scores, such as Glazunov piano music and Anton Rubinstein piano sonatas. For the Hyperion label, Howard has embarked on the monumental venture of recording the complete solo piano music of Liszt. The project is estimated to take fifteen years to complete and will total more than sixty compact discs. For those already recorded, he has been awarded three Grands Prix du Disque. Howard often broadcasts on radio and television, and has contributed to many music journals and symposia. He succeeded the late pianist Louis Kentner as president of the Liszt Society of Great Britain.

Writing of P. G. Wodehouse, *Punch* once wrote that "to criticise him is like taking a spade to a soufflé," and the same sentiment encapsulates the present writer's approach to Horowitz. There is an ephemeral magic in the man's art that supervenes over adverse critical appraisal, however one may be moved to remark upon the myriad of inconsistencies, stylistic anachronisms, and just plain bad taste that so often sat cheek by jowl with ineffable craftsmanship.

To appreciate the best qualities in him, it is impossible to neglect the annoying: Horowitz's playing has almost no purely intellectual fibre to it—for all the fanfaronade, his late Mozart recordings are merely full of inappropriate ear-catching tricks at the expense of what cricketers term "line and length," and the many beauties of his early recording of the Liszt Sonata (the later one is of little importance) are not shored up by an apparent musical understanding of the philosophic backbone to the work. It may be generally observed that the hectic desperation to titillate the public stands in the way of a mindful interpretation of almost every great large-scale work that he played. And yet, in smaller repertoire, where most modern players fear to venture, ostensibly for its want of imposing substance (and how boring most modern recital programmes have become as a result) but almost certainly because of the want of charm in their own playing, Horowitz has few peers. The price of this dichotomy was a repertoire brimful of music of the second rank alongside the great character pieces of the Romantic era, and performances which ranged from the crudest (the last Rachmaninoff *Etude-Tableau* or the First *Mephisto* Waltz) to the tenderly revelatory (Rachmaninoff's D major Prelude or Liszt's Third Consolation).

None of this can alter the essential quality of his playing: almost no player, past or present, can begin to compete with the variety of touch and sound that the man brought to his best endeavours: variety over the length of a phrase, a movement, an evening, and variety in the vertical combination of tones so diversely coloured that harmony and line perfectly graced each other. The underlying secret of this—not secret because undetectable but because impossible to replicate—is the unforgettable impression that, before a key was depressed, Horowitz knew *exactly* what sound would be produced. Of course, Horowitz knew, too, that he could afford to smile at his adoring public from the keyboard as he was about to deliver an act of musical prestidigitation because he knew beforehand that the trick would be a success. It is this skill, applied to a keen understanding developed over a long career of how to silence criticism in advance by having an attentively cajoled audience's fanatical support, which ensures that any shorter piece from Chopin or Scriabin to Moszkowski or Mendelssohn is memorable in his hands. Whilst one may question the way he went about it, there is no doubt too that Horowitz saw a genuine duty to his public to entertain, especially in the unabased sense of retaining the interest of the listener, a duty which he saw too many of his contemporaries neglect. He was certainly right to cite boredom of the audience as the greatest crime in performance; the perennial problem of how to manage to avoid musical travesty in the pursuit of attention seems often to have been a pitfall to him, as to many others.

The least defensible aspect of Horowitz's work is surely his textual alteration on a large scale of great works which stand in no need of surgery: his rewriting of Mussorgsky, Rachmaninoff, or Liszt is as unnecessary as it is destructive. His "version" of the Rachmaninoff Second Sonata (which he varied considerably between performances, *pace* Mr. Browning's excellent edition of the original) does not advance our comprehension of why Rachmaninoff should have emasculated a fine work in a period of depression; his "tarting up" of the First *Mephisto* Waltz, the Nineteenth Rhapsody, or, most lamentably, the Scherzo and March does nothing to advance Liszt's cause as an intellectual heavyweight in a world where he has often been misunderstood as meretricious. This sort of intervention is quite another thing from the often happy habit of the great Romantic pianist to leave small musical fingerprints in the text of character pieces, a habit at which Horowitz was congenially capable.

But, love him or hate him, or even both simultaneously, Horowitz's career remains the greatest in twentieth-century pianism because his phenomenal abilities simply cannot be ignored. One can imagine many an artist of more profundity, of broader repertoire, cringing at excesses of taste in Horowitz's playing whilst inwardly regretting his own puny command of things pianistic. It is an idle speculation, but the thought springs unbidden that some kind of genetic engineering that combined the best of Horowitz with, say, the best of Schnabel, Petri, or Fischer would have produced the total musician at the piano, the virtuoso in every aspect.

However, the famous dead can look after themselves without fear, and we living practitioners of the art of piano playing are as well aware of the difficulties which arise from a stage-managed career as we are of the potential damage of unsolicited criticism. Only a fool or a churl would deny Horowitz his singular place in the pantheon of the great: his winsome account of the Schumann *Humoreske*, his barnstorming A-flat major Polonaise, his serious interest in Clementi and Scriabin (what a pity he did not have the inclination to dig a little further here), his very personal un-Baroque Scarlatti, all of his miniatures—pensive or frivolous, the electric pianism in the first and second recordings of the Rachmaninoff Third Concerto is unfailingly moving or exciting, and, on a personal level, it was his recording of the B minor Sonata, which I listened to as a lad, which started my lifelong investigation of the music of Liszt.

Emanuel Ax

Born in Lwów (then part of Poland), Emanuel Ax moved to Winnipeg, Canada, when still a child. He studied at the Juilliard School with Mieczyslaw Munz and in 1974 was the victor at the first Arthur Rubinstein International Competition in Tel Aviv. In 1979 he received the Avery Fisher Prize. He recorded over twenty albums for RCA; since 1987 he has recorded exclusively for Sony Classical.

Ax performs in solo recital, as soloist in concertos, and in chamber music, often with Isaac Stern, Jaime Laredo, and Yo-Yo Ma. Besides the standard repertoire, he has given many performances of twentieth-century composers, performing solo and concertos by Schoenberg, Tippett, Henze, Previn, Schwanter, Bolcom, and Laderman. His recording of Haydn sonatas was named one of Stereo Review's *"Records of the Year" in 1989.*

One of the great assets of being a music student in New York during the 1960s was the opportunity to hear all the great artists of the day. No matter how often or rarely they performed, virtually all of them played here sooner or later. A young pianist could go to one of the many halls of the city several times a week and be uplifted, amazed, moved, and indeed sometimes disappointed by a major artist.

In spite of this cornucopia of delights for the piano enthusiast, there was always the regret of not having heard the pianistic legends of the past. My teacher, Mieczyslaw Munz, spoke at almost every lesson of the incomparable playing of Hofmann and Rachmaninoff, whom he had often heard in Carnegie Hall, and also people like Lhévinne, Moiseiwitsch, Barère, and many others.

Included in these reminiscences invariably was Vladimir Horowitz. His piano playing was as legendary as that of the greatest names from the past, and of course his recordings bore out everything that was said about him.

All this is to explain why, when the announcement of Horowitz's return to the stage came in 1965, it was as though Rachmaninoff had returned from Paradise to favor us with a concert. Horowitz to us was not a living pianist but a legend of mythical proportions. I was one of the first one hundred people to line up for tickets to the recital scheduled for May 9. I was able to secure seats (in the front row of the balcony at Carnegie Hall), but until the actual moment when Horowitz walked on stage, I had no sense of reality about the event—how could a legend of the past actually be here to play in the flesh?

That recital remains as the most thrilling listening experience of my life. From the first notes of the Bach-Busoni, there was a sense of sorcery that I had never heard evoked by anyone else. The sheer range of sound, and the fact that it was produced by a figure who looked totally still and controlled, whether the piano thundered or whispered, made each note electric. I have listened to the recording of the concert many times—the Schumann Fantasy remains my favorite performance of that work—and each time, I am transported back to my balcony seat at Carnegie Hall, drinking in my share of pianistic history.

I heard Horowitz many times after that and, of course, listened and continue to listen to his innumerable recordings.

The pianistic qualities that made him unique are:

1. A huge dynamic range, achieved through complete control of subtle shadings in the soft music, so that he was able to differentiate without having to resort to great volume—when he played fortissimo, it sounded much more enormous than anyone else, because our ears had been so sharpened and engaged by the delicacy of the dynamics from before. It was as though an extra switch had been thrown and the power was doubled.
2. An extraordinary sensibility for the agogics of melodic line. Horowitz was a great devotee of bel canto singing, and his phrasing reflected his love—the melodic line never sagged, and he was able to stretch a line almost out of shape, thus creating great tension and interest, but always retaining the continuity.

There was never a dead note in his playing—each note, whether loud or soft had a special ring.

3. His unbelievable ear for polyphony, which allowed him to cultivate an independence of fingers that led to an independence of line in everything he touched. Never did the bass slavishly follow the treble, never did inner voices serve only the function of filler—again, each note, whether on top, on bottom, or in the middle had a special ring and sound.
4. His seemingly electric physical ability. Even in his eighties, Horowitz was able to play octaves, repeated notes, and runs with a glittering sound which was inimitable. His unique technical achievements had very little to do with being able to play more accurately or faster than anyone else, although these things were probably also true. They had to do with being able to make the difficult sound either easy or impossible, whichever he chose, and with making a truly unique sound. I believe that Horowitz is one of only two or three artists in our century of whom the old saying is true: "One can recognize his playing from one phrase."

We all aspire to better ourselves as pianists and musicians. We are privileged to have before us such examples of the pianist's art as Horowitz's, for it is playing like his that gives our profession its greatest joy—the possibility of being a student forever.

Yury Boukoff

Yury Boukoff was born in Sofia, Bulgaria. At 12 he gave his first recital. He graduated from the Conservatory of Sofia, and won first prize at the National Competition of Bulgaria; shortly after, he went to France, where he continued his studies at the Paris Conservatoire with Yves Nat.

Boukoff has played under such distinguished conductors as Cluytens, Markevitch, Rodzinski, Dorati, Masur, Prêtre, and Ozawa. He has performed in Europe, North and South America, and Africa, and was the first European pianist to perform in the People's Republic of China, in 1956. He has recorded the Menotti concerto for Pathé-Marconi, concertos by Khachaturian, Rachmaninoff, and Tchaikovsky for Philips, and the complete Prokofiev sonatas for Westminster.

My encounter with Horowitz's art came to me quite late, when I settled in the West after the Second World War. In Bulgaria during the war it was practically impossible to get his recordings or have the chance of hearing many important pianists. Of the few foreign pianists who visited us, Nicolas Orloff occupied the first place in the hearts of the public.

Finally, in 1946–47, I was able to hear Backhaus, Fischer, Gieseking, Kempff, Rubinstein, Lipatti, and others. They were all wonderful. Besides their own personality and the various levels of technical skill, I found in them a normal and logical continuity in the history and evolution of piano playing. They followed in the footsteps of Thalberg, Liszt, D'Albert, Busoni, Anton Rubinstein, and Paderewski. However, one person stood out for me, although I only heard his recordings, and that was Rachmaninoff. Here, I felt, was a personality far above all others, with a technique and imagination that revealed the music in a different light. Unfortunately, I heard too few of his recordings to judge the universality of Rachmaninoff's art, but when I later heard Horowitz, I distinctly felt Rachmaninoff's presence.

I sincerely think that I do not know of another pianist (of my generation) who has had as much influence on his contemporaries as did Horowitz, and whom so many people unfortunately tried to imitate in vain. When I finally heard Horowitz, I was confronted with an unsuspected phenomenon that totally jarred everything I had learned from childhood on. Horowitz had a sound so particular that one recognized it immediately from the first notes. He took liberties that were almost shocking to traditional minds, with both dynamic indications and tempo; he brought out hidden voices to astonishing prominence, creating a polyphony where there seemed to be none. Indeed, in some works he stripped away all tradition, and his performances gave the wonderous impression of being improvised on the spur of the moment. I seemed to rediscover the composition he was playing. I, like most everybody, set about imitating Horowitz: his octaves, his voicing, his nervous and electric presence, and, most especially, the plasticity of his way of singing a melodic phrase. However, one does not become a Horowitz by wishing.

There are some people who say that Horowitz excelled in the miniatures and not in large-scale works. That seems to be a major error. I do not even take into consideration his great success in the Brahms, Tchaikovsky, and Rachmaninoff concertos, in which one could say the conductors contributed to the structure. There remain, however, amazing conceptions and an architectural magnitude in his Liszt B minor Ballade, the celebrated reading of the B minor Sonata, the Barber, Prokofiev, and Kabalevsky sonatas, the Mozart sonatas, his amazing structural grip of the fragmentary sonatas by Scriabin, and his control of flow of time in Mussorgsky's *Pictures at an Exhibition*. These are hardly miniatures or *minor* works; each requires a very different sense of construction and grandeur, which Horowitz projected to the ultimate.

To my mind, his inventive spirit reaches its summit in the Chopin mazurkas. Under his fingers, these so-called miniatures become epic poems, beyond all dimension. Nor can one ever forget his Scarlatti playing. Never had this composer been more fortunate in an interpreter. He certainly had a formidable influence on the Soviet pianists; Emil Gilels told me, "For me, Horowitz remains at the top of the world." Of the great Romantics, his Chopin, Liszt, and to a lesser degree Schumann offer wonderful achievements. It is difficult for me to say if Chopin's Fourth Ballade enchants me more than his Liszt Sixth Rhapsody, or whether the Brahms B-flat major Concerto is more wonderful than his incomparable Rachmaninoff Third Concerto. I think that in Mozart, Beethoven, and Schubert—these masters are farthest from Horowitz's temperament.

When comparing the great pianists, it is important to understand and make distinctions between the German tradition of Backhaus, Kempff, Fischer, Serkin, and Arrau and those bred in the Latino-Slav tradition of Cortot, Hofmann, Arthur Rubinstein, Rachmaninoff, and Horowitz.

I had the pleasure of meeting Horowitz once. It was during his return to the Paris concert stage in the 1960s. It was Horowitz's old friend, the pianist Jacques Février, who had invited Daniel Wayenberg, Pierre Barbizet, and myself to meet him. We spent a charming afternoon playing and discussing music and piano technique with him, as between old friends and colleagues. He was relaxed, without any pretension whatsoever. He seemed to possess a simple and kind disposition and was able to put us all at ease. Of all musicians during my own lifetime, it is the creative playing of Horowitz who has fascinated me the most. His death deprives me of many joyous emotions that he so generously bestowed during his lifetime.

Gilbert Kalish

Born in New York, Gilbert Kalish graduated from Columbia University and studied piano with Julius Hereford, Leonard Shure, and Isabella Vengerova. He has been active as soloist, chamber player, and teacher. He has often appeared as a member of the Contemporary Chamber Ensemble and was the lifelong duo partner of the late mezzo-soprano Jan DeGaetani. For many years he was a member of the Boston Chamber Players, and he has had a close association with the Boston Symphony Orchestra while directing the chamber music and keyboard programs at Tanglewood.

Kalish has a discography of over eighty recordings. Notable discs include his five-volume traversal of Haydn sonatas and his Ives Concord Sonata, *both on Nonesuch, as well as his many award-winning discs with Jan DeGaetani on the Bridge, Arabesque, and Nonesuch labels.*

During the 1940s, while the war raged throughout the world, the arts continued to flourish as always, bringing inspiration, solace, and simple pleasure to millions of people who carried a burden of sorrow and anxiety. Life then, however, was perhaps not much different than today for middle-class American families. Despite the torrent of cataclysmic events that inundated the world, there was a sense of order and relative tranquility.

Born in 1935, I was a small child at that fearful time. When I was 3, my mother discovered that I had perfect pitch and could remember and identify pieces of music. She was convinced that I was God's gift to the world of music, and her life's work became clear to her.

Each year during that period, Horowitz appeared in solo recital at the Brooklyn Academy of Music. His concerts were, of course, always sold out. I can still almost taste the atmosphere of that event fifty years ago. We were seated on the stage, my parents on either side of me. The auditorium was buzzing with expectation and excitement. I felt giddy sitting in the first row of stage seats, some fifteen feet from where the great man would be seated at the Steinway. The lights dimmed, and out he came, intent, serious, totally absorbed in the task at hand. I believe he played the *Kinderscenen* of Schumann, a piece I was working on at the time. When he played his incredible Fantasy on Themes from *Carmen,* I felt an almost visceral sense of contact with Horowitz as the piano thundered at me. I can still feel the roar of the audience, a sound I have never since experienced at any concert hall.

For the next few years, I studied with a series of teachers of German-Jewish origin, all of whom felt that their young students must be protected from the demonic powers of Horowitz. I am certain that this phenomenon occurred throughout the world. "Horowitz is an athlete," they complained, "not a musician. He distorts the rhythm in a willful and arbitrary manner and he doesn't always follow the composers' intents. He is more interested in demonstrating his own prowess than in the music." These complaints were spoken in sorrow rather than anger. Naturally, a ten-year-old was inclined to believe his teachers. A little voice inside my head, however, said, "If he was so *wrong*, why was Horowitz so stupendously riveting?"

As an adult, I never had the opportunity to hear Horowitz's "return to action" recitals. But the recordings document this man's phenomenal gifts and achievements that put him in a category by himself. I hate comparison in life or in art, for it always pits one person or thing against another, thereby belittling the unique qualities of an individual. And so it is for pianists as well. Yet one must recognize that Horowitz was a force of nature, the equal the world is unlikely to see.

Constance Keene

The American pianist Constance Keene first came to national attention when she won the Naumburg Award. A tireless performer, she plays recitals and chamber music throughout the world. Keene's orchestral engagements have included appearances with such orchestras as the Philadelphia, Chicago, New York, and Berlin Philharmonic. Recently she performed in Shanghai and Beijing, and with the KBS Symphony of Korea.

As well as serving on the piano faculty of the Manhattan School of Music, Keene gives master-classes and is an adjudicator of many piano competitions. She has also contributed articles on music and musicians to various publications. On the Protone label she has recorded a large repertoire ranging from the complete Rachmaninoff preludes, Chopin preludes, and sonatas by Hummel and Dussek to the four sonatas by MacDowell.

From childhood, I was fortunate in having heard many great performers, and to me Horowitz was the ultimate. As a teenager, I met Horowitz through my teacher, Abram Chasins, who knew him. After shaking his hand, I was so excited that I said, "I will never wash this hand again."

It was years later that I had the opportunity to play for Horowitz. Chasins asked him if he would listen to me and perhaps give me some instruction. Horowitz told Chasins that he would not give any suggestions unless Abram was present, for, as Horowitz put it, "Perhaps I will say something with which you will disagree." I was not nervous when I played for him. When I concluded the E-flat minor Rachmaninoff Prelude, he complimented me and told me to "Try making an accelerando at the coda. You must remember the box office." That afternoon he also gave me some wonderful fingerings for Liszt's *Dance of the Gnomes* that created dazzling effects. I remember to this day that the thrill of the afternoon was indescribable.

Meanwhile, my own career was established through winning the Naumburg. I was managed by Arthur Judson, the impresario who was the head of Columbia Artists Management. During my first season, CAMI had prearranged only two engagements, but they knew that I was ever ready to substitute for some of their fabled artists. One evening Helen Traubel couldn't sing. Instead I played. One day the call came to substitute, but this time it was for Horowitz. You can imagine my excitement but also my apprehension. Ada Cooper (in charge of the bookings) said that 4,400 people were waiting in Springfield, Massachusetts, and that 4,400 people were expecting Horowitz. His piano had already arrived, and Paderewski's bench was in place. The public had paid for the tickets, and they needed somebody to appear. I was the replacement. A representative came along for the ride, and, I suppose, to be certain that I did not defect. There were no printed programs, and so I had to announce my program! The audience was fabulous, and supported me throughout the evening. The press was present for both the news portion of the event and for the review. The only person a bit displeased was the president of the concert series, who had been through this once before with Horowitz; she was aptly named Mrs. Sweat.

Due to the car crush, some patrons had to park far away from the hall. A couple of ladies had driven miles and were devastated to find the program already in progress when they arrived. They pleaded with the usher to let them in, but he adhered to the usual rule of no admission until the conclusion of the first work. However, in order to be courteous he opened the door a crack so that they could hear. They also peeked, and suddenly in hushed horror one said to the other, "My God, Millie, Horowitz is a woman." That evening was a boon to my future, and the publicity received helped establish me. Through all our years together, this event was never mentioned by the Horowitzes, and as far as I know they were not aware that it was I who performed on that series in VH's place.

Once, while Wanda Toscanini Horowitz was abroad, Abram, Horowitz, and I did many New York fun things together. We went to the Stork Club with the columnist Leonard Lyons, we went to see *Guys and Dolls*, the Broadway hit show. When the theatre had misplaced our seats, we sat on the floor in the aisle, and when we departed Horowitz queried, "What is a guy and what is a doll?" So after years of living in the States and in New York he still was not street-savvy. Abram and I were newly married, and I was indulging myself by having many parties. Horowitz came to quite a few, and during one of them, a famous woman showed that she was a bit tipsy and said to Horowitz, "Everybody calls you Volodya, and your name is Vladimir, what should I call you?" He replied firmly, "You may call me Mr. Horowitz."

He and I went to the theatre together one evening, while Abram had a rendezvous with Jorge Bolet. It was that kind of chummy relationship. Horowitz had a great desire to go to the Electric Circus, one of our first rock discos. Leonard Lyons arranged that, too. The blasting sounds exhausted us, and we could only hope to take leave as soon as possible. But VH was all smiles and was full of enjoyment. And why was that? He had brought along ear plugs and, while observing the crowd was fun, he didn't have to listen! Shrewd, and how!

Soon Mrs. Horowitz returned and took over her role of attending to Volodya's every wish. She dedicated herself to pleasing him. Musically, she was the person who brought scores of the Clementi sonatas. These works tempted him to practice and to return to active concert life. She advised him on his programs. When he performed a complex Liszt work, not often heard, she advised him to drop it from further programs. She would make dry runs of the proposed cities and countries that his manager had urged for consideration. She tried out the hotels, she discussed the menus, she made the plans for the necessary dark window coverings, for taking Lily, their beautiful white French poodle. The picnic basket was readied by her for the tour, lest some provision would not be available. And the same precision was applied to the New York recitals. She was meticulous about going through the press lists and the guest lists for the backstage group and for the party at home, which usually took place at about 9:30 P.M. after the 4 P.M. recital. Wanda Toscanini Horowitz had been born to this, having supervised her father's life as well.

Fortunately we were in harmony, and so were invited to Fire Island, to recitals, to run-throughs. One time Abram arranged for WQXR to broadcast the second half of one of the Horowitz recitals, which also included the encores. According to the New York press, "That was the night television was dead." At that event, Paul Buttenwieser was one of my young students. Since Abram was backstage officiating, Paul was my date. It was his first Horowitz "live." He was dazzled and speechless during the recital, but when VH played the *Stars and Stripes* and the piccolos entered, another piercing sound emerged—and the audience heard, "Keenie, Keenie, where is his third hand?"

The daughter of Gitta Gradova and Maurice Cottle, close friends of the Horowitz's, was married in our home. Wanda came for the ceremony and reception while Volodya arrived only at reception time. The groom's mother's comment was, "With all these great pianists present, how come there is no music?" I responded, "Well, we couldn't ask Horowitz to play, and the rest of us did not want to perform unless he brought up the subject." Soon after, Wanda was asked to join the Harlem School of the Arts and prevailed on me to go with her to the first meeting arranged by Mrs. Artur Rodzinski. It was a much needed project in New York, and soon we were both heavily involved. I became vice-chairman to Wanda, who was chairman. This put us into daily telephone contact, and we also were together several times a week, usually at the Horowitz mansion. Horowitz was not going out socially much, but when we gave our first big charity blast with Peter Nero, my protégé, playing at the Buttenwieser home, Volodya said, "Nero is my favorite jazz pianist, and so I will buy a ticket and come." We were happy to tell him that it was too late because we were sold out. When Peter Nero heard this, he quipped, "Tell Horowitz he can have my seat." Of course we made a special seat for VH and he didn't have to miss a thing except for the fingerings, for he and Abram took positions in the downstairs library of the duplex apartment. All the keyboard seats were taken well in advance.

This association led to more and more intimacy, and when canasta became the rage we learned to play and would get together several evenings a week. There were usually two more guests, so that when Horowitz tired and needed a break we could continue. He was a shrewd player, and would con you into making his decisions for him. When he felt that he had to give the pack, he would say "You choose." We were not taken in by his boyish charm, and when he lost, he always paid up, even to Wanda. It was great fun, and there were many times that Horowitz would go to the piano during his rest period from the game and play through some new music. There were also many evenings when at midnight he would say, "You do not wish to hear my new Scarlatti sonatas? Or the rest of my new program?" Often these new works were performed with the music, and I turned pages. It was late and Wanda would say, "You are making so much noise, all the neighbors will complain."

Before a four-hand recital with Serkin I sight-read the scores, playing the top to Horowitz's bass. Fun for me. (That show never came off.) Both the Horowitzes were great animal lovers. There were two dogs and two cats in the house at one point. Fussy, an orange striped alley cat, was the mascot for VH. Then one night Fussy just disappeared. We never knew whether it was sex or death that took him.

Knowing Horowitz meant hearing those Horowitz sounds over and over again, seeing this genius at work, being transported to Paradise. This man had the highest standards, and while he said that he practiced only an hour and a half a day, he never counted the practice of playing for his friends as time at the instrument. He was a driven perfectionist, and nothing was left to chance in his preparation. He knew his works so well that he never played anything out of mechanical habit; he re-created. Each performance was different, and since I went to all within the New York area, I can tell you that each was its own musical adventure. On a couple of occasions I went to Cleveland, and once to Washington, where I spent the weekend with them and Lily. It was fascinating to be with the family on concert day. We all breakfasted together, but didn't speak. He needed complete quiet for his concentration. His breakfast was simple: a mountain of toast, Sanka, and tomato jelly. I don't recall any cereal or eggs. Then, after a brief rest, to the piano to play some exercises that he made up on the spot. Somehow we got to about 3:30 P.M. and left for the recital without uttering a word. Wanda took her precious husband backstage. Naturally the house was sold out and full of electricity. The audience reception was the usual frenzy: a delerium repeated throughout his lifetime. Even in Washington the inner circle gathered after 9 P.M. at the Horowitz hotel suite. The only exception, to my knowledge, was after the White House recital. I was present at that gala, and the fruit punch and sandwiches were served immediately after the music. What fun it was for me to exchange pleasantries with President and Mrs. Carter. There we were standing toe to toe and conversing.

During the New York appearances I was often able to purchase a large number of seats and use them to benefit the Manhattan School of Music. Those resold seats ultimately enabled me to arrange the purchase of two Steinway concert grands for our auditoriums; one in memory of Sonia Horowitz was dedicated by Gina Bachauer when she came to give a master-class at Manhattan. On that day both Wanda and her sister came, and we had a beautiful tribute to Sonia. By now that piano has been replaced by one that I contributed, but the placque on it reminds everybody that the instrument is in memory of their daughter, Sonia Horowitz.

At this writing Horowitz has been dead for three years. Fortunately he will never be gone, for we have his legacy of recordings. For me he is ever-present in my ears. Who has ever given us such sounds? Who has ever given us such intepretations?

Peter Frankl

Budapest-born Peter Frankl won several first prizes at competitions in Paris, Munich, and Rio de Janeiro. He made his London debut in 1961; his New York debut with the Cleveland Orchestra under George Szell took place in 1967.

Besides orchestral engagements and chamber music and recital dates, Frankl performs at numerous international music festivals. At the Edinburgh Festival he performed the Britten Concerto with the composer conducting. He has made twenty-one appearances at the Henry Wood Promenade Concerts, and his Far Eastern tours have taken him to Australia, New Zealand, and Japan.

He opened his 1990 season with performances of Schnittke's Piano Concerto at the Berlin Festival, with Ashkenazy conducting. He records on many labels, and his discography includes the complete piano music of Debussy and Schumann. Recently he has released compact discs on the ASV label. Since 1987 he has been visiting professor of piano at Yale University.

On a dark November afternoon in 1989 I was browsing in a bookshop in New Haven and I found a copy of Glenn Plaskin's Horowitz biography. For a long time I had been toying with the idea of buying this book, but this time, without any hesitation, I picked it up and bought it. Right away I became involved and fascinated with the book and, thus, the shock was even greater when, early the next morning, I turned on the radio and heard the news that Horowitz had died the day before.

What a coincidence! I found the timing very spooky indeed. But somehow I thought it was very appropriate and fitted well with his personality. Since my early childhood, he had been a legend in my life. I heard incredible stories about his debut recital in Budapest in

1926. As an unknown pianist, he played in the Redoutensaal for a very small audience, but all present became so wild with excitement that during intermission they rushed to the phones to alert their friends, who then flocked to the hall, filling it by the end of the concert.

We grew up with his legendary recordings, the two concertos with Toscanini, the Liszt Sonata, and so on. Later I acquired the pirated recording of his last concert in 1953 before his first retirement: the Tchaikovsky with Szell, which is somewhat crazy but much more electrifying than the commercial one. Szell kept up with him admirably until the very last page, when it became an incredible race, won, of course, by Horowitz. In a way, it is quite understandable that, at this point in his life, he had to stop playing.

I already lived in London when the BBC transmitted his comeback recital in 1965. I was glued to the radio from beginning to end, and in spite of his obvious nervousness, the impact he made on me was tremendous. I was particularly fascinated by his interpretations of the Bach-Busoni Toccata, Adagio, and Fugue, and the Schumann Fantasy.

In person, I was able to hear him only on three occasions. One of them was at Carnegie Hall in 1969, where he started his recital with a beautifully played Haydn C major Sonata, followed by *Kreisleriana* and Rachmaninoff's Second Sonata. I remember that the Schumann was heavily criticized, but I will never forget the mysterious last movement, which is also so beautifully captured on the record. And what an unforgettable encore: *Au bord d'une source*! And then the two London concerts, erratic, but still full of wonderful things, like the six Scarlatti sonatas. I have never heard Scarlatti played like that: it was simply magical.

Of course, he created plenty of controversy, especially in our very objective time. His playing was unique, not to be followed; he had a towering personality and was a very great artist. When, at his death, the *Guardian* interviewed several of us pianists in its obituary, I was a bit disappointed that many colleagues talked about him dismissingly. To me, he certainly will remain, as a performing artist, one of the giants of our time.

Idil Biret

Born in Ankara, Idil Biret graduated from the Paris Conservatoire at age fifteen. She studied piano with Cortot and Kempff, and composition with Nadia Boulanger. Since the age of sixteen she has given concerts worldwide. Over the years she has performed more than eighty concerts in Russia. In 1990 she made two tours to Japan.

Her discography includes Scriabin's Tenth Sonata, the Liszt transcription of Berlioz's Symphonie fantastique, *the Boulez Second Sonata, piano works by Kempff, Miaskovsky's Second and Third Sonatas, Liszt's transcriptions of Beethoven's nine symphonies, and many others. She is now in the process of recording the complete piano music of Chopin for Naxos Records. Her many awards include the Harriet Cohen/ Dinu Lipatti Gold Medal and the Chevalier de l'Ordre National du Mérite from France.*

Vladimir Horowitz has greatly influenced the contemporary pianistic world by opening new perspectives. The technical perfection of his playing, the brio, and the formidable virtuosity have become the ideal that, consciously or not, every pianist dreams of achieving. Musically and technically, the near-perfect playing of great pianists like Hofmann, Godowsky, or Rachmaninoff was well known among the connoisseurs. But with Horowitz these qualities became more accessible to everyone. His numerous recordings were in every musician's collection, and a new era started for pianists. Yet only the superficial and the most obvious part of Horowitz's personality was imitated. Playing stronger, faster, with the least mistakes and wrong notes, was the aim of many. The deep knowledge of the keyboard and the culture that lay behind Horowitz's interpretations were seldom perceived.

To fully understand the personality of Horowitz, one has to go back in time to the archetype of all the Romantic virtuosos, Franz Liszt, and his totally new and orchestral conception of the piano. The fascination of the countless possibilities that the modern piano offered inspired composers and interpreters who were the followers of Liszt. Anton Rubinstein, the tremendous virtuoso who would be a father figure to generations of Russian pianists, was among those strongly influenced by Liszt's vision of orchestral color on the piano. He used to point out that in the sound of the piano not only a single but one hundred instruments were contained. Rubinstein's heritage was transmitted further by Josef Hofmann, his disciple. Felix Blumenfeld, who had a close musical association with Rubinstein, conveyed his approach to the young Horowitz. As the true representative of the Romantic piano tradition, Horowitz's interpretations reflected his personal vision of the works rather than an objective and cooler approach to the music. For the Romantic virtuoso, the score is only the key that opens the gate to his own perception of what lies behind it. The score itself has only an abstract existence. It is the interpreter who has the power to endow it with the vital spark.

Because of his incredible technical capacity, one tends to consider Horowitz only as a fantastic virtuoso. In fact, like most of the great Romantic pianists, he conceived and played music as a composer. Even in his most debatable interpretations, there is an amazing sense of creativity and imagination. In this context, it is particularly enlightening to quote from an interview given for his eighty-fifth birthday, where he said he had two regrets in his life. One was that he never performed in public Liszt's piano transcriptions of the Beethoven symphonies. Faithful to the Lisztian approach, Horowitz explained, "For me, the piano is an orchestra. I do not like the sound of the piano as a piano. I like to imitate the orchestra—the oboe, the clarinet, the violin, and, of course, the singing voice." His second regret was that he did not become a composer. Horowitz also mentioned that he had a large number of compositions that he never played. Some of his transcriptions for piano are exemplary in this respect.

Orchestrating a piano score and playing orchestral transcriptions on a keyboard are identical in spirit. Certain of Horowitz's "excesses," like unusual accentuations, arbitrary rubatos, and a tendency to bring out some secondary melody lines (and partly neglecting in that process the main line) were possibly the result of a totally orchestral and creative spirit. Probably, even to Horowitz, ten fingers were not enough to produce the sounds he was hearing in his mind's ear.

To generations of pianists, musicians, and music lovers, the name of Horowitz has become a source of admiration and also of irritation. To some, only the negative side of his genius was apparent. To others, his amazing pianism and some nearly perfect interpretations that he was able to achieve were enough material to admire. In Horowitz's playing, opposites could easily coexist. These were the vital elements of an art where intelligibility had to have its counterpart—obscurity—so as to achieve the final goal, which is the ideation of a most complex universe of sound and its embodiment in the artist's performance.

Charles Wadsworth

Charles Wadsworth is a native of Newnan, Georgia. He studied piano with Rosalyn Tureck, and in Paris he studied vocal repertoire with Pierre Bernac and Poulenc. His identification with chamber music began in Spoleto, Italy, in 1960, when Gian Carlo Menotti invited him to create a midday chamber series at the Festival of Two Worlds. In 1969 he organized and developed the Chamber Music Society of Lincoln Center, which he guided and with which he regularly performed for twenty years as its artistic director. Under him the Society gave over a thousand concerts and performed over seven hundred works by more than two hundred composers. He received New York City's highest cultural award, the Handel Medallion. Among his other honors are the medal and rank of cavaliere ufficiale *from Italy and chevalier in the Order of Arts and Letters from France.*

I was raised in Newnan, Georgia (thirty-five miles southwest of Atlanta). I began studying the piano there when I was 8. In my first four years of study, I was the only "live" pianist I had access to. When I turned 12, my mother decided it was time to take me to Atlanta to hear some piano recitals. It was the 1941–42 season, and by chance the first pianist to appear in my series was Rachmaninoff and the second was Horowitz. I thought "Wow! So this is what it's like to play the piano." Sadly, I discovered later on there weren't too many others like these two.

At that time the overpowering quality in Horowitz's playing was its laser-like intensity. I shut out everything around me. The old auditorium held some four to five thousand people, but nothing that night could disturb the strange trance that this man's playing induced. The details of the music making remain very vivid to me. The quiet melodic line in Schubert's G-flat major Impromptu was projected throughout the vast space with exquisite yearning—floating over the perfectly articulated broken-chord accompaniment. The opaning of the familiar E-flat major Sonata of Haydn was majestic in a way I've never heard from anyone else. In the A minor Waltz of Chopin there was an overall sweetness and simplicity. But one was aware of Horowitz's infinite gradation in the voicing of the different lines of the music. Horowitz's virtuoso technique and individual sonority as displayed in his arrangement of *Stars and Stripes Forever* and in his Fantasy on Themes from *Carmen* excited me with their combination of abandon and control.

I heard Horowitz frequently over the next eight years. For me, these were his greatest. I had become familiar with his playing of the Romantic repertory, but his presentation of new twentieth-century works had a profound influence on my own musical direction. I was privileged to hear him play the Prokofiev Seventh Sonata in its premiere season. In the rhythmic ostinato of the last movement, Horowitz's demons were unleashed with extraordinary fury. Later he presented the Barber Sonata in its first season and with similar brilliance and power. This happy period in my listening reached a peak in the late forties. I had just arrived at Juilliard, and I got a front row ticket in NBC's Studio 8H to hear Horowitz play the Brahms Second Concerto with Toscanini conducting the NBC Symphony.

The high points of Horowitz's artistry defy description in those works in which he excelled. He set the standard and I doubt if we'll see the likes of him again in our lifetime.

Malcolm Bilson

American pianist Malcolm Bilson is professor of music at Cornell University. He has been in the forefront of the period-instrument movement for over two decades. His performances of Haydn, Mozart, and Beethoven on originals and replicas of five-octave late-eighteenth-century pianos have been a key contribution to the restoration of the fortepiano to the concert stage. During 1991 he concertized on three continents. He has recorded the complete cycle of Mozart concertos for Deutsche Grammophon/Archiv, the solo piano sonatas for Hungaroton, and the piano-and-violin sonatas with Sergiu Luca for Nonesuch.

Since the mid 1980s Bilson has been focusing his attention increasingly on the piano literature of the nineteenth century. He has recorded the Schumann Piano Concerto and the Fantasiestücke *Op. 12, and he has begun recording the complete piano sonatas of Schubert for Hungaroton.*

I have frequently read or heard the charge that Horowitz was a genius without taste. I take issue with such a view. We generally describe as tasteless those who demonstrate a taste quite opposite to our own, and I think that applies dramatically in this case. We live in a rather peculiar age of musical performance, an age almost obsessed by a sense of faithfulness to the score and fidelity to the composer's intentions; this aspect of performance has become almost universal, with some going back to original sources and instrumentation. Horowitz represented another class of musician altogether, one for whom such considerations seemed to matter little. Music, whenever it had been composed, was to be brought to life by an imaginative performer, each time in an individual and personal way. It was a different way of thinking from today's, and with the passing of Vladimir Horowitz its last disciple has gone.

The type of music making espoused by Horowitz can probably not be taken up by a young musician today; it is simply too foreign to our basic aesthetics. While one cannot really succeed, it would seem easier to aspire to be the next Artur Schnabel than the next Vladimir Horowitz. Horowitz's interpretations were sometimes masterful, sometimes odd, sometimes quite off the mark, but they were always riveting. I would hesitate to call him a showman. When he was playing the piano, it was sheer concentration—no extraneous movements or gestures, no quirks; everything was aimed directly at the music as he saw it. Of taste there was plenty, even if it was an odd taste formed in a kind of hothouse in which he enclosed himself in New York.

There were two things about Horowitz that always fascinated me. With all his towering technique, his precision and extraordinary sense of the color of the instrument, he does not seem to have been blessed with very good hands. I watched him often on television: fifth finger cramped under, fingers literally flailing out in scalar passages. When he was young, it seems to me, he must have had to work out very painstakingly every tiny hemidemisemiquaver. This peculiarity, combined with an uncanny ear, must have helped in some odd way to form the mastery we knew.

The other object of my admiration was his concentration, to my mind second to none. There never seemed to be a moment of wavering, and one was compelled to listen and to concentrate with him. Again, this was not showmanship; it was the effect of a life spent focusing everything on his art, like a French master chef boiling down several gallons to a few ounces. This was transmitted through his playing, and seems to me an irreplaceable standard.

Maurizio Pollini

Born in Milan, Maurizio Pollini studied at the conservatory in his native city. In 1960, at the age of eighteen, he won the International Chopin Competition in Warsaw. Pollini has since performed with all the leading orchestras and important conductors. His recitals exhibit a wide diversity: all-Beethoven, Schumann, Chopin, and Schubert, or the complete Well-Tempered Clavier. *He pays devoted attention to the twentieth-century repertoire, playing Debussy etudes, Bartók etudes, the Boulez Sonata No. 2, Webern's Variations, and works by Manzoni, Stravinsky, Prokofiev, and Nono.*

An exclusive recording artist for Deutsche Grammophon, Pollini recently released a disc with the Liszt Sonata and the Schoenberg and Schumann Concertos. He has won the Grand Prix International du Disque, the Prix Caecilia Bruxelles, the Grammy Award for best soloist with orchestra, and the Deutscher Schallplattenpreis.

Writing about Vladimir Horowitz is an occasion to reflect upon what we all owe to this outstanding artist and what he will always mean to the world of music.

During the fifties, we, in Europe, were able to listen to all the great pianists of the time except, of course, Horowitz. Even still, we knew about his fabulous playing through musicians and music lovers who had the good fortune to have heard him before the war, and there were also the recordings.

Only many years later did I have the opportunity to listen to Horowitz play in person, once in Rochester in the late sixties and later in Chicago during the eighties. The programs included works by Haydn, Clementi, Schumann, Liszt, and Rachmaninoff. The concert fully reaffirmed to me the impression made earlier by the recordings, only the sound was much more beautiful, and I could better understand this wonderful musician's special eloquence. What fascinated me most was his utter freedom of expression, a sense of improvisation which highlighted every harmonic and melodic detail.

Horowitz had an unforgettable way of playing the lyrical parts of the Schumann *Humoreske,* where, at the beginning of the piece, the music does not seem to have a definite onset, as though it had been going on somewhere all the while, even before the notes were actually heard. This, for me, was a moment of unsurpassed musical emotion.

I later had the privilege of meeting Horowitz and he was kind enough to play for me some Clementi, Scriabin, and Chopin.

For me, as well as for other young pianists, his recordings of Mussorgsky's *Pictures at an Exhibition,* Liszt's *Funérailles,* and the Third Rachmaninoff Concerto undoubtedly were the epitome of pianistic greatness. Horowitz showed his stature especially in his rendering of the Romantic composers, and his insight of the poetic vision of these composers was prodigious.

Clearly, Horowitz was close to an essential aspect of Romanticism. With a sense of powerful individuality and freedom, he made masterpieces even out of very brief musical moments. However, these moments were Goetheian in the sense that they could also extend throughout longer works, untrammeled by any formal limitations. I remember his Schumann *Humoreske* and the Fantasy in this sense, which he played so movingly in his return concert in 1965.

One clearly understands why Schumann was so intimately congenial to Horowitz along with Chopin. One can hardly imagine Scriabin without this revolutionary poet, and with Scriabin, Horowitz had a very special affinity.

Horowitz was one of the few *real* virtuosi of our century. His manner of playing was highly personal as was his incomparable intensity of tone and the variety of sonorities. These characteristics make Horowitz unique and all true music lovers will miss him.

Gary Graffman

Gary Graffman is a native of New York. In 1935, at the age of seven, he entered the Curtis Institute and studied with Isabelle Vengerova. In 1949 he was awarded the Leventritt Award. His career was curtailed in the late 1970s by an injury to his right hand. In 1981 Doubleday published his autobiography, I Really Should Be Practicing, *and in 1986 he assumed the post of director of the Curtis Institute. In 1991 he was honored by the Commonwealth of Pennsylvania as recipient of the Governor's Arts Award. In 1993 he received an honorary doctorate from the Juilliard School.*

Graffman has continued his performing career by playing compositions written for the left hand alone. Besides many appearances in the Ravel Concerto, he gave the American premiere in 1985 of the Korngold Concerto for Left Hand and has frequently played works by Richard Strauss, Prokofiev, Britten, and Franz Schmidt. In February 1993 Graffman gave the premiere of Ned Rorem's Piano Concerto No. 4 for Left Hand at Carnegie Hall.

My teacher, Isabelle Vengerova, and Horowitz were good friends, and through her I had met him and even played for him a few times when I was a teenager. Now she called and told me that since he was not giving concerts at that time—this turned out to be his longest sabbatical, the one that ended with his return to Carnegie Hall in 1965, when he worried, "Nobody will remember me!" only to learn that eager fans were bivouacked overnight by the box office—he wanted to do a bit of coaching. He told her that he would be willing to give me some lessons.

Strange to say (or perhaps not strange, since I was so stubborn), I was ambivalent about this at first. I admired Horowitz immensely. But as with all great artists, he had such a strong personality. And I had *my* ideas about certain things. I wasn't sure I wanted to be closely influenced by him, and I made all of this abundantly clear to Vengerova, who told me to shut up and go play for him.

His method of teaching me, after the first or second visit, erased irrevocably all doubt in my mind about whether I wanted to be taught by him. At no time did he ever even hint at imposing his ideas on mine. In fact, it was quite the opposite. After criticizing and making suggestions, he tried to find ways within my conception—or what he thought was my conception—of playing a phrase more intensely, or more lyrically, or both. He almost never would go to the piano and say, "Here's how to do it." He showed me how he practiced certain things, and how I could solve certain technical difficulties by practicing in different ways.

Above all, he wanted me to learn how to treat melodic lines as if they were sung by the human voice—an interesting contrast with Serkin, who, in Marlboro, frequently described different figurations as representing various orchestral instruments. This is obviously an oversimplification, as of course Horowitz conceived of something like the Mussorgsky *Pictures* orchestrally, and Serkin sometimes even sang a theme that he played while playing it. But nevertheless, in Marlboro the talk was mainly about a left-hand passage representing, say, a cello rather than a bassoon, while a certain right-hand melody might bring to mind the quality of a viola. And I remember the revelation I felt at Serkin's suggestion that some staccato notes that I made extremely short were actually the equivalent of a pizzicato in a stringed instrument and therefore should last *longer*, as the sound of a plucked string vibrates for a while before it disappears. But Horowitz was more concerned with trying to make the piano sound like a human voice, and continually analyzed how a great singer would phrase a certain passage. To illuminate this philosophy further, he introduced me to the recordings of great bel canto singers such as Battistini and to operas that I didn't know, such as *Pique Dame*. My lessons covered a lot of territory.

I think I must have played almost once a week for Horowitz for a couple of years, and then about once a month for several years after that. He was a "night person," and our sessions would usually begin at eight or even nine in the evening. Although he might have been considered something of a recluse at that time because he didn't go out much, he was always (in my presence, at least) extremely cheerful, enthusiastic, and full of enormous vitality and bounding vigor and energy that left me breathless when, as sometimes happened, it was

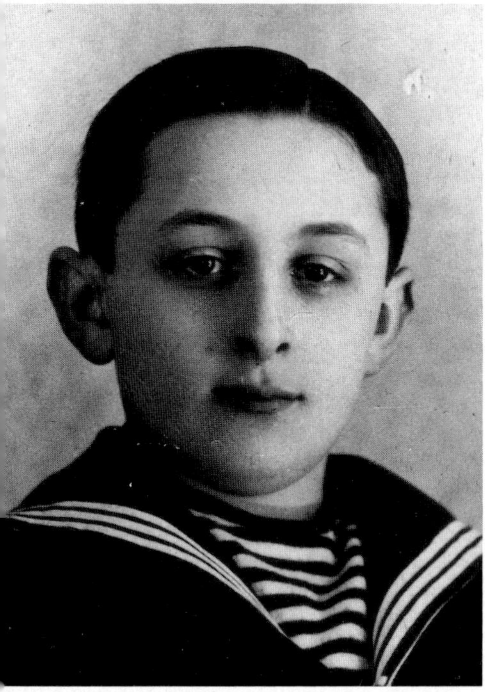

Horowitz while at the Kiev Conservatory. His talent was already startling, although he was not a prodigy on the level of Mozart or Hofmann. (*From the Vladimir and Wanda Toscanini Horowitz Archives in the Music Library of Yale University*)

It was a big decision for Horowitz to have his hair cut. From Liszt to Paderewski, long hair symbolized genius to the public. However, Josef Hofmann, Schnabel, and Rachmaninoff's "convict" cut produced a closer-to-the-scalp fashion. (*From the Vladimir and Wanda Toscanini Horowitz Archives in the Music Library of Yale University*)

Horowitz with two Steinway executives at the Steinway offices in Berlin. Upon arriving in Berlin, as Horowitz said later, "I went to Weber, to Bluethner, Bösendorfer, Steinweg, to Bechstein, everywhere, and then to Steinway. And when I played the Steinway in Berlin, I said, 'That's my piano.' " (*Courtesy Steinway and Sons*)

ABOVE LEFT: Photograph from the Carnegie Hall program for Horowitz's New York debut, January 1928, with Sir Thomas Beecham in the Tchaikovsky Concerto No. 1. Horowitz was not pleased with Beecham's slow tempi. Later in the month, he made his solo debut at Carnegie Hall. *(Courtesy Steinway and Sons)* ABOVE RIGHT, AND BELOW: After leaving the Soviet Union, Horowitz concertized for three sensational years in Europe, then made his first American tour. He fell in love with the United States instantly. *(Courtesy BMG Classics)*

Schnabel and Horowitz relaxing after Horowitz played the Schumann Fantasy privately for Schnabel. This was highly unusual, as Schnabel had only taught masterclasses. While in Russia, Horowitz had hoped eventually to study with Busoni, who, however, died in 1924. *(Courtesy James Dick)*

Horowitz with Alexander Greiner, Steinway's Director of Concerts and Artists. Horowitz had a special affection for Greiner, who made sure in the early days that the finicky virtuoso was always pleased with his pianos. *(Courtesy Steinway and Sons)*

Horowitz with his early manager, Alexander Merovitch, and Alexander Greiner in Paris in 1930. Merovitch, who also handled Nathan Milstein and Gregor Piatigorsky, was the mastermind of these young Russians' early careers. Without Merovitch, Horowitz might never have got to the West. *(Courtesy Steinway and Sons)*

ABOVE: Returning from Genoa to New York in 1934 aboard the Italian luxury liner *Rex*: Horowitz, Milstein, Piatigorsky, Arturo Toscanini, and Bernardo Molinari. Horowitz had married Toscanini's daughter, Wanda, in 1933; she was to become the true backbone of his life and career. *(Courtesy Steinway and Sons)* BELOW: Horowitz and his father, Simeon Horowitz, with Wanda Toscanini Horowitz, London, January 1935. The elder Horowitz had received permission to leave the Soviet Union for a few weeks and visit his son. Shortly after his return, he was arrested without explanation and sent to a prison camp. The date of his death is unknown. *(From the Vladimir and Wanda Toscanini Horowitz Archives in the Music Library of Yale University)*

The hands of the maestro, 1937. Even in old age, Horowitz's hands were beautiful to look at and immensely supple. *(Courtesy Steinway and Sons)*

Frédéric Chopin (1810–1849), the poet of the piano. The largest segment of Horowitz's discography is devoted to the Polish master.

Franz Liszt (1811–1886). The great Hungarian was the unequaled pianist of the nineteenth century. Toscanini thought Horowitz's renditions of Liszt "superhuman," and his 1932 performance of the B minor Sonata continues to astound pianists. The last Liszt he recorded, only days before his death, was Liszt's transcription of Wagner's *Liebestod*.

Pyotr Ilyich Tchaikovsky (1840–1893). Horowitz performed his Piano Concerto No. 1 more often than any other in his small concerto repertoire. At the celebrated Tchaikovsky War Bond Concert at Carnegie Hall in 1943, he and Toscanini raised over $10 million, which was promptly turned over to the Treasury Department. *(Courtesy Alexander Poznansky)*

Anton Rubinstein (1829–1894), the father of Russian piano playing. His name remains sacred in Russia. Horowitz was very proud that his own teacher, Felix Blumenfeld, had been Rubinstein's assistant.

BELOW LEFT: Sergei Rachmaninoff in 1937. Meeting Rachmaninoff, Horowitz said, was "even more important than my debut." Days after his arrival, he played Rachmaninoff's Third Piano Concerto in the basement of Steinway Hall, with the composer at the second piano. Rachmaninoff once said Horowitz "devoured it like a tiger." *(Courtesy Steinway and Sons)* BELOW RIGHT: Horowitz with Rachmaninoff. *(Courtesy Ruth Laredo)*

Horowitz with his daughter, Sonia, born in 1934. *(From the Vladimir and Wanda Toscanini Horowitz Archives in the Music Library of Yale University)*

Toscanini and Horowitz around 1940. Horowitz made two recordings of the Tchaikovsky Concerto No. 1 with Toscanini, as well as one of the Brahms B-flat Concerto. *(Courtesy Steinway and Sons)*

Horowitz became an American citizen in 1942. In 1945 he transcribed Sousa's *The Stars and Stripes Forever* for piano, and performed it in Central Park on "I Am an American Day" at the invitation of Mayor LaGuardia. *(Courtesy BMG Classics)*

Horowitz looked his most debonair during the 1940s. *(Courtesy BMG Classics)*

suddenly two o'clock in the morning and Mrs. Horowitz would come into the living room and shoo me out.

My lesson didn't go on for all that time, though. After the formal part was over—about two hours or so—Horowitz would then (like Vengerova) ask me about all of my colleagues, the music business in general, and then on to the politics, museum exhibitions, and the many other subjects that interested him. He read voraciously and his curiosity was wide-ranging, his ideas thoughtful and his way of expression uniquely pungent. But, fascinating though our discussions were for me, I was always waiting for the moment—usually around midnight—when he would ask a question like, "Do you by chance know the Sixth Sonata of Scriabin?"

"No, not really . . . ," I would reply apologetically.

Then the evening would begin.

Horowitz would stride to the piano, saying, "It's a very great work . . . you should hear it. I would like to play it for you, but of course you understand that I cannot play the piano anymore." Then he would sit down at the instrument. "If I could play, I would play it for you." His hands would hover tantalizingly over the keyboard. "Since I cannot play the piano anymore, this is not possible. However, I'll try to give you just an *idea*. But please forgive me, because, of course, you understand . . . " and he would proceed to tear through the piece, often in a performance so brilliant and so perfect that it could have been recorded on the spot.

The first piece would remind him of other works by the same composer that he "could not play," and these, too, were amply demonstrated during these unforgettable evenings, when he must have played for me over the years practically all the Clementi sonatas, scores of Scarlatti sonatas, and many works of Scriabin and Medtner. He also played for me some of his own compositions written many years earlier. They were extremely beautiful and impressive, and I have no idea why he has always hidden them. They had their own individual stamp, but also reminded me, not surprisingly, of Rachmaninoff, who was, of course a good friend of Horowitz, and whose photo, among a large collection of pictures of relatives and friends placed on the piano, stared somberly down at me during those evenings.

Once it did more than stare. I was playing a Rachmaninoff prelude. Horowitz had suggested to me a different way of attacking a certain passage that was giving me trouble, and when I tried to play it with the new fingering, every single note came crashing down wrong. As I lifted my hands from the keyboard, there was yet another crash; the photo of Rachmaninoff, alone among all of those on the piano, had fallen to the floor, its frame and glass smashed. Both of us were quite shaken for the remainder of the evening, and we avoided playing any music by anyone whose photo was anywhere in the room.

In spite, or, perhaps, because of their very different temperaments and outlooks, Horowitz and Serkin had always been friends. But I don't think they saw each other very often in those days; Serkin's headquarters were in Vermont and Philadelphia, and he toured most of the time, seldom visiting New York except to perform or record. One of the evenings that the two of them were together I'll always remember vividly because it was then that I managed, in one fell swoop, to bend both of these individualists to *my* will.

This came about when Horowitz had started to go out occasionally. He had taken a box for Rubinstein's Carnegie Hall recital, invited the Serkins, and then called to ask us to join them, too. We had just returned from Hong Kong, where I'd had a splendid new tuxedo made, and in the same breath with my eager acceptance I inquired, "Black tie?" Horowitz said he hadn't thought of it, but no, probably not. He detected my disappointment at his reply, and when I confessed that this would have been my first opportunity to wear the new suit, he obligingly said, "Oh, in that case, all right." The evening arrived and we gathered in the box. Serkin looked very uncomfortable in his dinner jacket and stiffly starched shirt, which seemed to be scratching him—and with a stud that refused to stay buttoned. Although white tie and tails is, or was, normal attire for concert performers, dinner jackets were neither fish nor fowl, and I have the feeling that when Serkin wasn't wearing his business uniform he would have much preferred his usual civilian garb. Horowitz, on the other hand, looked elegant, as always, if a bit odd in a beautifully tailored dinner jacket, double-breasted and with extremely wide lapels, that looked like something William Powell might have worn in a *Thin Man* movie. He sat down next to resplendent Hong Kong me, smiled confidentially, opened his jacket, and let me look at the label sewn in the lining, which bore the name of a famous tailor and the date 1936. A good year for tuxedos.

Alexander Slobodyanik

The Ukranian-born pianist Alexander Slobodyanik studied with Heinrich Neuhaus and did postgraduate work at the Moscow Conservatory with Vera Gornostayeva. He won prizes at the Chopin and the Tchaikovsky Competitions and he has appeared with orchestras throughout the world, collaborating with Bernstein, Jarvi, Masur, Kondrashin, Rostropovich, and others. He has recorded on Angel, Melodiya, Eurodisc, and Art and Electronics. In 1968 he made his New York debut at Carnegie Hall.

Slobodyanik has concertized extensively with the Borodin Quartet and with Gidon Kremer, Yuri Bashmet, and Viktor Tretyakov. He has appeared at the Newport, Santa Fe, Schleswig-Holstein, and Lockenhaus Music Festivals. In 1988 he returned to the United States after a nine-year absence, when cultural relations were broken between the United States and the USSR.

Two generations of Russian countrymen awaited a meeting with Vladimir Horowitz in their homeland. The authorities took away from the people their history, and their past, and divided the indivisible culture.

At the beginning of the 1920s, the young Neuhaus, Pasternak, and Horowitz worked in Kiev. They performed concerts, wrote poems, fell in love. . . . Later, in the classes of the Moscow Conservatory, Neuhaus exclaimed, "God! Just to think who in our time was born in the Ukraine? Heifetz and Prokofiev, Nijinsky and Archipenko, Burluk, Oistrakh, Richter and Stern, Lorolev and Sikorsky, not to mention the parents of Stravinsky and Tchaikovsky."

So many were scattered in the tempest of political experiment that ended in spiritual excrement and confusion. The new generation sensed the dishonesty of power and listened to the elders narrate about the elders, the distant ones, and their names became legend.

My teacher, Heinrich Neuhaus, characterized the young Horowitz as a "very clever musician." Truthfully, only a wise artist/musician could allow himself to be childishly naive and unpredictable. His individuality was displayed in everything: his unique creation of musical phrases, playing with "time," and unexpected dynamics. He very often irritated "conventional" critics, apologists, those followers of boring homework on stage rather than live art.

In life, he was also astonishing. When I was on concert tour in Kharkov, I went to visit Vladimir Horowitz's sister, Regina Samoilovna, to tell her of my meeting with Maestro in his home in New York. His own dear sister, of one blood, who lived on the other side of the barricades far away from him, was obviously proud of her brother. But she was also proud of her own work. She taught at the Conservatory all her life from sunrise to dark. Regina said, "Ah! Volodya! Do you know what he sent me as his first present after many long years? A record player so that I can listen to his recordings better!"

Yes, Horowitz unified people.

His art synthesized time and us.

Before the gaze of eternity, his face in the coffin was solemn, and stern as before his piano.

I was among the lucky ones who heard him and shook his hand.

Bela Siki

Bela Siki was born in Budapest. He worked with Dohnanyi, Leo Weiner, and Dinu Lipatti. He won the Liszt Society Competition and became a professor at the Budapest Conservatory at the age of twenty-three. In 1947 he won the Geneva Competition. He has been guest soloist under such eminent conductors as Barbirolli, Ansermet, van Otterloo, and Susskind. He has recorded a considerable discography on Columbia Parlophone, PYE, and Nippon Columbia.

Siki was professor of piano and artist-in-residence at the University of Cincinnati's College-Conservatory of Music. He now teaches at the University of Washington at Seattle and is also on the faculty of the Banff Music Center. Schirmer Books issued his Piano Repertoire: A Guide to Interpretation and Performance *in 1981.*

I never had the chance to meet Mr. Horowitz in person, though his talent, his pianism, and his personality provoked tremendous admiration in me since I first laid my hands on a piano. In my native Hungary, only a few of his recordings were readily available. His Liszt Sonata, the Mazurka in C-sharp minor, the *Carmen* Fantasia, Schumann's Presto appassionato were the choice recordings in my collection. In the beginning, I listened to them many times, but then I realized that those 78-rpm recordings were quickly wearing out and I had to exercise restraint.

The impression of his artistry was indelible on the fourteen-year-old apprentice. For me, he was the reincarnation of Liszt, the fabled virtuoso who started it all. Horowitz's artistry, to my mind, reached right back to the past century, when virtuosi liked the danger of taking technical risks because they loved the exaltation of the triumph in overcoming them. At the same time, Mr. Horowitz worked hard and with discipline, with which he offered us an admirable perfection. He loved his profession like only the best craftsman can love it; he wanted the work well done, clean and finished.

As wonderful as his perfection was, it would be a terrible mistake to consider Mr. Horowitz as only a perfect craftsman. Even as an adolescent, I understood that besides his immense technique he also had a great capacity to understand the composer's intentions and shape phrases in a unique way. My first hearing of his Liszt Sonata was a shattering experience that all other artistic experiences since could not erase. Was this because of the unbelievable dynamic range—he was able to achieve fortissimos that never blurred, and the most delicate of pianissimos? Or was it because of his incredible sense of timing, where each fermata or breathing became an essential part of his artistic expression and provoked the superlative excitement of his audiences? Or was it because of his inimitable singing tone he produced on the keyboard?

In his lifetime, Mr. Horowitz influenced several generations of pianists, and I am convinced that his art will be a model for many generations to come.

Ruth Slenczynska

The American pianist Ruth Slenczynska studied with Cortot, Schnabel, and Boulanger. She was a child prodigy and made her New York debut at the age of eight. Her life story has been featured on television programs and in magazine articles. She has written an autobiography, Forbidden Childhood *(Doubleday), and* Music at Your Fingertips *(Da Capo Press), as well as articles for* Piano Quarterly, Music Journal, Clavier, *and* Keyboard *magazine.*

Slenczynska has performed more than 3,000 recitals in both hemispheres and appeared with most of the world's important orchestras. Her discography includes a dozen recordings and she has received the Golden Cross of Merit from Poland. In Spring 1988 she performed fifty-two concerts in Asia. Slenczynska is artist-in-residence at Southern Illinois University.

During the years 1958–67, when I saw Vladimir Horowitz most frequently, he was preoccupied with creating bel canto, super-legato phrasing on the piano. He had brought from Italy to his Manhattan home scores of old recordings by historic operatic stars of another era. Tito Schipa and Beniamino Gigli were the most familiar names, but there were many others whose art he prized.

Horowitz would listen admiringly to a tenor voice moving liquidly from one tone to the next in a rubato phrase, study the same passage many times, then reproduce that phrase on the piano either with his right or left hand *without pedal.* He experimented with touch, hand position, wrist position, the height of the bench, and fingering, and, above all, he *listened.* His aim was to create the special lyrical sound his concept required. When he achieved this new skill he transferred it to the music of Scarlatti, Clementi, Mozart, and Beethoven, and later to Chopin, Rachmaninoff, Liszt, and

Prokofiev. His very own bel canto sound evolved, grew more polished, and became recognizably his.

Many young pianists today display speed, strength, precision, and bombastic virtuosity in their attempts to "sound like Horowitz." Until now, however, the special lyrical Horowitz artistry remains elusive.

Geoffrey Douglas Madge

Geoffrey Douglas Madge is a native of Adelaide, Australia. He began piano lessons at the age of eight. He left Australia in 1963 after winning first prize in the ABC Piano Competition, and settled in Holland in 1970 following his appointment as senior lecturer of piano at The Hague Conservatorium. Madge has appeared throughout Europe in recitals of challenging scope exploring a dense variety of repertoire.

Among Madge's many recordings are the Xenakis Piano Concerto Synaphai *and the monumental* Opus clavicembalisticum *by Sorabji. The piano works of Busoni were issued by Philips on a set of six CDs. For this accomplishment he received the Edison prize and the German* Schallplattenpreis. *He has also recorded a large quantity of Godowsky's music, as well as works by Wolpe, Reubke, Krenek, and, most recently on Danacord, the three piano concertos by Medtner.*

Listening to Vladimir Horowitz, either on record or live, has always been an active experience. One is immediately struck by the tremendous colour and dynamics in his playing, the daring interpretations, his use of the acoustic possibilities of the instrument, and the expression of his personality, even though at times it may be in conflict with the music. It is so easy to criticize when a pianist reaches such heights of achievement, but there is plenty of provocation! Yet in every performance he had the ability to present a view and a direction. He once said that "it wasn't necessary to always like what you do; dare to do otherwise."

At times I am both puzzled by and filled with admiration for his recordings. They are often most disturbing, and yet this can be a relief in an age when the music industry is turning more and more toward sickly sweetness in performance fashions. Similarly, other giants of the first half of the century (I refer here to Busoni, Medtner, Moiseiwitsch, Cortot, or Rachmaninoff, just to name a few) did not pander to the fashionable public taste of the day; they adopted a new aesthetic approach.

One thing that has always intrigued me is the way in which Horowitz could, almost by an illusion—either by the use of the pedals, accentuations, or the acoustics of the hall or the instrument—make his legato sound as if it were created by non-legato attacks, which was, according to Busoni, the basis of piano playing. (Busoni considered all legato to be an acoustic illusion.) With Horowitz what happens between the notes is more important than the notes themselves. He often said that he was more concerned by how the notes came up than by how they went down. He created dynamic tensions by using the pedal, giving a feeling of contrast when the pedal was released. Horowitz once told me that he was very sad never to have heard Busoni in a live performance. I sometimes wonder how close they were in pianistic practice.

My interest in the phenomenon of Horowitz has, over the years, led me to make a careful study of several of his idols. The influence of Toscanini, constantly imploring the orchestra to sing, must have been very strong. Horowitz wanted the piano to sing. He mentioned singers as a strong influence in the development of his style. These were the bel canto singers at the turn of the century. One who was especially important for an understanding of Horowitz's playing and for any in-depth study of interpretation is the baritone Mattia Battistini (1856–1928). Fortunately for posterity, he left many intriguing recordings, giving a last glimpse of the bel canto style of the nineteenth century.

What is the connection with the great bel canto singers? One element is the art of making diminuendos, retaining the impetus within the phrase. Some fine examples can be heard in several Horowitz recordings: the Czerny Variations from the forties, a number of the Haydn and Mozart Sonatas, the early Schubert B-flat major Sonata, and some of the Schumann recordings.

Horowitz was daring in the way in which he made long groups of notes, even phrases, for example in the Mozart and Haydn sonatas. Many performers, especially today, give vertical clarity to each note, almost as if playing a typewriter. It is the element of illusion in his cantabile touch and the dialogue he produced and developed between phrases which, for me, constitute the basic style and personality so characteristic of Horowitz. I will never forget a performance I heard of the Mozart Sonata in B-flat K. 333; it was monumental in its scope and design, producing a sound as if it had been orchestrated with horns (particularly in the last movement), with unique timing. I spoke to Horowitz after the recital, and mentioned to him that during the performance the sense of dialogue in the first movement, the sustained second movement, and the orchestral sound of the third showed an incredible understanding of the proportions of the work. He explained his approach to the interpretation whereby he created an "opera," each theme being a character in the drama.

During live performances the audience's reaction was immediate, almost as if breathing *with* the cadence of the playing; even members of the audience with no special musical knowledge would be subconsciously captivated. It was fascinating just to watch the audience during the performances. As a pianist myself, aware of the force of the audience, I believe that Horowitz made use of this energy during his performances, which helped make them so "electric." Horowitz, of course, was not the only pianist to achieve this feeling; I have sensed the same in live performances by masters such as Horszowski or Richter. But the way in which it happened with Horowitz made time truly appear to stand still. The effect is difficult to achieve in smaller halls or studio recordings. Bring an interpretation by Horowitz into a small auditorium, and the sound will inevitably be altered and most certainly distorted. A number of the studio recordings show Horowitz as excessive in his interpretations. I wonder whether such less distinguished recordings will stand the test of time. They will certainly not help future generations understand what the impact of a live Horowitz recital really was.

Misha Dichter

The American pianist Misha Dichter studied with Aube Tzerko and Rosina Lhévinne. His international career was launched with a top prize at the 1966 Tchaikovsky Competition. For Philips he has recorded music by Beethoven, Brahms, Mussorgsky, Schumann, and others. For BMG/RCA he has released the complete Hungarian Rhapsodies of Liszt. In addition to performing with the world's foremost orchestras, he has appeared at the Ravinia Festival for twenty-four consecutive seasons, and has also appeared at the Aspen Festival for nineteen consecutive summers. He often performs in two-piano recitals with his wife, Cipa Dichter.

Dichter has frequently given master-classes at leading conservatories and universities, as well as appearing in chamber works. He has contributed articles to many publications and was the subject of a television documentary.

Perhaps no single musician or pianist has had such an *impact* on so many generations as Horowitz did. When I was growing up in California, the Horowitz record that had the greatest impact on me was an album titled *Homage to Liszt.* I still put that record on occasionally, just to remind myself what the piano is capable of doing. For me, Horowitz's performances on that album absolutely expand the limits of what the piano can do, through a combination of his own sound and his diabolical musical mind.

There is a sound to certain passages that makes the listener cower. It was scary to me then and still is to this day. He had a sound that went deep into my mind and is impossible to erase from my psyche.

However, one must not characterize Horowitz as the man who played Liszt extraordinarily and that was all. For instance, his Scarlatti is unforgettable. So are many of the astounding miniatures in his repertoire. One of my all-time favorite recordings is his Schumann *Kreisleriana*.

During my teen years, the biggest musical influence on me was my teacher, Aube Tzerko, a pupil of Artur Schnabel. Listening to Schnabel and Furtwängler records contributed most to making me want to be a musician. Hearing Rubinstein live in Los Angeles contributed to my wanting to be a touring musician because there was something so glamorous about how he went triumphantly from city to city giving concerts. But it was hearing Horowitz records that made me want to practice the piano. Hearing Horowitz first was in a way a backwards process. I should have heard Rachmaninoff and Hofmann records before Horowitz's, so as to have been exposed to the roots of his world. I think Horowitz took the Russian tradition and brought it to diabolical heights.

There is, however, an aspect of Horowitz's playing about which I am ambivalent. His playing, taken to extreme, says, "Now listen to me. Enough about you. What do you think of my playing?" If every musician had this attitude of the performer first and the music second, which I feel was the underlying philosophy of his playing, I would fear for the state of music.

Tzerko once told me about one of the last, if not the last, performances Schnabel gave of Beethoven sonatas at Hunter College, which included the Op. 90 Sonata. At the end of that work, the pianist walked off stage almost in tears, saying, "I think that was the closest I ever came to the piece." That, to me, has remained the ideal of why I make music. And not, "Hey, not bad for an old man, ha? How do you like my playing now?"

I have nothing but reverence for what Horowitz accomplished, and at the same time, it also frightens me.

Stephen Hough

Stephen Hough was born in Cheshire, England. In 1983 his career was launched with his victory at the Naumburg Competition. He is a frequent guest of the major London orchestras, the City of Birmingham Orchestra, and the BBC Philharmonic. Hough is also guest at many of the world's leading festivals. In 1992 he made his Australian debut during a five-week tour.

His discography has been highlighted by his recording with the English Chamber Orchestra of two Hummel concertos; this was named "Concerto Recording of the Year" by Gramophone *magazine. On the Virgin Classics label his most recent releases include the complete solo works of Britten and the Brahms Second Concerto. For the Music Masters label he recorded the ten Beethoven piano-and-violin sonatas with Robert Mann.*

I came to know the playing of Horowitz rather late in my studies—in fact, around the time I changed from a push-bike to a small motorbike. Hearing the old 78-rpm recordings of Scarlatti sonatas and the famous *Stars and Stripes* transciption for the first time was rather akin to the reckless thrill of twisting the handlebars of my new bike—with an effort truly *leggiero*—and surging forward, if only at the thirty miles per hour that British law allows for sixteen-year-olds.

Soon after this "baptism" came my confirmation of interest in Horowitz's playing, particularly with some Scriabin recordings—the Fifth, Ninth, and Tenth sonatas. Here the sweet flame of the composer's imagination seemed to merge in one conflagration with the performer's; Horowitz's fingers were like ten singeing tongues of fire burning out the melodic contours, his pedalling a clinging cloak of smoke suffocating the poisonous harmonies.

Next came Rachmaninoff, and Horowitz's fabulous ability to

combine ardent melancholy with an unsinkable rhythmic buoyancy, the expressive character never sagging into a stretched and burdensome torpor. The Third Concerto (in the 1930 recording), the Second Sonata, selected preludes and etudes—lean, lithe, leopard-like playing, the Steinway's thunderous bass a growling yet tamed beast.

I only heard Horowitz live once, at the Metropolitan Opera in 1982. My clearest memories are of a poor performance of Beethoven's Sonata Op. 101 when I was longing to hear Solomon, and a stunning Rachmaninoff G-sharp minor Prelude when I thought I *was* Noah, gazing at a rainbow of pianistic colour. It was an experience that left me reluctant to breathe, for fear of disturbing the tiniest feather of nuance.

In a way, I am glad that my acquaintance with Horowitz's art did not come too early. It is probably unwise to dip one's fingers into a rich and exotic icing when the pale cake is still gently rising in the oven; or to consume interlocking octave passages in one's practice studio, piranha-style, with only milk teeth. Like the motorbike, there could be a danger for younger pianists to try to drive too fast too soon. It is important to have good balance and a sense of responsibility before finally twisting the handlebars and watching the landscape of a composer's work pass by through the thrilling but tinted hue of the Horowitz crash-helmet.

I have to admit that other pianists have been a greater inspiration to me through the years, particularly Cortot. I have never heard in Horowitz the sort of spiritual vision that Cortot imparts in, say, his Franck *Prélude, Aria, et Final* recording; or the deeply personal and private tragedy of his 1933 Chopin preludes; or, for that matter, the sheer elegance and delicate charm in his recordings of some of the waltzes and etudes. However, I know that when I next hear Horowitz in the *Carmen* Fantasy, I shall be totally won over again, caught in the jaws of a technique and rhythmic control so biting and utterly addictive, so completely genuine, the teeth-marks buried in the purest gold.

Lazar Berman

Lazar Berman was born in Leningrad and made his first public appearance at the age of four. He attended the Special Music School in Leningrad and then went to the Moscow Conservatory, where his teacher was Alexander Goldenweiser. Berman graduated from the Moscow Conservatory in 1953 and began to concertize extensively within the Soviet Union and in Eastern and Western Europe. He won prizes in the Budapest Liszt Competition as well as in the Queen Elisabeth Competition in Brussels. Berman has made several tours of the United States, appearing as recitalist and as soloist with major symphony orchestras. His many recordings on Melodiya, Columbia, and Deutsche Grammophon are well known to connoisseurs. Berman now lives in Italy and continues his concert and recording activities throughout the world.

My first meeting with Vladimir Horowitz took place in the fall of 1976, during my first visit to the United States. I traveled throughout the country, and it was a hectic tour. However, one of my goals was to somehow meet the greatest legend of the piano, Vladimir Horowitz. I wrote him a letter in which I expressed my admiration for him. I said, "Your way, the path in music you follow, has set an example for me in my life." I was overjoyed when I received an invitation to see him.

In the evening I went to visit him, Wanda Toscanini Horowitz opened the door herself. Mr. Horowitz was very charming and friendly. Suddenly he asked me to play something. I was not quite ready for this and I gently refused, asking instead to listen to my recording of the Liszt A major Concerto, which I had brought him as a gift. He said, "You can't really have the right idea about a musician from a recording. One must hear one live. A recording is like a postcard; it shows you the place but is not at all real, and just like looking at a postcard, it leaves you indifferent. Listening over and over to a recording leaves one wanting to hear the composition in a new way."

Nevertheless, Horowitz listened to my record of the Liszt Concerto, and said that he liked it. He also made an interesting comment about one of the episodes in the work (in D minor), which he said should be played much faster as Liszt himself had marked the tempo. Horowitz said this is the usual mistake pianists make here. "When I used to play this concerto, I too played it too slowly." I was surprised that Horowitz had played this work as he had never recorded it. He casually went to the piano and played the episode for me. It was very impressive, not only in the playing and his sound, but also in watching him.

A friend of mine, the pianist and teacher Vladimir Tropp, had given me a facsimile edition of Mussorgsky's *Pictures at an Exhibition* to give to Horowitz if I got to see him. Horowitz was glad to accept this gift. We began talking about this composition in which he had made many changes, resulting in a more colorful and picturesque work than the original. I told him that somebody in Russia had learned his version from the recording. Horowitz said, "I don't want my transcription to be played by anybody else." I had been offered the copy of the transcription, but after hearing this judgment, I knew I would not play it. And of course, he was right, one could not copy Vladimir Horowitz.

Mrs. Horowitz had coffee brought in, and the conversation turned to musical life in Russia and abroad. He gave me his assessments of certain artists. He spoke with bitterness that the Soviet government still would not let his beloved sister Regina visit him. He had not seen her since 1925. I looked at my watch and was amazed it was nearly 2:00 A.M. As I left, he gave me a gift of his record with Fritz Reiner of the Rachmaninoff Third Concerto. I was deeply touched. I walked down Fifth Avenue very slowly on my way back to the hotel, thinking about the whole evening. For me this was a historic meeting.

In the autumn of 1977, fortune brought us together for the second time. Horowitz was to give a recital in San Francisco, and we were staying at the same hotel. As I passed by his room, I heard the incomparable sound of Horowitz as he practiced. His concert took place in the afternoon. He told me that he much prefers to play at 3:00 P.M. because he is done by five, at six he has forgotten about it, and at seven he sleeps like a child.

It was at San Francisco that I was first able to hear him live. I was astounded! It was amazing, I had never seen any musician and his audience so at one with each other. There was not a sound in the audience. He gave his audience everything, he loved them and he made the people feel that love. How could a recording or a video ever create such an atmosphere? I felt Horowitz to be an honest person, and an honest musician. His playing was addressed to the audience on many levels. Above all, it was so human.

After the concert, I was joyous and excited, and I wanted to see the great Maestro but was told that nobody was allowed to see him. Fortunately, he heard I was there and I was brought to him. He looked at me and said, "What do you think? Are my fingers still *able to run*?" I told him, in all truth, that nobody has ever had such "electric" fingers. I also noticed that he played without consideration of age. He then asked me with the sincerest genuine interest how I was doing back in Russia, where I had played, and what I had played since our last meeting. We only spoke in Russian, and I noticed that in his speech, he had kept old Russian words that had already been lost in our time.

Unfortunately, this was our last meeting. Much to my regret, I was not in Moscow when he made his historic return to Russia in 1986.

For me, Horowitz was more than a unique pianist. He summed up the history of twentieth-century pianism, a century of many changes, fashions—the advent of recording, musicological investigations, as well as the great change that music occupies in the life of contemporary man. Horowitz had a searching spirit and had a big influence on the interpreter's role in music. I feel Horowitz developed very deeply throughout his long career. Although his early recordings exhibit a unique pianistic professionalism with their elegance and the passion for external imagery, they always left me indifferent. This early playing is reminiscent of the elegant virtuosi of the past, and I think they are somewhat shallow. However, all great virtuosi go through stages, and Horowitz's years of virtuosity were passed with honor, where he received the attention and admiration of a great public. However, the great mass of dilettantes are often without good taste.

After Horowitz retired, he developed deeper traits that are at the very roots of the Russian school of piano playing: the grand sweep, depth of psychology, polyphonic thinking in the voicing of compositions. It was Horowitz from his sixties until his very last year that is the greater Horowitz. For me, he is akin to Vladimir Sofronitsky, another great figure who had a big influence on music lovers as well as pianists.

We were all blessed that Horowitz had so long a creative life. It was fortunate that he was able to play for so many years on the same piano, a piano that was so responsive to him. This was an important decision that almost all pianists cannot make. It is a waste of time to have to get used to a new instrument and often without good results. His personal piano was always capable of realizing what he wanted to say artistically. Very few people understand what artistic despair occurs when a pianist is confronted with an unknown instrument. I am glad that Horowitz did not have to waste his time developing relationships with new pianos.

Ronald Turini

Ronald Turini was born in Montreal, Canada, and studied at the McGill Conservatory and at the Quebec Conservatory, where he graduated with first-place honors at the age of sixteen. In New York, he studied with Vladimir Horowitz. He was one of the few official students whom Horowitz acknowledged.

Turini has won prizes at the Queen Elisabeth, Busoni, and the Geneva competitions. He made his Carnegie Hall debut in 1961, and has since played with such outstanding orchestras as the Chicago, National, Toronto, Montreal, London Philharmonic, BBC, and Leningrad Philharmonic. He has made four tours of Russia and has frequently played throughout South America. Turini's recordings include works by Hindemith, Schumann, Ginastera, Schubert, and Rachmaninoff. He is a founding member of Quartet Canada and teaches piano at the University of Western Ontario.

Vladimir Horowitz was a unique artist with a very strong musical personality. He was one of the last and greatest of the so-called Grand Manner pianists. To have the opportunity to study with such a person would be something almost any young pianist could aspire to. When he agreed to take me as a student, I was naturally most grateful.

Horowitz the teacher was again quite unique, perhaps one could say a little unorthodox. I had previously been studying in New York City with Isabelle Vengerova and Olga Stroumillo—two very excellent teachers in their own right. One day, Madame Stroumillo at a lesson asked me if I would like to audition for Horowitz, as he was looking for a student. Flabbergasted, I agreed and subsequently went to play for the master.

One of the first things he said to me was that he was *not* a teacher, but that he would take me on for a three months trial period. "Perhaps I will not be good for you," he said. As it turned out, he was excellent for me, as he gave me the other side of the coin as compared to my other teachers. He was a great performer, which they were not, and his technical approach was quite different. He worked on my dynamic range and projection (which I needed). "More guts, more guts," he would say. He urged me to greatly increase my finger strength, especially in the fourth and fifth fingers. He did not teach very much technique, but the few suggestions he gave were most important.

He usually taught from a reclining position on his sofa. I would have to play a complete work or movement, after which he would give his comments. He concentrated very much on sound, pedalling, and especially "mood" or character. Before almost every lesson, he would say, "Make a mood with this piece." Often he had difficulty explaining, or perhaps did not wish to explain, how to make this mood. Likewise with pedalling, he would say, "More wet," or "More dry." He seemed to fully expect that if I was good enough to work with him, I was good enough to figure out how to do most of these things myself. One thing he was most emphatic about was to project the melody very strongly, sometimes even more strongly than I like—characteristic of his era of pianism.

A bit unorthodox also was his frequent use of demonstrations. These were perhaps the most enlightening features of his teaching. He would say, "Do something like this," then he would do it at the piano in wonderful fashion, after which I was to try it myself. Sometimes, after several tries and a few hints, he would say, "Go home and practice it." I learned a great deal through these demonstrations, since Horowitz was not always the most articulate teacher. I feel he himself did not know exactly what he was after until he played the passage in question.

One thing I wanted to do was to improve my octave playing, and I asked Horowitz how he did his marvelous octaves. All he said was, "I have lots of nervous energy," and recommended slow practice from the wrist.

Horowitz gave very few exercises but insisted I learn *all* the Chopin etudes. He expected a new etude at each lesson (usually every two weeks), memorized. He expected all the right notes and the right character, touch, and so forth at the first lesson. One thing I really appreciated, even though he was very demanding: he always taught me in a gentlemanly manner.

There were also a few drawbacks associated with studying with such a musical superstar as Horowitz. First, the tendency to imitate many of the individualistic mannerisms of such an artist is very hard to resist. This imitation, of course, can never be successful. I had to work hard to discard some of these mannerisms in order to retain my own style and personality. His playing was very extroverted; this did not always fit well with my natural approach. Secondly, I did feel a certain amount of pressure because of being Horowitz's student. It does tend to raise expectations in audiences and critics alike. As a result, I do not feel I played as freely or as well while studying with him. Most of the benefits came later, I think.

Horowitz gave me some advice and support concerning my concert career. One of his favorite sayings was, "You will have many bad concerts, bad pianos, bad halls, bad critics, but you must learn to take it if you want to be a concert pianist." He meant, of course, there would be good experiences as well. We generally had a very businesslike relationship. I paid for my lessons, though he often gave me extra time. Occasionally I would have supper with him and Mrs. Horowitz after the lesson. He was also a big factor in my being accepted by Columbia Artists Management after the Brussels Competition in 1960. Many years later, he helped to set me up with Shaw Concerts Agency in New York, a relationship that was to prove unsuccessful. In the late seventies, I began a new career as a teacher and performer in Canada.

To this day, my lessons with Horowitz have had a very strong influence on my own way of teaching. I do admit to using many of the ideas of the Vengerova-Stroumillo "method" in spite of Horowitz's seeming dislike for them. In this way, I feel I can try to give my students a more varied outlook on piano playing and music. In summary, I would like to say that I am most grateful for having had the chance to study with Horowitz. For me it was an extremely worthwhile experience and one I will never forget.

Evelyne Crochet

The French-born American pianist Evelyne Crochet studied at the Paris Conservatoire with Yvonne Lefebure, where she was awarded first prize in piano. She also worked with Nadia Boulanger and Edwin Fischer. At the invitation of Rudolf Serkin, she came to the United States to study under his sponsorship. She made her United States debut playing Poulenc's Two-Piano Concerto in its Boston premiere, with the composer at the second piano and Charles Munch conducting.

For Vox Records she recorded the complete piano works of Fauré, and in concert she has played the complete Debussy piano music. On a Philips disc, she recorded newly discovered pieces by Fauré, and with Alfred Brendel she recorded Schubert duets. Evelyne Crochet has taught at Brandeis, the New England Conservatory, Rutgers, and the Curtis Institute.

What makes me want to listen to Vladimir Horowitz's playing is not so much his astonishing virtuosity but rather his inexhaustible ability to understand and explore the piano sound, give it a shape, and transform it into a magical world of colors. His ear was keen; he could re-create orchestral, instrumental, or vocal sounds and translate them into a very personal language. Of course, none of this phenomenon would fully capture the attention if it were not springing from a perfect sense of harmonic relationships and musical cohesion as well as motivated by a distinct personality.

The concept behind his performances was not always orthodox. In fact it was more often than not subjected to his own instinctive perception. In that regard, he did not give the impression to approach a score in a scholarly fashion. Not to suggest that he did so without deference, but he was prompted first and foremost by his own involvement with the music, and that seems to have been his priority. In the end, his conviction was such that it won us over. To be exact, there was no need to argue about it: such was his way, whether it met with your taste or not. In an age where performers often lock themselves into a safe haven of manufactured performances, this precious quality—direct involvement—and the courage to take risks and let the music carry one away are rare and represent an important part of what was so admirable in Horowitz's playing.

Judging from his choice, he seemed to never settle for a work that he was not truly in love with. It would appear that his ambition was not to conquer the complete works of a composer but to select pieces that were keenly suited to him. I happen to believe that no one is universal and should ever assume to be a good ambassador to all of music or, for that matter, to all composers. How arrogant and what an abuse of power it would be to believe that we can translate and do justice to all original creations! As musicians we have affinity to all music but not necessarily the ability or the temperament to perform it. Peter Ustinov would not play Hamlet and Laurence Olivier would not play Falstaff—this comparison just to illustrate the point. One had the feeling that each work he chose to play committed him to a total relationship with it and engulfed all of his faculties as if the piece were the very center of his life at the moment. It was not just another work in his repertoire, it was an event.

His eloquent lyricism attested to his love for the opera. Few people can make the piano sing and handle the musical phrase as a language as he did. On stage, he did impress the audience with his pyrotechnics, often exhibiting his pleasure in athletic pianism, but his real gift of communication lay in the sharing of his vision and his world of fantasy, poetry, and emotions as he transported us into his adventure at the piano. Everything in his playing was essentially alive and imaginative, and there was an infallible sense of timing in his spacing of the music, the true mark of a consummate musician.

A whole portion of the pianistic repertoire was revealed to me by Horowitz. Under his fingers, the music of Scriabin and Rachmaninoff was exciting and beautiful because he played it with nobility, clarity, great feeling, and temperament, without the indulgence of sentimentality. It is very difficult for me to hear this music played by anyone else. And what should we say of his Scarlatti and Clementi sonatas, played with such exquisite elegance and style?

One can hardly count the pieces he immortalized. One day, my teacher, Rudolf Serkin, told me that Mr. Horowitz was very impressed with my Fauré recordings and that he was going to learn some of his works. Needless to say, it meant a lot to me. A little later,

I had the privilege to hear Vladimir Horowitz in his home, shortly before his Carnegie Hall return to the stage in 1965. It left an indelible impression on my young years: his candor, intensity, and vulnerability, his child-like sense of wonder at his own music making and his stance as a purebred thoroughbred waiting for his best race. There was fear, anticipation, and enormous spirit; his playing was free, full of fire and poetry: his incredible mastery of sound(s) was staggering. It was unforgettable. Yet, he was worried about the trill in Scriabin's Tenth Sonata and turned to me as for advice! It was incongruous of me to offer a suggestion, especially when the trill in question (on fourth and fifth fingers!) was electrifying, and I could only reassure him that it sounded stupendous and that I did not see why he should be concerned. As he insisted, I told him that what I listen for in a trill is evenness rather than speed, and we went on talking about Ravel's trill at the end of the second movement of the G major Concerto. I don't know if he agreed or not (it is unimportant), but it spurred his energy and he could not wait to play the Scriabin trill again, which he attacked with a vengeance.

How many pianists can we recognize after hearing only a few notes of their playing? Horowitz's playing is unmistakenly nobody else's, and can be singled out among all pianists. There is no question that he contributed to the evolution of piano playing by broadening its spectrum. No pianist can deny having been marked or influenced by Horowitz's playing, even those who for reasons of their own reject his artistry (perhaps especially those who criticize him the most!). He was inimitable yet emulated legions of imitations. Yes, he did open new horizons for the piano. His unlimited ability as a virtuoso allowed him to create a variety of colors and sounds never heard before, enabling him to illuminate each layer in the sound fabric with pristine clarity. This was a formidable tool to serve his creative imagination. He left a strong legacy.

Artur Balsam

Artur Balsam received his early training in his native Poland and later studied at the Berlin Hochschule. While still a student, he was engaged by Yehudi Menuhin for a tour of the United States. Five more North American tours and innumerable European performances followed before he settled permanently in the United States.

As a soloist, Balsam has performed with many of the leading orchestras. He has taught at the Eastman School of Music, Boston University, and the Manhattan School of Music. He has been on the juries of the Rubinstein, Montreal, Leeds, and Naumburg piano competitions. His recorded legacy is vast, numbering more than two hundred fifty recordings. He has collaborated with Milstein, Szigeti, Kogan, Oistrakh, Francescatti, and the Budapest and Juilliard quartets. Artur Balsam's influence has been felt by the dozens of musicians he has taught and with whom he has performed.

Horowitz was a god of the piano—one of the great virtuosi in history. He had the ability to inspire me, and he could arouse an entire concert hall to feverish excitement. Such a gift is unusual and one that comes infrequently. Such matters are mysteries. Horowitz, however, was not my favorite pianist. That affection was reserved for Rachmaninoff.

I knew Horowitz personally through his close friend, the great violinist Nathan Milstein, whom I worked with as his accompanist for a quarter of a century. I will never forget when once we played the Franck Sonata and Horowitz exuberantly congratulated me.

I must say that I knew more about Horowitz from what others said rather than what I discovered about him when I was with him. Milstein himself was not a man given to gossip, and he told me nothing of their long friendship, which went back to their teen years, and I never asked. Milstein and Horowitz made one recording together, the Brahms Third Sonata. The performance perhaps has too much of the piano in it, the piano being quite loud. But one must remember that this was Horowitz. Nobody should or did criticize the performance, and I'm certain that the playing was exactly as they wanted it.

I had dinner on occasion with Horowitz and Milstein. As I remember it, these dinners were spontaneous events. I especially remember when Mrs. Balsam and I were invited to the Horowitz home. He was in a first-class mood and he played the *Stars and Stripes Forever* transcription. It was fascinating sitting next to him and seeing those amazing fingers at work close up. I think that was the time he was working out his arrangement of Liszt's Second Hungarian Rhapsody. He played parts of it, and his articulating three different themes at once was a magnificent juggling act. It was unforgettable to hear him during these casual moments at home.

Somehow, I never heard him play the Tchaikovsky Concerto in public. But fortunately I heard several times the Rachmaninoff Third Concerto. It was not to be missed. In this concerto, he was the greatest in the world. Nobody could touch him in this score, not even Rachmaninoff. That was a fact and everyone knew it.

Horowitz was, of course, a major Liszt player. He adored Liszt and his interpretation of the Sonata was marvelous. He had the right sound. He was born for him.

His Schumann was always fascinating, although once when he played the *Traumerei* I came close to hating him. I thought, "This is somewhat excessive to say the least." He tried to make each note important. But I also heard him play that same little piece very simply and directly. With Horowitz a great deal relied on his mood.

I once heard him in a very symphonic Beethoven "Appassionata," and we decided that this particular work was not suited to him. However, that does not mean that he had no ability with the Classical repertory. In my opinion, Horowitz's playing of Scarlatti is the greatest playing of that composer by any pianist. He played Clementi wonderfully and with deep insight. Most important was that Vladimir Horowitz created a style altogether his own. There has never been anybody that has sounded like him. He was the supreme individualist. He was of himself, by himself, and for himself.

Claude Frank

Until the age of twelve, Claude Frank lived in Nuremberg. Later he studied at the Paris Conservatoire. After coming to the United States he studied with Artur Schnabel in New York and with Koussevitzky at Tanglewood. A noted teacher, Frank has given master-classes at many universities and is on the faculty of the Curtis Institute. He also is professor at the Yale School of Music and artist-in-residence at Kansas University.

Frank has appeared with the great orchestras of five continents. A frequent chamber artist, he has appeared with the Tokyo, Guarneri, Juilliard, and Emerson quartets. He has recorded a great deal on RCA, Sine Qua Non, and Audiofon; the thirty-two sonatas of Beethoven have been released on CD on the Music and Arts label. Frank appears often in performances with his wife, the distinguished pianist Lilian Kallir.

I heard about Horowitz as a child in Germany. "The most sensational young pianist!" my mother said. "Unfortunately, he can no longer come here."

Fortunately, I was allowed out of Germany, and I heard his recital in Brussels: the Chopin B-flat minor Sonata, among other music. I found it extraordinary. He was so different from Gieseking, Fischer, Erdmann, Backhaus, and all the others who *were* allowed in Germany. "He plays Jewish," I told my father. No greater praise would have been possible.

About five years later, a friend and I sat in Schnabel's music room, awaiting our lessons. I asked sotto voce about the Rachmaninoff recital he had heard the night before. He said nothing for a while, then shook his head judiciously and said, "Not good." Though this conversation was about Rachmaninoff, it helps to explain why I did not rediscover Horowitz till much later. He represented something so different that an active endorsement to find him would have amounted to a betrayal.

But one grows up, and much later, at age twenty-five, I had a chance to visit Horowitz and play for him. The meeting was arranged by Gary Graffman and Eugene Istomin, who thought that I was not too old to be under the influence of a pianist who overtly celebrated the relation with the instrument. The pre–music-making dialogue went something like this:

"You studied with Schnabel for a long time? Wonderful adagios. But he often forgot that there was music in allegros, too!" I found the remark rather unfair. Schnabel constantly stressed the importance of *the music* in technically difficult pieces. And I couldn't help thinking of some things Schnabel said about Horowitz, such as, "He is half man, half piano."

Horowitz continued, "And I hear you did not win the Leventritt Competition and were unhappy about it. Also, you have some mechanical problems, I hear." I then played the "Wanderer" Fantasy, all twenty-odd minutes of it, to a most attentive paternal, or at least avuncular, maestro, who even donned his glasses for the occasion.

Long silence. "You have no mechanical problem. You just have to practice more."

This verdict could easily have been construed as a dismissal, had it not been followed by a most inspiring two hours of illustrated monologue.

"The most important thing to work for," he said, "is the direct line between head and heart on the one end, and the *finger tip* on the other. It is not enough to feel and think if the playing is independent of feeling and thought. The playing by the fingers must constantly be the direct result of the other processes." There followed many illustrations at the piano, mostly Schumann.

"And there is not enough color!" More Schumann.

"Pedalling is enormously important!" More Schumann.

"And your chords are not together!" And down came seven fingers on the opening chords of the "Wanderer" Fantasy in shattering togetherness. "*This* is together!"

Then several Scarlatti Sonatas followed without comment.

It was magnificent. My feeling of betrayal had vanished. I felt most privileged to hear Horowitz play at a time when no one heard him "live."

More than ten years later, we heard him again live in Carnegie Hall, and few eyes remained dry. While most colleagues realistically observed that his playing was nothing that could or even should be imitated, it was an event to be remembered forever.

Seymour Bernstein

Seymour Bernstein studied with Alexander Brailowsky, Sir Clifford Curzon, Jan Gorbaty, Nadia Boulanger, and Georges Enesco. He has received many awards and grants, including the first prize and the Prix Jacques Durand from the International Competition held at Fontainebleau, France. His performing career has taken him to Asia and Europe, where he appeared in solo recitals and as guest artist with many chamber groups and important orchestras. Bernstein made his debut with the Chicago Symphony Orchestra, performing the world premiere of the Villa-Lobos Piano Concerto No. 2. He has had an extensive teaching career, and has given countless lectures and master-classes. His book With Your Own Two Hands, *published by Schirmer Books, is now in its eighth United States printing and has been translated into Korean and German.*

I first heard Vladimir Horowitz when I was fifteen years old. The occasion was the Distinguished Artists Series at the Mosque Theater (now Symphony Hall) in Newark, New Jersey. It is a cavernous hall with a seating capacity of 2,800. The sheer mania associated with the name *Horowitz* was as strongly in evidence then as it is now. It was not unusual, therefore, that the hall was sold out months before his appearance.

At 15, I had already decided to become a performing pianist. Not that I had very much to go on in those days—my technique was shabby, and my repertoire was extremely limited. But I did have one asset—a passionate love of music—and with this came a burning desire to overcome my fear of performing. I had another passion as well. It derived from two recordings I owned, the Concerto in B-flat minor by Tchaikovsky and the Concerto in B-flat by Brahms, both played by Horowitz and conducted by Toscanini. To me, those old

78-rpms were like living things. Thus I tenderly lifted them out of their albums, being careful not to scratch them, or—the worst of horrors—to break them. For that would have been tantamount to injuring Horowitz himself. And, finally, when I positioned the discs on the turntable of our old Magnavox console and subsequently listened to those demoniacal phrases and thundering chords and octaves emanating from the mono speaker, goose flesh broke out over my entire body, and my hair stood straight up on end. Awestruck though I was, that sound kindled a fire within me: "I can play like that," I thought. "I only need more time to work things out."

Such is the feeling that great performances and great things can engender in young people, and even in those adults who have retained that wide-eyed wonder associated with youth. In other words, the very *rightness* of extraordinary accomplishments can awaken something within us that not only admires the object of our inspiration, but actually feels capable of emulating it. Thus did those recordings of Vladimir Horowitz spur me on beyond myself.

Considering all of this, one can imagine just how charged with emotion I was when I actually sat in a concert hall and heard Horowitz play for the first time. I was fortunate in procuring a seat in the pit directly beneath his right hand. I not only heard him, therefore, but I also watched each and every gesture he made. I was stuck by three things in particular: his tightly curved fifth finger, his flat-fingered position on black keys, and the fact that he played everything detached—melodies as well as fast passages. Yet, when I moved to the center of the parquet after intermission, his playing sounded perfectly legato. From that moment on, I adopted a whole new philosophy of sound in my own playing. I suddenly realized that true legato on the keyboard depends foremost on physical comfort and the ability to control a wide range of dynamics. For one thing, I began using my first and fifth fingers exclusively for almost all octave passages; and I simply connected the sounds with my right pedal. And like Horowitz, I detached all fast passages, feeling all the while that I was playing as brilliantly as he did. Not everything I emulated, however, produced favorable results: For when I actually succeeded in stretching out my fourth fingers while keeping the tips of my fifth fingers curled, my hands and my forearms grew stiffer and stiffer. And soon I was hardly able to play at all.

One other thing struck me when I watched Horowitz at close range: I noticed with great distress and disillusionment that my idol's hands trembled from the beginning of the recital to the end. "He is not a god, after all," I concluded, "but simply a frail human being who gets nervous just like I do." By the time I returned home, however, I admired him all the more for surviving that performance—in spite of his nerves. And I had another thought, too: "Perhaps he plays like that *because* of his inner terror."

Through the years, I have purchased most of the Horowitz recordings; and I have heard him perform many times in public. I remember two concerts in particular. One at Carnegie Hall marked the twenty-fifth celebration of his debut with Arturo Toscanini. It was the concert at which he played the octave passage at the end of the first movement of the Tchaikovsky Concerto so fast that he finished the movement at least a bar before the orchestra. The other concert, in the spring of 1965, unquestionably the most memorable one I have ever attended, signified his return to the concert stage after twelve years of retirement. Most of us there wondered if, in fact, he would go through with it. My joy, everyone's joy, at seeing him walk across the stage of Carnegie Hall sporting a smile and looking every bit as amazed as we were, will remain in my memory forever. It was not one of his best performances. But, frankly speaking, it did not matter in the slightest. He was performing again, and everything seemed right with the world. Deeply moved by that event, I wrote him the following note:

> *Dear Mr. Horowitz,*
>
> *When President Kennedy was assassinated, I was sorry to have been born. But when I saw you walk across the stage of Carnegie Hall last Sunday afternoon, I was glad to be alive!*

His secretary at that time, Dorothy Pritchett, happened to have been my pupil. She told me how moved Horowitz was by my note. And much to my surprise, I received a gracious thank-you note from him.

I tried often to play for Horowitz; and I even made an attempt to interview him for my book, *With Your Own Two Hands.* One excuse followed upon another, and no meeting ever took place. In the meantime, I pursued my career and went on many State Department tours, including three trips to Korea. There, in 1960, I met a young pianist, Lee Kong Ju, whom I helped to bring to this country. Like so many other pianists, Kong Ju hero-worshiped Horowitz's playing, and was particularly taken with the Horowitz transcriptions. Through the years, Kong Ju collected all of the existing Horowitz recordings of these works. Being blessed with ears that can detect every pitch no matter how complex the sounds may be, he painstakingly wrote down each and every transcription, including three versions of the *Carmen* Fantasy. The whole project took twenty-five years—years of listening and refining until, finally, Kong Ju himself was convinced that he had written down the transcriptions exactly as Horowitz had played them. Thinking that Horowitz would be as amazed by this accomplishment as I was, I sent him a copy of the *Stars and Stripes*. But here, too, Horowitz remained aloof. And one day, his friend, the late Olga Stroumillo, telephoned me to say that something most unfortunate had occurred: Horowitz's servant had accidentally thrown out the envelope containing the transcription. Needless to say, both Kong Ju and I were devastated to hear of this. And I, for one, resolved never to contact Horowitz again.

Years later, I spoke with Thomas Frost, Horowitz's producer from Columbia Records. Mr. Frost agreed that the transcriptions ought to be published. He spoke to Horowitz about this, and the master finally consented at last to see the written-down transcriptions. More and more delays followed; and alas, Horowitz died shortly before we were to meet with him.

Now, it seems, Mrs. Horowitz is eager to have these transcriptions published. Quite recently a meeting took place at the Horowitz home, attended by Thomas Frost and his wife, Lynne, Lee Kong Ju, and me. Mrs. Horowitz sees the project as a fitting testimonial to her husband. Moreover, she welcomed the prospect of having her husband's transcriptions available at last to other pianists. During the entire meeting, my heart broke as I stared at Horowitz's concert grand stretched out like a black coffin in front of the impressive windows of the drawing room. It is silenced forever, I thought, like my idol. Prominent on the closed lid of the piano was a red brocade pillow on which rested a bronze cast of Horowitz's hands. During tea and the best cookies I have ever tasted, I asked Mrs. Horowitz if we might see the hands at close range. "Yes, of course," she said; and she graciously ushered us to the piano. Lynne Frost, who had often wanted to see those hands up close since Horowitz's death, whispered to me that she had never had the courage to ask this of Mrs. Horowitz. We all, then, walked solemnly to the piano as one would to a shrine.

Seeing the bronze cast up close, and having the details of Horowitz's hands etched clearly in my memory since that first concert I attended at the Mosque Theater, I knew at once that something was wrong: "Mrs. Horowitz," I exclaimed, "I know this may seem strange to you, but these do not look like your husband's hands!" Being taken completely aback, she retorted, "What are you saying! You know, he did not have large hands." "That may be true," I responded, "but please look at the finger tips, especially the fifth fingers. Your husband's finger pads were much thicker than the ones we are looking at." Without another word, Mrs. Horowitz left the room and returned a few minutes later with the original plaster model of her husband's hands. She held this model next to the bronze cast for comparison, and at once, all eyes met in utter astonishment. My assessment had been correct: The final product was far different than the plaster model. Thomas Frost then suggested to Mrs. Horowitz that she consult with the artist. And she agreed to do this. The rest of the story remains to be told some day.

We are all saddened to think that we will never hear Horowitz play again. My own sadness, however, extends beyond this; for I feel cheated that Horowitz, who was often thought of as the modern-day Liszt, did not, like Liszt, compose his own sonata, and his own rhapsodies. For he was, as everyone knows, a gifted composer during his teenage years. That he neglected to develop his formidable gifts in this area remains for me an unmitigated tragedy. I am saddened, too, that he did not have the inclination to teach more than he did; and it also troubles me that whatever attempts he did make at teaching proved, in many cases, to be disastrous. Many of my musician friends have chastised me for my complaints. They have accused me of being unreasonable. As far as they are concerned, we should all be grateful to have lived in the same century with such an artist. Much as I agree with this, I feel, nevertheless, that geniuses are, by the very definition of the word, unlimited in their capacities for doing the impossible. Horowitz was undoubtedly a genius. And to think of those unborn masterpieces, which, I am sure, must have resounded in those miraculous ears, fills me with a sense of inconsolable loss.

Leonard Pennario

A pupil of Guy Maier and later of Isabelle Vengerova, Leonard Pennario, born in Buffalo, New York, made his debut at the age of twelve in the Grieg Concerto with the Dallas Symphony. He made his New York debut in 1943 with the New York Philharmonic. Pennario has had a worldwide performing career and has created an extensive discography. He often collaborated with Heifetz and Piatigorsky. In 1967, he gave the premiere of the Mikló's Rózsa Piano Concerto, which is dedicated to him.

Pennario has made recordings with major orchestras and conductors of many romantic piano concertos. His discs of the music of Louis Moreau Gottschalk have helped considerably in establishing the composer's position in American music. He has also recorded large segments of music by Rachmaninoff and Chopin.

In May of 1942, I had the pleasure of playing for Vladimir Horowitz at his apartment in New York. I had long been an admirer of his, having been dazzled by his incandescent virtuosity, so it was an exciting experience to perform for him. He was generous with his time, and listened to me for about two hours. I had not as yet attained my eighteenth birthday, and still had that youthful obliviousness to difficulty that so soon vanishes. Looking back, I marvel that I played, among other pieces, both books of the Brahms-Paganini Variations.

He was very kind and complimentary in his comments, and encouraged me to pursue my career. As a final offering, I played for him a composition of my own, written the previous year in Newport, Rhode Island, depicting waves pounding on the rocks on the famous cliffwalk there. Entitled "Midnight on the Cliffs," my little paean to the sea elicited the following unforgettable comment from the great pianist: "That's a beautiful piece, but hard, isn't it?"

I will always treasure the memory of that afternoon with Horowitz.

Ursula Oppens

Ursula Oppens is a native of New York. She studied with her mother, Edith Oppens, as well as with Leonard Shure and Guido Agosti. In 1969 she won first prize at the Busoni Competition. In 1976 she ws awarded the Avery Fisher Prize.

Oppens is a dedicated exponent of the music of our time. She has premiered works by Braxton, Davis, Harbison, Nancarrow, Picker, Wolff, and Wuorinen, and in 1992 performed Lou Harrison's Piano Concerto with the Atlanta Symphony and Francis Throne's Piano Concerto at Carnegie Hall. Her recording on the Music and Arts label, American Piano Music of Our Times, *received a Grammy nomination, as did her Vanguard disc of Rzewski's* The People United Will Never Be Defeated. *Recently, an all-Beethoven disc was released on the Music and Arts label. Ursula Oppens performs regularly in recital and with the world's leading orchestras.*

I remember one moment when I was about fifteen years old, I was terribly sad after hearing all the Beethoven string quartets because I knew I could never again hear any of them for the first time. Of course, these first times are really a matter of consciousness and receptivity, for one can hear almost anything as if for the first time at many unexpected moments in life. Nevertheless, the past few months have been truly revelatory for me as I have listened to many of Horowitz's recordings absolutely for the first time, and, in consequence, have been experiencing some of the headiness and excitement that is normally the prerogative of adolescence.

Horowitz was *the* pianistic legend of my youth. With his return to the stage in the late sixties and early seventies, I, as much as anyone else, was caught up in the wonderful drama of the lost past becoming the attainable present. At that time, however, I was very much involved with the German repertoire, searching for certainty of interpretation. When I heard him, I was almost terrified by the utter spontaneity of his performance.

Horowitz was truly the solitary romantic figure who could inspire the listener to ecstasy or leave him speechless with awe. With Horowitz around, there is no way that one could imagine classical music to be effete or something that existed simply for the passive pleasures of a snobbish cultural elite.

If the nineteenth century was the heyday for classical piano music, Horowitz certainly retained all the romanticism and charisma of a nineteenth century hero. But Horowitz was not of a lost age. He had all the qualities of an ongoing creative musician as well. Like Schnabel, Anton Rubinstein, Heifetz, and Liszt, he was a composer. Perhaps he was not a first-rate composer, but he certainly seemed to enjoy inventing sounds out of whole cloth as much as playing exactly what someone else had written. It is impossible, of course, to play exactly what another has notated; these symbols must be brought to life.

No one made music more alive than Horowitz. We pianists have spent our lifetimes trying to imitate his sound and to duplicate his extraordinary dynamic range. We cannot do it. Many have tried to produce what seemed to be his hundreds of different articulations in the Scarlatti sonatas. We can only produce a few of them. Others have tried to play as he did, so that every note and phrase sounds as if it has just been discovered. We cannot do it the way he did. But we must try to play with intention as clear as his was.

Rudolf Firkušný

Rudolf Firkušný was born in Napajedla, Czechoslovakia. As a child in Brno, he studied with Leos Janáček; he made his Paris debut with Cortot conducting. Firkušný made his first United States Tour in 1938. In May 1990, he performed for the first time in forty-four years in his native country.

Firkušný holds an honorary doctorate from Charles University, the Gold Medal of the Performing Arts Academy of Prague, and honorary citizenships in both Prague and his home town. In October 1991, he was awarded the Order of T. G. Masaryk, the highest civilian honor bestowed by the Czechoslovak government.

During his distinguished career, Firkušný has appeared with all of the world's major orchestras and conductors. He has recorded a large discography, including Czech music from Dussek to Dvořák, Janáček, and Martinů. His disc of piano music by Janáček won the French Diapason d'Or and the Japanese Ongakuno-tomo Award.

I was fortunate in knowing Horowitz and especially during his finest years of pianism, which I judge to be the thirties and forties, until his retirement in 1953. I met him in 1941 when I first came to the United States, and we became quite friendly. Both Horowitz and Mrs. Horowitz were always charming to me. He could be very witty and often amusing. He had a wonderful sense of humor and he could be funny and sarcastic.

There was a time in the late forties that we were often together with Samuel Barber, who adored him and wrote his great Piano Sonata for him. I was crazy about the piece and had to learn it myself. We were together frequently, Barber, Menotti, and their crowd. Horowitz was very at ease with us.

I remember once he was supposed to play in Baltimore, and he had for some trivial reason cancelled the performance. However, he was in such a rare and wonderful mood because he had cancelled. He smiled, and laughed like a child: "How wonderful!" he screamed. "I don't have to go to Baltimore. I don't have to play!" He was elated. He said, "Let's do something fun. Let's go to Chinatown." He asked Sam, "Do you know any crazy places?" Sam replied, "There are some amusing spots in Chinatown." After several adventures we were told to go to a nightclub where there was a woman dancing with a snake and that it was amusing and daring. So we all went to find it. But the previous day, the woman was arrested, not because the act was obscene, but for animal cruelty because she taped shut the mouth of the snake.

I do not think he was always completely at ease with his father-in-law, the great Toscanini, whom he revered as the supreme musician. It must have been a strain for Horowitz to have such an awesome father-in-law. When occasionally at parties I saw them together, Toscanini never seemed to talk to Horowitz. I remember Toscanini was morose, and I went to talk with him, and it was a wonderful conversation. We spoke of Smetana and the soprano Emmy Destinn. I asked him about Puccini's opera *La Rondine*, and Toscanini screamed gleefully in Italian, "You are not a pianist, you are a musician!" From that moment, he was friendly. Horowitz and Toscanini did not play often enough together, but, fortunately, they left their recordings of the Brahms B-flat and the Tchaikovsky, which are wonderful, especially the Tchaikovsky.

There was something in Horowitz's sound that was electrifying, combined with a breathtaking palette of contrasting colors. I first heard him when I was still in Brno as a youngster. It was unfortunately only on the radio, but I was extremely impressed. It was in many ways a rather new kind of playing. We were used to the old Austrian School exemplified by the old fashioned elegance of Emil Sauer. When I first heard Rachmaninoff, it was a revelation, and then came Horowitz, who was again also a revelation.

I was instantly fascinated by this man. I couldn't wait to hear him in person. This occurred in Paris, where he gave a recital, I think in 1933. It was superb. He played the Bach-Busoni C major Toccata, Beethoven's Sonata in F-sharp major Op. 78, Ravel's *Jeux d'eau*, and other things such as mazurkas of Chopin—not really a large-scale program, but it was fantastic. I was entranced. From that moment, I became an ardent admirer of Horowitz. I adored his playing. I went to every possible performance of his.

After his retirement in 1953, we unfortunately lost touch. In his earlier years, there was a certain naturalness and simplicity that was beguiling. Everything was simple. After his retirement, he became more exaggerated. He had become too studied. He started studying the recordings of great singers and his playing began to sound mannered. I feel he was a pianist of instinct, and he had to be free as a bird. I was pleased to hear in his last period that some of the naturalness of his youth surfaced again in a relaxed and happy way. Horowitz was an extraordinary artist, one who will loom ever large in the history of the piano. I am glad that I was able to hear those extraordinary hands in public, where his very presence caused such an unprecedented and deserved musical sensation.

Maurice Hinson

The American pianist Maurice Hinson is active in many fields: performing, writing, lecturing, and teaching. He is a major authority on the piano literature, and has edited fifty volumes of the most diverse piano music. He has written many books, such as the Guide to the Pianist's Repertoire *and* Music for Piano and Orchestra *(Indiana University Press).*

Hinson studied piano with Olga Samaroff and Edwin Hughes. He has performed in forty-eight states as well as in Asia and Europe. He was founding editor of the Journal of the American Liszt Society, *and for his service to Liszt's music he received the Liszt Commemorative Medal from the Hungarian government. Hinson is professor of piano in the School of Church Music at the Southern Baptist Theological Seminary in Louisville, Kentucky.*

Horowitz has been my pianistic idol ever since I heard him in Jacksonville, Florida, when I was fourteen years old. That experience was unlike anything that had ever happened to me. I had a stage seat about four feet from him and I could not believe my eyes or ears. He played Scarlatti, Chopin, Schumann, and Mussorgsky, and, for an encore, his Variations on Themes from *Carmen*, among others.

I was fortunate enough to hear him over a period of approximately forty years—in person and numerous times on the radio and television. I have tried to answer the question: "What was it that made Horowitz so special to me?" and would like to share some of my answers with the reader.

His octaves were surely heaven-storming! I have yet to hear another pianist who came anywhere near Horowitz's octaves. They looked and sounded as if they were on a "fast-forward" film—but always fit the exciting musical situation. His dynamic control was incredible—from the quietest pianississimo to the most sonorous fortississimo, and without banging. His articulation was the clearest and most crisp imaginable. This was especially the case in his Scarlatti. Horowitz never tried to make the piano sound like a harpsichord when he played this great composer; he was never afraid to use color effects, those the modern piano does so well. I have one record, all Scarlatti sonatas, that has literally been worn out due to repeated hearing (for me and my students) over the years. His rhythmic and technical control in these pieces, plus the amazing pianism, is simply technically fabulous and breathtaking. These performances were convincing proof that the piano was a wonderful instrument for playing Scarlatti.

My first experience with the Barber Sonata was through Horowitz's recording. After hearing the recording for the first time, I remember dropping the needle again at the beginning of the fugue, just to make sure I had heard what I thought I had heard!

For years I would go to a Horowitz recital and try to figure how he did what he did. I never figured it out, and finally gave up and just went to hear him for the beauty, excitement, and plain amazement that a Horowitz recital always produced.

I could talk about his orchestral approach to the piano—his recreative process (more than just interpretation), his understanding and projection of the Romantic performance practice tradition (as I understood it), but I was asked to discuss what Horowitz means *to me.*

A Horowitz performance always meant something new, exciting, and extraordinary was going to take place. I heard him play the G minor Chopin Ballade on two different occasions, plus I own two of his recordings of this work. The performances were all different. His approach must have been like Chopin's himself, who never played a piece the same way twice. Every Horowitz recital was in a special category by itself. I was affected by each recital differently and more positively than by any other piano recitals, and I have been fortunate to hear some of the finest pianists of the twentieth century.

I read some words of Horowitz many years ago that described his approach to music. These pearls of wisdom have served as a guide for me and my students and deserve repeating here: "You must bring the spiritual, emotional, technical, and intellectual aspects of music together, combined into one. Nothing should stick out. Intellect and mind are only control, not the guide. The guide is the control of emotion. The first point of music is emotion." Horowitz always expressed the greatest amount of emotion in his playing. His intensity was always under control; you always felt there was much more to be had if he wanted to bring it out. He had quintessential simplicity when it was called for, as in a Chopin mazurka, or the free improvisational quality that infused his *Traumerei.* He could produce a singing line that left the listener limp.

Many people thought of Horowitz as a legend. He was never a legend to me; he was simply the world's greatest living pianist. It is because *all* these qualities—incredible technique, orchestral approach to the instrument, enormous dynamic range, simplicity, controlled intensity, exploration of the literature in his own unique way, the most gorgeous cantible line imaginable, and so on—that Horowitz was absolutely unique in the world of pianism. He was a beacon for me and had more pianistic influence on my life than any other pianist.

The entire twentieth century would have been much poorer without him. The world will probably never see another pianist like Vladimir Horowitz.

Leonid Hambro

Born in Chicago, Illinois, Leonid Hambro was trained at New York's Juilliard School. Later he won the Naumburg Award. He became the official pianist of the New York Philharmonic and was retained as staff pianist for WQXR, the radio station of the New York Times. *In this capacity, he gave live chamber, duo-piano, and solo recitals for fifteen years. In addition, for thirteen years he was pianist for the Sarasota Chamber Music Festival.*

Hambro has concertized extensively and has appeared as soloist with major orchestras. He made recordings of the standard repertoire and of music by Gershwin and Bartók, and was an early advocate of Charles Griffes piano music. Hambro was artist-in-residence at the Aspen Festival and has appeared on many television shows. For twenty years he was the head of the piano department at the Music School of the California Institute for the Arts.

I was ten years old when I first heard Vladimir Horowitz play. My father, who was my first piano teacher, had already taken me to hear all the great virtuoso pianists of that time—Josef Hofmann, Sergei Rachmaninoff, Josef Lhévinne, Benno Moiseiwitsch, and Ignaz Friedmann. They were all my gods, and Horowitz joined their ranks. Over the years, as I matured musically, I became somewhat more critical of my gods, even though their artistry always remained compelling.

In the case of Horowitz, however, I began to realize that here was a truly unique performer: despite his staggering ability to play with incomparable speed, impeccable accuracy, and a phenomenally thunderous sound, something was missing. For me, his musicianship did not match his pianism. I often found his musical judgment questionable and his choices inappropriate.

Rachmaninoff, as is commonly known, also expressed his reservations with Horowitz's playing similarly, and managed to exert some musical influence over him. Indeed, it was during the period of his friendship with Rachmaninoff that Horowitz seemed to do his best playing. Toscanini, Horowitz's father-in-law, also favorably influenced—albeit brutally, as many members of the New York Philharmonic orchestra will testify—Horowitz's musical interpretations. To me, it seemed that Horowitz's playing deteriorated after the loss of these two musical giants. Now, it might be reasonable to assume that a pianist's prowess wanes with age; yet there is the example of Arthur Rubinstein, whose mastery of all the elements of piano playing increased as he grew older.

My personal encounters with Horowitz served to corroborate my impressions of his musicianship. For example, one summer—it may have been in the mid-1950s—on Fire Island (a favorite vacation spot at that time for the artistic and gay communities), I saw Horowitz sitting on a bench watching a group of young volleyball players. I approached him with the intention of expressing my admiration. As I began to introduce myself, he interrupted with his thick Russian accent: "You are Leonid Hambro?! Best performance of Prokofiev Sixth Sonata I ever heard. Tell me—last movement—difficult passage. How you finger?"

"It's funny you should ask about that particular passage," I said, "because I dreamed that fingering."

"You too! I'm always dreaming fingerings."

"That makes three of us. My two-piano partner, Jascha Zayde, frequently tells me he dreams of fingerings that solve particularly nasty technical problems."

The following day, as I passed Horowitz's house, I heard him practicing and, just for the fun of it, I counted the repetitions of a particular two-bar passage—as I recall, it was a broken octave passage in a Liszt etude—and when I saw him the next day, again watching the volleyball players, I asked, "Do you know you repeated that passage ninety-nine times and every one was as good as the one before, and many were even better. Isn't it a waste of time to spend so much effort on something you already do so perfectly?"

"But you see, my dear," he replied, "I get so terribly nervous ven I play I must be able to play in my sleep. I must be able to play with house burning down. I must repeat so much that my fingers play without my head."

A few days later, again through the window of his house, I heard him practicing Chopin's G minor Ballade. When he came to the second theme, marked fortissimo, he hesitated so much before every downbeat that the interruption of the melodic flow was glaring and went against my grain. When I asked him why he distorted the rhythm so, he said, "I must have beeg bass notes." I then suggested could he not play the bass notes "beeg" and in time.

He replied, "Must be *special* loud bass notes."

I persisted, "But, Maestro, this extra time you take sacrifices the rhythmic flow of the melody."

His response—which I will never forget—was: "Well, you've got to sacrifice something!"

Roger Shields

Roger Shields was born in Arcola, Illinois. He displayed musical gifts from his earliest years. By the age of thirteen, he had composed two piano concertos and an opera, and had performed the complete etudes, preludes, and B minor Sonata of Chopin. His principal teacher was Soulima Stravinsky.

As a winner at various competitions, Mr. Shields toured Europe and the United States performing a large, eclectic repertoire ranging from the Well-Tempered Clavier *of Bach and the "Hammerklavier" Sonata of Beethoven, to operatic fantasies of Liszt, the twelve Debussy etudes, and avant-garde and serial music. George Perle dedicated his Six Etudes to Shields. For Vox he recorded several discs of twentieth-century piano music of Ruggles, Griffes, Copland, and others. He dedicates a great deal of his work to teaching and is the president of the Stravinsky Awards International Competition.*

The merging of passion and chasteness in the piano playing of Vladimir Horowitz engenders a mystery that enchants and enshrouds our senses of perception. While it is understandable that such Faustian artistry would generate torrents of debate, the intemperance of the dialogue is often tedious. It is true that dogs will always bark at caravans. Experience teaches us, as doges and beggars alike have always known, that the caravans will and must continue to come and go. One must surely realize that it is the mystery of Horowitz which is the source of both the commerce and the clamor.

One cannot reasonably deny that Horowitz's powers of communication were transcendental, perhaps beyond good and evil. It matters not that some choose to dote upon the perceived imperfections in his art. In spite of "wrong style," "wrong taste," "wrong conception," or "wrong whatever," nearly every note that Horowitz played was compelling. Perhaps the foundering intellect may find some relief in asking whether one would rather have the "right whatever" played the wrong way, or the "wrong whatever" played the right way.

Many pianists of the past three decades have tormented themselves trying to understand how Horowitz did what he did. Indeed there is much to be learned in the dissection of his art—the incredible sonorities, the limitless color palette, the sense of play, the clarity of structure, the intuitive grasp of texture, and the unfailing sense of harmonic and rhythmic polarity. One could, however, learn and project all of these components in performance, and still produce a result sounding like a dull lecture. There was something Horowitz did that transcended the cerebral, and vanquished analysis.

Most pianists are intrigued with how Horowitz used his physical equipment, seeming to break all of the rules. We can make sense of some of it—the often flat fingers and low wrists, for example. But how do taut shoulders and steely arms translate into the most fluid and resilient of sounds? It was wonderful to see just how easy playing the piano could be: the motionless sphinx sent forth a tsunami of sound and energy. In observing that Horowitz often appeared to be "untaught," we realize the truth: he taught himself.

Horowitz is a subject of confoundment only in our times. In listening to his contemporaries of the first half of this century, we discover many uniquely individual artists, each with personal and easily identifiable styles. Since the standards of that time demanded individuality, Horowitz was actually in the mainstream of keyboard artistry. But by the 1960s, Horowitz had been exiled, by the muzzle of academia, to the fringes of modern pianism. It takes some thought to understand what happened.

The dismal failing of academia since World War II is due to the quest for normalcy, which has led to the inevitable decline in the study of the "classics" and in the love and acquisition of "culture" in the most circumspect sense. With the loss of culture via the lifeline to the classics, the individual has been stripped of his most valuable attribute, the transcendental sense of aspiration, the belief that one can scale Parnassus. Since one can aspire only to fulfiull the ME, the individual has developed a rather total dependence upon ordinary and reasonable expectations, and society has devised the formula that equalizes the average and the heroic. Are we not, after all, all equals—so postulates the formula—and do we not, therefore, all have something equally important to say?

Naturally, in such a context, Horowitz was never, in my experience, played as an example in the studio/classroom. Obviously, he was unreasonable. Since the possibility of ascent to Parnassus was precluded, it followed that Parnassus itself should be dismantled. Horowitz was dismissed from our expectations, usually with great pontification and disdain.

We now reap the harvest: Endless numbers of bland "noodlers" dominating the concert stages, critics who can judge only by comparing to academically sanctioned performances, and audiences wanting to hear only what they have already heard many times before, much like Tolkien's hobbits. Perhaps those who say that people who really love music no longer go to concerts are correct.

Thus also the deflated position of Horowitz in our times. Yet there has always existed an underground that believed Horowitz was miraculous, and that was fanatic in its devotion. Horowitz was the only individual left, an imperfect hero who believed himself to be a part of the destiny of history; who had his own great cultural heroes; and who embodied that unique fusion of factual achievement and mythology that decreed no possible course of action other than aspiration to the loftiest heights. He composed, he arranged, and he pioneered new works. He found fault with his playing, was never satisfied, and often even felt that he could not play the piano. Obviously he was trying to live up to a great tradition to which he felt he belonged, but of which he probably never felt quite worthy.

Perhaps we will come to understand that what is crucial is not to play like Horowitz, but rather to be like Horowitz. Unfortunately, one cannot simply go out and acquire culture. Until society begins again to teach the classics and thus to infuse us with an inherent belief in the great romance of culture, in the value of aspiring to something beyond ourselves, and in the possibility of achieving the miraculous, the very concept of Horowitz will remain unimaginable.

The study of civilization reveals the mysteries of aspiration, the merging of individual passion with a chaste reverence for tradition, and the cyclical unfolding of our achievements. Our time will run its course, and one day another Horowitz will be possible.

Alicia de Larrocha

A native of Barcelona, Alicia de Larrocha studied with Frank Marshall. A child prodigy, she made her first public appearance in 1929 at the age of six. She received the Paderewski Prize in London, and her recordings of Granados's Goyescas *and Albeniz's* Iberia *brought her acclaim. During the last several years, she has recorded for BMG/RCA Classics and has embarked on recording the complete solo sonatas and concertos of Mozart.*

Alicia de Larrocha has received many awards, including four Grammys, the Dutch Edison Prize, the Grand Prix du Disque, and the Deutscher Shallplattenpreis. In 1979 she was honored as Musician of the Year by Musical America. In 1982 the city of Barcelona awarded her the Medallo d'Oro for artistic merit, and the Spanish National Assembly voted to award her its Gold Medal for Merit in the Fine Arts, which was bestowed on her by King Juan Carlos.

I am very happy to write a few words about Vladimir Horowitz. I met him only a few times, but I heard him play often, and he was of course a titan of our century. Such a strong and powerful technique, and with an incredible charisma! I still recall the amazement I felt when he came to greet me after one of my concerts in New York City, and we were honored together as Lincoln Center "lions"; I was very touched with his gentleness and serenity. After he passed away, I had the opportunity to make some recordings on his own Steinway, and the first time I touched the keyboard, I knew immediately that he liked his piano the same way I do—bright and clear, and with an easy and fluid action. It was a curious and illuminating moment. I also realized that we had a similar problem—the size of our hands! Mine are so small, and his were so large; it was the same problem, but from a different side!

Peter Serkin

American pianist Peter Serkin has a rich musical heritage. His grandfather was Adolf Busch, his father Rudolf Serkin. In 1958 he entered the Curtis Institute of Music, where he was a student of Lee Luvisi, Mieczyslaw Horszowski, and Rudolf Serkin. Peter Serkin made his debut at the Marlboro Music Festival in 1959. Ever since, he has been concertizing extensively. During the 1989–90 season, he played in eighteen cities in a recital program featuring eleven works that he commissioned from ten composers. In 1985 he gave the world premiere of Peter Lieberson's Piano Concerto and recorded it for New World Records. Toru Takemitsu has written seven works for him.

Serkin's recording of the six Mozart concertos of 1784 received the Deutscher Schallplattenpreis. He has also been honored as the first pianist awarded the Premio Internazionale Musicale Chigiana for outstanding artistic achievement. He is on the faculties of the Juilliard School and the Curtis Institute.

I knew Vladimir Horowitz a little. I had some conversations with him, visiting him in his home, where I also played for him, and he for me.

It was my father who really had a close friendship with Horowitz. They first met in 1928 in Basel, at the home of my grandfather, Adolf Busch. Introduced by mutual friends in the von Mendelssohn family, Horowitz seemed shy at first, so my father played some music for him first. Then Horowitz played Chopin's G minor Ballade and some Liszt pieces, I think, and my father was absolutely bowled over by Horowitz's fiery and brilliant playing. They were friends from then on.

Horowitz suggested a visit to introduce my grandfather and my father to Rachmaninoff. One of them responded by saying, "But he's dead, isn't he?" Horowitz told them that Rachmaninoff was living in nearby Lucerne. They both said, "He is?" And they sang out loudly the opening three notes of the C-sharp minor Prelude, laughing!

Each summer in those days, my grandfather and my father used to have their heads shaved. So when they met Rachmaninoff, who always had a similar very short haircut, they were thought to be playing a practical joke, making fun of him! Adolf and Rudi really hit it off with Rachmaninoff. They loved his sense of humor and sarcastic wit. The three pianists, Rachmaninoff, Horowitz, and my father took turns playing four-hand music together, mostly sonatas by Mozart, of which Rachmaninoff's favorite was the one in B-flat major, K. 358. I think that maybe the only pianist who impressed my father pianistically more than Horowitz was Rachmaninoff, whom they both adored.

Later on my parents, with my maternal grandparents and also Mieczyslaw Horszowski, had a further connection with Horowitz through their shared devoted friendship with Arturo Toscanini.

I remember my dad often on the phone with Volodya, talking about music, gossiping, and joking around. Sometimes they talked about performing some four-hand works together at Marlboro, but it never actually happened. During Horowitz's hiatus from concert performing, my dad often gave him warm encouragement to get back to playing concerts.

I myself heard Horowitz play a few times. I remember well his 1965 "return" recital in New York. I recall having had some nice talks with him, too. Once when he began an anecdote about the great Rubinstein, I remember how he growled, "*Anton* Rubinstein!"

Once, invited to Horowitz's home, I played some Messiaen (which he did not know) for him and Mrs. Horowitz, and he played Clementi's Grand Sonata in C major and much of Schumann's *Humoreske* and Liszt's *Mephisto* Waltz (with Horowitz's own little changes, which he pointed out, in the text). I believe that he had a recital in Washington two days later, with those pieces on the program. When he got momentarily lost in the rondo of the Clementi, he stopped, glanced, and looked up at his wife like a little boy to his mother, and said, "You see, I told you I couldn't play this!" And she sternly told him to get back to it and finish. His playing of the Schumann was very beautiful. I was really very taken with it.

Before I left, late at night, he said that I had to come back soon to visit. But the next time, I had to play for him Chopin etudes—so I never went back! I did call him again to congratulate him on his televised performance of the Rachmaninoff Third Concerto. As if promoting the music of some relatively obscure but deserving composer, he encouraged me to play some Rachmaninoff myself, saying, "You have the technique for it, if you can play Messiaen like that."

Reflecting back on this great pianist, I think that perhaps I did not have a deep affinity for Horowitz's musical mentality somehow, but I loved some of his playing, particularly what I heard in his home.

Dmitri Alexeev

Born in Moscow, Dmitri Alexeev began playing the piano at age five. He was brought to the Central Music School, and later, at the Moscow Conservatory, he studied with Dmitri Bashkirov. He participated in major competitions, winning top honors at the 1969 Marguerite Long Competition and the 1970 George Enescu Competition in Bucharest. In 1974 he won the Tchaikovsky Competition, and the following year was the victor at the Leeds Competition.

Alexeev made his American debut in 1976, with Giulini conducting the Chicago Symphony. He regularly returns to Russia and is frequently a guest soloist with the St. Petersburg Philharmonic. His solo recordings include the Chopin waltzes and preludes, Brahms solo works, and concertos by Prokofiev, Rachmaninoff, and Shostakovich for EMI. Recently he recorded the Grieg and Schumann concertos with Yuri Temerkanov and the Royal Philharmonic, on Virgin Classics.

For me and for many of my colleagues born in the Soviet Union and coming to maturity in the 1960s and 1970s, the name Horowitz stood like a shrine. He was a myth. We looked and looked for his records in the poorly stocked Moscow stores.

Although there were people in Russia who still remembered his concerts from the early 1920s, it was difficult to imagine that Horowitz was a real person who had himself studied in Kiev. It was said that he would call his sister in Kharkov, like a god talking through a telephone receiver. Once I read a very old letter where someone described Horowitz's concerts in Tbilisi and Leningrad in the 1920s. In the envelope, there were newspaper reviews of these concerts. I had never read anything so ecstatic. It all seemed to come from a vanished world.

Suddenly, after more than sixty years, it was announced that Horowitz was going to play in Moscow and Leningrad. Everyone involved with a piano tried to get tickets to the concert at the Great Hall of the Moscow Conservatory. It may not be well known, but two days before his recital, he gave an open rehearsal. It was unforgettable. Indeed, it was even better than the recital, which was televised and made into a video. At the rehearsal, we got to hear Horowitz warming up. The first thing we heard was endless scales played in extraordinary fast tempos. He also played some tunes with schmaltzy harmonies, reminiscent of a café atmosphere at the turn of the century. The harmonies also reminded me of those by Hofmann and Godowsky. After some time, the sounds of a Scarlatti sonata emerged, and it became absolutely clear that all the stories about the marvels of his "live" performances were in no way exaggerated. What we heard was not only a great master, but a genius of the piano. I will always feel gratitude for being able to have heard him. Those moments of beauty will live within me forever.

Ruth Laredo

Ruth Laredo was born in Detroit, Michigan. At the Curtis Institute she studied with Rudolf Serkin, and she made her orchestral debut under Leopold Stokowski. Her career has taken her throughout the United States, Japan, and Russia.

A three-time Grammy Award nominee, Laredo has recorded a large discography that includes the complete piano music of Rachmaninoff; she is the first pianist to fulfill this monumental task. In addition, she has recorded the complete sonatas of Scriabin and works by Barber and Ravel. After her Russian tour, Charles Kuralt devoted a profile to her on CBS Sunday Morning. *The Music Teachers National Association honored her for "Distinguished Service to Music in America."*

I shall never forget the impact of hearing Vladimir Horowitz for the first time in my life. I was eight years old and had already been studying piano for five years. Since the recital had been completely sold out, I sat with my parents in stage seats only a few inches away from the great man. After this concert, I vowed to become a pianist.

Although I never had any personal connection with him, Horowitz continued to influence me profoundly throughout my life. While my parents lovingly fostered my early interest in music, it was Horowitz who lit the spark that burned inside me ever since that unforgettable performance.

As a youngster attending elementary school in Detroit, I went to many great concerts in the cavernous Masonic Auditorium. I heard such immortals as Jascha Heifetz, Gregor Piatigorsky, and the Budapest String Quartet. But when Horowitz came to town, something extraordinary happened. He was not like anybody else; he had an aura. He cast a spell over the audience that defied analysis. His explosive playing seemed to unleash the power of a volcano; sounds erupted out of the piano like molten lava. I was mesmerized. I couldn't wait to get home to tackle every piece I had just heard.

During high school, I consumed such fire-eating works as the Rachmaninoff Third, the Brahms B flat, and the Barber Sonata, simply because I had heard Horowitz play them. My adolescent adoration grew into a much deeper love. During Horowitz's twelve-year hiatus from performing, I cherished every one of his recordings, and yearned for his return to the stage. Ultimately, I was privileged to witness his historic "return" to the concert stage at Carnegie Hall. I was lucky to get a seat in the very last row at the top of the peanut gallery. So astonishing was his performance on that fabled Sunday afternoon that I recall wandering up and down Fifty-Seventh Street in a daze. I wanted to stay there forever, near the place where I had just heard the most thrilling concert of my life.

I always liked Horowitz's gracious stage presence, his Old World charm. Striding from the wings dressed in an elegant grey morning coat and pin-striped trousers, he seemed to be welcoming the audience into his own living room, not Carnegie Hall. He usually gave seven or eight encores, culminating with the fiery *Carmen* Fantasy or the thunderous *Stars and Stripes Forever*. He whipped up such a storm of sound that the piano lid actually shook!

Horowitz's grip upon me from afar was balanced by the influence of my flesh-and-blood teacher, Rudolf Serkin, who came from an entirely different tradition. From Serkin, I learned Mozart and Bach, Schumann and Beethoven. I learned how to study music, how to prepare for a concert, how to develop stamina, sound projection, and intellectual rigor. His spiritual approach to music and reverence for the composer created an example I shall follow for the rest of my life.

But it was Horowitz whose alluring and sensual interpretation of Scriabin and Rachmaninoff intoxicated me like a drug. He was the incarnation of virtuosity who enticed me into a repertoire I never would have dreamed possible.

Much as I would have loved to have known him and played for him, it never happened. I did write him a letter, though, when I had just finished recording all ten Scriabin piano sonatas. I was engaged to perform them in New York and in many other places. These were to be the first complete "live" performances in America, and since I was intensely aware of Horowitz's relationship with Scriabin, I hoped he might come. The reply, written on creamy white engraved stationery, came not from him but from a secretary, who coolly informed me that "Mr. Horowitz never attends piano recitals." So much for *that* idea!

By the time I received this response, I was mature enough to know that Horowitz had never been a nurturing soul. Such a world figure did not especially encourage younger pianists. I have long since replaced my disappointment with the realization that it was Horowitz who probably did more to change the course of my life than anyone I have ever known.

Martin Canin

Martin Canin was born in New York City and studied at the Juilliard School, where he was a student of Rosina Lhévinne. After graduation, he became Lhévinne's assistant, a position he filled for eighteen years. After her retirement he was appointed to succeed her on the faculty of Juilliard. He is also artist-in-residence at the State University of New York at Stony Brook.

Besides his work as a teacher, Martin Canin has edited a number of piano works for Editions Salabert. He frequently judges international competitions, and has given master-classes in universities in the United States, Japan, and Korea. He has lectured a great deal and has written on musical subjects for several journals. Canin performs as a recitalist and in chamber ensembles. For the Spectrum label he recorded the Brahms F minor Sonata Op. 5.

My first memory of Vladimir Horowitz goes back to sometime in the 1940s when, as a teenager, I was taken to one of his concerts at Carnegie Hall. I do not remember any of the details of that particular program except that the final piece on the program was the Sixth Hungarian Rhapsody of Liszt. And what I best remember was seeing, from my vantage point in the top balcony, the entire audience leaning forward as one person, totally mesmerized by the thrilling explosiveness of the octave passage that concludes the piece. I remember also the pandemonium that swept through the hall as he finished, although I think that that experience was repeated at any number of concerts following that one.

Looking back on a lifetime of hearing recitals, there is no question in my mind that a Horowitz concert, when he was in his prime, was the most electrifying of any instrumentalist that I have ever heard. Other artists have given equal musical pleasure and, of course, every great artist is unique. But for the particular element of sheer musical electricity Horowitz stood alone.

We are fortunate that so much of his repertoire was recorded and that a good amount of it was done in the years when his technical wizardry was at its peak. To my own mind, the quintessential greatness of his art can be summed up best in the recording of his Twenty-Fifth Anniversary Concert at Carnegie Hall, which ended with his own extraordinary arrangement of the all-too-well-known Second Hungarian Rhapsody of Liszt. Utilizing every pianistic trick in the book (and some not even in the book), Horowitz simply overwhelms us with the brilliance of his sonority, the phenomenal sensitivity of the lyrical episodes, the dazzling speed of the finale, and an array of details that delight the ear even upon repeated hearings. It is the work of a gigantic performing personality.

The underlying qualities of Horowitz have been spoken about and written about for the last half century. Still, I would like to point to one aspect of his playing that I have not much seen nor heard being discussed. I think that he had a special knack for choosing just the right tempo for a piece. Despite his reputation as a "knock 'em dead" virtuoso, he really did not play faster than others. He did play, however, with an incomparable clarity of articulation and a splendid rhythmic sense that made for such a visceral sense of musical excitement. However, his gift of tempo, never too slow or too fast, was one of his undervalued assets, and very much a part of the tremendous strength and character of his playing.

Jeffrey Siegel

Jeffrey Siegel was born in Chicago and studied piano with Rudolph Ganz. At the Juilliard School he worked with Rosina Lhévinne, and in London with Ilona Kabos. He has appeared with every major American orchestra.

Siegel does a considerable amount of conducting each season, and is music director and conductor of the Mainly Mozart Festival at the Chandler Center for the Arts in Arizona. He has recorded for Denon an album of Rachmaninoff's solo piano music, and has recorded Hindemith's Third Sonata and the Piano Sonata of Henri Dutilleux. With the Saint Louis Symphony under Leonard Slatkin he has recorded Gershwin's music.

At 9:30 P.M. on June 20, 1969, I found myself trying to ring the doorbell of Vladimir Horowitz's home and realized that the butterflies in my stomach were already affecting my fingers. Eventually, I managed to ring and Horowitz himself answered the door—no butlers or assistants, the great man greeted me personally. That evening's appointment had been made by the late Peter Mennin, then president of the Juilliard School. Mr. Horowitz had approached Juilliard; he wanted to teach and asked that the school send him a couple of its pianists. I was one of the first.

As he ushered me upstairs into his music room, Horowitz sensed my understandable nervousness and suggested that he leave me alone to try his piano and get accustomed to the room. He would return in five minutes. I looked around and saw on the wall the famous Picasso, *The Juggler*, and signed photos of Rachmaninoff, Toscanini, and others. When Horowitz returned, I was not significantly less nervous than when he had left. Noticing this, he said something that I shall never forget. "Please don't be nervous to play to me because no one understands better than I how difficult it is to play the piano!"

He then invited me to sit down at a chair near him, and he lay down on a divan, propping his head up with his enormous hand, a hand unlike any I had seen before. He asked me many pertinent questions in a very friendly way. The questions ranged from my studies with two octogenarian piano teachers he admired and had known for decades (Rudolph Ganz in Chicago and Rosina Lhévinne in New York) to my current status, given the Vietnam War, with my draft board. Quite insightful and topical for a man who was supposed to have his head in the clouds.

He asked, in addition, about the music I listened to "just for fun!" Although he was pleased to learn of my great love of the orchestral and chamber music repertoire, he seemed disappointed that I had not, as yet, developed a similar passion for opera, and reminded me how important it was to listen and learn from great singers. After forty minutes of extremely relaxed and wide-ranging conversation, he motioned me to his piano. Interestingly, Vladimir Horowitz had wanted to know before my visit what I would be playing. The choice of repertoire had been relayed to him and his scores of these works were open on his piano. He had re-studied them before my arrival!

When I sat down, I found his chair too low for my short frame. He asked with a twinkle in his eye and his child-like laugh if I would prefer to sit on Mozart or Beethoven, and then placed a large volume of sonatas upon the seat. As I began to play, Horowitz took out his spectacles—he was only three feet away—the better to view my fingers. I played some Bach; the first two movements of the F-sharp minor Sonata of Schumann, a work he adored, he said, but never played in public; and the Prelude in B minor of Rachmaninoff, which he confessed was one of his favorites. After I played, he said some very kind things and added that I ought to be working on some musical "trash," works of perhaps dubious musical value, but compositions that stretch one's technical resources, and works demanding the artist's recreative abilities. He said, "It takes a Rachmaninoff to make a third-rate piece sound great!" How true!

By that time, Mr. Horowitz had made me feel welcome, appreciated, and at home, and I asked if *he* would play for *me*. "Oh, I haven't practiced for days," he demurred, "but I will show you something of my approach to the piano." He began to play *Au bord d'une source* of Liszt. Although I was just three feet away and saw keys being depressed and hammers hitting strings, what I heard were sonorities floating from the instrument that were a rare alchemy of mingled tones, infinite colors, and a sense of unreality. Could this be the same piano I had just tried to play? He then played some octaves, scales, and chords, explaining how he obtained such and such an effect by moving his wrist this way, or voicing the chord that way, or delaying the change of harmony a moment longer than expected (and playing it softer than that which had preceded it), how he mixed his pedals in this manner—all the while looking up at me like a sorceress with a sackful of potions and tricks we both knew only he possessed.

I left his home feeling that I had been in the presence of someone superhuman, a feeling I continued to have every time I heard him perform. And perform is what Mr. Horowitz decided to do, not teach—but my visit with him remains one of the highlights of my life.

David Burge

David Burge grew up and studied in the Chicago area. He has been on the faculties of numerous distinguished universities here and abroad. He is the author of nearly two hundred fifty articles on a variety of subjects, and in 1991 Schirmer Books published his Twentieth-Century Piano Music.

Burge has toured as a pianist for over forty years. He has brought to the concert stage an enormous range of twentieth-century repertoire as well as the standard literature. He has recorded for Candide, Nonesuch, Musical Heritage Society, and CRI. From the twentieth-century repertory he has recorded the Boulez First and Second sonatas, Kodaly's Seven Pieces Op. 11, Stockhausen's Klavierstück *No. 8, the Twelve Bagatelles of Rochberg, volume 1 of Crumb's* Makrokosmos, *Hindemith's Second Sonata, Wuorinen's Variations, and Krenek's Fourth Sonata, as well as works by Stravinsky, Schoenberg, Berio, and Albright. Burge is on the faculty of the Eastman School of Music.*

As he appeared from the wings, bursting through the overflow audience that sat in an uncomfortably conspicuous manner on folding chairs crowded in a wide semicircle behind the piano, his face displayed astonishment and delight to find, as if completely by surprise, such a vast crowd cheering his every step toward the keyboard. Bowing briskly, hands first clasped together, then spread wide apart, left, right, forward, and back, he greeted the excited throng. When, at last, he sat, the huge ovation ceased instantly and more than three thousand people, many of whom had waited anxiously in their seats for nearly an hour, held their breath in anticipation of the first note.

* * *

His taste was dubious, the critics had whispered, and the older, more knowledgeable students at the conservatory sneered over their afternoon coffee at his unstylistic rubati and his negligence toward indications in the score of such essentials as dynamics and tempi. Quite unforgivable, all agreed—meanwhile desperately coveting the faint possibility of matching for . . . oh, please! sixty seconds? . . . that bravura, that insouciance, that unbelievably compelling presence! Of course, no one would dream of not going to hear him if he played within a hundred miles. Such a thing was unthinkable.

* * *

For pianists and lovers of piano music, the years immediately following the end of World War II were good ones. Piano recitals, whole seasons of piano recitals, were major events in the musical life of city after city in the United States and in Europe. Year after year, people flocked to hear the knowns and unknowns. We grew up sensing that piano playing was important and that by learning to become pianists we were doing something valuable and respectable. The newspapers lent authority to these convictions, publicizing each recital beforehand and reviewing it in detail after. Concerts were remembered and performances compared—as were, incidentally, the reviews as well. People on the street knew the names Rudolf Serkin and Arthur Rubinstein, among others, and had high regard for their accomplishments.

Serkin appeared regularly, in fact, playing with such fervor and angular abandon that one feared for his survival until intermission. Walter Gieseking presided over the keyboard with regal calm, followed the next week by skyrockets from Rubinstein or teutonic verities from Wilhelm Backhaus. Guiomar Novaes melted hearts and Claudio Arrau cleared the senses. We heard of people named Richter and Gilels and hoped they would be allowed to come to America some day. Friedrich Gulda did come, playing Beethoven until about 10:30, then moving over to the Blue Note where his expert fingers embroidered jazz changes until many hours later. Another young fellow named Willie Kapell made us think that anyone who played so well and swayed back and forth so much must have something, so we all swayed back and forth, too. Lili Kraus bounced onstage and made that almost forgotten eighteenth-century composer, Wolfgang Amadeus Mozart, come alive and dance. And then there were Firkušný and Magaloff and Casadesus and . . . .

And, yes, Horowitz, but he was different.

* * *

He lurked in the backs of our minds as we practiced the Liszt Sonata or the Chopin etudes or whatever else we were working on.

There was no adjective such as "Arrauian" or "Casadian" or even "Serkinian," but one woke up in the middle of the night wondering if any critic anywhere might ever be so prescient as to pronounce one's technique "Horowitzian." One never said such a thing out loud, of course, but the adjective was there in our vocabularies, coated with envy.

* * *

He bent over his opening work, a sonata by Clementi, the severe curves of his face exaggerated by the intensity of his concentration, the flicker of his eyebrow an agogic accent to the stream of scales, arpeggiations, and other conventional figurations that streamed forth from the shining black Steinway. On occasion, as the hands moved apart, his head would pivot quickly back and forth, faster than the eye could follow, the unruffled, slicked-back hair gleaming with the same ebony as his instrument. Tempi were fast, but not too fast, as if to say "you have no idea how quickly I could do this if I chose." Each note, even those that others might consider unimportant, sounded individually handcrafted—the ping at the beginning, the connection at the end, the carryover between. The music was little more than ordinary; he illuminated its detail and filled its predictable harmonies with color and zest.

Finished, in his practiced way he feigned astonishment that we were still in the room, and, more than willing to be gullible, we applauded as he again bowed left, right, forward and back, always with the sharp-chinned, puckish smile, after which a raised finger let us know there was more to come.

* * *

Studying in Italy in the mid-fifties I became friends with Pietro Scarpini, a pianist of formidable attainments and a man whose Italian was so unimaginably beautiful that even I could understand every word. Among his wondrous stories—there was one that Scarpini himself had corroborated about Busoni declaring that a cathedral in Bologna was like the Goldberg Variations—he told about an evening with Horowitz and a number of other pianists. They were all students then, he said, and many of the egos in the room were large, but Horowitz was the one who took over one of the pianos and dominated the entire session.

"And, you know," declared Scarpini, "he never played a piece during the entire time! *Trucchi! Sempre trucchi!*" ("Tricks! Always tricks!") He would ask one of the others to play a glissando from the bottom to the top of one of the pianos. At the same time he would start a chromatic scale at the bottom of the other piano and beat the other person to the top. His *trucchi* went on, apparently, for hours, with Horowitz becoming more and more gleeful at his own prowess.

* * *

He had thundered through Liszt's *Funérailles* and was now embarking on the Etude in C-sharp minor Op. 10, No. 4 by Chopin—one of his favorites. One felt those clangorous octaves in every vertebra. They penetrated more deeply than the ministrations of the most resourceful chiropractor. He was able, somehow, to make the ear believe that each mighty bass sonority grew in intensity before it gave way to the next. This impossible crescendo was, well, "Horowitzian." Yes, that was the best word for it.

We journeyed down to Orchestra Hall in Chicago to hear him do the Rachmaninoff Third with Artur Rodzinski, in celebration of the twentieth anniversary of his first appearance with the Chicago Symphony. Of course, we shouted to one another over the shriek and clatter of the El going into the Loop, he would choose such an overblown cornball of a piece for such an occasion. He would undoubtedly play too loud and fast, we agreed. Probably he'd just try to show up the orchestra. (Oh, we *envied* his ability to do just that!)

* * *

Horowitz spoke a word or two to several members of the second violin section on his way downstage. He embraced the concertmaster warmly, greeted the audience more humbly than usual, and after taking his seat at the piano, waited a long time before quietly signalling the conductor to begin.

The concerto started from nowhere. The brook was flowing icy cold, high in the mountains of ancient Russia. It grew and grew, gaining intensity from other streams as it cascaded down the slopes with ever-growing speed and strength. By the cadenza, the audience was gripping the arm rests so as not to overturn from the force of the tumultuous sound washing over and around them, but then Horowitz, suddenly quieter, turned to the principal flute player, and they played together as the river calmed, flowing out onto the plain and warming in the sun.

The movement ended with a few staccato chords—pianissimo, scherzando, the ensemble between orchestra and pianist perfect—

and Horowitz threw up his head and laughed. We sat stunned, wondering what had possessed this audacious man, but then we saw that they were all laughing! The conductor, all the string players, all the woodwinds. They were having a *wonderful* time making music together!

* * *

First encore: Moszkowski. When he chose, his lightness of touch would defy gravity and various other laws of mechanical engineering—impossible that so many piano keys could move that fast and make sounds that soft.

And then Schumann, with inner voices coming from nowhere . . . .

* * *

We fretted over his dreadfully mannered, self-indulgent *Traumerei.* Our knowing glances to one another asked, how could anyone do such a thing in public? What would Schumann have thought? (Why are people crying? Why am I transfixed?)

A few years later, while I was in my first months in the army, I was able to get away from camp long enough to hear him play a recital in Richmond. It was 1952 and there was some question as to whether he would play. People in the know whispered about nerves and stagefright and tantrums.

The featured work on the first half of the program was the Schubert Sonata in B-flat major. I had never heard him do anything of that nature before and wondered what his bad nerves, if indeed he was suffering from them, would do to that transcendent work. If he tampered so egregiously with little pieces by Schumann, what would he do here?

There was no courting of the audience when he arrived onstage. The smile was perfunctory. He sat immediately and began to play the quiet opening in the simplest possible manner. He played for himself, rarely rising above mezzo piano for what must have been about forty minutes. I was, however, heedless of the duration of anything, and for the first time in my experience, listened to him unaware of his presence. There was only the music, played as devotedly and magically as I have ever heard it since.

The applause was light. People seemed to want to hurry to the lobby for the intermission.

* * *

Final encore: *The Stars and Stripes Forever.* With the first notes the audience burst into applause, anticipating the exhilarating pyrotechnics to come. The people on folding chairs behind the piano leaned forward, thus focusing everyone's attention even more fixedly on the sounds that came marching out of the piano. Everyone knew that at a certain moment *it* would happen: the trombones, tubas, and drums would keep the brisk rhythm going in the bass, while the trumpets, clarinets, and horns would blare out the famous melody in octaves in mid-range, and then, miraculously—for the man had only two hands after all, anyone could see that!—the piccolo would start its screeching obbligato high up in the treble.

One lady, sitting in the front row of folding chairs directly behind the pianist's back, was almost out of her chair. She leaned left, then right, desperately hoping (or so it appeared) to find out how he did it. The piccolo came in. She couldn't see! She leaned too far, and fell on the floor! The drums marched on, the trumpets continued, and, of course, the piccolo missed not a single sixteenth note.

When Horowitz leaped to his feet to welcome the cheers of more than three thousand standing, shouting people, he was unaware of what had happened. One person, at least, had preceded him from the room, and she was flying faster than Sousa ever imagined. For everyone else in the hysterically applauding hall, Horowitz had triumphed. As expected.

* * *

On a rare visit to my television set, I recently watched and listened to a rebroadcast of the return-to-Moscow recital he made not too long before his sudden death. For those of us who knew his playing in his prime, it was a strangely touching experience. The eccentricities, somehow exaggerated, were still there, in both his performance and stage demeanor. Or had they always been exaggerated before, but now seemed less acceptable from a man in his eighties? Or perhaps *more* acceptable coming from this grayed divinity, whose left hand struggled to keep up and whose right poked where it once caressed? Indeed, there were magical moments in every piece, and at no time was there the least intimation that he, himself, had any doubts about what he was doing.

It was clear that the members of that rapt Moscow audience still found the art of piano playing a valuable and deeply moving human endeavor. The people of what was until recently called the Soviet Union suffered greatly during the years since Vladimir Horowitz left his homeland. I suspect some of them would have preferred that cameras not be focusing on their private thoughts and tears as they listened and as they clearly seemed to comprehend the profound message of that evocative concert. Music is a temporal art, and a great artist can, for a brief period, seem to transform time. But stop it he cannot; time always moves inexorably on, and will continue to play its little tricks—its unpredictable *trucchi*—on us all.

Jean-Philippe Collard

Jean-Philippe Collard was born in Mareuil-sur-Ay, Champagne. At 16 he earned the Paris Conservatoire's first prize, and later he won prizes at the Prix Albert Roussel, the Prix Gabriel Fauré, the Concours International Cziffra, and the Marguerite Long/Jacques Thibaud Competition. In addition to playing recitals throughout Europe, North and South America, Russia, and the Far East, he has been soloist with the world's greatest orchestras and conductors.

Collard is a prolific recording artist for EMI. His disc of Rachmaninoff Etudes-Tableaux *was* Stereo Review*'s "Record of the Year." His recording of the two Ravel concertos with Lorin Maazel was* Gramophone*'s "Best Concerto Recording," and his Chausson Concerto Op. 21, with violinist Augustin Dumay and the Muir String Quartet, won the Grand Prix du Disque. With André Previn and the Royal Philharmonic he recorded all five Saint-Saëns piano concertos. In 1992, EMI issued an all-Liszt album.*

The grand piano will no longer sound . . .
Gone are the pirouettes, the winks, the cascades . . .
Blown away are the harmonies mingled like the colors of
  his paintings of which he was so fond . . .
Transfixed forever, the smile of this great child . . .

In the future, much will be written, much told. Who? What?

The biographers will gather the memories of each instant of an existence full of twists and turns.

The exegetes will play up the many contradictions of a musical journey marked by the seal of genius.

The listener will testify to the unique art which he communicated so well to us.

There is not one episode, not one misfortune, not one note that should be ignored at the moment of an homage. Every instant of this exceptional life—subtle amalgam of hypersensibility and sorceries, ranging from the whimsical to meditation—has never ceased to nourish an unfulfilled desire, an eternal quest.

For Horowitz was a seeker. A seeker in tone. Never did he rest on the pleasures of what he had acquired; his piano, which he attempted every day to tame, has nevertheless, thank God, remained "wild." . . .

He led this struggle with the perpetual thought of the "orchestra-instrument"; the steely-blue timbres, the bronze-colored basses, the emergence of counterpoint at unexpected moments . . . the rebounding of a bass note to prolong it or the resonances that blend with a deft manipulation of the pedal.

He led it also with a technique he largely created for himself, and for himself alone. How can one explain the strange position of his wrists, the unnatural curve of his posture, the little impulse his left hand required to chime out the basses?

But above all his fatal weapon was that of the heart. No one but he could entice from the instrument a range of emotions so rich, so varied, so vast. Storms unleashed with sudden violence, those deep rumblings that emerged out of nowhere (his own pianos had little to do with this, as I can attest) and, a moment later, the miraculous splendor of the colors of the sky depicted by the right hand, polishing the contours with a luminous phrasing, galloping like an urchin, with a pleasure he never tried to hide, or shrinking here and there on an interminable note. . . .

Possessing an active culture, that which is the quintessence of history and of the present, and endowed with a malicious humor, he liked to say of himself, laughingly, that he was "the last of the Mohicans," referring to the lineage of Romantic pianists who preceded and inspired him.

Mindful of the musical world, he examined with an increasing curiosity the rising cohort of young pianists, guiding his preferences toward tonal quality, choice of repertoire, and musical content.

"Do not imitate me!" he often said in a jocular tone tinged with a little annoyance.

Promised, sworn. Maestro, we will not touch the fruits of the garden of your life, provided you never cease to shoot arrows to the stars. . . .

Cyprien Katsaris

Born in Marseilles, France, Cyprien Katsaris began to play the piano at the age of four. In 1969 he completed his studies at the Paris Conservatoire with a first prize for piano. Katsaris has also received prizes in the Queen Elisabeth Competition and the Tchaikovsky Competition.

Katsaris has recorded on the Pathé-Marconi, EMI/Angel, Teldec, and Deutsche Grammophon labels. On Teldec, he recorded the complete Beethoven symphonies transcribed by Liszt. Among recent releases is a performance of the Brahms Second Concerto, with the Philharmonic Orchestra under Eliahu Inbal. In addition, Katsaris has undertaken to record the complete piano works of Chopin with Sony Classical; the first CD issued contains the three sonatas. He was awarded the Grand Prix du Disque Frédéric Chopin for his recording of Chopin's ballades and scherzos. Since 1977 he has been music director of the Echternach Festival in Luxemburg.

Vladimir Horowitz is one of the very few pianists whose playing is instantly recognizable. In his performances one enjoys his individual phrasing, unique sense of coloring, and a kind of three-dimensional transparency. Unfortunately, such qualities have been missing in the more academic, "modern" way of playing in the last four or five decades. Other characteristics of Horowitz's pianistic approach include a great ability in handling contrasts and in creating a constant tension that keeps the listener alert.

However, to me, the main quality of Horowitz is his powerful imagination, which is comparable to those of pianistic geniuses such as Ignaz Friedman, Moritz Rosenthal, Leopold Godowsky, Josef Lhévinne, and Sergei Rachmaninoff. Even if one initially disagrees with some of their interpretations, one easily becomes convinced by them after two or three listenings. These pianists, like Horowitz, had a tremendous magnitude and personality with which to *communicate* musical emotions. Through their imagination and wondrous technical tools, they projected a spiritual message. A great interpreter must be a highly developed spiritual being who is able to transcend mere technique. Such a spiritual being is always "one self" but never loses a moral integrity that remains within the scope and requirements of the composer.

I would like to mention another great pianist, at least as remarkable as those mentioned above. It is Georges Cziffra, who combines rigor and discipline. His recordings of Liszt, the Chopin etudes, the Brahms Paganini Variations, and many other composers, including his own amazing transcriptions, are unparalleled for their technical brilliance and spontaneity. Cziffra, without doubt, must, like Horowitz, take his place as one of the instrument's immortals.

Vladimir Leyetchkiss

Vladimir Leyetchkiss began his piano studies in Baku and later studied with Heinrich Neuhaus at the Moscow Conservatory. He emigrated to the United States in 1974. He has made several European tours, and has performed all-Beethoven, all-Schubert, all-Schumann, and all-Mendelssohn recital programs. In 1986, for the centennial of Liszt's death, he performed all-Liszt recitals.

Leyetchkiss has composed many piano transcriptions, the best known being his solo piano version of Stravinsky's Rite of Spring, *published by G. Schirmer. His recordings for Orian and Centaur include Beethoven's Diabelli Variations, "Russian Virtuoso Piano Music," "Great Piano Transcriptions," and, to honor the centennial of Tchaikovsky's death, solo piano works of the Russian master. He is on the faculty of De Paul University in Chicago.*

Horowitz! He is always with me. I listen to his cassettes in my car endlessly. Sometimes the illusion of his presence becomes too strong. I almost see him on the passenger seat with all his grimaces and mimics. I hate and love him at the same time.

The first time I heard his recordings as a young student in Baku, I thought, "who doubts that music has color?—*no!* Music may be even made of a certain material, and here is a pure marble.

Later, in Moscow, the old conductor Yakov Elyashkevich, who I studied with, shared with me his memories of young Horowitz's legendary recitals in Leningrad. "Particularly, he said, "I was amazed at the modesty of Horowitz and his desire to learn. After recitals there was a long line of admirers backstage, but Horowitz seemed not to enjoy all their adulation, dismissed them shortly, and looked for some musicians he knew and immediately asked them, 'Any criticism?' "

I remembered well the conductor's story. Consequently, many years later, in Chicago, in Orchestra Hall, I heard Horowitz for the first time in person. The impression was overwhelming. After the concert I went backstage and introduced myself to Horowitz. When he heard that I had studied with his old friend Neuhaus, he announced to everybody around that this man has studied with Neuhaus, and if so, he must be very good. Then, after some compliments, I asked him which edition of the Scriabin Fifth Sonata did he use? His face became immediately less friendly and he said, "The usual edition." I asked, "Russian edition?" He said, "Yes." This was the end of our conversation.

Later, I wanted to meet him, thinking that he would be interested to hear about Neuhaus's last years, which I had witnessed, and I wrote him a letter. But he didn't invite me. I received a letter signed by his secretary with best wishes from him. In the Fifth sonata of Scriabin, I wasn't going to criticize him for intentional changes on the last pages, but I thought I heard some real misreadings. That's why I asked him about the edition he had used. Also . . . I remembered the story of the conductor. Horowitz had responded in exactly the opposite way. So much for his desire to hear criticism!

When I came to America, I was surprised at the importance of Horowitz to the American school of piano playing. It seemed many artists tried to imitate him. It resembled greatly the dependency of generations of American composers on Stravinsky. Commenting on this, my friend Sheldon Shkolnik suggested that I listen to the recording of the *Mephisto* Waltz by Liszt, played by William Kapell. Sheldon said, "This is one of the 'followers of Horowitz' who could still be himself. Most others could not!"

Later I noticed that most American pianists, including Sheldon, seemed to emulate Horowitz. Sheldon once worked as a rehearsal pianist for Horowitz and became friendly with him. Once Sheldon asked him, "Why do you play Chopin's F-sharp minor Polonaise Op. 44 so differently from anyone else?" Horowitz replied, "I never heard anyone play this piece!" In his trying not to listen to others, there seems to be a resemblance to the young Beethoven, who also chose not to listen to the works of other composers lest he imitate them. Sheldon had a talent for mimicking voices. He also was great at mimicking Horowitz's playing and did play, by ear, the *Carmen* Fantasy and the cadenza to Liszt's Second Rhapsody. Sadly, Sheldon is no longer with us. Is there any musician who could sit and write these down for the rest of us?

As I watched Horowitz's Moscow concert on TV, I saw in the audience a man I immediately recognized, tears rolling down his face. It was my friend, the musicologist and transcriber Yuri Olenev, who was one of the greatest Russian admirers of Horowitz. Some years earlier he had sent a letter to Horowitz and had received a reply, to the great surprise of many. In the reply, Horowitz reminisces on how as a young boy he had visited Scriabin and had played for him.

From the U.S.A., I had sent Yuri several Horowitz recordings. He felt that this was a gift fit for a king. Upon recognizing my friend Yuri Olenev, I snapped several pictures of him on screen and sent them to him in Moscow. He didn't know that he had been on camera and was impressed and happy to see a snapshot of himself on American TV. It had been the dream of his lifetime to hear Horowitz in person. I'm happy that his dream came true. He died a year later at the age of seventy. Yuri Olenev, who himself was an excellent transcriber (Tchaikowsky, Debussy, and others) and who worked as a publishing house editor, was a great man in that he fearlessly promoted for publication my transcriptions—the works of a young Jewish musician. This required courage in Russia in those days.

Horowitz's return to Russia in 1986 made me angry and gave me many misgivings. I felt that his return to Russia would promote the Communist cause, with all the indignities, evils, and sufferings it caused to so many. "How could he do this?" I wondered, "he, who had also suffered so much!" But, seeing the faces and reactions on TV, I understood that it was a good thing that he went, although it is my feeling that others like Rachmaninoff, Siloti, or Chaliapin wouldn't have done so.

I feel that writers in their critiques of Horowitz and his playing do not consider or take into account the inherent Russianism of his boyhood and development. In the beginning of the twentieth century, the bacillus of rebellion and wildness shook all Russian art—with poets, writers, and artists like Alexander Blok, Andrei Byelii, Leonid Andreyev, actor Constantine Stanslavsky—founder of the Moscow Art Theatre—Vrubel, Serov, Benois, Chagall, dancer Nijinsky, and especially the great Chaliapin, singer and director.

Theirs were tremendously colorful and vibrant contributions. Perhaps those writers who reproach Horowitz as to "tasteless exaggerations" should hear once more recordings of Chaliapin as Boris Godunov and study more of the others I have mentioned.

Horowitz was a part of this constellation of Russian geniuses which had burst forth at this time.

Russell Sherman

Russell Sherman was born in New York. At 11 he began studies with Edward Steuermann and at 15 he made his New York Town Hall debut. Soon after, he played with the New York Philharmonic under Leonard Bernstein. At 19 he graduated from Columbia University.

Sherman subsequently has appeared throughout the world in recital and concerto performances. He has recorded the five Beethoven concertos with the Czech Philharmonic and an abundance of Liszt's music on the Albany label, including the Sonata, the Don Juan *Fantasy, and the complete* Transcendental Etudes. *Currently he is recording the thirty-two Beethoven sonatas. Some of his other releases include the Schumann and Grieg concertos, the Gershwin Concerto, and the twenty-four Chopin preludes.*

Early in his career, Sherman established a reputation for his dedication to contemporary music. In 1990 he was invited to join the faculty of Harvard University as visiting professor and artist-in-residence.

Making a distinction that was perhaps too facile, I used to think that Horowitz was more a great artist than a great musician. The premise for this distinction was grounded in the notion that music is but one of the sister arts belonging to the hierarchy of Art, which, at the top of the pyramid, contained all of the magical prescriptions disseminated among the several individual arts. But the individual arts—music, poetry, painting, and so forth—had their own specific canons of appropriate styles, idioms, and structures. It seemed to me that, on occasion, Horowitz would willfully contradict the accepted musical practice on behalf of a more demanding (or mischievous) Muse, one devoted more to the whole than to the part, or to the part than to the whole, more to the poetic atmosphere than to the prosaic creatures who breathed it, more to the multidimensional textures than to the discrete and organizing patterns of notes within.

Such a distinction, however, is based upon a rather mechanical model. There are several problems with it, of which one is expressed by an equally glib but pleasing thought. As more than one poet has suggested, all of the arts aspire to the condition of music. By this formula (which may even be defensible) the codes of Art and of Music would be at least equivalent, perhaps coincidental. If a musician then were a great artist, ipso facto he must be a great musician.

A second objection is more serious, however, and tends to sabotage entirely the original distinction. Namely, what is the essential constituent of music? Of course, sound. Which pianist has provided us with the most extraordinary lexicon of sounds? Sounds of every conceivable order and disorder, ardor, arbor, as well see and harbor, color, languor, not least star, volcano, and martyr? Of course, Horowitz. Is it possible, then, that the maker and molder of these sounds, the very stuff of music, could not be a great musician while yet being a great artist?

One reason I had developed this ungainly theory was to counter the occasional denigrations of Horowitz one heard from different quarters, even from very serious musicians. It was not merely criticism, but rather comments to the effect that he played and behaved like a buffoon, like a charlatan. It is something analogous to the way presumed connoisseurs and "classicists" turn up their nose toward Liszt. And just as short-sighted and foolish. Behind this critique there is often a moral pomposity that prizes the Apollonian world of sweet and sober reason over the "decadence" of the sensual, dionysian, and playful world Horowitz portrays. The judgment implied is no more valid than declaring that one prefers yin to yang. Behind the judgment is a premise that the universe can logically be separated into two opposite camps, a notion as artificial as it is convenient.

A notably serious, estimable, and famous pianist once said to me that the problem with Horowitz is that he could never be "simple." A rather offhand, provocative remark, yet one instinctively knew what he meant. For instance, by way of contrast, in Schnabel's recording of the Mozart B-flat major Piano Concerto K. 595, the unadorned, angelic stasis that he achieves in the larghetto movement is of a character one does not readily associate with Horowitz. Nevertheless, two caveats are necessary before one can trust such a casual comparison. The first Shakespeare provides in a line from his Sonnet 66: "simple truth miscalled simplicity." The performance of Schnabel may indeed reveal a simple truth, but it is one that could not be revealed without an arsenal of means entirely sophisticated and supple in the shaping of sound. The second caveat is an obvious truism that demands constant reiteration: there are many roads to Parnassus. What Schnabel does may be heavenly; what Horowitz (and others) might do could be equally luminous, with different characteristics, colors, and rhetorics.

I would divide the contributions of Horowitz into four particular areas that mean a great deal to me, and, I believe, to the history of piano playing as well. In doing so, I will leave the description of his incredible bravura, fire, and explosiveness to others. One: Horowitz embodies Rachmaninoff's wise and famous dictum that the pedals are the soul of the piano. No other pianist, including Rachmaninoff, has manipulated the pedals in such a way as to convert the piano into a device worthy of Scriabin's eternal dream, the color organ. Two: good pianists, if sufficiently blessed, will exploit the four conventional registers—soprano, alto, tenor, bass; for Horowitz there is an infinite number of registrations. One might even say there are eighty-eight, one for each key of the piano. The variety and personality of his voicings surpass the number and fantasy of Scheherazade's fables. Three: the character of his legato is influenced by a strategy that is perhaps as important as the usual shaping of the melodic line. I refer to the uncanny skill and discretion in the way that the harmonies displace one another, which, together with the general plasticity of the bass line, is a unique element of the Horowitz persona; in tandem, these become exquisite agents for the malleability of musical sound. Four: most precious and most potent is the magical deftness displayed in the handling of layers of sound. The universe of Horowitz indeed parallels that of Einstein, wherein space is curved, time is relative, and four or more dimensions are required to maintain equilibrium among the competing and infinite orbits.

The history of Western music is largely derived from two main sources, the minstrel and the church. The oeuvre of Horowitz rejuvenates the stature of the minstrel, and it reminds us that serenading and singing of the universe is no less worthy than praying to it. One approach describes the world, while the other gives thanks for its abundance. Each is contained in the other.

Edward Kilenyi

Edward Kilenyi was educated in New York and Budapest. He was a pupil of Ernst von Dohnányi at the Franz Liszt Academy, where he received the Artist Diploma in 1930. Kilenyi has appeared in performances with Beecham, Muck, Klemperer, Szell, Munch, Paray, Ormandy, and Knappertsbusch. He made recordings on the Pathé, Columbia, and Remington labels. He often gave Beethoven sonata recitals, where the audience selected four sonatas from the set of thirty-two.

Kilenyi has had a distinguished career as a teacher on the faculty of Florida State University. In 1986 he received the Liszt Centennial Medal from the Hungarian Government. In 1990, at the governor's mansion, the Florida secretary of state named Kilenyi the Florida ambassador of the arts on his eightieth birthday.

Without doubt, Horowitz was the most powerful force to which aspiring virtuosi were subjected. This influence on pianists lasted to some degree throughout his career and beyond. I came under his spell around 1927, through the marvel of recordings. In my case, this power was mitigated by the influence on my musical life of Dohnányi, with whom my association lasted for thirty-nine years.

I first heard about Vladimir Horowitz in 1926 from Gusztav Barczy, head of Rozsawolgyi, the famed music publishing house. He had heard Horowitz and raved about him. I asked my fellow student in Budapest, Boris Goldowsky, who seemed to know everything connected with Russia. His comment was that we have heard many new and fine pianists, but Horowitz was "something else." In 1927 I was in New York, where I received a letter from my friend John Huberman, the son of the great violinist Bronislaw Huberman. John wrote he heard Horowitz in Budapest and that it was marvelous beyond belief.

It was in January 1928 that New York was treated to a double-barrelled sensation: the American debuts of Sir Thomas Beecham and Vladimir Horowitz on the same concert at Carnegie Hall. In retrospect, this was a historic performance, as both artists stayed at the very top of their professions to the end of their lives. At that time, the New York Philharmonic concerts were given in pairs—Thursday evenings and Friday afternoons. I was frustrated, as I wanted to hear them on Thursday. However, the Friday matinee turned out to be the better performance because the two protagonists had smoothed out the tempo discrepancies the critics mentioned at the first performance. My feeling right from the start was that Horowitz's playing was a model, even an ideal. By the time the young man cut loose with the triple forte double octaves in the last movement, I just about fell over. In all my concert-going—and I had heard the greatest virtuosi of the period—I had never heard anything like that, or even approaching it.

However, the "battle of the tempi" left a lasting impression on both Beecham and Horowitz. In October 1929 Horowitz gave me a vivid description of what happened. "I have nothing against Beecham personally," he said. "He is a nice fellow, but when he conducted"—here Horowitz mimed a conductor waving his arms all over the place—"I could not stay with him. For two movements, I tried to make music. But then I decided, all right, mein lieber, you take your tempi and I'll take mine." According to Olin Downes's review in the *New York Times*, that is just what happened. Nevertheless, the ovation Horowitz received was tumultuous.

In March 1935 I met Sir Thomas for the first time, when I played for him, and he engaged me for the London Philharmonic, the Liverpool Philharmonic, and the Hallé Orchestra as soloist. In the course of conversation with guests, he was asked his opinion of various pianists. His comment on Horowitz was, "He would be fine, except that his conception of a concerto is to be one bar ahead of the orchestra."

A few weeks after Horowitz's blazing orchestral debut, he made his solo debut in Carnegie Hall. The big works were the Bach-Busoni Toccata in C and Liszt's B minor Sonata. I was hypnotized by his explosive octaves, and I regret not being more impressed by the Sonata than I was, since I was used to hearing Dohnányi's rendition, which I felt to be on a musically higher plane. It was the following year, 1929, that I heard him again, this time in Budapest. Besides hearing his concerts, I had a fine and long visit with him in the Gellert Hotel. Horowitz was a charming, friendly, and rather modest young man. He spoke of all the things he said he was unable to do on the piano. In fact, the way he spoke, one thought he was almost unable to play. Of course, when he sat down and did play, the impression was quite the opposite.

He claimed that he could not play the "Winter Wind" Etude of Chopin. He said for three pages he could play it wonderfully, and then his hand felt like it was ready to fall off. This was because he used a kind of super-energetic windmill motion of the fingers. I played it for him, and he was most kind and generous with his comments. I was swept off my feet, and, with this experience, I was even more receptive to his concerts.

About ten months later, I once again heard Horowitz at a small but packed hall in The Hague. It was the first time he played the F minor Sonata of Brahms. It was beautiful, I thought that he was developing very well. The most memorable recital I heard him give in those early days was at the big Salle Pleyel during the spring of 1935. The audience went wild.

I had one more conversation with him in Berlin, in 1930. He told me that he had once composed a lot, indicating with a gesture what a big pile it became. I asked him, "In what style?" He replied, "Modern, Debussy and Ravel." He talked about the Third Rachmaninoff Concerto, saying that he had played it early in his career in Moscow. It was with a conductorless orchestra! They rehearsed it for half a year, and it was an awful trial.

After 1930 I never had occasion to talk with him again. But through recordings, I and the rest of the world kept up with Horowitz's art as his playing continued to reach new depths. He is still with us. Very much so.

Daniel Pollack

Daniel Pollack enjoys a worldwide reputation as concert pianist–teacher and adjudicator at international piano competitions. Highlights of Pollack's career include five concert tours in Russia, a tour of China, and chamber music concerts with Jascha Heifetz and Gregor Piatigorsky, as well as appearances with major orchestras. He has also performed in Bangkok, Tel Aviv, and Seoul. In 1990 he was a judge in the Ninth International Tchaikovsky Competition, where he had been a prize winner in 1958. Pollack studied at the Juilliard School with Rosina Lhévinne. His recordings have appeared on Melodya and Columbia.

It was springtime, 1965. The time, 4 A.M.—an ungodly hour to be out in the streets of New York City. But there we were, my six-months pregnant wife and I, standing on Fifty-Seventh Street somewhere between Sixth and Seventh Avenues. Actually, we had already hung around for about seven hours in the night chill. Things were looking up, however, in this wee hour of the morning. Some nice lady was engineering a giveaway of hot coffee and doughnuts to the crowd that had, by now, swelled to well over a thousand people.

It turned out to be Wanda Horowitz, who was hosting this early morning breakfast for the enthusiastic fans that braved standing all night for the privilege of hearing her husband, Vladimir Horowitz, perform in Carnegie Hall for the first time after an absence of twelve years. And a privilege it was. . . .

Much has been written about Horowitz's virtuosity, uniqueness, electricity. It all falls short for me as compared to what truly happened when Horowitz crossed a stage. Words, no matter how eloquent, cannot describe the experience. It needed to be felt. For what would compel music enthusiasts and professionals alike to stand in lines for Vladimir Horowitz as for none other? The experience is an emotional one.

From time to time, an artist appears in our lives who makes such an impact that we, who are touched by him, are never the same. Horowitz did that for me. He literally changed the way I viewed pianism and took me past the limits, into a realm of thinking and listening that I did not believe possible.

For me, Horowitz transcends musical explanations. Words that most performing artists would covet in describing a performance, such as superb phrasing, marvelous technique, amazing scope, and so on, became meaningless in the light of the experience that was Horowitz. It didn't even matter if we agreed with his interpretation of a work or not. He was easy to disagree with, for he broke most rules that were once sacred in our musical heritage. He had the uncanny ability to convince us with his concepts, even if that meant changing a legato to a détaché or "rearranging" dynamic ranges. He touched a raw nerve in the listener and carried that listener onto emotional paths rarely crossed.

Horowitz transcended today's classical adage of performers—that of being at the service of the composer, thereby subjugating the artist's personality toward that effort. After all, he evolved from the so-called Golden Age of Pianism, an era in which the primary lure was the interpretation of the performer. In essence, that concept is not unlike what happens in the pop world. Do people really care what Madonna sings, or do they come to her performances for what "happens" on stage as she interprets works written by others? A legacy of the Horowitz decades are the new standards he set for critics in reviewing would-be Horowitz pianists. To be recognized as one with a Horowitzian technique or a Horowitz-like dynamic range, architecture, electricity was tantamount to achieving the top plateau in the piano world.

But although many tried, it was impossible to copy him. Answers could lie in the unpredictability of his approach to phrasing; his uncanny ability to manipulate fingers, causing each to have a voice of its own that formed lines of music that could be followed for pages, if not whole movements; his pacing of the music that could rouse tidal waves of sounds within seconds or last the length of whole works; his willingness to take chances, risking the cleanliness of technique that most would strive for as their number one goal in performance. One could dissect his performances, analyze them, learn from them—but not copy him. It proved impossible, much to the despair of generations of pianists.

I was lucky to have first experienced Horowitz when I was only six years old, at a Los Angeles performance. His recital program included many of his signature pieces: Mussorgsky's *Pictures at an Exhibition*, Schumann's *Kinderscenen*, Sousa's *Stars and Stripes Forever*, Bizet's *Carmen* Fantasy. What in effect does a six-year-old remember or retain? In this particular case, a life-lasting impression. Even today, those works carry Horowitz's stamp on them for me, and I find it difficult to avoid comparison to that first impression as I listen to others.

Over the years, Horowitz and I crossed many paths: backstage encounters, at formal social receptions as well as more casual ones. Just two weeks before his death, most of us were with him at John Steinway's memorial in New York. Still, for me, the person that was Horowitz had absolutely nothing to do with the personality that crossed the stage. It was as if they were separate beings. How can the clown-like person that TV viewers so often saw in interviews be reconciled with the pianist that seemed so often to be possessed by the devil as he delved into the souls of Scriabin or Rachmaninoff?

It can't be, nor is it necessary. Suffice it to say that Horowitz happened in our lifetime.

Herbert Stessin

A native of New York, Herbert Stessin studied piano with Clarence Adler, José Iturbi, and Sascha Gorodnitzki. He made his New York debut at Carnegie Hall in 1950, followed by annual tours of the United States and Canada as recitalist and soloist with orchestra. Stessin has had numerous radio broadcasts in Europe and the United States, and has toured Holland, Germany, and England. Since 1962 he has given master-classes in many countries, including Japan and Israel, and since 1983 he has taught at the Aspen Summer Music Festival. He has also taught at New York University, and is currently visiting professor of piano at Hunter College. In addition, he is on the piano faculty of the Juilliard School.

Horowitz was more than a performer; he was a creator at the piano. The music sang from his every pore. His technique in the largest sense of that term was formidable. His feeling for the sonority of each chord was unforgettable. It was not necessary for him to play faster and more brilliantly than other pianists, for he just made it sound faster and more brilliant. How he attained such feats, nobody ever figured out. He could also build climaxes like no other pianist of our time. Somehow, Horowitz had more power, more sound.

I always marvelled at his pedalling. It was a separate art with him. He must have studied the pedal in a very different way than most other pianists. Anton Rubinstein called the pedal the soul of the piano. With Horowitz, that was true. I also marvelled when Horowitz did not use the pedal.

Like all the great Romantic pianists before him, he had a memorable sound, and a beautiful singing tone that he used to create a balanced musical line. He was sometimes accused of tampering and distorting the intentions of the composers, but I always felt convinced of his own musical judgments, even if they were different than mine. This was because Horowitz was deeply committed to his own ideas. Although he was widely imitated, it was foolish to try to be another Horowitz. Even if we could clone two Mozarts, two Rembrandts, or two Horowitzes, we would not want them. Unfortunately, too many pianists pathetically tried to be like him. After hearing him, they contracted Horowitz fever. It was a hard disease to get rid of, and it killed many a pianist.

I had never met him, but several years ago, Maestro was invited to hear one of my students perform the Prokofiev Third Piano Concerto at Carnegie Hall. He was sitting in the adjoining box, and somebody was thoughtful enough to introduce me to him. We shook hands, and then, in his inimitable manner, he looked over the railing, pointed to the stage, and indicated that he, too, had performed on that stage. I thought to myself, "Yes, you certainly have played on that stage. And for the so many of us who heard him at Carnegie Hall, we would never forget it!"

Oxana Yablonskaya

Born in Moscow, Oxana Yablonskaya studied at the Moscow Conservatory with Alexander Goldenweiser. She won the grand prize at the Marguerite Long–Jacques Thibaud Competition, and the gold medal in the Rio de Janeiro and the Vienna Beethoven competitions. Yablonskaya has made recordings for Melodiya and the Connoisseur Society. Her Liszt-Schubert album received the Grand Prix du Disque from the International Liszt Society. She has performed in over thirty countries. In 1977 she emigrated from Russia, where she had been professor at the Moscow Conservatory from 1965 to 1975. She returned to Russia in 1990, when she performed in Leningrad's Great Hall. Since 1983 she has been on the faculty of the Juilliard School.

I recall first hearing the name of Vladimir Horowitz at the age of about five. My mother once took me with her to visit a woman friend who had studied at the St. Petersburg (Leningrad at the time) Conservatory. Standing on her grand piano, she had a portrait of a young man, mounted in an antique silver frame. The man had a finely shaped nose and shielded his chin with a large white hand. I remember being struck by the fact that this portrait seemed to look you straight in the eye. "That," said my mother's friend, "is Vladimir Horowitz." Both the way she pronounced that name and the manner in which Mother scrutinized the portrait conveyed a feeling that here was something especially important. And I also remembered that name: Vladimir Horowitz.

On various occasions after that, I regularly heard people talk about Horowitz. Sometimes it took the form of recollections by the so-called Horowitz girls. These were some frenzied devotees of his at the time when he still resided in Leningrad; they never missed a single performance by him and were identified by a distinctive green bow worn on their breast.

Or else, someone with loving care would place a disc on the turntable, and a stream of magical tones would pour forth, as if the actual instrument itself were singing rather than a pianist playing on the keys. And in a reverential whisper listeners would utter the name, "Vladimir Horowitz!"

Or else, some lucky person who had managed to visit America would return, bringing back tales of Horowitz. For example, there was a Moscow Conservatory professor, Yakov Zak, who had been in New York and had the good fortune to get to know the great pianist and visit his home. Zak regaled us with tales of Horowitz, the Jewish boy from Kiev who had studied with Blumenfeld, one of Russia's greatest teachers.

Or else, there were people like Heinrich Neuhaus, who had known Horowitz when he was a student in Kharkov in the first few years after the Revolution. Neuhaus talked with admiration of the young pianist's hours of labor to perfect every single note, striving after the desired dynamic and tone color and polishing each phrase of the whole composition in tireless pursuit of his musical ideal.

All this helped create a magical sense of Vladimir Horowitz's "presence" in the lives of myself and other musician friends. Despite the fact that we had seen only photos of him and never heard him except on disc and tape recordings, we were, nevertheless, aware of him as an artist who lived and worked somewhere in close proximity. Sometimes I would catch myself wondering whether I would ever manage to see Horowitz and hear him in the flesh rather than on records. Fifteen years ago I left the Soviet Union and emigrated to the United States. Now Horowitz really was close by. It was announced that he would give a concert at Carnegie Hall, which I walked past at least twice every day. It seemed as if my dream was about to come true. But no. I was unable to attend that concert. As a newly arrived refugee in New York, I simply did not have enough money to pay for a ticket. Then, suddenly, one day a musician friend of mine offered me a ticket to hear Horowitz rehearsing the Rachmaninoff Third Concerto.

So there I was in Carnegie Hall; I saw and heard Horowitz rehearse the Rachmaninoff Concerto. I was bowled over. I played that concerto myself and knew every single note of it. No question, I was staggered by his virtuosity. Yet that was only one facet of his wizardry. He enthralled listeners with the peculiar lyricism, lushness, and variety of his tone. He created the impression that his piano sound really was a combination of the tones of various instruments. It was as if this was not a concerto for piano and orchestra, but for one orchestra accompanied by another. As a musician, I can say that his knowledge of the instrument was impeccable and boundless. That first impression of Vladimir Horowitz playing and rehearsing at the piano has remained with me ever since.

Later on, when listening to Horowitz, I might accept or disagree with some of his interpretations. At some moments, he might fail to convince me, or else prompt me to question his approach. But that was not the main thing. Most importantly, one felt the presence of a great artist, a sense of contact with a gigantic, original personality that was a law unto itself. And one could only judge him by the laws which he himself had set. In that respect, Horowitz was inimitable. And to be like that, you had to be born Vladimir Horowitz.

The first thing about him, I think, was his ability to create an atmosphere in his concerts. Nothing in the performance was left to chance; everything was worked out, down to the finest subtle detail, from the details of his program and his dress to the way he gestured, smiled, walked out onto the stage, the way he approached the instrument and placed his hands upon the keys. Everything was governed by the image he created and cultivated—that of a great Romantic artist.

Vladimir Horowitz left his homeland as a young man of 23. He had no intention of ever returning there. But circumstances changed, and not long before his death he visited what was then called the Soviet Union. Of course, his concert was not attended by the same people that had admired him in days of yore. In the words of the poet, "Some had gone, and others were away," and only very few of his former admirers were able to meet up with him again. On the other hand, there were many young people at his concert, and for them the name of Horowitz was a legend, a dream, just as it once had been for me.

Many people have called Vladimir Horowitz the modern-day Liszt, the second Rachmaninoff or the second Anton Rubinstein. And his bravura, artistic daring, virtuosity, and lofty artistry do indeed set him alongside the greatest pianists of the past. But for me—and, I am sure, for many others—he always was, and will remain, the legendary Vladimir Horowitz.

Garrick Ohlsson

Garrick Ohlsson was born in White Plains, New York. His principal teachers have been Claudio Arrau, Olga Barabini, Tom Lishman, Sasha Gorodnitzki, Rosina Lhévinne, and Irma Wolpe. In 1966 he took first prize at the Busoni Competition; in 1968 he won the Montreal Piano Competition, and in 1970 the Chopin Competition in Warsaw.

In 1989 Ovation *magazine chose his Arabesque recording of the complete sonatas of Weber as "Solo Instrumental Record of the Year." His Telarc disc of the Busoni Concerto, with Dohnányi conducting the Cleveland Orchestra, won a Grammy nomination as "Best Classical Album of the Year." In 1991 he received another Grammy nomination for "Best Classical Performance by an Instrumentalist with Orchestra" in Henri Lazarof's* Tableaux *for piano and orchestra, with Gerard Schwarz and the Seattle Symphony. He has begun a complete Chopin cycle for Arabesque Records.*

I first became aware of Vladimir Horowitz at around ten years old. The first great pianist I heard live was Arthur Rubinstein at Carnegie Hall in 1957. It was an incredible experience. Shortly after, Horowitz entered my life through recordings. Naturally, it was the sheer wizardry and overwhelming brilliance that first attracted me. I heard his dazzling transcriptions, including the *Stars and Stripes Forever.* I was astonished, I still am. My own teacher, Tom Lishman, was of a slightly different school. He had studied with Cortot, and admired Rubinstein more than Horowitz.

It was somewhat later that I realized that Horowitz was much more than loud and fast. By the time I was 14, I had become fascinated by those special "Horowitzian" harmonic shifts, the fascinating subito pianos, those almost erotically beautiful changes in timbre. As I listened to his Schumann *Kinderscenen,* I was intrigued by a certain intensely perfumed, decadent beauty. I know his performance of that work can indeed be considered to be tortured and distorted. However, it got deep into me, as only Horowitz could.

When you are a young artist, you are always comparing the greats. I remember heatedly discussing our idols with Emanuel Ax when I was growing up. As one matures, however, one realizes that one does not need favorites. I still love Rubinstein, even though his piano playing did not quite have the after-burners that Horowitz had. There were other qualities. In fact, I believe Rubinstein is underrated in the fingers department.

During my formative years, Horowitz had entirely left the concert stage. I desperately wanted to hear him. In the meantime, Richter magically appeared from dark Russia. I was staggered by his powerful personality, so different from Horowitz. Richter was a great master, a mighty intellect, and a virtuoso. When the news hit that Horowitz would play again, Richter had been giving an astonishing group of recitals at Carnegie Hall in all kinds of repertoire. Now, I thought, after all the excitement of Richter recitals, I would have something that would put even these in the shade.

Oddly enough, upon hearing Horowitz I was slightly disappointed. Yes, he was larger than life, but I had expected him to be even larger than that—a genuine live devil who would burn a hole through the piano and the stage, and who would ravage the entire audience. The recital, however, was merely a very great recital by one of the greatest pianists of all time. I was not prepared for an urbane, elegant gentleman who appeared master of the situation. He did not even play one of his spine-tingling arrangements for an encore.

By the time I was 17, I was becoming acquainted with many more musical influences. Although Horowitz remained one of my main role models, there were aspects of his playing, a kind of lordliness, a willfulness in his performances, that I no longer admired. He once said, "When I am playing, I am king." I had not yet understood Horowitz's predecessors. During those days of straightforward music making, I had not realized that Horowitz had come from a tremendous Russian and Polish tradition that had been dying out just before I was born. If I had heard the recordings of Hofmann, Friedman, Michalowski, I would not have been confused about Horowitz, who now stood alone.

Horowitz did almost everything that teachers told students not to do. For example, do not play the piano with flat fingers, do not add extra octaves, or bring out such and such inner voices, or accent certain notes, or exaggerate for an effect. Vladimir Horowitz seemed lawless. He did not, pianistically or musically, behave like he was at a tea party with his pinky in the air. He was sensual, physical, even infantile, sometimes wild and savage. He represented a civilized embodiment of the untamed. He was a magician, a conjurer, a wild man, who went for the jugular. He came out of the jungle, full of dangerous charms. He had no hesitation in rewriting Mussorgsky's *Pictures at an Exhibition* or improving upon Liszt's Rákóczy March or his Scherzo and March. He was never frightened to go over the top, to take his audience over the edge. Horowitz, to his more conservative uptight colleagues, was a naughty man indeed.

During the next years I heard every Horowitz recital I could, and realized more than ever his extraordinary range. I no longer went to hear God, I went to hear *him,* and I always had a knockdown-wonderful, fascinating, sometimes even an annoying experience. Around 1980, at Avery Fischer Hall, I heard him play Liszt's *Mephisto* Waltz. I was with the pianist Joseph Villa, a great Lisztian. We were looking at each other incredulously throughout the piece, as I imagine all the pianists in the house were. Horowitz was incorporating into the *Mephisto* everything but the kitchen sink. He used his version, Busoni's version, and God knows what else. As he entered the coda, we were thinking, how is he going to end this? I think he played Liszt's ending, then some of Busoni's, then his own.

It was sinfully outrageous, and it was tremendous. Quite legitimately, one may say that this is not acceptable, you do not do this to works of Art. But Horowitz worked from his own standards, and he knew Liszt did such things, too. If you did not accept his standard, then you could not easily accept him. But if you did accept what he did, then you had a wonderful time. There are people who say he was disrespectful, or he was too kitschy or exaggerated. But when one makes such statements, one usually tells more about oneself than the person one is talking about. There were many reasons one could disapprove of Horowitz, like any other distinctive artist. However, even his playing of the Classic repertoire cannot be dismissed because, in my opinion, there are some works of the Classical period that Horowitz played absolutely magnificently.

Horowitz was a great cultivator of his own mystique. Even as a child, I heard many tales of Horowitz. He was the last of the demonic nineteenth-century people, with whom one associated slightly otherworldly things. I was told, "Oh, Horowitz is in a mental institution.

He thinks his hands are made of glass, and if he plays a piano, his fingers will break." I am sure he was smiling to himself when he heard the stories, which he may have circulated himself. It all deliciously comes from Paganini.

I first met him at a party at our mutual manager, Harold Shaw's. Shaw had told Horowitz the previous year, "If you play all your concerts during the season without cancellation, I will give you a big party." So at the end of the season, Horowitz called Shaw and said, "I played all my concerts. I want my party now." I, of course, was happy to be invited. Horowitz had told Shaw that he would like to meet me. I was being very virtuous at the time and had lost a lot of weight. Horowitz, with a twinkle in his eye, said, "Oh, you're Garrick Ohlsson. I've heard a lot about you. My, you're much better-looking than your photos. You must have lost some weight recently." Watching and listening to him, I realized how disarming he was. He was a major diplomat of the cleverest kind.

Later, he summoned me over, saying, "I want to talk to my young colleague about music. But since I get up very late, I can't go to concerts. So the only way I can hear people is if they come and play for me. Would you come and play for me?" I said I would be delighted to.

We continued talking about repertory and Schumann for a while. He said, "I know you play Chopin. Do you play much of Schumann?" I told him that I have played a good deal, but there is something in my nature that does not always quite respond to him. Horowitz said, "Oh, I understand that. Schumann was really crazy, and it can be very disturbing music. But what piece by Schumann have you played most recently?" I said, "The F-sharp minor Sonata." He looked at me, "Oh, but that's the craziest of all. That's a scary piece. I wouldn't play that. Well, you must have an interesting dark side to you."

Horowitz was very gracious when I arrived at his house. He said, "Please try the piano and warm up. I will go upstairs so you won't be nervous." When he came down, I proceeded to play quite a bit—the Mozart B-flat major Sonata K. 570, the Brahams-Handel Variations, a Chopin mazurka, a waltz, a nocturne, and the F minor Fantasy. I felt rather at ease with him. Here was a man who had played two pianos with Rachmaninoff. I thought, I can't impress him, so I don't have to try. There is nothing I can do that is going to make him say, "Garrick, you are now the greatest pianist that ever lived."

Horowitz seemed pleased with my playing. He had asked me not to play the repeats in the Brahms-Handel. He told me he felt

Brahms was often ponderous. He criticized Rudolf Serkin for playing the Brahms-Handel after intermission, the first half being two Beethoven sonatas, ending with the "Appassionata." Horowitz said, "After the elemental power of the Beethoven the Brahms sounds too academic." He also made some interesting comments on my Chopin. He felt that in my Chopin playing I had a fault that virtually every young pianist had. He said, "When you make a crescendo in a melody in the right hand, you must support it in the left hand. You just can't be a melody man," and demonstrated what he meant. If you don't bring the left hand along with it in crescendo, you will get an ugly sound.

His most extensive comments were in the F minor Fantasy. He talked about stage make-up. He suggested to me ways of making things more dramatic. He said that in certain pianissimos that are dying away, let it really die away, even blurring the harmonies with the pedal. When you play very softly, you can blur a lot more without losing the harmonic intent. At one place, he said, "At the climax, don't be afraid of making an ugly sound. This is an ugly moment." Horowitz was a very conscious artist with an incredible ear and a marvelous acoustical sense. That evening, I received a wonderful music lesson.

During this century, Horowitz brought virtuosity to the maximum. Virtuosity on a high level is a rare thing. In the past, Hofmann, Rosenthal, Friedman, Lhévinne, Rachmaninoff, Godowsky, and Busoni had it. But it is certainly a select group. In my lifetime, he was the pianist that every other pianist was fascinated by; they hated or loved him—but indifferent, never!

Julien Musafia

Born in Bucharest, Julien Musafia graduated from the Royal Academy of Music in that city, where he studied with Florica Musicescu. He holds degrees in composition, ethnomusicology, and political philosophy. He has published The Art of Fingering in Piano Playing, *and also an edition of the Twenty-Four Preludes and Fugues by Shostakovich in collaboration with the composer, both published by MCA.*

A noted exponent of Shostakovich, Musafia performed the Seven Romances on Words of Blok *with Rostropovich and Vishnevskaya. During the Liszt centennial year of 1986 he performed four different Liszt recital programs, and in 1991 he played at the opening night of the First Lipatti Festival. He has recorded for the Orion label an all-Enescu disc, and is professor of music at California State University at Long Beach.*

A book such as the present one—a collection of views on a great pianist by his contemporaries in the profession—would be of immense interest to us today if the subject were Liszt, Anton Rubinstein, Thalberg, Tausig, or any other who has not left recordings to show the reasons for their fame as instrumentalists. But is a book on Horowitz somewhat superfluous because we do have an extensive discography? Could not future generations always dip into that treasure to form an immediate impression, without the aid of any contemporary testimony? And wouldn't the reaction of the masses as captured on live recordings, delirious shouting, and frenetic applause say it all from the point of view of popular sentiment, and thus complete the picture?

I do not believe so. Listeners of the next century will certainly have a different attitude toward pianism, derived from *their* prevailing aesthetics and concepts regarding literalism, objectivism, structuralism, or expressionism. Their feelings toward eighteenth- and nineteenth-century music, the bulk of Horowitz's repertoire (by that time two and three centuries old), will certainly be different from those of today. One needs only to listen to recordings made in the first quarter of this century by Busoni, de Pachmann, Reisenauer, Friedman, or Paderewski to recognize that tastes have changed. For example, the practice of arpeggiating chords, though intended to clarify the leading function of inner voices in the chord, has now fallen out of fashion. Similarly, sliding between intervals in violin playing—as heard from Kreisler—is now considered in bad taste. Yet, in matters of good taste is the present always wrong and the future right? Is the history of art largely the history of improved discernment? The question can be resolved only by recognizing the present-day anomaly of artists of one century playing for the most part the music of another. In the past, only contemporary music was performed, and usually by the composer, who knew what he wanted, and by those under his instruction.

At a Horowitz performance all issues of authenticity, veracity, and correctness of style seemed to most of us present to be resolved by the magic of his art. His musical solutions were not only right but inevitable. He had discovered some fundamental truths about rhythm, about phrasing, and about sound, which we would recognize but could not duplicate. He had two whole generations of imitators, but he remained inimitable.

He was an intuitive musician. He knew that music was born of ecstasy, that it expressed the substratum of our emotions—not a particular sadness, pain, or joy, but the essential nature of feelings that could stir our thought and imagination. His cool and supremely lucid mind, however, which dominated his skill in terms of aims as well as means, was entirely at the service of this intuition.

He was a realist. His tactile approach to the keys was clearly derived from an accurate perception of the task, that is, of relating physical action to the resistance of the key as it changes with the volume of sound and point and angle of application. In a video tape made in his home, one can see his method of producing a sudden diminution of sound by pressing the key very close to the fulcrum, where the resistance is greater. The flat-finger technique Horowitz acquired from his teacher, Blumenfeld, must have been crucial to this aspect of his playing. It opened up opportunities for sound exploration that other approaches do not encourage, and must have influenced his interpretations as he observed the results he was obtaining and learned from them.

He was an original as he gave us a new view of the expressive content of sonatas by Scarlatti, Clementi, Mozart, and Scriabin that was non-academic but vital, dramatic, and virtuosic.

At most of Horowitz's concerts in Los Angeles I sat near Abram Chasins, his long-time friend. He said flatly after one of his recitals: "You cannot learn anything from Horowitz." I quite agreed, because I felt that there was a secret in his playing that could not be penetrated. He had discovered how to encode the import of the musical message in the unique and specific language of the instrument. He could reveal the innermost nature of any composition by means that my reasoning faculty could not comprehend. Although the pitches are given in a score, and the timbre of the piano is given as well, he accomplished all his artistic aims by the full understanding of the interrelation of the two remaining sound qualities, duration and volume. His bracing and indomitable rhythms, his mixing of harmonics as a new layer of harmony (as they were generated through the well-gauged loudness of the bass notes coupled with savant pedalling), his simulation of many touches—from maximum brilliance to mellow tenderness—was the result of this knowledge, which he possessed to the highest degree.

In a 1951 interview in *Etude* magazine, Horowitz was quoted as saying: "The performer must strive for that perfect coordination of mind, heart and means which allows none to predominate and balances all in the well-rounded whole of finished musical performance." Such a balance always seemed to me to have been fully attained by him. The visceral impact of his emotional projection, springing as it did from the near-opposites—instinctive abandon and complete awareness—an amalgam possible only in art—was obtained in his softest playing as well as in the loudest. He presented the music of any composer as his own creation, fully comprehended and assimilated in all its aspects: style, phrasing, structure, harmonic meaning. Listening to him play, I was constantly astounded at the immense amount of sonic information per unit of time I was receiving. Every note had a different intensity, in chords and horizontally. The effect was kaleidoscopic and delightfully surprising.

The importance Horowitz gave to each note stimulated the concentration of his listeners, who awaited eagerly the advent of the next new sound. He thus stopped the flow of time. The lengths of a Liszt sonata would evaporate in space without time. No perfunctory note marred his playing, and no wrong note disturbed the music in the least, as the ear was always drawn to what the pianist wanted us to hear.

Watching Horowitz play, one understood how Schopenhauer's Will worked through him. His position at the keyboard was purposefulness objectified. His straight torso inclined slightly forward allowed the arms to hang at the vertical, out of action. His forearms, thus freed, took full advantage of man's anatomical construction, which is designed for speed. In fortissimos, his playing apparatus assumed the skeletal position, all bones in the fingers, hands and wrists lined up to absorb without stress the reaction of the keys to his ferocious attack on them. He looked always at his fingers and gave no inkling of his feelings at the moment. Total concentration on each note was the only visual message in his facial expression.

I shook his hands on two occasions immediately after his recitals. His muscles felt soft and non-tetanic, as though they had not been exerted in the least. This was to me the strongest clue to his friendly relation with the keyboard, his unmatched control of nuance (a task made even harder by the reportedly very light action of his piano), and his exhilarating bursts of velocity—abilities he maintained and even improved upon to the end of his life.

James Streem

Born in Cleveland, Ohio, James Streem studied at the Juilliard School with Josef Raieff and later with Theodore Lettvin. After his successful debut at Cleveland's Severance Hall, he taught at the Cleveland Music School Settlement. His New York debut in 1966 led to appearances as soloist with such major symphony orchestras as Boston, Cleveland, Detroit, Miami, and New York. He has continued to perform recitals as well as to give master-classes throughout the United States, making annual appearances at the Juilliard School in lecture-recitals.

Streem has consistently championed the music of Scriabin and has done research on Chopin's mazurkas. He is professor and coordinator of piano at Florida State University.

To have seen and heard Vladimir Horowitz perform was for most pianists an unparalleled phenomenon. Not since Liszt has a pianist emanated so much influence. One didn't merely listen and watch Horowitz; one studied him. I, as many pianists before and after, would be continuously searching for that secret Horowitz ingredient. Was it all in the pedalling? Impossible! If anyone else used that pedalling it would be a total blur. Then it must be the articulation . . . but I've known many pianists whose digital prowess is on that level. So now we are left to speculate on his enormous dynamic range of color, his penchant for unusual voicing, or is it all contained in his ability to couple the demonic with the ethereal? And so it continues.

My first impression of Vladimir Horowitz was his RCA recording of Chopin's Andante spianato and Grand Polonaise, and as a child I remember how taken I was with the beauty, grandeur, and glitter of that performance. Now, many years later, I still find it unrivaled. There have been, however, several recordings he allowed to be released later in his life, such as Liszt's *Mephisto* Waltz or certain

Scriabin works, which I believe are not up to the level we came to expect from him, but are nevertheless worth our attention.

Studying the art of Vladimir Horowitz is both fascinating and mystifying. It is astonishing to find some of his later recordings of the Chopin mazurkas, for example, Op. 30, No. 4, to be so similar to his circa-1930 renditions even to the slightest detail, and yet the Scriabin "Black Mass" Sonata recorded in 1953 (approximately 6′30″) goes through a complete transformation in his 1965 performance (half again as long).

With regard to the Chopin mazurkas, I can think of no one save Ignaz Friedman who could perform them with such beautiful imagery. The opening canon of Horowitz's 1931 recording of the Op. 50, No. 3, in C-sharp minor defines the flirtatious female dancer in the right hand, followed by her more straightforward male counterpart in the left, as one might expect a couple to dance the slow *kujawiak*. It is interesting to note that Horowitz opted not to repeat the first sixteen bars, probably due to the time limitations imposed by the old 78-rpm process, where four minutes and thirty seconds was considered the outer limits. As a result he was able to deliver a far more imaginative opening than we hear in his later rendition of this opus. The later rendition, however, shows the mature Horowitz, with greater restraint, new inner voices, and a wash of pedal that only he could bring off.

In his performance of the Op. 24, No. 4, in B-flat minor, he shows his scholarly awareness of how Chopin told his students, "The hammers should not strike the strings but must merely brush them." I would point out that in his circa-1931 performance of the E minor Op. 41, No. 2 mazurka he not only abandons all sense of a scholarly approach, but takes such enormous liberties with the score that he has all but written his own little variation. I hasten to add that it never really bothered me, as I could appreciate it as much as his 1968 performance, where he evidently decided Chopin's score was the preferred model.

My close friend and colleague Edward Kilenyi told me of a conversation he had with Gusztav Bárczy, who, in the late twenties, managed many of Horowitz's appearances in Hungary as well as several other countries. It seems that Bárczy was sitting with the great Polish violinist Bronislaw Huberman at a Horowitz concert where he performed some mazurkas. Bárczy reported Huberman making motions for the music to move, and afterward both agreed Horowitz had played the mazurkas more like nocturnes than mazurkas.

When considering the textual liberties taken by Horowitz, one must assume that his prime concern was for a composition's aural impression above all else. While I personally do not disagree with this philosophically, for those of us who diligently worked out the technical problems of the Op. 42, No. 5 Scriabin etude it was always a disappointment to hear one's model of pianism resort to such oversimplifications.

Perhaps the greatest legacy Horowitz left us was his uniqueness. How few pianists are identifiable by their sound. Like it or not—it was special. It was this very singular approach in his playing that I, in the role of a teacher, would hope to focus my students' attention upon: finding their own particular sound, their own individualism.

Joseph Banowetz

The American pianist Joseph Banowetz studied in New York with Carl Friedberg, and later at Vienna's Hochschule für Musik with Josef Dichter. During his career he has performed on five continents.

Banowetz has been an active editor of music and has written on music in many journals. His book The Pianist's Guide to Pedaling *(Indiana University Press) has been published in four languages. He has made recordings of standard concertos and of the Anton Rubinstein concertos. In 1987 his recording of Balakirev's scherzos and mazurkas was given a Deutsche Schallplattenkritik citation.*

For part of each year, Banowetz holds classes in piano performance at the University of North Texas. He is on the advisory board of several international competitions, and often serves as judge. In 1992 he was on the jury of the Arthur Rubinstein Competition in Tel Aviv.

Pianists of my generation, whose most formative musical years were in the forties and fifties, inevitably found Horowitz to be not only a potent but in many respects a dangerous musical lodestar. Yet, although during that time of my artistic adolescence I cheerfully would have sold my soul for some of the famous Horowitz speed and brilliance, I mercifully was never infected by "Horowitzitus" in its most virulent strain. At that time, this was a well-known musical disease accompanied by copycat symptoms that musically maimed so many young performers of my generation. American pianists seemed especially susceptible. My comparative immunity may in part be explained by my not having heard Horowitz in life until after his return to the stage in 1965. Too, I had early on formed strong musical crushes on Fischer, Gieseking, Solomon, and above all Cortot. To have slavishly aped, as so many then tried unsuccessfully to do, Horowitz's sonority, machine-gun octaves, and his highly personalized sense of coloring, rubato, and phrasing was to me at the time both physically impossible and stylistically unthinkable.

But in spite of consciously keeping my distance from Horowitz as far as direct imitation was concerned, I nonetheless both idolized and was fascinated by him—an attraction that has remained compelling to this day. One aspect of his playing that always especially intrigued me was his sense of rhythmic projection. Rhythmic tension in any performance usually has to do with rigid metronomic playing, and a strict mechanical beat will in fact often of necessity be distorted and displaced (as in a mazurka, waltz, or polonaise rhythm) in order to achieve such tension and projection. In strongly expressive melodic material, such avoidance of a metronomic beat becomes critically important. Horowitz was a master of this, and for me towered over any other pianist in achieving this rhythmic intensity and flexibility. To my ears, I only later felt him to have possibly been rivalled in degree and consistency by Hofmann, judging from recordings in particular of live Hofmann concerts. Hofmann also was able to inject an at times overpowering amount of rhythmic energy into every note of his playing, yet achieved entirely different musical results. Both Hofmann's and Horowitz's abilities to pull melodic lines, each injected with varying degrees of tension and rhythmic impulse, and to relentlessly thrust and project phrases in a rhythmic direction, bordered on the uncanny.

Horowitz's rhythmic imagination in Chopin mazurkas was always to me something very special, and his earliest 1920s and 1930s recordings were some of the most treasured and well-worn discs in my fledgling collection of 78s. I am not certain that he ever fully matched the unforced suaveness of some of these performances in subsequent recorded versions. The musical impact of these was only matched when in my early teens I stumbled across the now legendary Ignaz Friedman album of Chopin mazurkas in a secondhand store. To have then been able to compare mazurka performances of Horowitz and Friedman and the Rubinstein recordings of 1938–39 (Rubinstein's first traversal of the Chopin mazurkas, and still in some respects my favorite of his three recorded versions) was a humbling yet invaluable experience for me. With all three artists, I sensed vast similarities in their feeling for rhythmic tension, yet heard enormous differences of detail. A few of Rubinstein's readings (and Malcuzynski's later mazurka recordings as well) apply Chopin's own lengthening of first beats (as documented by the composer's own contemporaries such as von Lenz and Hallé). In the opening page, for instance, of the Mazurka Op. 30, No. 3, both Rubinstein and Malcuzynski play with a rubato that crosses over into a duple meter. The first beat in effect becomes stretched to two beats, and the last two beats are played within the third beat. Horowitz, on the other hand, clearly favors Friedman's general approach to the Chopin mazurkas, and uses some shortening of the first beats, followed by compensating lengthened second beats. Everywhere, there are fantastic colors, highlighting of inner voices, and the like.

Horowitz was capable of projecting rhythm in the most aggressive, even brutal, manner, yet when he so wished could achieve this in a tempo that might be slower than that chosen by most other performers. His 1947 recording of Prokofiev's Toccata clearly demonstrates this, where with a relentless rhythmic drive and explosions of accents, rather than by sheer speed, he achieves a terrifying, near-sadistic intensity. Each note seems bathed in electricity, pounding bass rhythms become orgiastic, and long pulses are balanced with a feeling of great tension within and between each note. An equally striking deliberate use of such rhythmic tension is to be found in Horowitz's 1945 recording of Prokofiev's Sonata No. 7. In the first and last movements in particular, where there seems entrenched a Russian tradition of hurdling through much of the score pell-mell, Horowitz again opts for rhythmic intensity rather than high velocity, which allows him greater latitude for color and dramatization.

Horowitz's incredible instinct for manipulating rhythmic tension dominates and directs the highly personalized way in which he shapes and stretches phrases, and examples are legion of how he is able to infuse simultaneously different respective levels of tension into accompaniment figuration and one or more strands of melodic material. Over a long, slow pulse that will serve to maintain forward direction, primary and secondary melodies will often writhe and pull against each other, with the hands and music at times threatening to break apart entirely. Extreme rubatos frequently become consequences of different levels of rhythmic intensity and tension being applied against each other.

Nowhere is all of this more evident than in Horowitz's performances of Scriabin. Horowitz was arguably the greatest interpreter alive for the music of Scriabin, and in many of his Scriabin performances he reveled in exploiting multiple levels of rhythmic tension as a means of conveying the music's exotic neuroticism. In a Carnegie Hall recital in 1953, Horowitz performed two Scriabin etudes. The recorded performance is a unique documentation of an interpretative genius at his zenith. The Etude in B-flat minor Op. 8, No. 11 is drenched with a sick, longing quality. Horowitz uses several levels of melodic intensity, these being always counterbalanced by a longer, more relaxed pulse in the accompaniment figuration, to heighten the music's heavily perfumed sensuality.

Even more electrifying is his performance of the Etude in C-sharp minor Op. 42, No. 5, where multiple rhythms and streams of melodic tension are simultaneously locked together in a twisting musical mass that threatens to erupt from the erotic to the obscene. Here, Horowitz's mastery of rhythmic tension is exploited to its fullest, and is used to reveal nakedly every neurotic aspect of Scriabin's —and Horowitz's—psyche.

Horowitz's mastery of rhythm in its widest sense still remains for me one of the fundamental keys to understanding his complex art. Yet, like so many other facets of his playing, in the end he only used it as a tool for exposing through the music his own colorful yet disturbing personality, never for a cosmetic effect or as a gimmick. Perhaps no artist has ever used it more imaginatively. Many of the pianists of my generation who tried to copy Horowitz's rubato and complexities of rhythm, in addition to not having a scrap of his genius, simply did so without understanding what he was trying to do musically. Most of the time, their mini-Horowitz interpretations had as much artistic depth and originality as an Andy Warhol print. They could not have picked a more dangerous role model.

Although Horowitz's art can be broken down and superficially analyzed in terms of rhythm, color, rubato, pedalling, sonority, and the like, such discussions somehow still provide only the faintest glimpse into the musical wizard that was Horowitz. Genius has its own inscrutable laws, and Horowitz was one of the very few performers, in this time of publicity representatives and outrageous hype, who truly deserved this designation. I shall miss him greatly.

Michael Boriskin

Michael Boriskin was born in New York, where he studied at the Juilliard School. He has performed at the Kennedy Center in Washington, D.C., at Lincoln Center, Carnegie Hall, the BBC in London, Paris's Théatre des Champs-Elysées, the Smithsonian Institution, and elsewhere. He has given concerts for the United States Information Agency and has appeared as soloist with many important orchestras. During the 1992 season he toured Japan. Boriskin is also an accomplished chamber musician and a busy recitalist. His repertoire ranges widely, from Brahms and Tchaikovsky to Virgil Thomson and many other contemporary composers. He recently recorded an album of American piano music on New World Records. Other of his recordings appear on Newport Classic, Delos, Music and Arts, and Musical Heritage Society. During the 1993 season he gave the premiere of George Perle's Second Piano Concerto with the Utah Symphony.

Vladimir Horowitz was the first legendary performer I ever heard live. I was 14 at the time, and the occasion was nothing less than his 1965 "historic return." Little did I realize, upon entering Carnegie Hall that Sunday afternoon, that I was about to have one of the most exhilarating concert-going experiences of a lifetime. Even though I was then quite unsophisticated and unable to grasp more than a fraction of what was transpiring on the stage, Horowitz's magnetism, inimitable sound, and sovereign musical voice made a colossal impression. It was a transforming event for me, and an awesome display of what it meant to be a concert performer. My reaction was identical to that of another young pianist upon meeting Josef Hofmann for the first time in the 1920s: "I had finally encountered standards, Olympian standards," Abram Chasins wrote, "and a conception of music and performance which had never before touched me at all." I succumbed to Horowitz's sorcery, and he immediately became my pianistic hero. I began to acquire and study closely all of his recordings, and did not miss a chance to hear him locally at that time. From his live and recorded performances, I learned nearly as much about piano playing as I did from the Juilliard professors with whom I was working during that formative period in my life. That my own musical attitudes eventually diverged considerably from his does not alter the importance his work held for me in my student years (or since).

Like so many young pianists, I was mesmerized initially by Horowitz's supreme command of craft and the sheer brilliance and electricity of his playing. Later on, I came to value other aspects of his art that were not as often noted as his more spectacular attributes. His consummate workmanship was a revelation to me. As a teenager, I fancied myself as being pretty diligent about practicing the piano, but Horowitz demonstrated what real craftsmanship involved. Every nuance and passage was honed to an exquisite sheen; even the smallest detail was comprehensively prepared, considered, and refined, yet there remained a sense of spontaneity. The élan and utter authority of his playing made it appear as if he were actually creating the composition at the moment of performance, and his delivery left no doubt as to his musical intentions.

Despite his volatile temperament and notoriously eccentric behavior offstage, I saw that his attitude when performing was one of complete earnestness, and his magic was conveyed solely through his playing. On the platform, he was all business; he maintained a subdued demeanor, affected no false poses, and sat dead still while working his pianistic miracles. This was consistent with Horowitz's intensity of absorption as he played, which struck me from the beginning. While many concert performers are bedeviled by occasionally fickle memories, Horowitz's extraordinarily assured performances seemed to have been built upon granite; in all the many times I heard him live, I recall only one or two lapses of the most insignificant kind.

Although his programming tended to be rather conventional, it was fairly serious in tone, and he usually saved the "potboiler" for his grand finale. While not nearly as substantial as those of Serkin, Curzon, Petri, Arrau, and others drawn to a more monumental kind of repertoire, his programs were not the "circuses" of some performers who feel the need to dazzle at every point during a concert. I admired the fact that Horowitz, unlike many musicians who repeatedly rely on the same compositions, continued to learn or revive works until the end of his career. I also eagerly looked forward to his occasional, though always notable, ventures beyond repertory staples, including works like the Schumann F minor Sonata and *Humoreske*, Rachmaninoff's Second Sonata, and sonatas by Clementi, Scriabin, and Scarlatti.

As my perspectives widened, my reaction to his work naturally evolved as well. During my twenties and early thirties, I went through a stage in which I became very serious indeed, and was aghast at what I perceived to be Horowitzian extravagances and mannerisms. (That this period coincided with the years when Horowitz's playing was perhaps at its most wayward and idiosyncratic made my revised stance even easier to justify.) Hearing his performances during those years, and going back over his earlier recordings, I began to notice many puzzling aspects of his playing, including the unexplained accents, broken melodic lines, clangorous sound, and curious interpretive decisions. Many of his conceptions sometimes seemed to be imposed arbitrarily upon the music rather than drawn out of it. With all the righteousness of youth, I was indignant about what I felt was an interpretive attitude that exalted the performer over the composer. Horowitz also had an unfortunate tendency that, for me, often marred otherwise well-shaped readings: despite his reputation as a thundering powerhouse with a generous tonal palette, he often turned climaxes requiring big, "orchestral" sonorities bearing heightened musical expression into trite, athletic displays rather than hard-earned emotional apotheoses (like those in Mussorgsky's *Pictures at an Exhibition*, Chopin's *Polonaise-Fantaisie*, the *Vallée d'Obermann* by Liszt, and dozens of other pieces he played over the years).

Finally, I grew up. My initial enthusiasm for this singular figure returned, now somewhat tempered, and, I think, more discerning. While I did not abandon all of my reservations, it became clear to me that regardless of how fervently one might disagree with Horowitz's treatment of a piece, his performance commanded attention, and could not easily be dismissed. This was due, in large part, to an underlying consistency and principle in all of his work. The extraordinary conviction inherent in his playing made almost everything seem organic and logical, at least during the performance, which is the key to a compelling interpretation. This was one reason why his many Scarlatti readings, for instance, rank, for me, among the glories in the annals of pianism, even though they are stylistically unidiomatic and "all wrong."

I still regret that he was not more involved (especially after 1950) with contemporary repertoire, since his performances and recordings of music by Stravinsky, Barber, Prokofiev, Kabalevsky, Poulenc, and other then-current composers constitute some of his most electrifying, persuasive playing. The attention he occasionally devoted to such works (as well as obscure pieces from earlier periods) demonstrated an adventurousness and curiosity all too rare among headliners. Had he regularly applied his technical genius and considerable powers of imagination to the music of his time, it is not an exaggeration to say that he could have reshaped recital life in the second half of the twentieth century, as to both repertoire and our approach toward programming. As Harold Schonberg once noted in a *New York Times* review, "where Horowitz goes, everybody else follows." Were this pianist to have regularly championed worthwhile new works, he would have greatly enlarged the repertoire; this, by itself, would be an invaluable investment in the future of music. (That Samuel Barber's Piano Sonata, for instance, so quickly entered the active repertoire is surely due, in significant measure, to Horowitz's advocacy of it, both in concert and on his incendiary 1950 recording.) Furthermore, Horowitz would, by example, have encouraged a creativity in programming that is sorely missing from most concerts; today's performers offer recital repertoire only marginally different from that heard in the 1920s.

In his later years, it became fashionable to consider Horowitz "the last Romantic." (I thought it was interesting that when he started out in the 1920s, he was regarded as the archetype of the modern pianist. How the musical world changed around him in the ensuing seventy years!) For me, that sobriquet does not merely involve interpretive approach and repertoire inclinations, but also an aesthetic of performance that is essentially lost and maybe even irretrievable. When I listen to recordings of the great artists from past generations (regardless of the differences of style and character among them), I am struck by the sense of daring, danger, originality, and, for want of a better term, natural informality with which these performances are imbued. This was surely true of Horowitz, as well. Increasingly absent in modern-day performances, and even somewhat suspect in the musical life of the late twentieth century, are the very things that, I felt, set Horowitz's playing apart from that of so many of his contemporaries, and from the routine, uninvolved performances of most of his younger colleagues—risk, adventure, and passionate commitment. I valued his work for this perhaps above all.

Ivan Davis

Ivan Davis was born in Texas. At North Texas State University he studied with Silvio Scionti and, after receiving a Fulbright Scholarship, he worked with Carlo Zecchi in Rome. He won top prizes at the Casella, Busoni, and Vianna da Motta competitions, and in 1960 he won first prize in the Franz Liszt Competition. Soon after, he studied with Horowitz.

Davis has appeared with many of the world's orchestras, and has recorded on Columbia, Decca/London, and the Audiofon label, for whom he has issued an all-Grieg recital and works of Beethoven, Schumann, Liszt, and Czerny. The city of New York has honored Ivan Davis with its Handel Medallion for his outstanding contribution to American cultural life. He is pianist-in-residence at the University of Miami in Coral Gables, as well as visiting professor of piano at Indiana University. He has given master-classes throughout the United States, and has served on the juries of international competitions.

My knowledge of Vladimir Horowitz began at about the same time my interest in music was born. I was twelve years old and had been sent to Hobbs, New Mexico, to spend the summer with my aunt, a piano teacher. I had never had a lesson, but as I was surrounded by budding virtuosi my curiosity was aroused. I learned quite rapidly, and after a few months was mauling the A major Polonaise of Chopin, among other helpless musical victims. And I listened constantly to my aunt's record collection (78s, of course). In particular I remember Rachmaninoff's own performance of his C minor Concerto, an album of Chopin mazurkas by Maryla Jonas, and, above all, Horowitz playing the Tchaikovsky First and the Brahms Second with Toscanini.

The opportunity to hear live classical music in this small town in southeastern New Mexico was limited in the extreme—unless you particularly enjoyed Mildred Dilling on the harp or the Great Rubinoff on the violin. I did hear Jonas and José Iturbi in Lubbock, Texas, and Clifford Curzon in Fort Worth while in high school. Luckily, things changed when I went to college in Denton, Texas, at North Texas State. My teacher, Silvio Scionti, a Sicilian who had taught for many years in Chicago before coming to Texas, awakened me to everything musical and was certainly the most influential person in my life until I met Horowitz. Silvio's two favorite pianists were Claudio Arrau and VH (rather strange bedfellows to my mind now), and he insisted that I take advantage of the bustling musical scene in Dallas. The *only* time I heard Horowitz before his Carnegie Hall return in 1965 was in 1950 or 1951, when he performed the Tchaikovsky B-flat minor with the Dallas Symphony. My feet didn't touch the ground for days, yet how could I possibly have known that within ten years I would be both a musical and personal friend of this living legend?

In 1960, after several years in New York City and Italy, I entered and won the Franz Liszt Competition in New York City. The jury, chaired by Dimitri Mitropoulos, included Ania Dorfmann and Byron Janis, both close friends of Horowitz. Early one morning, in the week after the contest, I was awakened by an inimitable voice asking to speak to "Ee-von Dah-vees." After clearing my morning throat, I inquired for the name of the caller and was told: "Vladimir Horowitz." Incredulously I said, "Okay, come on, who *is* it? Is this Johnny Woods?" (a pianist friend known to pull such shenanigans). Finally, reality dawned and I accepted an invitation to dinner at the Horowitzes.

What an evening! I don't remember who was there—although I think Ania was; I don't remember what was served—it could have been foi gras or Alpo; I was in a delirious and delicious daze. I was asked if I wished to play; Horowitz and I went to the music room alone. I performed some Scarlatti and the Schumann *Abegg* Variations, and then VH said, "I understand you play Sixth Rhapsody." I thought, yeah, coals to Newcastle, took a deep breath, and plunged into D-flat major. Actually it went pretty well, and Horowitz said, "Ho Ho! You have good wrists but I bet you get tired. Later I will give you octave secrets!" Any pianist would kill for that info. At the end of the evening he said, "You know, I don't perform any more but I *have* had some experience. You are already a formed pianist with a real personality but sometimes I don't think you listen to yourself and if you like, I will be big ears for you." Hosanna in the highest!

This started almost two years of 9:45 P.M. sessions of music making, music listening, and conversation. I was making my first recording for Columbia—an all-Liszt program—and I played all the repertoire for Volodya. In particular, I remember discussing and then combining the original *Mephisto* Waltz and the Busoni version as well as some alterations to the Sixth Rhapsody. Soon after this, Horowitz was making *his* first recording for Columbia, and he played for me several versions of the Nineteenth Rhapsody before committing it to posterity. I have always thought that VH was the supreme interpreter of the Liszt Rhapsodies—a perfect medium for his blend of imaginative freedom, sense of the dramatic, and diabolic and technical wizardry. The Second Rhapsody from the 1953 Carnegie Hall Recital is one of the milestones of pianism. There was also a breathtaking performance of the Thirteenth Rhapsody in Boston that I wish had been recorded.

In concerto repertoire, I played the Liszt Hungarian Fantasy (again with textual additions) and the Rachmaninoff Second, which I recorded with Ormandy. When I told VH I was playing the Liszt with the Philadelphia Orchestra on television, he asked what network. I responded CBS, and he squealed "Good—that's a really clear channel!" I also played for him the Liszt A major, which he informed me he had played often when young and always repeated the lyrical D-flat major section; what conductor would allow *that* today? Also the Saint-Saëns Fourth and the Rachmaninoff-Paganini Rhapsody (which was the only time he accompanied me on second piano). I thought I was playing with the combined Philadelphia, Chicago, and Leningrad orchestras!

He rarely discussed technical matters—only in terms of color and voicing. He would illustrate by playing three melodic lines with the right hand (improvising an accompaniment with the left hand) while changing the dynamics of each voice in the most dramatic fashion. We also agreed that sometimes it was far easier to play thirds with one hand than attempting to keep the hands together with two. The famous "secret of the octaves" was something I and thousands of other pianists had been doing for years, that is, practicing high from the wrist and in rapid, propulsive groups.

Personally, I found Volodya one of the most charming of men. His child-like sense of humor was irresistible and his enthusiasm was contagious. During this period Horowitz was rarely seen in public—certainly not at musical events. To my surprise, one day he called and asked if I would like to go to Carnegie Hall with him to hear Rudolf and Peter Serkin perform the Mozart two-piano concerto (the elder Serkin, a close friend, had sent him tickets). I delightedly said yes, and Volodya picked me up in a limousine. At the end of the concerto he informed me he would like to go backstage, which, as usual, was packed with pianists. Rudolf introduced Peter (who was about 12 at the time) to him saying, "At last, you have met your favorite pianist!" Horowitz looked increasingly nervous and whispered loudly that we must go. In the limo, I said, "Volodya, did all those people upset you?" And he said, "No, the Emmy awards are on and I want to see if *The Naked City* will win!"

One time he wished to go out on the town and asked me to suggest some locale. I puzzled, and wondered where do you take the pianistic Garbo? Eventually we went to a sidewalk café in Greenwich Village, where he informed me that if I saw anyone I knew I must introduce him as Mr. Howard. Needless to say I told several of my friends that if they wanted to see Horowitz in person to walk past the café, and, on point of death, say nothing! They did that, but suddenly I saw a group of obvious piano students, carrying yellow Schirmer scores, point at our table. Volodya said, "Tell them I'm Mr. Howard!" The group selected a representative, sent him to the table with a score of the Liszt Sonata, where he asked, "May I have your autograph, Mr. Davis?" I will never forget the look on Mr. Howard's face. Later he said, "Ivan, they didn't *know* me!" And I said that they were too young to have heard him; after all, I was an old man of 28 and had played three times in New York City that season. I truly believe that on this evening he decided to return to the concert stage.

We listened to a great amount and variety of music together. I was immensely interested in Italian opera before I met him, particularly after two years in Rome, where I heard and met Maria Callas—but VH introduced me to several unfamiliar Russian operas and singers. I also heard acetates of his recitals from the forties and early fifties with many works he never recorded. I also remember hearing a wild performance of the Sixth Rhapsody, accompanied by the famous Horowitz giggle and interpolations of "This is really naughty—you think too fast—the critics would *kill* me!"

I was always so impressed with his debonair appearance—crisp shirts, perky bow ties, et al.—particularly since I have always been a tee-shirt and jeans person—but not in his presence. When I first went to London to perform, I was subtly ordered to bring back his favorite fragrance—Stephanotis by Floris. I complied and even purchased a small amount for myself; it didn't help my octaves either!

I was very protective of my friendship with Volodya. He never even met my wife, but there were two people whose acquaintance I thought would be mutually beneficial. First I introduced him to John Ardoin, a friend from college days who became the critic for the *Dallas Morning News* and was an opera and keyboard fanatic. The evening went swimmingly. The second was Robert Berkshire, a former roommate from Italian days and a very successful painter whom I knew would be mightily impressed with the Horowitz art collection. He was, and Horowitz liked him immediately. Unfortunately, the evening evolved into a festival of hilarious and often risqué stories overheard by his wife, Wanda—never widely known for her charm or sense of humor—who remained in the room stonefaced as a Buddha. Things were never the same after that evening.

Of course I was in the audience for the 1965 Carnegie Hall return, and heard him many other times. Some of the most indelible aural memories are of the Chopin *Polonaise-Fantaisie*, the trio of Chopin's funeral march (where no one dared breathe for fear of breaking the ultimate pianissimo spell), Liszt's *Vallée d'Obermann*, and the Mozart B minor Adagio and D major Rondo.

Fortunately, we have a vast recorded legacy left to us. I know of no artists other than Callas and Richter who have been so extensively documented on CD—sixty years of constant recording, with almost every note available today. What a range of music also—from the lapidary elegance of the Scarlatti sonatas and demonic lyricism of the Liszt Sonata done in the early 1930s to the profound magnificence of the late Chopin nocturnes recorded in 1989. I have always thought that, other than Liszt, Horowitz's greatest affinity has been with the three Ss—Scarlatti, Schumann, and Scriabin. Not quite so with the fourth—Schubert. The ultimate romanticism of Schumann, so elusive for most pianists, was mother's milk to Volodya. I remember when I recorded the *Carnaval*, VH refused to hear it, declaring that it was the only work of Schumann's that he didn't like. However, he did perform it one season (during a bad medical period), and the tapes from Philadelphia and Tokyo sound like late Cortot on cocaine. But his recordings of the Fantasy, *Kreisleriana*, the *Humoreske*, and the F minor Sonata are incomparable.

For many years Horowitz was, I think, a harmful (if unwitting) influence on young pianists—at least those without the intelligence and imagination to realize that loud and fast does not equal virtuosity. I remember Volodya being mightily impressed with a tape I played for him of Martha Argerich. But he was not so impressed with her extraordinary technical equipment as he was with the daring individuality of her musical personality. In these days of IBM pianists, I hope that the recordings of Vladimir Horowitz will now serve as musical proof that the piano *can* be a vocal instrument as telling as any great singer. Just listen to his late recording of the Schubert-Liszt *Ständchen;* it says it all.

Morton Estrin

Vermont-born Morton Estrin studied in New York with Vera Maurina-Press. He made his New York debut at Town Hall in 1949 and has since performed throughout the United States and Europe. His many recordings for Connoisseur Society include the Preludes Op. 32 by Rachmaninoff and the Scriabin Etudes Op. 8.

An advocate of worthy but neglected works, Estrin has recorded for Newport Classic Joachim Raff's monumental Suite in D minor Op. 91, Anton Rubinstein's Six Etudes Op. 23, and Tchaikovsky's Sonata in G major Op. 37. He has played a good deal of contemporary music and has recorded music by Meyer Kupferman for the Serenus label. Estrin has been professor of music at Hofstra University since 1959.

Horowitz! The very mention of his name sends shivers up the spines of generations of pianists worldwide. The commanding personality, the electrifying mechanics of those hands, the adulation of those immense crowds waiting in line to have the honor of buying a ticket to his concerts—these are the immediate thoughts that come to mind. But there is more, oh, much more. When I was a student, having long been infected with that incomprehensible virus that committed me to devotion to the mastery of the piano, Horowitz was the deity before whom I trembled and whom I set as an ideal. No, maybe not my *total* ideal. That was Arthur Rubinstein. He of the joie de vivre and healthy Romantic interpretations sharply contrasted in my mind with the neurotic bizarre genius Horowitz, who could touch three notes on the piano and immediately reveal a sound that could be recognized as belonging only to him. Maybe I was intimidated—probably every pianist was! Even my beloved Rubinstein admitted that Vladimir had a better technique, but that he, Rubinstein, was the better musician. I suppose every pianist, at one time or another, had to reckon with this terrifying monster. My contemporaries, faced with the Horowitz challenge, often would offer a facile dismissal of the great man by saying that he "was all technique" with no soul. How this must have served as a convenient self-justification for the more modestly endowed students who filled the conservatories.

His legendary technique was only a small part of the Horowitz mystique. To understand him was to appreciate his performances as supreme acts of creation. His limitless imagination and sense of rightness, which stemmed from a seemingly inexhaustible creative energy, was more to the point of his uniqueness. Yes, his octaves could leave one breathless, but it was the visceral excitement of his insights into tonal possibilities, sudden turns of a phrase, cataclysmic dynamics, and sheer daring that were his glories. His way with a melody gave a whole new meaning to the term "lyrical" in piano playing. And not to be underestimated was his reverence for Beethoven. This was not a wayward approach to the Bonn master, but rather a revelation of the dramatic significance of every sforzando, every subito piano that abound in the sonatas. Horowitz's recording of the Sonata in D major Op. 10, No. 3 has always been, for me, the way Beethoven must have visualized his intentions in this masterpiece. And, again, in the Sonata in F major K. 332 of Mozart, he showed a side of lyrical beauty seldom achieved even by so-called Mozart specialists.

But all is not praiseworthy. The dichotomy of Horowitz the pianist and Horowitz the man has always disturbed me. This great artist could become, instantly, the spoiled ten-year-old who never really grew up. The stories one reads of his incorrigible behavior make one uneasy. His treatment of people, his total disregard of certain obligations, his cruelty toward friends, his cavalier attitude toward his students . . . one could go on.

But I suppose we must set aside these memories of him in favor of the extraordinary artistic legacy he has left us. His presence in this world will always remain an ultimate challenge, even in death. How does one dare to play the Mussorgsky *Pictures at an Exhibition* with the Horowitz version lurking? Or the octave passages in the Tchaikowsky B-flat minor Concerto? Everyone tries to outdo this supreme physical display, all the while maintaining one's musical vision. Or Liszt—his B minor Sonata has never left my aural consciousness. And the Brahms B-flat major Concerto, where, we have been told, Toscanini called the shots but his son-in-law prevailed brilliantly. I could go on and on. I recall, when I was a student, that there were three versions of the Tchaikowsky Concerto on records—Egon Petri, Arthur Rubinstein, and VH, again with Toscanini conducting. My peers and I would argue for hours on end about the relative merits of these great performances. We would almost come to blows! I won't say that Horowitz always won the arguments, but, somehow, we always seemed to end up comparing the other two to his. That would have to tell us something!

And, of course, there is Scriabin, a subject that is very close to me. Some years back I recorded, for the first time in history, the entire cycle of Etudes Op. 8. Horowitz never recorded the entire opus, playing some half dozen or so of these incredible pieces. I am grateful to him for leaving the rest to me!

Now that Horowitz is gone, and with him so many other giants of the twentieth century, including Rubinstein, Serkin, and Arrau in recent years, we wonder about the future of our glorious instrument and its incomparable literature. So much of our love has been reduced to a series of contests to determine who is the "best" that we forget that it is the very diversity in art that is its glory. Horowitz often commented with disdain about the machine-like sameness of our younger generation of pianists. He fairly cried out for an expression of individuality. He would even comment that perhaps some of the young virtuosi had faster hands than he but that they created little of consequence as interpretive personalities. This message, which he repeatedly sent to the world, may become his ultimate contribution to us. What he has left us in his immense recorded legacy will, in retrospect, set a model for the future. It is the democratic ideal of the worth of the individual. One must first be worthy. Then one must demand to be reckoned with by the sheer force of personality. For me, this is the message of Vladimir Horowitz.

John O'Conor

John O'Conor was born, and lives, in Ireland. In 1973 he won the International Beethoven Competition in Vienna, and soon after took first prize at the Bösendorfer Competition. A prolific recording artist, he will complete his nine-volume recording project of the Beethoven piano music on Telarc in 1994. He is also working his way through the concertos of Mozart with the Scottish Chamber Orchestra under Sir Charles Mackerras. In addition, he has recorded the Irish composer John Field's four sonatas and nocturnes. O'Conor has performed on an international scale, and has toured the United States, Europe, Japan, and the Soviet Union.

A familiar figure on television and radio in Ireland, O'Conor is actively involved in improving educational and performing opportunities for young musicians there. He has been instrumental in the establishment of the GPA Dublin International Competition.

When I was growing up in Ireland, the name of Horowitz had a sort of mystical sound to it. It never occurred to me that he might still be alive, because nobody I met had ever seen him play. In my mind, he was already as legendary as Anton Rubinstein, Paderewski, and my other childhood idols.

It was soon after I went to study in Vienna, in the early 1970s, that Horowitz became real to me in a way that made me very grateful to him. My professor there, Dieter Weber, was a Horowitz "nut." He adored his technique, his aura, his mystique, his disappearances from the concert platform; but above all he loved his sound.

Weber also was a great teacher in improving his students' facility. He tried valiantly to lower my right wrist (a legacy of my first piano teacher), which he felt was too high for good technique. I was so much in awe of him that everything he said was like divine revelation to me. But try as I might, I couldn't get my wrist as low as he wanted. Then one day he came into his studio, asked me to play something, and to my astonishment announced that my wrist was now fine. When pressed for an explanation, he informed me that Horowitz had been on Austrian TV the previous night, and his wrist was high, too. If Horowitz managed that way, he supposed I could, too! I was eternally grateful to Horowitz.

I then began to borrow Horowitz recordings and came across his famed *jeu perlé* for the first time. I understood Dieter's fascination with Horowitz, and felt that another musical door had been opened. I began experimenting with the tonal possibilities that he made sound so simple, and read everything I could on the man. I was not a great admirer of his Beethoven interpretation—I don't feel it was his *Fach*—but I was convinced that his vast tonal range could be incorporated into more traditional Beethoven interpretations.

I regret that I never saw him play live. Of course I have seen the TV broadcasts, but those who were there at the performances speak of the special atmosphere of a Horowitz concert. Though not everything may have been perfect, everybody talks of the hushed expectancy and then the spine-tingling thrill when the magic happened.

It has only happened to me once. About ten years ago, at a Dublin recital, Shura Cherkassky created that magic when he played Rachmaninoff's *Polka* as an encore. The audience held its breath and exploded in rapture afterwards, and I wanted to press the rewind button to experience it all again. But it was gone; only the memory of the magic was left.

It is the memory of that magic that Horowitz has left behind. I can watch the videos and listen to the recordings and wonder and marvel at his genius; but I will always envy those who saw him live on stage at his greatest.

RIGHT: Horowitz listening to a playback after a recording session. He was immensely particular about the quality of his recordings; the closest he ever came to expressing satisfaction with the finished product was "Oh, that's not bad." *(Courtesy BMG Classics)* BELOW: At a wedding in the 1950s: Therese Milstein, Alexander Greiner, Horowitz, Nathan Milstein, and John Steinway. *(Courtesy Steinway and Sons)*

With Oscar Levant, John Steinway, and Alexander Greiner. Levant was friendly with Horowitz in the 1940s. His reputation as a wit obscured his very real attainments as a pianist; in addition to his well-known recordings of Gershwin are numerous others, including Anton Rubinstein's Fourth Concerto. John Steinway, with his impeccable manners and beautiful speech, was the mainstay of the house of Steinway. *(Courtesy Steinway and Sons)*

Horowitz collaborated with the great Greek conductor Dimitri Mitropoulos, who was himself a superlative pianist. His specialty was playing Prokofiev's Third Piano Concerto while conducting the orchestra from the keyboard. *(Photo by Sedge LeBlang, courtesy BMG Classics)*

Horowitz around 1950, a few years before his unexpected retirement. *(Courtesy Steinway and Sons)*

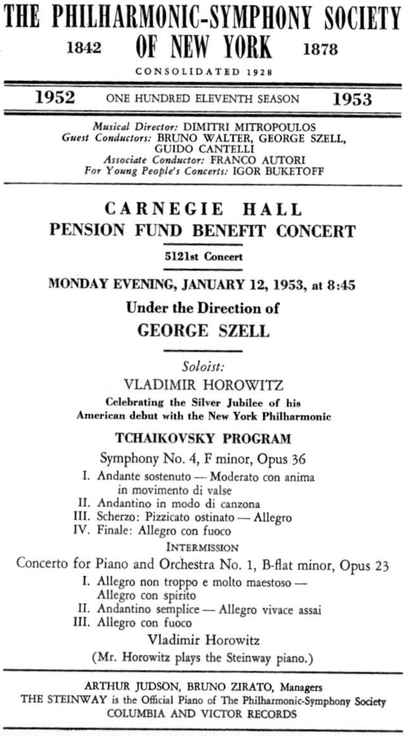

THE PHILHARMONIC-SYMPHONY SOCIETY
1842 OF NEW YORK 1878
CONSOLIDATED 1928

1952 ONE HUNDRED ELEVENTH SEASON 1953

Musical Director: DIMITRI MITROPOULOS
Guest Conductors: BRUNO WALTER, GEORGE SZELL, GUIDO CANTELLI
Associate Conductor: FRANCO AUTORI
For Young People's Concerts: IGOR BUKETOFF

CARNEGIE HALL
PENSION FUND BENEFIT CONCERT
5121st Concert
MONDAY EVENING, JANUARY 12, 1953, at 8:45
Under the Direction of
GEORGE SZELL

Soloist:
VLADIMIR HOROWITZ
Celebrating the Silver Jubilee of his American debut with the New York Philharmonic

TCHAIKOVSKY PROGRAM
Symphony No. 4, F minor, Opus 36
I. Andante sostenuto — Moderato con anima in movimento di valse
II. Andantino in modo di canzona
III. Scherzo: Pizzicato ostinato — Allegro
IV. Finale: Allegro con fuoco

INTERMISSION

Concerto for Piano and Orchestra No. 1, B-flat minor, Opus 23
I. Allegro non troppo e molto maestoso — Allegro con spirito
II. Andantino semplice — Allegro vivace assai
III. Allegro con fuoco
Vladimir Horowitz
(Mr. Horowitz plays the Steinway piano.)

ARTHUR JUDSON, BRUNO ZIRATO, Managers
THE STEINWAY is the Official Piano of The Philharmonic-Symphony Society
COLUMBIA AND VICTOR RECORDS

The program for Horowitz's twenty-fifth anniversary concert. A pirate recording was made of this concert that is completely different from the Toscanini collaborations. Its reckless bravura has never been equaled. *(Courtesy Carnegie Hall)*

Sunday Afternoon, May 9, 1965, at 3:30 o'clock

THE CARNEGIE HALL CORPORATION

presents

Vladimir Horowitz

Pianist

Bach-Busoni Organ Toccata in C major
Prelude
Intermezzo: Adagio
Fugue

Schumann Fantasy in C major, Op. 17
Fantastic and with passion
Moderato, energetic throughout
Lento sostenuto sempre dolce

"Through all the tones that vibrate about Earth's mingled dream, one whispered tone is sounding for ears attent to hear."

FRIEDRICH SCHLEGEL

INTERMISSION

***Scriabin** Sonata No. 9 in One Movement, Op. 68
Poem in F sharp major, Op. 32

Chopin Mazurka in C sharp minor, Op. 30, No. 4
Etude in F major, Op. 10
Ballade in G minor, Op. 23, No. 1

---

*In memory of the composer on the 50th anniversary of his death, April 27th, 1915.

COLUMBIA RECORDS STEINWAY PIANO RCA VICTOR RECORDS

Net Proceeds for the Program Fund of The Carnegie Hall Corporation.

The program for Horowitz's return to public performance, May 9, 1965. Note the respect for Scriabin expressed in the commemoration of his death. During the years of retirement, Horowitz had had time to study in depth the music of the composer for whom he played in 1914 when Horowitz was 11. By 1965, Scriabin was rarely performed. *(Courtesy Carnegie Hall)*

Ticket lines for Horowitz's return concert in May 1965. Had Horowitz performed at Madison Square Garden, there would still have been a vast line for tickets. Judging by the number of people who claim to have attended this concert, Carnegie Hall's seating capacity was temporarily inflated from 2,800 to 10,000. *(Courtesy Steinway and Sons)*

Horowitz on his way into Carnegie Hall, May 9, 1965, accompanied by Schuyler Chapin. *(From the Vladimir and Wanda Toscanini Horowitz Archives in the Music Library of Yale University)*

Horowitz in the 1960s. After his celebrated comeback, Horowitz played only infrequently in the late 1960s. He peaked in 1969 with ten recitals, quit suddenly once again, and did not return until 1974. *(Courtesy Steinway and Sons)*

A rehearsal for Horowitz's first appearance at Lincoln Center's Avery Fisher Hall, in 1979, for the Rachmininoff Third with Zubin Mehta. The concert was nationally televised. *(Courtesy Steinway and Sons)*

Horowitz signing a recording contract with RCA in 1975. *(Courtesy BMG Classics)*

In 1978 Horowitz performed at the White House for President and Mrs. Carter. Horowitz performed again at the White House in 1986, for the Reagans, after the President had conferred the Medal of Freedom upon Horowitz. *(Courtesy Steinway and Sons)*

With Isaac Stern at a party for Horowitz's birthday in 1976. *(Courtesy BMG Classics)*

ABOVE: Horowitz's third and final recording of the Rachmaninoff Third in 1978, for the fiftieth anniversary of his Carnegie Hall debut, the RCA performance with Eugene Ormandy. He recorded it in 1930 with Albert Coates, and in 1949 with Fritz Reiner. *(Courtesy BMG Classics)*

BELOW LEFT AND RIGHT: Horowitz and David Dubal at a Deutsche Grammophon press conference, September 1985. *(Courtesy Shawn Randall)*

Horowitz in the 1970s. *(Photo by Henry John Corra, courtesy Steinway and Sons)*

John Browning writes: "After a recital by Alicia de Larrocha at Avery Fisher Hall, Horowitz, Claudio Arrau, and I found ourselves waiting outside her dressing room to congratulate her. As she came off the elevator she saw us, then went directly in front of Horowitz (whom she had never met), knelt before him, and kissed both his hands. Horowitz beamed and said, 'My dear, you should have played more. I think there is more music in these little hands.' " *(Courtesy John Browning)*

These photographs, by the pianist Mordecai Shehori, were among the last pictures taken of Horowitz. Born October 1, 1903, Horowitz died November 5, 1989. He is buried at the Cimitario Monumentale, Milan, in the Toscanini family tomb. *(Courtesy Mordecai Shehori)*

Harris Goldsmith

A native New Yorker, Harris Goldsmith is a pianist, author, critic, and musicologist. He studied piano with Verna Brown and Robert Goldsand and graduated from the Manhattan School of Music. Since his Town Hall debut in 1965, Goldsmith has performed throughout the United States and Canada. In 1979, and again in 1981–82, he was visiting professor of music at the State University of New York at Binghamton, and has coached chamber music at the Yale Summer School of Music in Norfolk, Connecticut.

Harris Goldsmith's articles on music have appeared in many periodicals. He has recorded music by Beethoven, Brahms, Mozart, Schubert, and Schumann for MHS, RCA Victrola, MMO, AAG, Crossroads, Music and Arts, and Stradivari Classics.

Horowitz was an artist surrounded by paradox. He became a U.S. citizen in 1942, and his adopted country regarded him as a national treasure. Even the great pianist's detractors tended to equate the sensationalism that often surrounded him with a quintessentially American preference for the bigger and better. Yet in both his art and his persona, Horowitz remained, to his dying day, the very soul of old Russia. Consider his blood-stirring performances of Rachmaninoff's Third and Tchaikovsky's First concertos; his mystical, indeed possessed, Scriabin; his molten Prokofiev.

But consider, too, his love for refinement and his self-proclaimed (and usually unsuccessful) quest for "simplicity"; his incomparably volatile artistry, and much about the man himself, remained as quintessentially true to imperial Russia as the many artifacts of Peter Carl Fabergé. Fabergé (1846–1920), a jeweler and goldsmith, lovingly crafted cigarette cases, picture frames, parasol handles, and miniature animals and flowers for two czars, Alexander III and Nicholas II, as well as for the delectation of other members of the Russian nobility. Above all, he became deservedly famous for almost indecently decorous Easter eggs that are still unique more than sixty years after the fact. Let me suggest that many of Horowitz's performances are like Fabergé eggs set to music!

The analogy is not all that far-fetched; the two art forms (Fabergé's and Horowitz's) share many stylistic features: both display endless patience, immense pride, and lapidary skill; they share a penchant for riotous color and intricate ornamentation; they share, too, a certain temperamental unpredictability. And for some, such refinement and opulence verges on garish decadence.

Many consider Horowitz the greatest pianist of the twentieth century—indeed, perhaps of all time. The mere announcement that he was planning to give a public concert created a virtual stampede at the box office, and even now, more than three years after his passing, the release of yet another of his recordings creates a Pavlovian response even among professional musicians. Conversely, the article (by Michael Steinberg) in the *New Grove Dictionary of Music and Musicians*) contains the following bit of opinionation:

> In music that has characteristics perfectly complemented by those of his playing—Moszkowski, Liszt, Prokofiev, for example—he is brilliantly effective, and he has illumined some interesting music like Schumann's *Kreisleriana* and much of Scriabin. Horowitz illustrates that an astounding instrumental gift carries no guarantee about musical understanding.

What Horowitz *does* guarantee is unpredictability. It is his infinite ability to surprise that sets him apart from so many other artists. And it is precisely this quality that makes him such a complex and difficult figure to write about. His quasi-improvisatory interpretative approach frequently means that even the same composition will vary drastically from one Horowitz performance to another. True, many prize this inconsistency—but it *does* sometimes make it difficult to get a handle on his musical approach.

But, then, there are many parts to the Horowitz whole, and if he is a great musician (a moot point for some), I think there will be little argument about his being a conjurer, a magician. Sleight-of-hand is part and parcel of every magician's arsenal, and so it was with this wizard virtuoso. It was, in a way, imperative to his modus operandi that his audience somehow came away from his concerts feeling awed and also tricked. And often enough, they were indeed tricked: as with so many of the "Romantic"—make that *necromantic*—pianists, there were, in most of his performances, countless adjustments and redistributions; little, and sometimes considerable, tinkerings with the printed text; inner voicings brought to the fore by way of left hand anticipation; and so forth. This does not explain the hold that Horowitz had over his many believers—for similar liberties can be found in the playing of other artists: the volatile, but far less magnetic, Shura Cherkassky, and even such "antivirtuosi" as Horszowski, Kempff, and Edwin Fischer.

No, it was something more than that. Horowitz's mastery of his craft—the powers he exercised over his instrument, over the managerial and commercial aspects of concertizing, and over just about all who came under his spell—was truly diabolic. Both as a vivid onstage presence and on a one-to-one basis, many had the feeling that a supernatural force was holding sway. There was something terribly manipulative about Horowitz—in the way he twisted and colored musical compositions to his personalized whim of the moment; and also in the way he seemingly mesmerized our powers of judgment. A distinguished musician, one of the world's outstanding young pianists, told me of his once having listened to Horowitz's recording of Mozart's Concerto K. 488 in the Maestro's presence. He was convinced that it was splendid, his resistance completely broken down. Only later, at home and without the great man at his side, did a second hearing help him regain the use of his critical "antibodies." And I think that there was a bit of the *Histoire du Soldat* legend about the way this devil Volodya attracted young footsoldiers (fingersoldiers?) to gather 'round his flickering flame, and then charmed and enticed them with his remarkable resources, and even on occasion (but shh! don't tell anyone) hinted that he might even show them his wonderful book filled with all sorts of supernatural things (e.g., on page 13, how to play octaves so quickly that one has finished playing them before one has even started). I won't say that all the Horowitz "pupils" and imitators relinquished their souls (or even their Saint Ravinsky medals), but some of them *did* end up with muscle cramps and severe psychological problems.

There has always been for me a lifelong fascination—and, yes, a love-hate relationship—with Horowitz and his music. It began early;

I recall his recording of some Chopin mazurkas circa 1950 and, in particular, how his overdrawn contrasts in Op. 30, No. 3 (in D flat) made me cringe in anticipation of the imminent risoluto outburst and its aftermath. It was only after hearing Arthur Rubinstein's far more emotionally balanced account of the same piece, and studying it myself, that I realized that fortissimo and pianissimo alternations didn't, ipso facto, mean nuclear warfare. I also remember with extreme distaste Horowitz's mincing little caprices in Chopin's B minor Scherzo and F minor Ballade, his hypertense voice-leading and sentimentality in an early recording of Beethoven's "Waldstein," and an utterly tortured and pretentious Schubert B-flat major Sonata D. 960 (*pace* Harold C. Schonberg, I don't agree that only the later, 1986, Horowitz recording of that masterpiece is "labored and artificial"; that description seems equally applicable to the 1953 Carnegie Hall concert recording).

On the other hand, I adore the steady, architectonic Horowitz recording of the Chopin E major Scherzo (1936); both accounts he left us of Haydn's last sonata (1932 and 1951); Czerny's *Ricordanza* Variations (1944), and even a goodly portion of his Classical and Romantic fare (such as the provocative Beethoven *Pathétique* (1963), his surprisingly straightforward, unmannered "Emperor" Concerto (1952) and Mozart Sonata K. 332 (1947). Indeed, I find almost all of his explorations into Clementi's oeuvre an enlightening and delectable bequest, and his amazing Scarlatti is simply a source of perennial wonderment—a bubbling delight. And yes, I think well of his 1940 recording of the Brahms Second Concerto (though I like his 1948 concert broadcast even better). Interestingly, Horowitz himself disparaged both his interpretation and the music itself toward the end of his life, also whining that Toscanini had coerced him into doing it *his* way. The truth is, however, that the Horowitz of the 1930s, 1940s, and 1950s was a far less unbalanced musician than his much older self, and that it was unquestionably Toscanini (and Rachmaninoff, too) whose musical maturity and rectitude supplied him with a sense of stylistic morality, a morality with which the shrewd and sensible pianist readily complied. (The unequalled Tchaikovsky, Prokofiev, and Scriabin, the Rachmaninoff surpassed only by the composer himself, have already been cited.)

Another great Horowitz paradox was the fact that, in his technique, this paragon of pianistic perfection contradicted the strictures of all the instrument's recognized pedagogues. His flat finger position, upward-curled pinky, and seemingly tense arm position confounded all textbook folderol about "correct" piano playing. Horowitz was a magnificent colorist, yet he used the pedal sparingly. "Because my playing is very clear," he once explained, "when I make a mistake, you hear it." His performances, even on recordings, were not always note-perfect, but there can be no denying that his pianism—the dazzlingly even scales, the breathtaking clarity of articulation, the incredibly electrifying energy—established new technical standards that none of his successors could ignore (and that few have equalled, let along surpassed).

Also paradoxical was this most sensational showman who, particularly in his fire-eating prime, was one of the *least* sensational artists to watch. Utterly unlike his good friend Rudolf Serkin, Horowitz sat quietly at his instrument, his overpowering feats achieved with a total economy of movement. In that respect he resembled Jascha Heifetz, another virtuoso champ. But whereas Heifetz became increasingly laconic and remote with age, Horowitz in his later years revealed an almost child-like glee in delighting his audiences—a characteristic that made his infrequent concert performances as much media events as they were sublime musical experiences.

There was also something contradictory (thus, again, paradoxical) in the way Horowitz viewed himself: on the one hand, he was a self-proclaimed devotee of "simplicity," on the other, he openly acknowledged altogether fustian musical ideals—an admiration for the bel canto extravagances of the baritone Mattia Battistini, in particular. Those who prefer the more direct singing of a Björling or an Aksel Schiøtz (which is to say, true simplicity) are duly forewarned.

I have saved the biggest paradox for last: how strange that the pianist most celebrated for approximating a whole orchestra—that extraordinary transcription of Sousa's *Stars and Stripes Forever*, or the piano reduction of the Ravel orchestration of Mussorgsky's *Pictures at an Exhibition*—should have sounded so *un*-orchestral in the Alla marcia of Beethoven's Sonata Op. 101 and in the second movement of the Schumann Fantasy (influenced by Op. 101). I venture a partial explanation for this seeming anomaly: Horowitz's technique, for all its superhuman brilliance and incisiveness, favors point and attack over mass and line. One suspects, too, that, in music that has the reputation for being "intellectual" (and that certainly applies to Beethoven's Op. 101!), Horowitz may have been responding in a slightly garrulous, insecure, and psychologically nervous manner.

In any event, the man himself is now history: he takes his place in the annals of pianism alongside Liszt and his beloved father-figure, Rachmaninoff. The story of Horowitz's excitement-filled career—his early tours in Russia and Berlin, his New York Philharmonic debut with Sir Thomas Beecham, his unforgettable War Bond concerts with his father-in-law, Toscanini, his various "retirements" and subsequent comebacks—will doubtless gather barnacles as fact petrifies into legend. But his ample legacy of recordings, warts and all, will be invaluable to generations of music lovers intent upon rediscovering truths behind the inevitable myths and falsifications. It is anyone's guess what Vladimir Horowitz's influence will have upon music making in the twenty-first century.

Jon Kimura Parker

Jon Kimura Parker was born in Vancouver, British Columbia. He appeared with the Vancouver Youth Orchestra at the age of five and won the prestigious Leeds International Competition in 1984. In 1985 he was chosen "Performer of the Year" by the Canadian Music Council, and soon after, at André Previn's invitation, he recorded on Telarc the Tchaikovsky Concerto No. 1 and the Prokofiev Third Concerto. In 1988 his first solo disc was released.

At the request of Canadian Prime Minister Brian Mulroney, Parker performed a recital to open officially the new Canadian Embassy in Tokyo. In November 1992 he was one of the judges at the first Helen Honen International Competition in Calgary.

While I was growing up, I constantly listened to Vladimir Horowitz's recordings and marvelled. I wondered if such thundering sonorities and unrivalled octaves were actually performed by a real person.

After Horowitz retired from the concert stage, his name had become a legend. Although he seldom performed, I was hoping that one day I would hear this phenomenon. However, it was my father who heard Horowitz live before I did. It was in the mid-seventies at the Seattle Opera House. I will never forget his description of that concert. He told me the hall was packed and the atmosphere was charged with excitement and anticipation. A special contingent of classical music connoisseurs had flown in from Japan just to hear the maestro. Horowitz sat at the piano almost immobile, like an image graven in stone, and produced an extraordinary range of color. After his encore—a Rachmaninoff etude—the audience exploded in a frenzy of applause. Horowitz deflected the ovation from himself by pointing to the inanimate piano. A consummate showman, it was a brilliant way of eliciting further encores from an already happy audience.

It was not until the early 1980s that I first heard the master. I was twenty years old and studying with Adele Marcus at the Juilliard School in New York. It was announced that Horowitz was to perform, and I camped out overnight at the box office hoping to make certain I would be among the lucky ones to get a seat.

I was ecstatic the day of the recital. As Horowitz stepped out on stage, it was as if the world stood still. Musically, the recital was a revelation. He had arranged the music beautifully, balancing the great sweep of the Rachmaninoff Sonata with a group of exquisite miniatures. I found myself ashamed of my previously condescending attitude toward Clementi when I heard Horowitz's performances of the composer's music.

I particularly remember his rendering of the Liszt Consolation in D-flat. It was so magically attenuated that the playing seemed overheard rather than heard. It was more ravishing than anything in my previous listening experience. I remember a brief moment of humour at the end of the recital when the maestro, with a childlike look of disdain, stared down a patron who had the gall to try to leave before hearing his last encore. Horowitz the legend *was human!* I left the hall deeply moved.

The next time I heard him was in 1986 at the Metropolitan Opera House. He was already eighty-three years old. While other pianists had often lost a great deal of their agility in the eighties, it was clear to me that Horowitz was as fleet as ever, only he had replaced his trademark fortissimi with a new range of subtle dynamics.

Certainly there is no such thing as a single greatest pianist, for each artist brings his or her own specific gifts and insights to the keyboard literature. The golden tone and generosity of spirit of Arthur Rubinstein, the integrity and power of Emil Gilels, and the flawless command and contrapuntal mastery of Glenn Gould were each unique. However, Horowitz, without doubt, possessed the most electrifying, indeed terrifying technical mastery of any pianist in modern times. He brought to piano playing superhuman control of the instrument and the most subtle nuances of musical expression. And the mere presence of Horowitz on a concert stage was spellbinding.

Personally he gave me the highest standards to strive for, even if these be unattainable in my own playing. Musically, Horowitz demonstrated to me the importance of being true to one's own interpretive muse. I would not exchange his occasional bizarre turn of phrase for a more prosaic musical utterance; whatever he did was the honest expression of his own musical persona. I remember Vladimir Horowitz as a pianistic genius who is forever enshrined in the musical history of the twentieth century.

Barbara Nissman

Barbara Nissman was born in Philadelphia, Pennsylvania. In 1971 she began her international career with a tour under the sponsorship of Eugene Ormandy. Subsequently she has appeared with many major conductors such as Muti, Slatkin, and Skrowaczewski. During the 1970s she championed the works of Ginastera and gave the Dutch and English premieres of the Argentine composer's First Piano Concerto; Ginastera dedicated his Third Piano Sonata to her. Included in her discography are two CDs of the complete solo and chamber music of Ginastera.

In 1989 Nissman became the first pianist to perform the complete piano sonatas of Prokofiev, in a series of three recitals at Lincoln Center in New York. Her recordings of Prokofiev's piano music are on Newport Classic in three CDs. Recent releases include a Liszt CD and the Chopin nocturnes and scherzi, as well as recordings as soloist in the five Prokofiev concertos.

I think of Horowitz in the same way as I think of an old and dear friend: years might pass, but when we meet again, the friendship flourishes and continues to provide nourishment and inspiration. And so it has been with the piano playing of Vladimir Horowitz. He has inspired an entire generation of pianists and left us with a great legacy, and we keep returning to listen.

As a young student, I was initially attracted by his sheer virtuosity. It was staggering to hear the *Stars and Stripes* or the *Carmen* transcriptions. All the piano students called him the "piano monster"; we were convinced that there was an extra hand creating all those inner voices and helping with those double thirds. It was inhuman—demonic! We listened to Horowitz with disbelief and then rushed home to practice. His joy for the piano and his love and respect for the instrument were contagious. And that sound of his—some claimed it was the piano; then the day came when we all sat down at his Steinway and realized that the exciting sound was unique to Horowitz. Horowitz had the genius to ravish the piano yet leave it chaste.

He redefined virtuosity for us. For Horowitz, virtuosity was not a dirty word but was used to serve the music. Virtuosity gave him the freedom to go beyond the instrument and allow his imagination to flourish. His virtuosity at the keyboard was responsible for his wide color palette, his vast dynamic range, and the varieties of touch he could achieve. He was master of the pyrotechnical as well as the lyrical. Horowitz's playing attracted many followers, pianists with wonderful techniques who tried to play just like him but unfortunately lacked his imagination, personality, and talent. For these imitators, virtuosity assumed a different meaning and deteriorated into a caricature of the real thing.

He was truly "to the instrument born"—a natural pianist, but that did not mean that he didn't seriously work at it. I remember a conversation we once had about the Tchaikovsky Concerto, which I was about to perform. Horowitz shook his head, and with a worried look on his face said to me, "Oh, those octaves—they are so, so difficult." I had to laugh. Yes, even Horowitz practiced his octaves; even he wrestled with the everyday problems of piano playing, and even he was humbled by the instrument. Yet when we watched that natural mechanism at the keyboard, it was easy to forget that he had done the homework.

To me, Horowitz represents the essence of what it means to be a performer. He is able to capture the excitement of each moment and use every possibility. Nothing is ever thrown away; nothing becomes filler. Every phrase, every note, every crescendo has its special meaning. Yet his attention for detail never dominates nor overloads the structure. Horowitz makes us aware of the uniqueness of that particular moment which will never again be the same. He reminds us why we continue to go to live concerts.

What I find so refreshing is his child-like innocence, combined with his natural virtuosity. It is fun to hear him show off at the keyboard; every time I hear his Schubert-Tausig *Marche militaire,* I have to smile. His enjoyment is obvious. He revels in the sudden accents, the dynamic contrasts; he teases us with agogic accents and flirts and cajoles and delights. He possesses a comedian's sense of timing; the tempi are stretched as far as they can go without interfering with the rhythmic vitality. And it wears well; it seems as if we are hearing the piece always for the first time. It is fresh, exciting, witty, interesting—never mannered, never boring!

Horowitz dared to risk. With every crescendo and ritardando he saw how far he could go, and then proceeded to take the listener right to the edge of the cliff—but always within the boundaries of good taste. Listen to his Scriabin Etude Op. 42, No. 5. It is almost obscene the way he shapes the melody, and the primitive raw energy he produces takes us nearly over the edge. It's addictive; we crave hearing it again and again. Horowitz seems possessed of the demon. Is it Scriabin or Horowitz? I believe Scriabin needs Horowitz to bring him to life. Horowitz might be obscene, but he is never vulgar. The listener can never predict where he will go. You might not agree with his concept, but it is convincing, and it is always his own.

His gift of spontaneity is also captured in his legacy of recordings. Horowitz recorded in the studio as if he were playing a live concert. He had no interest in achieving the note-perfect recording. He criticized the younger pianists for their technical perfection but lack of personality. Horowitz never recorded the same composition the same way twice. These differences are taken to their extreme when we compare his older recordings with his most recent issues. Compare his earlier transcriptions with the Wagner *Liebestod* of his last recordings and see how far Horowitz traveled. Even in his earlier years, the difference between two performances of the Brahms No. 2 with Toscanini in 1940 and in 1948 is staggering; we hear how the conception has gelled in those years in between. Horowitz and Toscanini convince us that their tempi are the "tempi giusti." As Horowitz liked to say, "It is Brahms without his beard"—certainly faster than we are used to, but it works. The Brahms No. 2 of 1948 is one of those rare and great performances when orchestra and piano mesh. The question becomes, Whose conception is it? How much credit should be given to Toscanini or to Horowitz?

My definition of a serious artist is someone who is constantly exploring, rethinking, reevaluating, and growing. Horowitz is such an artist; he seems able to fully utilize his potential and fulfill his responsibility to his unique talent. He plunges in with his child-like sense of wonderment and discovery, unshackled by the limitations of the academic mind-set. He is able to "follow his nose" to wherever it might lead, while at the same time retaining a true passion for the material. I remember the last time we met; we each asked what the other was practicing. Horowitz's eyes lit up when he talked about reworking Liszt's Tarantella. What always emerges from his journey is a personal approach to the music, built upon a solid foundation of extensive research. His nose has led him to explore the complete repertoire of Scarlatti, Clementi, Fauré, Haydn, Scriabin, among others.

His Scarlatti recording on CBS is a wonderful by-product of this curiosity. Horowitz studied all of Scarlatti's sonatas for this project. He returned to the original manuscripts, researched the period, and even consulted with the expert Ralph Kirkpatrick. As a result, Horowitz transformed these pieces from sonatas for harpsichord into virtuosic piano gems. He did not set out to imitate the harpsichord, but by using the modern keyboard was able to explore a wider color palette. He imitated orchestral colors and exploited a wide range of rhythmic and percussive effects, heightening the Spanish character of the sonatas. There is a vitality and ongoing energy here. Contrasts abound and serve to underline the form and structure of these works. Creating a richer texture, he still retained the clarity of every voice. He respected the stylistic limitations of the period, but was not inhibited by them. These performances represent virtuosity at its best.

What comes through in everything Horowitz played is his passion—his passion for both the music and the instrument. And this passion is contagious: when Horowitz plays, he makes us listen. He is able to reach out and touch the heart. That is why audiences keep returning to concerts; that is why pianists keep practicing. But what exactly is the Horowitz legacy? It goes far beyond his wealth of recordings and performances; it is much more than his dynamic pianism and virtuosity. He represents something unique in our society: the freedom of soul and the strength and belief in one's talent to proceed one's own way—wherever that might lead. He possessed a fearlessness; he wasn't frightened of venturing into areas unknown and exploring.

Balzac once wrote that "time is the sole capital of people whose future depends on their talent." Horowitz understood that. He led the charmed life—a life lived totally within his music. He has left us all a great legacy. But for me, Horowitz is one of those rare examples of a natural talent who was able to work and realize his full potential. And that is my inspiration!

Mordecai Shehori

Israeli-born Mordecai Shehori studied in Tel Aviv with Mindru Katz. At 9 he gave his first public performance. Later he received first prize in the Beethoven Competition and received the American Israel Cultural Foundation Award. In New York, he studied with Claude Frank at the Mannes College of Music and graduated from the Juilliard School.

Shehori made his New York debut after winning the 1974 Jeunesses Musicales Competition. He concertizes in the United States, Canada, and Europe and has performed at various music festivals and at the White House. He has given seventeen different recital programs in New York in as many years. He records for Connoisseur Society; his releases include music by Beethoven, Chopin, Scarlatti, and Liszt.

It was my first record player—a small box with a measly three-inch speaker. In Israel those days, a radio was rare, a record player a great luxury. I took the vinyl out with great care and put it on. The next moment changed my life forever. It was an EMI 1932 recording of the Liszt Sonata in B minor played by Vladimir Horowitz. I was in a state of shock, not because of musical inexperience—for I had been studying piano from the age of five, had given recitals, and had already heard many great performers live, including Rubinstein, Michelangeli, Arrau, and Rudolf Serkin—but because I recognized instantly that this was a higher level of music making.

For me, his playing was magnetically seductive. There was a tremendous sense of daring and an imagination that often flirted dangerously at the very edge of the compositions' possibilities. I realized that he was a pianist who held incredible secrets of music making. From that moment on, an irrepressible desire to unlock those secrets led me to an often maniacal quest of learning from him, although the idea of meeting him seemed beyond reality.

In 1970, I came to New York City to continue my piano studies at the Juilliard School. Although Vladimir Horowitz became geographically closer, he remained elusive. As a Horowitz fanatic, I had naturally accumulated all the articles about him as well as taped interviews. I listened to every recording with rapturous attention, and even taped off television his 1978 White House recital in order to study his hand and finger movements frame-by-frame on a film editor.

On the infrequent occasions when his concert was announced, no long lines or freezing nights stopped me from getting a ticket. Each performance was unforgettable. I quickly realized that even his finest recording did not do him justice. The recordings were merely snapshots of something so much larger and complex. It had to be experienced hearing in person.

I met Horowitz's piano before the pianist himself. Once when practicing before a concert, at the Steinway basement, I noticed in a far corner the only piano that was covered. My friend and Steinway head technician Franz Mohr told me in great secrecy that it was Horowitz's piano, and that he had played most of his concerts on it since 1943. Since I am a great believer that dogs as well as pianos adopt the personalities of their owners, I could not resist the temptation to play on it in order to further understand Horowitz's approach to the piano. One night I managed to open that instrument. Touching those keys with their hair-trigger feel and listening to the particulars of the sound—the endless possibilities of tone production, the awesome power of the bass, and the flute-like timbre in the soprano—I was in ecstasy.

In the beginning of February 1987, Thomas Frost, Horowitz's record producer, called me and asked, "What are you doing on Tuesday? Would you like to play the orchestra part of Mozart's A major Piano Concerto (K. 488) with Mr. Horowitz?" I answered, "Is the Pope Catholic?" I immediately went to rewrite the awkward orchestral reduction in order to make it more pianistic. On Tuesday I arrived early at Steinway's basement. Franz Mohr positioned Horowitz's piano and another Steinway side by side. Shortly afterwards, Horowitz entered. He went straight to the piano and warmed up his fingers with the Busoni cadenza for the concerto.

Knowing that most pianists, when rehearsing a concerto, prefer to skip the initial orchestral tutti, I asked him if he would like to hear it from the beginning. "Every note, I want to hear," he answered. I was in Paradise; imagine playing two pianos with Vladimir Horowitz!

Besides the colossal privilege and honor, it presented some very practical application in my quest to decipher his musical mind. When you play with another musician, you often find out subtle features in their playing that are impossible to recognize through passive listening.

We played the complete piece from beginning to end, with very good ensemble. His phrasing was so clear in its direction that following him was child's play. I showed him that I marked my score with some different dynamics than those in print because I had anticipated that he would change them in that particular way. He not only fulfilled each and every one of them, but also commented that "I was sensitive to his musicianship," which made me happy.

On June 24, 1988, I played for several hours on Horowitz's concert piano, but this time legitimately. Thomas Frost asked me to play on the instrument at the Metropolitan Museum of Art, in the Grace Rainey Rogers Auditorium. Horowitz wanted to record in a different space than the RCA recording studio, closer to home. The idea was to use me to spare Horowitz the suffering of countless audio tests. Frost knew that I had spent years studying Horowitz's style and could approximate his sound, and thus the tests could be done without him being there. The test piece was Mozart's Rondo in D major K. 485. I was intoxicated by the sound of his piano, since it was, by far, the most responsive and explosive piano I had ever played on. It gave me everything I could ask for, and responded to my wishes instantly. Since the action was feather-light, it presented a certain risk of losing control. One could easily play wrong notes in a relatively short time unless one's mind and ears were quicker than one's fingers. Certainly this facility was a main feature of Horowitz's pianistic arsenal.

Horowitz was due to arrive at 3 P.M., and I was due to leave the premises at 2:50 P.M. No one was to be at the hall when he arrived. At this point, I have to make another confession. Instead of leaving the hall, I hid, lying under the first-row seats of the balcony. He came and played the entire record repertoire with the music, while explaining to Frost some intricacies of the scores. This was his way of preparing himself for the project: reading it from the music and sharing his enthusiasm and fascination for it with a few chosen people around him. This illustrated another important quality he possessed: the never-diminishing love affair and enchantment with music and the need to communicate its beauty. His amazing success, both artistically and financially, never diminished his commitment for achieving excellence or his maniacal drive to give a memorable performance each and every time.

On November 23, 1988, I was invited again to do the recording test at the Maestro's home. I was excited to see his home and to play on his new Steinway. It was similar to the other piano, but a little tamer and not as capricious. Knowing he was no longer young, he felt that a more stable instrument would be easier to control and also better fitted acoustically for recording at home. I played the rondo many times, imitating his tempos, dynamics, his patented hesitations, pedalling, off-beat accents, and articulations.

A few hours later, the door opened and he walked in. While greeting me, he said: "A very difficult morning." Complaining and laughing, he explained, "You see, the tailor came and measured me for pajamas, and it took him three hours." He went to the piano and played "our" rondo in a totally opposite way, reversing the accents, the dynamics, and the articulations. Apparently he was listening to my playing from the floor above, and, after recognizing his own interpretation, he decided to play a joke on me and on himself at the same time.

On October 24, 1989, exactly at 3:00 P.M., I rang his doorbell on East Ninety-Fourth Street. I was invited to turn pages for him on what turned out to be the sessions for his last recording. By then, I had already discovered much about his unique way of playing the piano, but there were still some puzzles to be solved: What happened in his mind when he saw a musical score for the first time, and was there any kind of order and logic in this intuitive genius mind? Those meetings from October 24 to November 1 supplied the answers. They were also the greatest musical experience of my life. Since he had to repeat several works numerous times during the recording sessions, I was able to observe the subtlety of his phrasing, the virtuosity of his pedalling, the way he listened to himself, and his overwhelmingly creative musical imagination at work.

While discussing and sharing his thoughts, he said, "I have no idea what I am doing. It is all by intuition, but I know when it is wrong." I understood that this was part of his playfulness. He was not merely an intuitive genius. Rather, he prepared a number of possible interpretations and chose one spontaneously for each occasion. His playing during those sessions was miraculous. In Isolde's *Liebestod*, the left-hand octaves in the climax toward the end were so furious and powerful that the room was literally shaking. When he finished, he looked at me to see how I liked it.

I commented, "My God! How do you produce such sound?"

He lifted his left hand and replied, "Eighty-six, you know. Not bad for an old man."

The truth is, no pianist at age twenty could make half the sound. The reason for this was that he had the sound-image first in his musical mind and only later in his hands. All pianists who try to imitate Horowitz are doomed to failure because they merely imitate his unorthodox position at the piano, his musical gestures, or his repertoire. They unfortunately do not possess his mind or his ears.

When Maestro passed away on November 5, an era came to an end. He was considered to be "the last Romantic." However, Horowitz resented this "honorary" title and repeatedly proclaimed that all music was romantic. He was right. He was not the last Romantic; he was the last great pianist to have character, imagination, and unheard-of brilliance. To be at his concerts was to live through a musical adventure, one of joy and revelation.

Michael Ponti

Michael Ponti was born in Germany, but his early studies were in Washington, D.C. Early on, he won prizes in several competitions, and in 1964 he took first prize at the Busoni Competition. In 1972 he made his New York debut at Alice Tully Hall, performing a gargantuan program that included an encore sheet from which the audience could select from a vast array of encores. In the two decades since, Ponti has recorded works by a staggering number of composers, including the complete piano music of Tchaikovsky and music by Alkan, Rachmaninoff, Moscheles, Scriabin, Thalberg, Henselt, and many others. Ponti's career has taken him everywhere. He has played with literally hundreds of conductors in one of the largest concerto repertoires of our time.

I first heard Horowitz play the piano in person at Constitution Hall in Washington, D.C., when I was about nine years old. My father, who took me to concerts—not always my first choice of an activity at that time—had probably told me about the great pianist. In any case, my interest was not too high and, indeed, I don't remember much about the concert except for the encores. The piece that really caught my attention was Horowitz's own arrangement of Sousa's *Stars and Stripes Forever*. Now *that*, I thought, was really something. There was another encore that faded out in a funny sort of way, leaving the audience giggling—*Sparks* by Moszkowski. Those two pieces impressed me the most.

At that time, Horowitz had already been a figure of international celebrity for more than twenty years. His famous and sensational recordings of the First Tchaikovsky Concerto with Toscanini, the Liszt Sonata, and Mussorgsky's *Pictures* were already legends. I was just a little too young to appreciate fully what I was witnessing.

Down through the years, I heard him play a good number of times, but I think that the most memorable occasion for me was the night of Eisenhower's inauguration, the twentieth of January, 1953. It was at Constitution Hall again. However, this time, at age fifteen, I was fully aware of the extraordinary nature of what I was hearing and seeing. Every piece held my attention. I immediately fell under his spell.

By the time I became serious, or better yet fanatical about playing the piano (at age seventeen), Horowitz was the ideal toward which I set my sights. I wanted to be able to reproduce the excitement he generated and the brilliance and the sonority that he was able to get from his piano. Not that I wanted to copy him—but it was that kind of piano playing that I aimed for as a goal. There was a special excitement in hearing him live: the way he entered, the way he sat at the piano, the expectancy and the fulfillment. It was unique, and the mystique of it was fed further by the infrequency of his performances. He disappeared from the public for as long as twelve years at a time. I also had twenty years of experience behind me when I next heard him, and though I never failed to be enormously impressed, it was never again so overwhelming as that twentieth of January, 1953.

Earlier, I had been more attracted to the more obviously appealing works, such as the Chopin A-flat major Polonaise and the Liszt and Rachmaninoff pieces. On this occasion, the Chopin B minor Scherzo was electrifying, and the pyrotechnics of the Liszt Second Hungarian Rhapsody were mind-boggling as usual. Could it be that, having reached the ripe old age of fifteen, I found this recital different? Through him, I realized for the first time in my life that Schubert and Scriabin were great composers. The Schubert B-flat major Sonata was a revelation, and Horowitz's playing of the Scriabin Ninth Sonata was still a vital living memory when I was eventually asked to record Scriabin's complete works.

That Schubert of 1953 remains one of my favorite recordings, the *Danse macabre* of Saint-Saëns is another, and my favorite of his Beethoven recordings is the Op. 101. Of the orchestral recordings, one often hears the Rachmaninoff Third Concerto from the 1930s with Albert Coates, and the second one with Reiner is often raved about, but my own favorite is his third recording with Ormandy. I have myself performed the Rachmaninoff Third well over a hundred times, and I can still enjoy listening to the Horowitz-Ormandy performance of it. I can't say that about many other pianists' recordings of works I play that much.

I am never bored listening to Horowitz recordings, though I am not sure that I am as fond of Clementi as he seemed to be. Now we are fortunate in having the videos, most of them made when he was in his eighties. A lot has been written about Horowitz recently, some of it less than kind. It is, I suppose, possible to criticize him and to point out perceived shortcomings. I'm sure that many will honestly do so. I will not. I will remember the aura of light around him—the electricity in the air—the thunderclap when he appeared—the excitement of being in the same room with him—the wire stretched taut—the existence on the brink—the marvelous, thrilling pianist—and the music, the rarefied level of the music making.

Charles Rosen

Charles Rosen was born in New York City and made his New York debut in 1951. As a pianist he regularly tours the United States and Europe. He has made dozens of recordings; his recording of piano works by Boulez won the Edison Prize in Holland, and he received a Grammy Award nomination for his recording of Beethoven's Diabelli Variations.

A distinguished scholar, Rosen has received honorary doctorates from Cambridge University, the Peabody Institute of the Johns Hopkins University, and Trinity College, Dublin. In 1980, he was appointed Charles Eliot Norton Professor of Poetry at Harvard University. He is also Professor of Music and Social Thought at the University of Chicago. His first book, The Classical Style: Haydn, Mozart, Beethoven, *won the National Book Award in 1972.*

In the 1940s Horowitz was already a legendary figure. People literally stood on their seats to watch him play the octaves in the Tchaikovsky Concerto. He was, however, too idiosyncratic a player to have a really profound influence. In fact, the greatest influence on pianists of my generation was not a pianist at all but Horowitz's father-in-law, Toscanini. There were very few young pianists who successfully imitated Horowitz's style of playing, in which both the rubato and the accentuation took one by surprise; the accents were dramatic, unprepared by what preceded them, and yet most often convincing.

I remember a typical Horowitz program as being shorter in actual playing time than the programs of most other pianists, and also that the playing was inconsistent, ranging within one program from breathtakingly superb to disappointing. Other famous pianists of the time, notably Rudolf Serkin, would also vary wildly from one night to the other. A program played to perfection by Serkin could be repeated a few weeks later sounding as if it was out of control. One Horowitz program began, if I remember correctly, with the D major Toccata and Fugue of Bach-Busoni, not yet warmed up. Horowitz could not deal convincingly with the famous parallel sixths. Then followed Thirty-Two Variations in C minor of Beethoven, a work he often played without doing it justice either musically or even technically. Horowitz's scales were never very even. Then came the Prokofiev Seventh Sonata in a performance of such dramatic power that it made everyone else's pallid; it even made Horowitz's own recording seem cautious. After these three works, none of them very long, there came an intermission, and afterwards only two short groups. A Chopin group of two mazurkas and two etudes (including the F major from Op. 10, which I remember Horowitz finishing with a rather coy pianissimo), and two pieces of Liszt: the *Sonetto 104 del Petrarca* and the Sixth Rhapsody. The Sonnet was incredibly moving and the Rhapsody overwhelmingly brilliant. The famous *Carmen* Fantasy was one of the encores.

Horowitz's manner was distinguished by both its power and its limitations. In a sense, he had two styles: the way he played Scarlatti, and the way he played Scriabin—two composers in which he was never surpassed. He played Prokofiev like Scarlatti, and it was wonderful. He treated Chopin like Scriabin, and it was beautiful but excessively mannered. With composers like Schubert or Mozart who could not be fitted comfortably into these two styles, he was generally at a loss in spite of many beautiful passages, and it is paradoxical that he tended to be academic with these composers when he thought he was being most original.

What was unequalled about his playing was its intensity: he seemed to be playing not only with everything he had but even to be forcing himself beyond his means. A pianist who knew Josef Hofmann told me that Hofmann heard Horowitz play the Chopin Ballade in G minor at the Bohemian Club, and commented, "The technique is wonderful, but it can't last. It's based on nerves." Looking back, this prediction of Horowitz's eventual breakdown (from which he emerged some years later as a very different pianist) was reasonable. That breakdown was implicit in the incredible intensity of the playing at its best, an intensity that made Horowitz literally inimitable.

Horowitz's technique never had the solidity of Backhaus's, or the evenness of control of the widest variety of tone color of Hofmann, or the ease of Lhévinne. But he had something else found in no other pianist: a desperate passion.

Abbey Simon

Abbey Simon, a native of New York City, was educated at the Curtis Institute of Music in Philadelphia. In 1940 he won the Naumburg Award, and he has also been honored with the Elizabeth Sprague Coolidge Prize and the Harriet Cohen Medal. Simon's concert tours span six continents, and he has played with many of the world's finest orchestras. He has recorded the complete Rachmaninoff concertos and the solo piano works of Ravel, and, for Vox, has been recording the complete works of Chopin.

Abbey Simon has been teaching at the Juilliard School since 1977. In addition, he holds the Cullen Chair for Distinguished Professor at the University of Houston.

One cannot write about Vladimir Horowitz without listening—or relistening—to his records, nor can one write about him without comparing him to the present-day scene. It is only then that it is possible to single out the qualities that set him apart from all others. Certainly his fingers were extraordinary and the octaves remarkable, but it all adds up to the one word that everyone looks for when entering the theater—"magic." There is always a moment in a performance when the public is gripped by the intensity of what is taking place on the stage. That was the quality that Horowitz transmitted to the listener in his performances and which, unfortunately, does not seem to exist any longer in the concert halls.

Let us also examine Horowitz as a stylist. Certainly his Scarlatti was without equal. The clarity, the color, the rhythm, the sense of registration really represent the ultimate in performances of music of that period. The sonatas of Haydn, Clementi, and Beethoven that we heard and that have been recorded should satisfy the most demanding scholar of those works. With Schubert, Chopin, and Liszt, we again hear the most remarkable performer, the most astonishing magician of our time. The wondrous sound and his ability to change color in the briefest amount of time were part of this magic.

Those great octaves and fingers were ruled by great ears. Horowitz heard (or pre-heard) every note in a way that no other pianist has been able to do and that present-day pianists seem to be uninterested in doing. One has to listen to some of the rhapsodies of Liszt to appreciate the moments of the most tender poetry. And, of course, let us not forget the wit of his playing, which is so apparent in his Scarlatti and in his transcription of *Stars and Stripes Forever*. These are not just demonstrations of virtuosity; these are aural pictures on the grand scale displayed with the greatest detail.

When we come to the twentieth-century literature, we should not forget that it was Horowitz who popularized for us the music of Scriabin, Prokofiev, and Barber. In fact, Horowitz, who gave the first performance of Prokofiev's Sixth and Seventh sonatas and of Barber's Piano Sonata, performed an important service in encouraging young American pianists (like myself) to introduce contemporary piano music. There was even a period in the forties when it was considered chic and "the thing to do" to have a first performance on a New York recital program of the music of contemporary composers.

In many ways, to us teenagers or those in their early twenties at that time, Horowitz was also a destructive influence in that we were overwhelmed by him. Most tried to imitate him, and none succeeded. It took us a long time to grow up and become ourselves, but when we listen to his records today the awe still remains. What a pity that the magic seems to have been bred out of the pianists of the present day.

Israela Margalit

Israela Margalit grew up in Tel Aviv. She first performed in public at age twelve at a kibbutz. By 15 she had performed the Grieg Concerto with the Haifa Symphony. Following her debut in Munich she has performed on five continents, appearing with leading orchestras.

Margalit has recorded on Telarc, Chandos, and Decca. Among other concertos, she has recorded the Brahms Concerto No. 1 and the Rachmaninoff Concerto No. 2 with the London Symphony. For Koch International she recently released a disc of Grieg's Lyric Pieces. *In addition, Israela Margalit has written and produced programs on musical themes for television. In 1985 her PBS special "The Well-Tempered Bach, with Peter Ustinov" earned her an Emmy nomination. She also wrote "Immortal Beethoven" and "Mozart Mystique." These programs won the National Education Association's Excellence in Broadcasting Award.*

People came back from trips abroad telling wonderful tales, but only three things caught my young imagination: The wide lance of Boulevard Champs-Elysées, where eight cars could roll side by side, the self-service restaurants where you could eat as much food as your heart desired, and the greatest living pianist, who could not perform well in concert until he reached the encores.

Who was that man who so many called the great living pianist? I had always been told that this description was reserved to Arthur Rubinstein! Rubinstein was a frequent visitor to Israel, and his dignity of phrasing, the warmth of his touch, and his straightforward music making became the yardstick by which excellence was measured.

Horowitz, however, never came for a visit, and over the years his image became imprinted in my mind as a mystery, a phenomenon to explore, an experience worthy of a pilgrimage, but when I finally made my way to New York, he had retired from the concert stage. All I had to content myself with were old recordings and the sounds of hundreds of pianists, unsuccessfully trying to emulate the master's style by exaggerating dynamics, accelerating already too fast tempi, over-phrasing, and distorting lines and rhythm.

When Horowitz announced his comeback, my excitement was boundless. At last, the real thing! It was a cool day in Cleveland and people were bundled up as they entered the concert hall, tape recorders bulging under their coats and a sense of anticipation causing them to rush to their seats without the habitual chatter. Horowitz sustained his reputation: engulfed by nervous tension, he could not relax and did not reach his peak until the encores, and even then his playing was far surpassed by his old recordings.

I sneaked out of the hall that was still buzzing with people exchanging enthusiastic remarks, refusing to admit that the king had come to their concert hall half-naked. "Too late," I thought. "I have missed the good days." I put on a recording of a recital that he had played fifteen years earlier. There was no doubt about the magic of his playing: tone quality that was both virile and velvet-like, virtuosity that grabbed you by the throat, bursts of sensuous passion that went through your body like electrical current, modulations that were executed with extreme sense of freedom, a gamut of colors that created a canvas of light and shade. Like a few who preceded him—Rachmaninoff, Rosenthal, Friedman, and Hofmann, he gave a new meaning to the notion of individuality and style. Yet there was a strange inconsistency in his music making: crystal-clear Scarlatti but mannered Mozart, superbly crafted Chopin but tasteless Schubert, and then unbelievable Liszt and breathtaking Scriabin. It crossed my mind that he would not have made it through the preliminaries of most piano competitions, with their insistence on an overall stylistic mastery, but did he make it in the grand competition for the hearts of audiences everywhere!

The next time that I saw Horowitz, he was playing at the White House in celebration of his fifty years on the concert stage. The television cameras focused on his hands with their extraordinary long fingers and the end-joints that seemed to have a life of their own. His hands were trembling and his face was contorted with an obvious effort to take hold of himself. Fifty years on stage and he was still scared! I felt sorry for Horowitz, who gave so much joy to others while inflicting such torture upon himself.

I did not expect to hear him in a live concert again, but when a few years ago he scheduled another comeback. I took my son along and eagerly headed towards Carnegie Hall. A smiling man walked on stage, winked at the audience, and played a relaxed, spirited, magnificent recital.

Was it old age? The liberating effect of a biography that told all? Perhaps he had discovered beta-blockers? Gone were the nerves, the tension, the fear. Here was a great pianist who had made peace with his instrument and ended his career, at last enjoying what he did like nobody else.

Louis Lortie

Born in Quebec, Louis Lortie made his debut with the Orchestre Symphonique de Montréal at age thirteen. After a Toronto debut in 1978, he became guest soloist with the Toronto Symphony during its tour of Japan and the People's Republic of China. In 1984 he was a prize winner in the Leeds Competition and winner of the Busoni Competition.

In 1991 Mr. Lortie's Chandos disc of Beethoven's "Eroica" Variations received the Edison Award. For that label he has also recorded the complete Chopin etudes and the complete piano works of Ravel. Recently he recorded Gershwin's Rhapsody in Blue *with Charles Dutoit, and Schumann's Concerto and Chopin's Second Concerto with Neeme Jarvi. He has completed several compact discs of the Beethoven Sonatas in a project that will include all thirty-two. In 1992 Louis Lortie was named an officer of the Order of Canada.*

Every human being who has ever been a more or less active participant in any form of interpretive art knows that the interaction between interior vision and physical will is always somewhat limited. The artist constantly strives to surpass that limit. The first step is to listen, to understand better, then to order the body that is our reluctant slave to respond to the imagination. Through the changes that it does succeed in making, the body in turn feeds the imagination, which is then encouraged to send it new stimuli.

This perpetual interdependence causes the profound suffering that marks the performing artist. Occasionally an individual actually manages to perfect this dialectical interplay beyond all expectation. I believe this is the reason the Horowitz phenomenon fascinates and affects us so much.

It certainly must not have been easy to be that mutant, that pariah, that *Homo horowitzus* with no one to follow him. His was a unique experience, with problems that could bring only disorder and confusion, as seen in the lengthy cessation of performance from 1953 to 1965. From this would arise a resurrected being who was henceforth less a prisoner of his public, which tended to "reduce" him only to his virtuosity, and more a slave to his idiosyncrasies, which would carry his imaginative fancies to much higher poetic flights.

Master of his career's progress from then on, he would play when and where he pleased, always using the instrument he preferred. He could finally indulge in the introspective voyage that would take him to the peaks and valleys of Schubert and Mozart. A new richness could now emerge in a man who used to "re-paraphrase" Liszt and re-embellish Mozart in the purest of styles. At a time when so many virtuosi were allowing their own incandescence to reduce them to ashes, Horowitz was able to make extraordinary changes in himself, astonishing the world with an unceasingly thorough musicality and an ability to reunite discreetly the octogenarian with the sparks of his own electrifying youth.

The development of Horowitz's sound will remain legendary because of the strange way it coincided with developments in technology, the artist's maturity reaching its peak when stereophonic and digital sound were developed. Even his death is legendary, since it has occurred at the time when the two powers to which he gave so much of his life's blood are laying down their arms and hopefully moving toward a greater understanding of humanity.

Jerome Rose

Jerome Rose was 15 when he made his debut with the San Francisco Symphony. He studied with Leonard Shure and Rudolf Serkin at Marlboro and soon after was a Fulbright scholar in Vienna. In 1961 he won the Busoni Competition at Bolzano, Italy.

For his series of Liszt recordings, Rose was awarded the Grand Prix du Disque, and the Ministry of Culture of Hungary conferred on him the Franz Liszt Medal. Rose serves as artist-in-residence at the College of Musical Arts, Bowling Green State University, Ohio. He has organized several festivals and served as artistic director of the International Festival of the Romantics in London. Recently he recorded for Newport Classic the complete ballades and sonatas of Chopin, and the Liszt concertos with the Budapest Philharmonic.

In reflecting over the career of Vladimir Horowitz, I have thought what makes this musician through sound, phrasing, and nuance dig so deeply into the ultimate reaches of the human heart, while others, seemingly well equipped, only scratch at the entry way, never to exalt in that transcendental world. How can the rational mind explain the messages that Horowitz could portray and transmit in his art?

Reading his biography, one sees that his education and development are steeped in the Russian tradition of the piano: Anton Rubinstein, Essipova, Blumenfeld, Scriabin, Rachmaninoff, and Hofmann. In his youth he established lifelong friendships with Nathan Milstein and Gregor Piatigorsky. In 1928 he met Rachmaninoff, who raised his standards even higher. They remained close associates for fifteen years until Rachmaninoff's death in 1943. Through his marriage to Wanda Toscanini and as the great conductor's son-in-law, Horowitz was steeped in the operatic and symphonic repertoire. Truly, his musical pedigree was amazing.

Running parallel to Horowitz's musical and pianistic life was an utterly tragic family history. If an artist is the sum total of all that he has experienced and felt, then Horowitz reflected these many different ingredients in his tonal world. Few pianists could communicate on so many levels.

For Horowitz, a concert was no polite activity. I think he felt an almost prophetic role. Music was there for him to transform and create a cathartic effect on the listener. He seemed to demand that his listener participate with him. Often this sense of responsibility was too great for Horowitz himself. But he had incredible tenacity at self-development, and he continued to grow as an artist.

Thank God he was here for all those many years. We were swept along willingly with his hypnotic style of playing, never to be the same. He is now forever of the ages—part of the eternal world of Art.

Walter Hautzig

Born in Vienna, Walter Hautzig studied at the Vienna State Academy, at the Jerusalem Conservatory with Mieczyslaw Munz, at the Curtis Institute, and with Artur Schnabel in New York. Hautzig's career has taken him to more than fifty countries in Europe, North and South America, the Near and Far East, Australia, and New Zealand. He has often appeared with the world's finest orchestras, such as the Berlin Philharmonic, l'Orchestre de la Suisse Romande, the Japan Philharmonic, and the Baltimore Symphony. He is also a regular participant in many prestigious music festivals. In 1979 he was chosen by the State Department to be the first concert artist from the United States to perform in the People's Republic of China. He has recorded for RCA, Vox, Monitor, Turnabout, and the Musical Heritage Society.

When I was a boy in Vienna, the big names among pianists were Backhaus, Schnabel, Rachmaninoff, Cortot, and Brailowsky. They were the ones who played in the biggest halls, the Grosse Konzerthaussaal or the Grosse Musikvereinssaal and were usually sold out. Curiously enough, Rubinstein and Serkin played in the medium-sized Mozartsaal and the great Egon Petri in the even smaller Brahmssaal. I remember seeing one announcement for a Horowitz recital. Probably he gave other concerts which I must have missed. But then the radio started to play his recording of the Third Rachmaninoff Concerto, and suddenly everyone seemed electrified and talked about it. The next news came in the summer of 1938, when the press was already controlled by the Nazis. It was a newspaper report saying, "Horowitz Dead [headline]. The piano Jew Horowitz, to whom Toscanini had sold his daughter, has died in Switzerland." Fortunately, the report was false.

In the early forties, after I had arrived in America, whenever people discussed pianists, it seemed to be Horowitz and all the others. When I started to hear more of his recordings and concerts, I understood why. His playing captured one's attention immediately with its brilliance, clarity, and intensity. Leschetizky described the Russian school of piano playing as full of passion, powerful drama, and extraordinary force. Horowitz's playing combined all of these with an incredible command of the keyboard and an exceptional range of sonority, especially in the louder register.

Others, like Rubinstein, Schnabel, Serkin, and Arrau, had great careers and a big following, but Horowitz seemed to be in a class by himself. Of course, Rachmaninoff was also in a class by himself, a wonderful composer and what an incredible pianist! But, unfortunately, he died in 1943. A great part of the American public did not seem to be aware of some of the other "giants" among pianists, like Moriz Rosenthal and Emil Sauer—both Liszt pupils—and the fabulous Ignaz Friedman. One reason was the fact that the recording industry was in its infancy when they were at the height of their careers. Even the incomparable Josef Hofmann had not recorded very much and, although still playing, was past his prime. The important Russians, like Gilels and Richter, were not yet allowed to play in the West, so we really did not know enough about them. But every new Horowitz recording or concert was an event eagerly awaited and thoroughly discussed.

There were those for whom Horowitz could do no wrong. There were others who, while admiring him in the Russian and Romantic virtuoso repertoire, had reservations about his performances of the Classical composers. I vividly recall his Tchaikovsky and Second Brahms concertos with Toscanini. They were superb. I never heard him play Bach in the original version, only in the transcriptions by Busoni. I thoroughly enjoyed the orchestral fullness of his sound and the transparent clarity of his voicing. The latter quality was also characteristic of his Scarlatti. While some disagreed with his Romantic approach and liberal use of the pedal, I found his interpretations very appealing. When it came to Tchaikovsky, Mussorgsky, Scriabin, Liszt, or Rachmaninoff, the sheer brilliance and power of Horowitz's playing was often overwhelming. But in Chopin or Schumann, I personally found the interpretations of others, like Rubinstein, Moiseiwitsch, or Lipatti, more spontaneous, more colorful, and simply more beautiful, although some Chopin mazurkas were marvelous.

If I may be permitted a very personal digression—our daughter heard both Horowitz and Rachmaninoff when she was nine years old.

When my wife asked her to compare them, she said, "Well, to me, Horowitz seems to play in black and white and Rachmaninoff in full color." An interesting observation, especially from a child. With all due respect to Horowitz's unique position in history, I myself was never greatly convinced by his Mozart, Beethoven, or Schubert. It was all very well played, but at least to my ears, he played "with it," almost toyed with it, and never really immersed himself deeply in the spirit of the music. Of course, there were passages that sparkled. I may have been dazzled by them, but I was not moved as by Schnabel, Serkin, Myra Hess, or Clifford Curzon.

But I also learned from his playing. His free and Romantic approach to all music was a refreshing change from some of the pedantic puritans among pianists, especially of the younger generation. He even dared to make occasional changes in the printed score, a common practice in the past, but often frowned upon today. For instance, he added his own ending to one of his favorite encores, Moszkowski's *Etincelles.* It is delightful, and I gladly admit to doing it now, too. When we read of Liszt's performances, we find many examples of far greater liberties.

Some years ago, I picked up a newspaper while touring out west. In the sports section, a columnist was exploring the question how a certain tennis player would compare to the legendary Bill Tilden. This set my thoughts in motion, and the next time I saw Mieczyslaw Munz, the distinguished Polish pianist and my major teacher, I asked him, "How would you compare Horowitz with your teacher, Busoni?" He thought for a moment, then his face broke into a broad grin and he replied, "What Busoni has forgotten Horowitz will never learn!" This may sound mean. But one must consider that Munz revered Busoni and also couldn't resist turning a witty phrase.

All in all, no one can deny that the meteoric appearance of Horowitz on the pianistic horizon left an indelible imprint on all of us, and music and piano playing are the better for it.

Karl Ulrich Schnabel

Karl Ulrich Schnabel was born in Berlin. His mother was the lieder singer Therese Behr and his father was the pianist Artur Schnabel. His principal teacher was Leonid Kreutzer at the State Academy of Music in Berlin from 1922 to 1926. He made a debut in Berlin in 1926, followed by recitals, broadcasts, chamber music, and appearances with orchestra.

Schnabel has played in eighty-three towns in the British Isles, and in some cities he has performed in as many as fourteen consecutive seasons. In 1948 he played fifty-three concerts in Britain. In 1971 he made his first tour of New Zealand and Australia.

Schnabel has given master-classes from Italy and Scotland to Brazil and Japan, and is the author of a book, Modern Technique of the Pedal. *He has taught at the Dalcroze School of Music in New York, and is on the faculty of the Manhattan School of Music.*

The year was 1925, the country Germany, and the city Berlin, my home town. I was fifteen years old and was just learning Tschaikovsky's B-flat minor Concerto. My father, Artur Schnabel, asked me whether I would like to come with him to a concert in which a new young pianist from Russia was playing "my" piece. We went and there came the tremendous surprise—for the whole audience: great pianism as never experienced before. Not only expression and beautiful virtuosity, but there was something unbelievable, new for the world: considerably faster octave passages than had ever been heard. For everyone present, this was a historic concert. Everyone knew it and was overwhelmed. The young pianist was Vladimir Horowitz.

The next morning, when I was practicing, my father sent someone to the room to tell me, "The difference between your octaves and those of Horowitz is like that between a snail and a greyhound." I was not even hurt because I knew it was the truth.

In the following years, I started giving a large number of piano lessons to prepare students for lessons with my father. Most of my pupils were older than I and played better. But I knew what my father expected and was able to show it to them. Those pupils who had already very swift octaves wanted to know Horowitz's "secret," and it became an obsession of mine to discover it. Through good "connections" I obtained seats nearest to the piano, where I could watch his hands. I did learn much, but nothing was entirely helpful.

Meanwhile, Horowitz had let my father know that he would like to study with him. My father was extremely pleased, and arrangements were made. During all of his life, my father gave all of his lessons in the presence of many of his students. Horowitz wanted to be alone with my father, but my father was unfortunately very stubborn, saying that he *could not* make an exception. In that way, it did not work out; Horowitz played only twice for my father, then it was given up. Both meetings took place while I was away from Germany, which made me very unhappy. For Horowitz, there was probably very little difference, but my father missed a great joy and I missed everything.

Much later, when Leon Fleisher was fourteen years old (he had worked with me since he was 9½), I suddenly had a "flash" about octaves. Without having time to test it, I showed it to Fleisher. He had already very good octaves, but somehow was unable to increase their speed beyond that of other pianists. I recommended to him to try the new idea. In two weeks, he returned and his octaves were sensational. Then I knew I had found the "secret" and would be able to show it to others.

Thomas Schumacher

Thomas Schumacher has sustained a distinguished career as a pianist, appearing throughout the United States, Europe, and Asia. He has played with the National Symphony, Tokyo Philharmonic, Toronto Symphony, and Warsaw Philharmonic. He studied with Robert Goldsand at the Manhattan School of Music, and with Adele Marcus and Beveridge Webster at the Juilliard School.

Schumacher gave the world premiere of David Diamond's Piano Concerto with the New York Philharmonic at Lincoln Center. For the Elan Label he has released a compact disc of sonatas by Scriabin and Prokofiev. He is a recipient of the Maryland Creative and Performing Arts Award.

In addition to maintaining a full performing schedule, Schumacher appears as a lecturer, in master-classes, and as an adjudicator. He is on the music faculty at the University of Maryland, where he is professor of piano.

My initial encounter with Vladimir Horowitz occurred at Len Waters Music Store in Butte, Montana. I was in the fifth grade or thereabouts, and browsing in the record section one day after school. In those days one selected albums off the shelf and "test-heard" them in listening rooms. I spotted a 78-rpm album of Horowitz playing Chopin, and listened to several of the polonaises, among them the famous one in A-flat; I already owned the Rubinstein version (having established with my parents early on that I only wanted record albums as Christmas and birthday presents). I was mesmerized by playing of such high voltage, and of course suddenly preferred it to the slower (and perhaps more nobly eloquent) performance of Rubinstein. I had never imagined the piano creating an ambiance like that, and I became hooked on the Horowitz sound. (I have not heard either of those versions of the polonaise for years, and my perception has since been colored, I am sure, by my hearing Rubinstein several times in live performances of the piece, the impact from which no one escaped.)

So I collected all the Horowitz recordings I could, and when I moved to New York and went to music school every pianist I knew was a Horowitz worshiper. We wallowed not only in the superhuman pyrotechnicism but also in that elusive, magical ability in pacing, which only he seemed to possess and we all tried to imitate in one way or another. Since this was during his first retirement period and none of us had yet heard him live, we knew every note of his recordings and of course set him up as the model to emulate in our own performances, often to the profound disapproval of our teachers. I remember a studio class of Marcus's in which each of us in a discussion described our first steps in learning a new piece. When it came to one of my friends, Miss Marcus said, "And what do *you* do, dear, put on the Horowitz recording? You know, when I was a student we *never* listened to records before learning a new piece." (I heard my friend say under his breath, "When you were a student, I doubt the phonograph had yet been invented.")

Although my perspectives have changed over time and I am perhaps less tolerant of some of the aspects of Horowitz's playing than I used to be, I still react with the white-hot enthusiasm of my youth when I hear his recordings. His Liszt and some Chopin, especially the mazurkas, are still without equal; his Scarlatti is enchanting; the Twenty-fifth Anniversary recital recording of the Scriabin etudes and Ninth Sonata was my first real introduction to that composer, and I still think of that performance when I play that sonata. I remain captivated by most of his Schubert B-flat major Sonata, even though friends and colleagues sometimes try to make me feel guilty for liking it as much as I do.

Concerts in Poland during April and May of 1965 prevented my being at Horowitz's Carnegie Hall return, although several weeks before I had stood overnight in the ticket line along Fifty-Seventh Street with my friends. Jack Romann later sent to me in Warsaw the morning-after front-page piece in the *New York Times* with the note, "Yep, he *really* did it!!" I first heard Horowitz in public in 1966, and vividly recall that I was so ecstatic at finally hearing him live it didn't really matter that I hated some of the things he did to the Mozart A major Sonata. I heard him every time he played in New York during that period, including one season when he was first at Yale in New Haven and then in the same program a few weeks later at Carnegie.

I will always remember my reaction to the two main "forces" on those recitals—the Schumann *Kreisleriana*, and the Rachmaninoff Second Sonata. The Schumann was schizophrenic, violent yet excruciatingly tender; it was the most (and for me appropriately so) tortured performance of the work I had ever heard. Many totally disagreed; Adele Marcus told me at the Carnegie performance that she hated the overt neuroticism he brought to the piece. The Rachmaninoff sonata was a revelation, in that it took someone of Horowitz's wizardry to endow rather weak material with the ambiance of great art; I had the same feeling hearing him upon another occasion do the Liszt *Vallée d'Obermann*. Later performances that were memorable if much less successful include the Beethoven Sonata Op. 101 (not his territory) and the Scriabin Fifth Sonata at the Met (which I had made a trip up from Washington especially to hear, and in which I was surprisingly disappointed. For years I had taken fantasy trips imagining what he would do with that piece, and I returned home unquenched).

Horowitz's 1974 recital at Constitution Hall in Washington has to be among the more unforgettable experiences of my life. A ravishing performance of the Chopin Introduction and Rondo in E-flat major was followed by more Chopin, including the G minor Ballade, which stylized interpretation everybody always admired but nobody ever liked. The program also included the Scriabin *Vers la flamme*. Oh, to have a videotape of Horowitz swooping down on the climax chords of that piece like some gigantic bird-of-prey, his face out of a Goya *capricho*! The impact was unbelievable; I was hoarse for days after screaming *BRAVO!* (I was often hoarse—and hysterical—in those early days after one of his concerts, and I can even recognize my own voice shouting on the recording of his Carnegie Hall performance of the Scriabin Tenth.)

There were subsequently quite a few times when I personally found his interpretations not to my taste, and not just in the Classical composers but in works long considered his personal turf; in fact I stopped making trips to New York to hear him because I found the playing increasingly mannered, and indulgent to the extreme. He was becoming a caricature of himself, parodying those aspects of his playing that were the most personal and controversial. It's heartening to know now that he himself did not like many of these performances for the same reasons (just as it is to learn that Horowitz disliked the TV camera close-ups, revealing some "forbidden" hand positions he would never tolerate from his students). Like his playing or not at that time, however, I couldn't miss the opportunity to hear his 1978 "Golden Jubilee" performance of the Rachmaninoff Third with Eugene Ormandy and the New York Philharmonic. That concert was a "double whammy" for us all—*witnessing* Horowitz sculpt that "sound" and *watching* Ormandy transform for a time the Philharmonic's sonority into that of the Philadelphia.

I have a wish-list for performances/recordings, including more chamber music. Hearing his exquisite performance with Rostropovich of the slow movement of the Rachmaninoff Cello Sonata only whets our appetite for the rest of the piece. I wish we could hear all the other Scriabin sonatas, the big sonatas of Miaskovsky, and Medtner. One reads about his early all-Medtner programs in Russia—how disappointing that he contemplated but abandoned the same later in the seventies. My list would include all of the Prokofiev concertos (imagine him with the cadenza of the first movement of No. 2!). And one wonders what he would have done with Messiaen, Boulez, Stockhausen, and the more avant-garde.

Jerome Lowenthal

Jerome Lowenthal was born in Philadelphia. He studied with William Kapell and at the Juilliard School with Edward Steuermann and worked with Cortot in Paris. Lowenthal has had an extensive performing career, appearing with major orchestras throughout the world. He has performed a great deal of contemporary music and has presented all-Rochberg recitals. He gave the world premiere of Rorem's Piano Concerto (in six movements) and recorded the work. With the London Symphony under Sergiu Comissiona, Lowenthal has recorded the complete works for piano and orchestra by Tchaikovsky.

For over twenty years Lowenthal has taught in the summer at the Music Academy of the West in Santa Barbara. He is frequently on the juries of international competitions.

An anecdote from the early 1950s: a Juilliard freshman pianist named Ronit, staring starry-eyed out of a bus window, spots a disconsolate figure on a park bench. She leaps out of the bus, runs up to the man she had recognized, and, seizing both his hands, cries: "You're Horowitz!" If her expression can be described as a radiant C major, his is a dark E-flat minor. He shakes his head from side to side in silent denial. No further words are spoken, but a long look is exchanged. Some weeks or months later, their paths cross on Fifty-Seventh Street, and this time it is he who, leaving two ladies with whom he had been walking, wordlessly takes her hand.

In 1955, when Ronit told me this story, Horowitz seemed already like a figure from the past, and it was being commonly assumed that he would never return to the stage. I thought of the last time I had heard him, in Philadelphia, playing a nervous Brahms E-flat major Rhapsody, a revelatory Schubert B-flat major Sonata, and a dumbfounding Liszt Second Hungarian Rhapsody. I had gone to that concert with my teacher, William Kapell. Three years later, Horowitz's silence seemed oddly congruent with Kapell's forever unacceptable death.

The years went by, not totally Horowitzless. A new electronic Horowitz was created by a fascinating series of records that did not so much reflect memories of concerts as they explored and illuminated unusual repertoire. I myself, during those years, had no opportunity to see Horowitz in the flesh, but I certainly knew a great many people who did. Almost every pianist I knew seemed to be receiving lessons from him. Even the magical Martha Argerich came to America to study with him, although, because of a misunderstanding, she never did get to see him, thus frustrating the expectations of those who, like Nikita Magaloff, imagined the two virtuosi playing octaves at two pianos.

I never heard much of what the great man had to say about music, but his feline remarks about other pianists were much bruited about. A particularly delicious account of Horowitz's conversation with Barenhoim about Rubinstein was later mirrored by Terry McEwen's account of *his* conversation with Rubinstein about Horowitz. The stories were not subject to judicial confirmation, but sometimes their very contradictions seemed to be mutually confirmatory. Pianist A, for example, told me that Horowitz had said there was no reason why A could not play as well as Horowitz, since they both had exactly the same

1. extreme and all-invading differentiation;
2. complexity—indirection—subtlety;
3. lucidity, clarity;
4. elegance, dandyism.

It is the miracle of differentiation that makes Horowitz's passagework so brilliant. Far from being even, his passages are composed of individually faceted jewels, each weighted dynamically and rhythmically so as to cast the greatest possible quantity of harmonic and melodic light. Similarly, in his famous cascades of octaves, not only does each octave differ from its predecessor and successor, but the upper and lower voices of each octave are eloquently individualized. As for the chords, a single Horowitz chord can be instantly recognized by the intensity of orchestral imagination that goes into its voicing. The passion for differentiation required the use of the widest possible palette. Horowitz's fortissimi were famous, but his pianissimi, which could somehow whisper to the top seat in Carnegie Hall, were even more remarkable. How much of his ability to effect those extremes was due to his spectacular physical means? The question is imponderable: at the level of Horowitz's art, technique and vision are one.

The commitment to differentiation cannot be separated from the expression of emotional complexity and indirection. For example: those vertiginous shifts of dynamics, those extreme withdrawals at a high point, those phrases that begin out in the open and then progressively find their way into the wood of mystery and loss, the basses that sigh rather than proclaim, the pedalling that abolishes barlines, and the inner-line orchestration that so often distracts the listener's attention from the tune. On the other hand, subtlety and indirection are not natural partners of lucidity. The conflict seems to engender for Horowitz difficulties that lesser pianists do not have to overcome, and there is something heroic about his determination to cast blinding light upon shadow. Sometimes he seems on the verge of self-parody as he engraves subtlety in steel, expressing tenderness with a positively brutal reversal of direction. Nor does his carefree elegance, his wonderfully profound sense of surface, always survive his need for clarity of outline and expression. At moments, charm and delicacy are subverted by an almost irrational explosion of clarifying brilliance.

And that brings me back to the first phrase of the Bach-Busoni Toccata in 1965. I have not heard the record of that concert, and it may well be that those notes sound perfectly normal, particularly if heard on a cosmeticized concert disc. But in the hall they rang with a stridency that was more than startling. As if the fear had been there without my realizing it, I thought, "He's gone insane!" The moment passed, and by the slow movement, the pianist was in perfect control.

What that moment, and others like it in the years that followed, meant to Horowitz one cannot know. For me, trying to understand the phenomenon of Vladimir Horowitz, it suggests that the intensity of his artistic vision and the greatness of his resources required from him a corresponding greatness of concentration to keep from falling into chaos. If I am right, it is no wonder that the man on the park bench shook his head as if to say, "No, I am not Horowitz." We must simply be grateful that the man on the Carnegie Hall stage accepted his destiny.

Rosalyn Tureck

Rosalyn Tureck was born in Chicago. At the Juilliard School she studied with Olga Samaroff, making her Carnegie Hall debut at age twenty-one. Tureck is the recipient of numerous honorary doctoral degrees, including one from Oxford. She has been a visiting professor at numerous universities, including London and Columbia, and is at present professor at Yale. She holds a life fellowship from St. Hilda's College. Her publications include the three-volume Introduction to the Performance of Bach, *published by Oxford University Press.*

Tureck has made the study and performance of Bach her most important work. She is currently making videos and CDs for Video Artists International. Her video debut took place with a recital given at the Teatro Colón in Buenos Aires in 1992.

Yes, I knew Horowitz, I attended his recitals throughout my life and we spent several evenings together. That may surprise many people, for, more likely than not, we are viewed as utterly alien to each other. But I respected his achievement and admired many aspects of his playing. I remember an evening in East Hampton during a period when Horowitz was not performing in public. We spent late into the night, he playing Scriabin sonatas and I listening—and both discussing the music. Later, when he was again active in the public concert halls, I had dinner with him and his wife at his New York home. Again he played for me late into the night. At this time it was the Clementi sonatas that enchanted us both. We discussed the idea of his programming them more frequently, and I urged him to do so.

Horowitz was, of course, the wizard of virtuoso pianism. His style of demonic energy was unique, and no pianists were his match, no matter how great their technical speed and brilliance. Though he emerged from the Russian school of piano playing, his pianistic approach was by no means representative of the original Russian schools of Anton and Nicholas Rubinstein, founders and directors in the late nineteenth and early twentieth centuries of the Petrograd and Moscow conservatories. Horowitz rocketed to a sphere totally his own.

The Russian schools of pianism are well known to me, for my own pianistic and musical foundations were also based on their teaching, in particular, that of Anton Rubinstein. My first and profoundly influential teacher, Sophia Brilliant-Liven, had been a student of Rubinstein and his teaching assistant in Petrograd. When she and her husband escaped to the United States from the Soviet Union and arrived in Chicago, I was nine and a half years old. My family, also being Russian escapees, knew immediately of their arrival. I was one of Mme. Brilliant-Liven's first pupils. What I learned and developed in my formative early years from her, between the ages of nine and a half and thirteen and a half was the original Russian/Rubinstein school of piano playing and standards of musicianship. These emphasized equality of tone and touch, finger technique, and uncompromising musical goals. Horowitz inherited the uncompromisingly high standards of that world.

The speed and clarity of his octaves were legendary. In this area he resembled Alexander Siloti. I heard Siloti play Liszt's *Totentanz* when he was 77 and I was 16. His octaves dazzled me. I have carried that memory throughout my life. Rachmaninoff, the composer of Romantic-virtuoso music par excellence, and a great friend of Horowitz, was more Classical in the programming of his recitals. His performance of Beethoven was an example of the most superb stylistic classicism.

Horowitz was anything but Classical in his tonal, technical, and stylistic art. However, strands of classical purity inherited from the old Russian school were evident in the structural clarity of his performance of Scarlatti and Clementi; added to that was his personal inimitable sparkle. As we all know, that combination was superb by any standard.

To a younger generation, however, he came to represent the demonic virtuoso, the speed king. The skyrocketing glamour of his career and the dazzle of his style hypnotized young people. They elevated these surface characteristics to the level of the ultimate desired goal for a successful performing career. The result was the spread of dazzle for dazzle's sake and of speed and technical prowess as the end to be sought for such a career. Deepening musicianship, maturity of thought, and the allowance for growth—inevitably slow—of aesthetic and spiritual expression lost their radiance. Such long-term demands were left behind in the race for producing the intoxication of the quick thrill that would sweep the audience off its feet.

Fundamentally, this was a misconceived development. I don't believe Horowitz meant to influence others in this way. But, too frequently, disciples tend to pick off and imitate only those features that they apprehend. They, not being the creators of an individual vision or style, or of a new technical approach (as was Horowitz), are apt to slice off the top, so to speak, or only a segment of an art or a style with which they can identify and carve their own way.

I shall never forget Horowitz's performance of the Brahms waltzes long ago at Carnegie Hall. His tone color was so sensitively wrought and so exquisite as to gainsay those who had emphasized his demonic qualities above all others. His imitators do not attain his level. Ultimately, Horowitz's pianism and unique artistry have not been, and undoubtedly never will be, replaced.

Ari Vardi

Israeli pianist Ari Vardi has won the Israel Chopin Competition and has appeared with the Israel Philharmonic, Zubin Mehta conducting. His career expanded to Europe after winning the George Enescu Competition. Vardi studied piano with Paul Baumgartner and composition with Boulez and Stockhausen. In 1992 he made his first tour of Russia.

In 1985 he was awarded the Omanut La'am Prize. He has appeared often on television in his series Master Class. *In 1987 he began teaching at the Hochschule für Musik in Hanover. He is also professor of piano at the Rubin Academy of Tel Aviv University, and has been an adjudicator at such leading competitions as the Tokyo, Munich, Sydney, and Leeds. He is also chairman of the music committee of the Arthur Rubinstein International Competition.*

Rubinstein and Horowitz were my most admired pianists throughout the years of my childhood and youth in Tel Aviv. I knew Rubinstein from close by. I heard him rather frequently at concerts and even occasionally had the privilege of playing for him. He was "one of us," a revered model—but attainable. He made me believe that if I practiced properly, perhaps, one day, I would be able to play as he did.

Though I always kept his records close at hand, Horowitz remained distant, somewhere over the seas. From my first record collection, I listened to Horowitz compulsively in the manner of a child who enjoys self-brainwashing, defenseless before this superpower. However, I never met him nor heard him live. One day, his image became intimately close to me. This happened when I discovered, to my great surprise, that my father-in-law resembled him like two peas in a pod. When I compared old photos, it was difficult to distinguish between the two. Horowitz thus escorted me throughout the years until he became a quasi family member by means of a double.

As a child, my love knew no bounds for anything Horowitz played. Hearing two tones was sufficient to identify him, so distinct were his fingerprint and his electrifying touch. I loved him as lovers are wont to do, "as he is," despite a feeling (or perhaps because of it) that Clementi looked squintingly toward Scriabin and that somehow, in everything he played, there nested a small Scriabinese genie. When I wanted to release that genie from the bottle, I listened to Horowitz's performance of Scriabin in order to trace the origin and the essence of his accent and to allow his supremacy with Scriabin to remain unchallenged.

Before I took pen in hand to write these following lines, I listened again to Scriabin's Sonata No. 3 in F-sharp minor in three superlative performances by Vladimir Sofronitsky, the closest to the source as he was Scriabin's son-in-law; Glenn Gould, the most original of all; and Horowitz, the greatest of them all.

One can hardly imagine a work more tailor-made for Horowitz than this sonata, from its thunderous opening in the bass to the monumental finale. The first movement, Dramatico, grows and rises up, attaining a Gothic architecture. Throughout the movement, which lasts about six minutes, only one approximately six-second idea is actually heard. This obsessive repetition in Horowitz's hands becomes a lesson for the rhythmic shaping of one single motif. The repetition of this motif gathers height and reaches gigantic dimensions, where physical power and greatness of spirit are interwoven. At the close of the movement, Horowitz takes leave without regret, erect and proud. One who departs in such a way is never forgotten.

The second movement, Allegretto, introduces rhythmic energy of a different variety. Here, there is no longer static energy seeking height, but forward motion beginning mysteriously and ending with unbridled trampling. Suddenly there appears a small trio section, a song filled with nostalgia and yearning for the enchanted world of childhood. One begins to ask where one left one's heart, where is his lost happiness? And in all this, where is Scriabin and what is Horowitz? The boundaries have vanished.

In the third movement, Andante, Scriabin and Horowitz introduce the true bel canto. When Horowitz sings, the sounds flow one into the other. Every note is sustained and stretched to the outermost limit and beyond. Contrary to the laws of nature and the limitations of the piano, the sound seems never to die out but to gain in strength and tension. The poetry and the almost indecent seduction of the music are with us.

The sonata concludes with the fourth movement, presto con fuoco. The Third Sonata being twice the length of Scriabin's Second, Fourth, or Fifth, the listener may be fatigued long before it comes to an end. However, it is in this movement that Horowitz draws his mightiest thrust and leaves Sofronitsky and Gould far behind. He demonstrates the force of crescendo, pressing and trampling all boundaries. The listener can do nothing but to yield and surrender himself to the pianist's satanic sorcery, to be swept along and allow him to lead one where he will. Then, exactly when you feel like saying, "No! I cannot go on any more," he begins his final assault for his real finish.

My record is now old and scratchy, but the sounds appear to have a life expectancy that no other pianist has succeeded in breathing into a recording. The secret and the riddle cannot be solved, even if the means can be figured out. The worn record still preserves spontaneity. In fact, it seems to renew itself down through the years.

Much to my regret, Vladimir Horowitz never visited Israel. Some years ago, I took part in an initiative that was finally to bring him to us. We chose him as the recipient of the Wolf Prize (a kind of Israeli "Nobel Prize" that has achieved prestigious standing in the world and carries with it a considerable financial reward) for music. The prize is awarded in the Knesset (Parliament) building in the presence of the president and prime minister of Israel. According to the precise regulations, recipients of the prize must be present at the ceremony. Horowitz was the only one of the many internationally recognized scientists and artists who did not come to Jerusalem and thus also remained the only Jewish musician of world renown who never performed in or visited Israel. There are those that carry with them echoes of dissonance until the last chord.

Yefim Bronfman

Born in Tashkent, Yefim Bronfman emigrated in 1973 at the age of fifteen to Israel, where he studied with Ari Vardi. In the United States he worked with Firkušný, Fleisher, and Rudolf Serkin. He made his New York Philharmonic debut in May 1978, and in 1991 was the recipient of the Avery Fisher Prize. He also played a series of joint recitals with Isaac Stern in Russia. He has performed with many of the leading orchestras and conductors, recently the Chicago Symphony and Daniel Barenboim, the National Symphony with Yuri Temirkanov, the Pittsburgh Symphony with Lorin Maazel, and the Los Angeles Philharmonic with Esa-Pekka Salonen.

Bronfman records exclusively for Sony Classical. Among his latest releases are the Rachmaninoff Concertos Nos. 2 and 3, and Prokofiev's complete piano sonatas and concertos.

I first met the great pianist in 1973. I was only fifteen years old. I was brought to the United States to do some benefits for the American-Israel Cultural Foundation. Growing up in Russia, it was difficult then to obtain recordings of foreign artists in the Soviet Union. At the time, Soviet artists were totally exalted in their validity and importance. Official thought pretended Horowitz's playing represented a type of bourgeois music making that was negative. But at a very early age I found his recording of the Liszt Sonata. I was blown away by the recording. I remember thinking, "Oh my God. This is of another world, another dimension."

It was the pianist Eugene Istomin who suggested that I play for Horowitz at his New York home, and he arranged the meeting. I remember being nervous yet puzzled. How can I so easily go to his house? It was 9:00 P.M. I don't remember if there was one or two pianos in the living room, but I remember a large Japanese screen. Several minutes after we arrived, Horowitz appeared impeccably dressed with a bow tie. I remember this vividly because I had never seen anyone greet me in their own house in a bow tie. Horowitz was very friendly, and he smiled brightly. His wife, Wanda Toscanini, was just as charming, too.

Horowitz began talking to me in Russian, asking me various questions. I was impressed with his Russian as he spoke it beautifully even though he had been away from his homeland for so long. I noticed he spoke to Wanda in French. Since I was only 15, naive and straightforward, I asked him why he spoke to Mrs. Horowitz in French. He replied, "It is our habit. We speak very bad French to each other."

Soon he asked me to play for him. I played the slow movement of Beethoven's Op. 10, No. 3 followed by the E-flat major Paganini-Liszt Etude and the finale of the Prokofiev Seventh Sonata. I suppose I was arrogant to be playing to him his own repertory. I also played some Scarlatti sonatas. I played for Horowitz for forty minutes without interruption. He said he was very impressed. He looked at Istomin and said, "He is very talented." Istomin and Horowitz were very comfortable with each other and Istomin asked Horowitz if he would give me some suggestions. Horowitz went to the piano and told me how to practice and what to practice, and he said to work on the Chopin Etude Op. 10, No. 1 very slowly.

At around 10:00 P.M., Horowitz sat at the piano. I was right next to him. He played for no less than two hours for us. That was obviously the highlight of the evening. I had never heard Horowitz live, and all of the sudden I was experiencing a private concert. There was a pile of music on the piano by Medtner, which he played for us. The way he played it, Medtner sounded like the greatest music ever written. He was unbelievable in his ability to convince the listener that what he played was the greatest piece.

The evening ended at midnight. The last thing he said was, "I hope to see you again and I'd like to give you lessons." I had to return to Israel, and this never happened. But that evening is enshrined in my mind as one of the most important musical experiences of my life.

I was deeply influenced by Horowitz. Perhaps every pianist goes through his Horowitz stages, like violinists go through Heifetz stages. Horowitz had such strong convictions that one begins to sink unknowingly into his ways of doing things. But it is all very dangerous because one cannot imitate greatness. I had to stop being influenced by him. Yet that never stopped me from loving his playing. In fact, my love for his playing has grown. He never ceases to amaze me, but when I listen to his recordings I always have to remind myself that only he can do this, or get away with that. For instance, many accents he makes in Schumann would sound mannered and ridiculous if done by others but sound right with Horowitz.

Once when talking to Rudolf Serkin about Horowitz, he told me that Horowitz had played the Beethoven "Hammerklavier" Sonata for him. Serkin, whose performance of this work was celebrated, said that he had never heard such a stunning performance, and that the fugue was electrifying. Yet Horowitz never played it in public.

Horowitz was beyond technique. That is what fascinates me. There are lots of people who play fast octaves and scales. But they do not necessarily say anything musically. Horowitz on the other hand seemed to create a different color for every note. After all, what is technique? It is not just fast and loud; it is pedalling, color, and many other things. However, it is the Horowitz sound that haunts me above all else.

Horowitz was daring. He was not afraid to go deep into the music, where he found inner voices that most pianists would not have the imagination to bring out. In this sense, Horowitz's conceptions could irritate purists. For those interested in easy-going, pretty, or conventional playing, Horowitz may indeed be hateful. His immense talent and volcanic power makes me shudder in such adventurous performances as Schumann's *Kreisleriana* and Sonata in F minor. For me, these gigantic and shocking performances are the true fulfillment of Schumann's dreams.

Ralph Votapek

Born in Milwaukee, Wisconsin, Ralph Votapek began his musical education at age nine. He studied at Northwestern University, and in New York at the Manhattan School of Music with Robert Goldsand and with Rosina Lhévinne at the Juilliard School. In 1959 he captured the Naumburg Award, and came to world attention as the first-prize winner at the first Van Cliburn Competition in 1962. In 1989 he served on the jury of the eighth Van Cliburn Competition.

Votapek has performed extensively throughout the United States as well as in Europe and Russia. In 1992 he made his first Asian appearance, in Seoul, as well as his fifteenth tour of South America. He was a judge at the 1990 Tchaikovsky Competition and is currently artist-in-residence at Michigan State University.

From my first awareness of the classical piano world, the name Vladimir Horowitz had inspired a sense of awe. How many hours I had listened to his recordings of the Rachmaninoff Third Concerto, the Prokofiev Seventh Sonata, and the Barber Sonata, among others. And how I regretted that throughout my formative years, which included a lot of concert-going, Horowitz had retired! At the time, it seemed like a permanent condition.

During the 1962–63 season, just after winning the Van Cliburn Competition, I was living in Milwaukee. Several times that year I made trips to New York for concerts, or to see my manager. On one of those trips, Grace Ward Lankford, the great organizer of the first several Cliburn competitions, arranged for me to play for Mr. Horowitz. She had begged from Fritz Steinway Horowitz's private phone number, with his permission, of course. I was to call him as soon as I arrived in New York, to confirm a specific time for a lesson.

I had protested to Mrs. Lankford that playing for Horowitz was not exactly my idea of fun. Part of awe is fear. I did not want my confidence severely shaken by Horowitz's brusqueness or lack of concrete advice. "I can't give you my technique" was a quote attributed to him that I imagined him saying to me. When I arrived in New York, my fear in calling him grew worse. I procrastinated. Finally, only hours before the departure of my flight out of New York, I telephoned, thinking more of Mrs. Lankford's disappointment than of the opportunity she was affording me. Mr. Horowitz answered in what I thought was an agitated voice, "Who is this?" I identified myself; but before I could assure him that I had gone through the proper channels, he asked me in an even more agitated voice, "How did you get my number?" To my relief, the tiny time slot I had purposely left for the lesson could not fit into his schedule. I left New York a happy man. Naturally, Mrs. Lankford, who was so concerned for my career, was not sympathetic with my youthful decision.

Not many years later, I was living in New York City with my wife and family and was present at Horowitz's second Carnegie Hall recital after his return from retirement, as well as one he gave at Queens College. For many of us young pianists who were doing something in the concert field but had long left our teachers, these recitals were lessons in the best sense. Horowitz charmed us by playing what then was a little-known Haydn sonata, and inspired us to look anew at a relatively neglected composer. His Scarlatti made us non-apologetic to play this composer on the piano, and taught us that clarity, like legato, is an ideal for which one can always strive. In Debussy, he made the piano sound like something other than a piano producing wondrous colors. I remember passages in *L'Isle joyeuse* seeming like beams of light. In Chopin and Liszt, his octaves and double note passages were naturally astounding, but from the recordings I had not realized that their excitement came as a result of their nuance as well as their velocity.

I thought back on the missed opportunity to play for Mr. Horowitz, now feeling more confident as a pianist. Maybe I should not have backed away. Yet his flame was so bright. I felt that, after all, I had learned much from him at a slight distance, without the danger of getting burned.

Michael Habermann

Michael Habermann was born in Paris. He studied composition at Long Island University and later graduated with a D.M.A. from the Peabody Institute. He made a New York debut in 1977 and has performed at many festivals in the United States and Canada. He has contributed articles to various musical journals.

Habermann has a large repertoire and is interested in many diverse styles. He became interested in the intricate styles of the piano music of the late English-Parsee composer Kaikhorsu Sorabji, who for decades forbade the performance of his compositions. This sanction was lifted for Michael Habermann, who has thus far recorded three albums of Sorabji's exotic work. Habermann teaches at the Peabody Institute of the Johns Hopkins University, as well as at Morgan State.

Horowitz's recorded performances of Czerny's *La Ricordanza*, Variations on a Theme by Rode Op. 33 (1944) and of Tchaikovsky's *Dumka Scène rustique russe* Op. 59 (1942) continue to fascinate despite numerous listenings. A fabulous technician he may have been, but it is the intense musicianship and attentiveness to character and inflection of mood that give these renditions enduring value. Contrary to what detractors claim, Horowitz places the needs of musical expression ahead of pyrotechnics.

The opening page of the Czerny opus charms us with its warmth, its leisurely nobility, and elegance of character. The variety in tone and ever-changing balance between the hands avoid hackneyed solutions. Ornamentation, played with exquisite delicacy, delightfully expands or rounds off a phrase. The playing is free, unmetronomic, yet perfectly balanced. Never do recurring patterns ever sound identical. Their location in a phrase, their relationship to the meaning of an idea determines how they will be delivered. The willingness to explore the ever-changing tendencies inherent in the unique combinations of melody, harmony, rhythm, and texture shows Horowitz as a true composer's advocate, willing to spare no effort in order to bring the essence of the music to the listener. Occasional rewriting of some passages illuminates; it is not an act designed to draw attention upon himself. As the piece closes, one is struck by the structural beauty of the whole. In Horowitz's hands the composition is transformed into a homage to Czerny's teacher, Beethoven. The prayer-like reprise recalls similar farewells at the end of sonatas Op. 109 and Op. 111. Placing his interpretative genius into a little-known composition shows him as a true servant of music.

The performance of Tchaikovsky's little-known *Dumka* Op. 59 is equally amazing. An overpoweringly melancholy Russian landscape is evoked with only a few opening chords. One wonders if one has ever heard sadder music. Horowitz's powerful inner continuity of musical thought molds all deviations from the rhythmic and dynamic norm as specified by the written score as contributing elements to a significant musical statement. His attention to musical clues embedded in the texture wrenches us into a fearsome world. Daring pedalling at the end of the first page transforms what could potentially be a monotonous right-hand ostinato into an emotional pleading below which enters a lament suggestive of a solemn brass intonation. The "Con anima" section is played with demonic rhythmic exactitude, and as the excitement builds the threatening tone seems to swell to the verge of explosion. The last page returns us to the mood of desolation and exhaustion. In barely ten pages is contained the emotional impact that would later appear as the *Pathétique* Symphony. Horowitz was like no other pianist in the world.

John Salmon

John Salmon has a multifaceted career. He plays a large classical repertoire, and has performed his own jazz works as well throughout Europe with his jazz trio; he also performs with the jazz quintet Spectrum. Salmon feels that the musical languages of jazz and classical can coexist and enhance each other. Since 1989 he has been on the faculty of the School of Music at the University of North Carolina at Greensboro, where he has organized several music festivals concentrating on the piano literature of various composers. His book The Piano Sonatas of Carl Loewe *has recently been published. Salmon has lectured at many conservatories and colleges.*

I heard Horowitz three times, twice in Texas in the mid-1970s and once in New York in the early 1980s. The times I heard Horowitz in Texas were formative experiences. From 1973 to 1978 I was a student at Texas Christian University in Fort Worth, home of the Van Cliburn Competition and a venue for many famous pianists. But Horowitz did not play in Fort Worth; the first time I heard Horowitz was in Houston. A group of students—two cars' full—drove the six hours from Fort Worth to Houston with the zeal and devotion of a pilgrimage. We were gong to hear a legend, and we felt fortunate that the maestro had picked a place for his recital within driving distance of our home. I was young then, maybe 19 or 20 (which would have made the year about 1974), and I was just learning to swoon to "great art."

The first half of Horowitz's program at that huge Houston theatre consisted of virtuoso works that caused the audience to go wild. I was impressed but I did not go wild. I remember thinking, "This is wonderful playing, but the audience is exaggerated in its unrestrained bravos and long applause. They're doing it because they know it's

Horowitz, because they know they're hearing a legend." But with the opening notes of the second half—Schumann's "Of Strange Lands and People" from *Scenes from Childhood*—my skepticism was totally wiped away. I started to cry. "Now," I thought to myself, "am I also getting caught up in this mass hysteria, or is there something genuinely, deeply moving about this man's performance?" I also gushed involuntarily during *Traumerei.* After the last notes of "The Poet Speaks" had died out, Horowitz left the stage and the house lights went up briefly. I remember looking down the long row at my friends, fellow pilgrims, and noticed their eyes glistening too; quite independently of each other—though we all shared the same artistic Weltanschauung—we had all been caught off guard by this disarmingly simple performance of Schumann.

My second Horowitz recital took place in Dallas a couple of years later. I remember being invited to the concert by a priest close to my artistic circle named Father George. The afternoon—going to hear Horowitz with a priest—again had something of the flavor of a journey to a holy place (though Dallas, a forty-minute drive from Fort Worth, now seems the pinnacle of the crassest kind of commercialism and the most bothersome bourgeois lifestyles). In those days, I spent a good bit of time around Catholics, and read a lot of mystical writings (Thomas Merton, Zen poetry), and the Horowitz concert seemed to me more an encounter with a Maharishi than a musical event. I remember feeling enlightened as much as thrilled. Horowitz opened his program with unfamiliar Clementi.

My third and final time to hear Horowitz was in New York, when I was a student at Juilliard in the early 1980s. My wife, who was also a piano student in those days, had never heard Horowitz. I remember getting up at 2:00 A.M. one night to trudge down to Lincoln Center and get a place in line. I got there about 2:45 A.M. and was number 100 in the already formed line. The ticket office did not open until 10:00 A.M., and before 11:00 A.M. all the tickets were gone.

We were newcomers to New York, freshly enchanted and even overwhelmed with Manhattan's array of cultural offerings. On the particular Sunday afternoon in November that Horowitz was to play at the Metropolitan Opera House, there were several other pianists of note playing in New York, none of whom we had ever heard. One of those pianists was Earl Wild, whose Carnegie Hall recital of transcriptions was to begin at 3:00 P.M. We decided to go to as much of the Wild recital as we could, then dash the six blocks uptown (on foot—certainly not in the slower taxi or subway) to catch the Horowitz show at 4:30 P.M.

Wild's first half ended around 4:00 P.M. It was great, but we had no trouble bounding out of our seats before Wild's first curtain call. We ran down at least twenty-four flights of stairs at Carnegie, dashed out onto West Fifty-Seventh, braved the thick and uncaring traffic, and headed north. We were breathless by the time Chagall's famous murals came into sight. I remember looking at my watch as we headed up Lincoln Plaza. "Five minutes to spare," I announced proudly. As I looked up from my watch, I glanced to the left and saw Murray Perahia also walking hurriedly toward the Met entrance. Only days afterward could I appreciate having spotted another musical luminary, and only years afterward could I appreciate the full significance of this image of Perahia—a great, great artist—running to hear Horowitz. To what other pianist in the world would Perahia have run with the same rushed gait and anticipation?

My fellow Juilliard students said afterward that Horowitz had played badly that day at the Metropolitan Opera House. You certainly could not have told from the audience's vociferous reaction. Though I do recall some banging in the coda of the Chopin G minor Ballade, the audience still went wild. I remember wondering at the tremendous aura and mystique one man could produce. That day, the audience applauded the man as much as the performance.

William Wolfram

William Wolfram made his orchestral debut with the Pittsburgh Symphony under the direction of Leonard Slatkin, and has subsequently appeared with many other major orchestras. As a bronze medal winner at the Tchaikovsky Competition in Moscow, Wolfram was prominently featured in the PBS television documentary on the competition. He has appeared at the 92nd Street Y in New York, the Cliburn Concerts, the Gardener Museum, the Prado Museum, the National Gallery, and many other recital series. He was the silver medalist at both the William Kapell Competition and the Naumburg Competition.

William Wolfram studied with Jacob Lateiner at the Juilliard School. He performs throughout the United States in chamber concerts and recently appeared with Rostropovich at Alice Tully Hall.

When I was young I heard a man named Vladimir Horowitz. He invited me into a private world of intensity and involvement—a world of evocative imagery, charged with musical grandeur.

His interpretations projected music onto the biggest possible canvas, with vivid colors. With the music as landscape, I would walk with him as he would tell of the amazing things that happened in that very place.

As I grew older, people told me that his tales were too vivid, his house too full. Others furnished their houses in a simple fashion, as not to overshadow the architectural design.

I visited those houses, and watched the people as they walked in silence, deferential to their surroundings. I found them to be cold and impersonal, lacking the stamp of personal commitment and human intimacy.

How rich they would have been had they breathed the air of musical vitality.

Horowitz's house was imbued with such vitality. One room was a homage to Liszt, yet another faced the sun in a soft reverie of *Traumerei.* And finally, the garden, where God's beauty was crafted by man . . . the permanent linkage between the Creator and those that pass the flame.

Earl Wild

Earl Wild was born in Pittsburgh, Pennsylvania. His teachers included Egon Petri and Paul Doguereau. In 1939 he became the first American pianist to give a recital on television, and in 1942 Toscanini invited him to perform Gershwin's Rhapsody in Blue. *He has conducted opera and symphonic works, and in 1962 gave the premiere of his Easter Oratorio* Revelations, *commissioned by the American Broadcasting System. Wild's latest composition,* Doo-Dah Variations, *based on Stephen Foster's "Camptown Races," was recently premiered.*

In 1986 Wild gave three recitals of Liszt's music at Carnegie Hall to honor the centenary of the composer's birth. He has received the Liszt Medal and made a documentary film called Wild About Liszt. *In addition, Wild's transcriptions of Rachmaninoff and Gershwin songs are played by many pianists. He has premiered many new works written for him, such as the Creston and Levy piano concertos. His discography is immense, including thirty-one piano concertos and four hundred solo piano pieces, on twenty record labels.*

During his long career Horowitz became a symbol of success for all pianists. Underneath his often eccentric behavior was a personality that dealt with reality in an imperial fashion—something his talent afforded. He disliked indifference in performers, loved all that was personal in musical thought, and succeeded in providing relief from the routine occurrences of our often arid musical scene.

His personal life, along with his unstable health, gave his jealous competitors a wealth of material for their cocktail hour chatter. At the same time, the adverse publicity he received during his bouts with various illnesses created a bond of public sympathy that has not appeared in the music world for many decades. That Horowitz triumphed over these adversities was a manifestation of extreme personal resilience, and it is a lesson to every musician who might be faced with similar circumstances.

My admiration for Horowitz was continually renewed by the musical boundaries he eradicated. From the first time I was privileged to hear him in performance, I was struck by the phenomenal physical electricity that emanated from the piano. His pyrotechnics were complemented by his extreme grace at the keyboard. Young musicians who never heard him in person may be a trifle skeptical about the adulation given him by the musical public. However, it was in the concert hall that Horowitz's spirit took wing, creating that indefinable combination of tone, technique, interpretation, and most important, inspiration.

The nineteenth-century miniatures he frequently programmed, such as Schumann's *Kinderscenen*, were predominantly of a sentimental nature. These were loved by the older people in the audience, who were raised on those tunes. The personal charm and nuance he brought to them indicated his regard for and love of that genre. I have always regarded Horowitz as a kind person, and that attribute was clearly evident in his performances.

Many of the larger solo pieces he recorded, such as sonatas, received rather capricious interpretations. In the concert hall, these same works would be remarkable in their adherence to the composers' wishes, possibly due to his ability to maintain an unswerving focus while performing for live audiences. Why the Horowitz discography contains only a handful of piano concerti is a great puzzle. Perhaps his rare orchestral appearances were due mainly to a dislike for many conductors. He always felt that most of them were not on his wavelength.

When Horowitz gave a bad public performance, critics had to make some of the most difficult decisions: to tell the truth with sympathy, to create a martyr, or just to do an old fashioned axe-job! I have always thought of him as a great artist, one of God's favored creatures. Vladimir Horowitz was the only pianist I ever asked for an autograph.

Ilana Vered

Ilana Vered was born in Israel. At 15 she graduated from the Paris Conservatoire with a first prize. She also studied with Aube Tzerko and at the Juilliard School with Rosina Lhévinne.

Vered has appeared worldwide with many important orchestras. She was the founder of several music festivals, including the SummerFest at Rutgers University and the Ken Boxley Performance Institute at Rutgers. On London/Decca she has released Mozart's Twenty-first and Twenty-third concertos, Schubert's "Wanderer" Fantasia, the Brahms Second Concerto, the Chopin Concerto No. 1, the Tchaikovsky Concerto, and the Rachmaninoff Second Concerto. On the Connoisseur label she has recorded the twenty-four Chopin etudes and the fifteen Moszkowski etudes, and, for the Musical Heritage Society, the five Beethoven concertos.

The other day I was looking through my very old score of the Rachmaninoff Third Concerto for a performance. The first thing I noticed was my own markings. They were all so "à la Horowitz." This struck me because I grew up in Israel, where the only performance I heard of Horowitz was his Rachmaninoff Third on radio. For a long time afterward, I longed to hear those incredible sounds again.

Later, while I was a student at the Conservatoire in Paris, I heard him play Moszkowski's Etude No. 6, and I remember my jaw dropped. I recorded the whole set of the Moszkowski etudes many years later, and because of these etudes I somehow felt related to him. I met him on the street one day in New York and mentioned them. He tossed off, "Oh,yes. Moszkowski. Very nice!"

For those of us who had the ephemeral glory of being compared to Horowitz, that accolade amounted to a bobby trap. A part of me wanted to have his daredevil panache, and so I emulated him. However, I felt ambiguous about this. I felt wrong doing it, but I did it anyway.

Horowitz's pull was irresistible. Once, I heard on the car radio, while driving, a piano sound that spoke to me. I found myself pulling over to listen more intensely, and soon discovered that it was again Horowitz—the sorcerer casting his spell.

As a woman, I have been constantly damned with the praise, "You play like a man!" I must say, a part of Horowitz's genius was that he allowed the side of him that was feminine to flower; he was engaged in his own Florestan/Eusebius dialogue.

Onstage Horowitz often appeared to be private. However, his magical sense of drama and timing never failed to ignite the music. One went on a voyage of surprises, filled with torrents of emotion, sensuality, and lightning. I used to be galvanized by his live performances. At times, he himself seemed astonished by the road he had just travelled.

Roads run forever
under feet forever
falling away
yet, it may happen that you
come to the same place again
stay! You could not do
anything more certain
Here you can wait forever
and rejoice at your arrival

–Samuel Menashe

Fernando Laires

Fernando Laires graduated from the National Conservatory in Lisbon. He studied with Isidor Philipp and Ernest Hutcheson. His performing and teaching career has taken him throughout the world. In 1989 he was appointed permanent guest professor of piano performance at the Shenyang Conservatory in China. He also is a frequent jury member of important piano competitions. He is a cofounder of and president of the American Liszt Society.

As a pianist, Fernando Laires has toured on five continents. In London he was awarded the Beethoven Medal in memory of Artur Schnabel for his performance in cycle of the thirty-two piano sonatas. He was the recipient of the Franz Liszt Centennial Medal, given by the Hungarian government, and he was decorated by the Portuguese government with the rank of Commander of the Order of Prince Henry the Navigator. He has taught at Catholic University and the Peabody Conservatory.

Vladimir Horowitz was a free spirit and a pianistic giant throughout his career, and the unequalled representative of the great Russian school of piano playing. He never departed from his cultural values and traditions and the romantic concept of art as larger than life. His visceral playing and colossal mastery were impelled by uncommon energy and fantasy.

I heard Horowitz in person for the first time in 1948 in Carnegie Hall. I was acquainted with most of his recordings, but hearing him in person was a revelation. What he heard and communicated from behind the printed notes was phenomenal. He contrasted brilliant and intimate works in the same program, which he played with extreme panache and intimate subjectivity, thus heightening the drama of his concerts. His playing did not lie within the central European traditions of performance and interpretation. He embodied, exclusively and without compromises, the great Russian culture he inherited. With a few exceptions, his choice of repertoire was wisely suited to his imagination, and he brought renewed honor and attention to significant works and composers not then in vogue, for example, Clementi and Scriabin.

His love of excesses, for which he was well known, was a logical part of his aesthetics of Romantic values and extravagance. Wonderful as they were, they could shock us in our time, as, for example, in his recording of Liszt's *Vallée d'Obermann*—a work imbued with Liszt's vision of life's variable nuances, too earnest a subject for overt showmanship. But one must acknowledge that audacious performances by creative artists of great stature are essential to the stimulation of concert life.

In order to create the phenomenal acoustics he heard, he paid special attention to the proper technological care of the piano for his concerts. The instrument response had to be rich in tone quality and allow for large, sonorous canvases. Physiologically, his posture, his low hand positions on the keyboard, and his reflexes all made possible his unfathomable skills. Uncanny, too, was his sense for oncoming inaccuracies in performance, which he seemed to camouflage by changing the energy of the attack in the last split second, often to the point of almost total inaudibility.

Fortunately, he succeeded in overcoming the immensely agonizing challenge of having to match his own astonishing standard of performance every time he played. Now that he is gone, his art will meet the fate that befalls all performers after they die. Recordings exclude the magic of human presence, and future judgments of his playing will inevitably suffer and be marred by the impossibility of experiencing the impact of his personality.

Ronald Smith

Ronald Smith was born in London, and was educated in composition and piano at the Royal Academy of Music. During his early career he composed a great deal, including a comedy overture and a violin concerto. However, his debut in 1948 with Sir Henry Wood heralded his concert career. During the following decade he performed over forty concertos, sharing the platform with such legendary conductors as Ansermet, Boult, Sargent, and Steinberg.

It was during the 1960s that Smith's interest in composers he regarded as unjustly neglected led him in particular to the music of Alkan. He has written a study in two volumes entitled Alkan: The Enigma *and* Alkan: The Works. *In addition, he has recorded an enormous amount of Alkan's music for EMI. In the last several years Smith has performed in Russia, the United States, Australia, Canada, and the Far East.*

My first experience of a live Horowitz recital was in 1951. The pianist was already in his late forties. As he had not appeared in Europe since the mid-thirties, no pianist of my generation had seen him play. Yet his position in the pianistic firmament was unassailable; his gramophone records had seen to that. Hardly any aspiring pianist could have escaped the intoxication of Horowitz's matchless fingers, his soaring bel canto, or his devastating octaves.

The atmosphere in London's brand-new Royal Festival Hall was electric. Amidst the buzz of anticipation, one could sense an underlying note of apprehension. Could some last-minute hitch still rob us of this long-awaited chance to see just how it was done? Two minutes to go, a loudspeaker crackled. There was a moment of doubt. Was Horowitz indisposed? Was a substitute already pacing the artist's room? Then came the voice, "I have a special announcement." The audience froze. "Mr. Horowitz would like to open his recital with the National Anthem."

Hardly had we registered our relief than a trim, spry figure emerged, gave a series of febrile bows, and struck up in huge, fat chords a rendition of *God Save the King* worthy of Mussorgsky's "Great Gate." The audience rose to its feet, as is customary for the anthem. At a stroke, Horowitz had proclaimed himself master of the game. By paying his host country an unsuspected compliment he had secured for himself a standing ovation.

The advertised programme started with Busoni's arrangement of Bach's C major organ toccata, the very same opener with which Arthur Rubinstein had so recently wooed his first postwar London audience. In the wake of Rubinstein's high-stepping audacity, Horowitz sounded urbane. It was all wonderfully executed, but despite the languidly sensuous central adagio one could scarcely escape the impression that Horowitz had yet to discover himself in an unfamiliar and somewhat impersonal acoustic. The audience responded encouragingly.

Horowitz adjusted his seat, placed a firm but mobile hand on the keys, and the miracle happened. With sensitive flat fingers, he started to explore the child-like contours of *Kinderscenen*, and any lingering doubt about the Festival Hall acoustic was stilled. In my experience, no other pianist, not even Horowitz himself, has ever coaxed such magic from his instrument. This must sound fanciful, but to my ear, each note seemed to form itself above the instrument and float down from a height. In an attempt to analyze the craft behind the art, I can only add that each individual note took on a life of its own, yet every note was artfully matched within a phrase or formed the perfect foil to its neighbor, and all this was achieved without loss of breadth or the slightest hint of coyness. Without recourse to that famed virtuosity that had become inseparable from his name, Horowitz had triumphed. Now he was to bring out his heavy guns and deploy the full gamut of his artistry.

Prokofiev's Seventh Sonata was no stranger to postwar London audiences. Horowitz's pioneering recording had already spawned a retinue of imitators and has since become a gramophone classic. However, the live performance of 1951 was more impressive. All the familiar ingredients were there: the morbid sensuality, the heady climaxes, the tight nervous rhythms. But there was an added sense of danger. One could almost smell the gunpowder in Prokofiev's war-wracked opening movement, while the uneasy truce that follows took on a kind of sleazy voluptuousness. The famous finale can easily resemble the sullen beat of a piledriver. With Horowitz, one became caught up in a stream of raw, nervous energy, its menace mocked by shafts of wry humor, its every detail etched out with newly minted clarity. As he approached the final bars, his hands became a confused blur in a gigantic climax that seemed to set the entire keyboard aflame.

After such a high-powered display, it must seem churlish to report that the remainder of the programme was less revealing. A popular Chopin assortment flanked by the G minor Ballade and A-flat major Polonaise was beautifully played but not deeply committed. In the ballade one sensed that the emotional expression was applied from without rather than compelled from within, and the polonaise, athletic rather than epic, aroused little more than a cordial reception.

Supreme showman that he was, Horowitz took the initiative. With impeccable timing, he returned to the piano and galvanized his audience into a frenzy with his own outrageous *Carmen* Variations—a feat that had to be seen as well as heard. Like some diabolical cardsharper, he dispensed trick after trick. And there seemed always to be a spare ace up his sleeve. As the pianist left the platform, I had the fleeting impression not of a great artist so much, but of a wizard. Little did I suspect that a generation and more might pass before I would again attend a Horowitz recital.

In May of 1982, after an even longer lapse of over thirty years, the pianist returned to London to give two recitals in the same hall. I attended the second and was hardly surprised to find the hall liberally peppered with musical celebrities like Solti, Brendel, and Jessye Norman. And no wonder—Horowitz had, like Lazarus, risen from the dead to become a living legend. At 77 the pianist's entry had become more measured—a touch, perhaps, of the Grand Seigneur. But he was still wiry; his glance was sharp, his expression artful, as though he were the sole custodian of some highly coveted primeval secret, and might be coaxed to divulge just a little of it.

Much of the recital came across as the playing of an elder statesman, suave, knowing, and self-communing. A dose of Scarlatti sonatas, exquisitely cultivated but a trifle unsettled, provided the springboard for some favorite Chopin. The Fourth Ballade struck me as speculative rather than purposeful, its melancholy outlines refracted through a haze of pedal. Each of the varied moods was elegantly introduced, but they failed to fulfill themselves, and one was left with the impression of a series of anecdotes rather than the unfolding of a sustained narrative. Then came a mazurka, the enchanting A minor from Op. 17, which he recreated in his own image, torturing its subtle harmonies, teasing its contours, and flirting with its delicate tracery. finally, the B minor Scherzo, a Horowitz speciality, generated some of the old fire and verve, and brought the first half to a rousing conclusion.

As I wandered into the foyer, pondering Schnabel's warning that a concert ticket is no insurance policy against disappointment, I was accosted by a dewy-eyed young colleague with, "Wasn't that simply *fabulous*?" followed by an excited lady friend who declared, "I never want to hear another pianist *touch* the keyboard." Clearly, Horowitz had been operating outside my framework of experience; but the second half was yet to come—Liszt: the B minor Ballade and the D-flat major Consolation. At a stroke, all doubt about his ability to play like "Horowitz" evaporated. Every aspect of the pianist's legendary powers came into focus: his acute ear for texture and color, his creative finger-work, and those prodigious octaves, powerful and electrifying as ever. The ballade became an incandescent epic, brooding, heroic, and imperious, while the Consolation was transfigured within a halo of pedal that neither clouded its transparency nor blurred its design. After this brief revelation, Horowitz, tantalizing as ever, went on automatic pilot. Some familiar Rachmaninoff and three encores were unexceptionable.

Older pianists, remembering Horowitz in his prime, left the hall with mixed feelings. Non-pianists were euphoric, younger pianists were euphoric, the press was euphoric. All were impressed by the pianist's quiet, undemonstrative demeanor at the keyboard, but it was his flat-fingered technique, levered from the metacarpals and applied to cantabile and filigree alike, that raised a flutter in the pianistic dovecotes. In contrast to a high-wristed "handstand" posture, Horowitz's "hang-gliding" technique must encourage a flexible wrist and an extended finger contact: vital ingredients of tonal control. I have noted from personal experience that such a position also precludes the necessity of over-shortening the nails and of exposing the quicks.

My admiration for Horowitz the pianist and my ambivalence towards Horowitz the artist were given a further twist as I recently happened on a video of an earlier performance of those same Scarlatti sonatas. The experience was quite different. One could but be fascinated by his spontaneous absorption; by his child-like exploration of every nook and cranny; by his delight in every harmonic inflection—even the enhanced placing of a single note—and most of all, by the self-congratulatory relish with which it was all accomplished. What a complex and paradoxical artist he was—equally capable of bewitching as overwhelming the public, equally liable to bewilder as to dumbfound his rivals.

Performers who are great creative artists are rare. Names like Paganini, Liszt, Rubinstein, Busoni, and Rachmaninoff himself spring to mind. All were seriously creative as well as being outstanding executants. The reputation of others, Heifetz for instance, rests solely on a matchless mastery of their instrument. Such was Horowitz. His place in the firmament of great pianists is assured; his position among the greatest interpreters is less precise. I very much doubt if a future generation will turn for enlightenment to his recordings of sonatas by Mozart, Beethoven, and Schubert. A stylish account by the twenty-eight-year-old pianist of Haydn's last sonata suggests that his subsequent career might have taken a different turn, but the greater introspection of his later years and his increasing absorption in minutiae of color and phrasing sit awkwardly in Classical attire.

I also sense that Horowitz's particular breed of virtuosity was only able to make its full impact in more spectacular music. His chance remark to the conductor Barbirolli that he would like to have rewritten the solo part in Beethoven's "Emperor" Concerto is revealing. For a truer insight into the Viennese classics one must turn to artists less preoccupied with their personal and pianistic reputation, to deeper if less glamorous pianists like Schnabel and Fischer. For me, the reputation of Horowitz is more likely to rest on his early recordings of Scarlatti sonatas, Chopin mazurkas, and dazzling miniatures like the Dohnányi Capriccio. Above all, it is his uncanny identification with the darker side of Liszt and his total involvement in certain major works from the twentieth century that ensure him a permanent place among the outstanding exponents of his time. In sonatas by Scriabin, Prokofiev, and Barber, Horowitz unlocks a Pandora's box of necromantic fantasy, unrelenting motor rhythms and iridescent color. In all these works, the argument is pursued with white-hot intensity and an imperious mastery that must remain the envy and despair of every other pianist.

Daniel Ericourt

Daniel Ericourt was born near Paris and studied at the Paris Conservatoire, where he won first prize in the advanced piano class. He studied with Roger-Ducasse and Nadia Boulanger and soon after won the Diémer Piano Competition, where the jury included Brailowsky and Eduard Risler.

During the war years Ericourt became friends with Claude Debussy. Later he recorded the composer's complete piano works. He has performed in over forty countries and has appeared as soloist with orchestras conducted by Fritz Busch, Jasha Horenstein, Eugene Goossens, Igor Markevich, and Sergiu Celibidache.

Daniel Ericourt has had a long teaching career. He has taught at the Cincinnati Conservatory and the Peabody Conservatory, and for many years was artist-in-residence at the University of North Carolina at Greensboro.

I first heard Horowitz in the early 1920s, when I was still living in Paris. He had come to the French capital with Milstein and Piatagorsky. They were accompanied by their manager, Mr. Merovitch. The three of them were an instant sensation, although I seem to remember that, perhaps, Horowitz had the edge over the two others. Their names were on everybody's lips. They had captured "le tout Paris." Then I heard him again in the United States: first, in Cincinnati, playing the Rachmaninoff Third Concerto under Fritz Reiner, and later in New York and other American cities.

Where is Vladimir Horowitz's place in the pantheon of pianists past and present? Being of the same age, I heard all the virtuosi of our time: Busoni, Paderewski, Pachmann, Josef Hofmann, Josef Lhévinne, Godowsky, Harold Bauer, Backhaus, Cortot, Gieseking, and Arthur Rubinstein. Few, if any, came close to his incredible pianism. As for the keyboard giants of a much earlier period—the likes of Czerny, Liszt, Chopin, Tausig, Thalberg, Anton Rubinstein, Kalkbrenner, Moscheles, Hans von Bülow, Teresa Carreño—I doubt if any amongst them ever attained his technical perfection. Horowitz had it all! Fingers of steel, wrists that produced octaves that lifted you out of your seat, a tone quality that could move you to tears, a rhythm that was electrifying. He was the epitome of the Romantic pianist.

I equate his Romanticism with the great nineteenth-century painter, Eugène Delacroix. Both had a rich and voluptuous palette. Some canvasses of Delacroix are awe-inspiring as was Horowitz at the piano. He had a demoniacal drive. He was monumental. I never ceased to be amazed at his uncanny facility. He seldom seemed to be making an effort. Scales would sparkle, arpeggios and octaves would cascade with terrific speed and clarity. There were times when you thought that he had reached the limit of his power. Yet, he would go on and carry you along with him. By the same token, he could also etch small pieces with the elegance and purity of a drawing by Ingres. His Scarlatti remains unsurpassed. His recording of the Chopin Mazurka in C-sharp minor Op. 30, No. 4 is a true masterpiece. His interpretation of the "Serenade of the Doll" from Debussy's *Children's Corner* is unbelievably beautiful. These, along with the Rachmaninoff Third Concerto, the B minor Liszt Sonata, the Toccata of Prokofiev, and the *Kinderscenen* of Schumann, are some of the pieces in which I remember him as a transcendental artist.

His Chopin interpretations may not have always been one's cup of tea. However, can anybody ever forget the technical wizardry that he displayed in his concert arrangements: *The Stars and Stripes Forever* by Sousa and his Variations on a Theme from *Carmen* by Bizet? He had an almost infallible instinct for style on a grand scale, and an innate gift for communication. His audiences the world over were mesmerized by such extraordinary playing. Whether in Europe or America, his brand of magic never failed. He had many imitators as well as a good many detractors. The latter is easily understandable, since he could often be less than orthodox. I, for one, was rather taken by his unorthodoxy. It was part and parcel of a Horowitz concert. One either accepted it or, yes, you could hate it.

If we go back to the nineteenth-century, we all know that during a performance, Liszt, on the spur of the moment could embellish a Classical piece that he was playing. He wanted to please his audience, who were not always receptive to the austerity of, say, a Beethoven sonata. I read that he first conformed to the original composition and then repeated it in his own style. Who else but someone of this caliber could take such liberties? Horowitz's "peccadillos" seem rather insignificant compared to what Liszt and others were wont to do.

Only two pianistic figures larger than life come to my mind when I think of the impact they have had on the musical life of their generation: Horowitz and, of course, Arthur Rubinstein, who were as different from each other as night and day. The Pole was perhaps more versatile, but he lacked the breadth and panache of the Russian. Their legacy to the art of piano playing will remain with us for years to come.

To end, I would like to quote what the English pianist and conductor Sir Charles Hallé wrote about Liszt when he heard him in Paris in 1836. "For him, there were no difficulties of execution, the most incredible seeming child's play under his fingers. One of the transcendent merits of his playing was the crystal clearness which never failed for a moment in the most complicated and, to anybody else, impossible passages. Such marvels of execution, skill and power, I could never have imagined. He was a giant."

Is not this a true representation, a hundred years later, of the pianist that was Horowitz? To be sure, it is a fitting and final tribute to the memory of two superlative artists.

Samuel Sanders

For over three decades, New York–born pianist Samuel Sanders has collaborated with some of the leading performers of our time. These include Håkon Hagegard, Jessye Norman, Mstislav Rostropovich, Yo-Yo Ma, Itzhak Perlman, Pinchas Zukerman, and many more. As a chamber musician Sanders has performed at the Mostly Mozart Festival, Tanglewood, Ravinia, Spoleto, Madeira, and elsewhere. He has recorded more than three dozen records, two of which won Grammy awards.

Sanders serves on the faculty of the Juilliard School, where he helped organize the degree program for accompanists, and at the Peabody Conservatory, where he inaugurated and heads the ensemble arts degree program. In 1966 Sanders received an honorary award in the Tchaikovsky Competition in Moscow. He has made seven appearances at the White House under five presidents.

Vladimir Horowitz is one of the pianistic giants of this century. I believe that Horowitz's art set the standard for modern day pianism.

One has other favorites, of course: Arthur Rubinstein and his plush sound and expansiveness of line: Rudolf Serkin or Artur Schnabel or Richard Goode with their intense probing of every note and phrase pattern; Daniel Barenboim and his architectural mastery; and so forth. But Horowitz's unique ability to be the most intimate and reflective of artists in certain works and a paragon of demonic virtuosity in others enabled him to both charm and electrify an audience. One is simply transported—sometimes to heaven, other times to . . . who knows where?

Horowitz is both a Romantic and a modern hero. The super high-tech digital equipment, the rock-solid rhythm that generates its own visceral excitement and around which the most elastic rubati could be shaped, the exquisite voicing and attention to inner melodic lines, the pacing and timing of phrases and individual notes, and the sheer daring and risk-taking—these are all part of Horowitz's magic act. Of all pianists performing publicly today, I think the artist who most closely resembles Horowitz in matters of communication and charisma is the great Argentinian Martha Argerich. As with Horowitz, Argerich has that rare ability to draw the listener into another realm, often scary, thoroughly exhilarating.

One can quibble about stylistic matters in Horowitz's performances. For example, his interpretation of Scarlatti sonatas is a far cry from what one considers "correct" Scarlatti. No matter. The minidramas that Horowitz creates from these gems most vividly illuminate their inner beauty. Horowitz creates his own musical truths.

Edmund Battersby

Born in Detroit, Michigan, Edmund Battersby studied with Barbara Holmquest. Later he was a student of Sasha Gorodnitzki at the Juilliard School. His many tours have taken him to Portugal, France, Switzerland, Germany, Africa, and recently to Russia.

Besides performing on the contemporary piano, Battersby has a deep interest in early pianos. He was invited to play at the Smithsonian Institution on an 1854 Erard piano that belonged to Prince Albert and Queen Victoria, and he has recorded works of Schumann and Chopin on an 1825 Graf piano. His recent recordings include Granados's Goyescas *and selected preludes and* Etudes-Tableaux *by Rachmaninoff, on the Koch International label. Battersby has collaborated in a variety of premieres, in works by Crumb, Bolcom, Schwartz, and Messiaen. With the American Chamber Players he has recorded Rochberg's Piano Quintet.*

One often hears of Vladimir Horowitz described as a wizard, demon, or magician—a pianist of extraordinary individuality and genius. His musicianly attributes recede into the background, if they are acknowledged at all. To be sure, Mr. Horowitz is the object of scorn by those who value the spiritual and intellectual in the pianist's art—this in spite of his having championed Scarlatti and Clementi when they were nearly forgotten, or introducing the now-classic Samuel Barber Piano Sonata to the world, or his own reworking of Rachmaninoff's B-flat minor Sonata from the two versions (with the composer's approval). I am beginning to think that pianists and critics of future generations, while still astonished at the pyrotechnics and wizardry of Horowitz, will have a surprising amount of praise for his "musicianly" traits. Distortions and mannerisms that disfigured some recorded performances will doubtless still create a negative impression, but a new generation of informed listeners and musicians might revere him for a whole new set of reasons.

A few years ago, I read an article in *Nineteenth-Century Music* by Edmund M. Frederick entitled "The Romantic Sound in Four Pianos of Chopin's Era." In this article, Frederick remarks that the kind of "unmarked" brilliant staccato that Horowitz employed in the fast-moving bass octaves of Chopin's "Military" or A-flat major Polonaise was exactly how the music would be revealed, whether one played staccato or not on pianos of Chopin's time. Frederick's observation is two-fold. It is a comment on Horowitz's understanding of articulation nowhere described in the score, but also on the curious and unique quality of early pianos, where the character and expression of the music is inevitable just by being set in motion by a player. This may be a difficult concept to grasp without detailed explanation by a true expert. Suffice it to say that the simpler mechanism of early pianos, especially those without metal, helps to produce the intent of the music written for them as naturally as can be. This "instrumental" ability on the piano is akin to bow changes on the violin and their significance in regard to phrasing (incidentally, something nearly lost today in favor of sleekness and speed) or the effects of breathing in singing or on woodwind instruments.

What is amazing about Horowitz is how very much of his playing epitomizes principles that are simply truths when one plays the music of the early, middle, and late nineteenth century on the instruments for which it was composed. Horowitz's seemingly infinite nuances, his separation of voices, fast cut-offs, pedalling and non-pedalling, and exaggeration of register (both in terms of sound and character) are hallmarks of *his* style and form the tenets and discoveries of what is known today as "performance practice" in regard to the piano. Even Horowitz's thundering and dramatic testing of the extent of the modern piano's capabilities resembles a more miniature but exciting drama that takes place on the limits of early pianos. Could it be that Horowitz's aural memory of instruments from the mid-nineteenth century affected him so? It is entirely within the realm of possibility that there were enough "old" (thirty-five to fifty years old) pianos around when Horowitz began to listen and play. Whether it was conscious or unconscious is not important.

I have vivid memories of Horowitz concerts and the controversies surrounding them in the late sixties and into the next decade. One student-colleague of mine was deeply offended by Horowitz's performance of Beethoven's Sonata in A major Op. 101. He complained, "It was all sound effects, something sticking out here and something sticking out there. And can you imagine, at the end of the last movement, those long notes in the bass sounded like bells?" The delineation of voices was too much for that student. Of course, it is much easier on the listener not to have to deal with clearly enunciated voicings all happening at once; that kind of listening demands too much concentration from the listener. The same student went on to say, "Why does he have to make everything sound like an orchestral transcription?" Poor Horowitz—his encompassing and all-embracing techniques got him into trouble.

Did Horowitz really know that the very first keyboard music *was* transcription (*Intavolatura*) and that piano makers added all kinds of gadgets (Janissary music) mostly activated by pedals to make sounds like drums and bassoons (parchment that buzzed more than sounding like a bassoon—which gave one the idea of what kind of sound might have been created on the bassoon in those days). Garish Turkish music was represented too by bells and triangles, until the instrument was capable of interesting player and listener for its own sound and the music played upon it. One thinks of Horowitz's *Stars and Stripes Forever* transcription. Indeed, Horowitz's talent and accomplishments cover four centuries of keyboard lore.

Today one frequently hears praise of a new piano described in this way. "It's marvelous—no register breaks, just one even sound from top to bottom." For those of us who are delighted by the difference in registers or the character that the hollowness between extreme treble and bass strings can create on an early piano, this is faint praise. Homogeneity was not always so prized by many pianists and builders as it is today. The resulting soup can sound as if all the notes were put through a food-processor! But maybe it is a matter of taste. The exciting part about being alive at the end of the twentieth century is just how much there is from which to choose and how really great the classics are, having been put to every test imaginable.

Arthur Loesser, in his incomparable book *Men, Women, and Pianos*, describes a definite shift in taste and dates it at about 1830—when metal found its way into pianos (an American invention)—tying it to politics, economics, and the change in the ruling class. Loesser says:

> The conception of what was desirable in a tone quality had completed its long period of change . . . a clear, well-defined, unambiguous statement of individual tone—such as the earlier eighteenth century had

> liked, was no longer wanted. The yearning was for a vague, mellow tone-cloud, full of ineffable promise and foreboding carrying intimations of infinity. A gulf lies between these two ideals of sound. The former belongs to a philosophy that values logic . . . the latter . . . harboring the mystical suspicion that anything might merge into everything. The former was gratified more by the distinctness—that is, the separateness—of tones; the latter, more by their fusion and their blend.

Arguably the most *questioning* great pianist of our time who openly and heroically wrestled with his uncomfortableness with twentieth-century pianos for eighteenth- and nineteenth-century music was Glenn Gould. Critics and musicians alike were amused and curious about Gould's choice of piano and then his tampering with paper clips and tacks to create a leaner, more austere sound in the Classical repertory. One does wonder why his instinct and genius did not lead him to the instruments of the period (save the harpsichord and organ, both of which he played and recorded on).

Gould's doctoring of modern pianos to create the sound he wanted seems more artificial to me than either going right to the source (early pianos) or dealing with the contemporary instrument in an imaginative way. Horowitz, on his beloved Steinway, proved that this instrument had the coloristic abilities for any music of any century. Listen to Horowitz's Scarlatti, which has a myriad of colors under mezzopiano, coaxed out by this musician-magician as if his finger sensitivity was the result of clavichord playing. Many other performances reveal every line's independence, as Loesser has described.

When the truths and the excesses of the period instrument/performance practice movement are gradually sorted out, what will remain is the fact that transparency and independence of voices is the rule to be cherished from Scarlatti and Mozart through Schumann and Chopin, and that every note and every line has its own context, beauty, character, and relationship. While this can be learned from serious compositional study, or from deep examination of the string quartet or the great choral literature, a pianist must, in the last analysis, return to his own instrument. Horowitz is still the master and guardian of this truth, and for many players of old and new pianos he will have been the most persuasive in confronting and often solving the dilemmas of translating the great classics on the instrument of our time.

Claudette Sorel

Claudette Sorel was born in Paris and studied in the United States with Olga Samaroff, Rudolf Serkin, and Horszowski. At age ten she made a Town Hall debut. She graduated from the Juilliard School and the Curtis Institute, and received from Columbia University a degree cum laude in mathematics. Sorel has taught at Ohio State University and the University of Kansas, and was Distinguished Professor at the State University of New York at Fredonia. She is the author of Compendium of Piano Technique, *which has been translated into Japanese, and* Mind Your Musical Manners. *She has edited three nocturnes of Rachmaninoff and the etudes of Arensky.*

Claudette Sorel has performed over two thousand recitals in her career, and has appeared with two hundred orchestras, including the New York, Philadelphia, Boston, London, and NBC Symphony. She has recorded for RCA Victor, Monitor, and Musical Heritage Society. She has been a judge at many piano competitions, including the Van Cliburn International Competition.

From the time I began playing professional concerts in 1943 at the age of ten, I never missed a Horowitz concert. His concert was never just another concert, but a transcendental event that left us in speechless wonderment. Today concerts end with artists playing at the most four encores. A Horowitz concert contained encores that in themselves amounted to another concert. If Horowitz did not play at least ten encores, the audience felt cheated. Only when an attendant came out to close the keyboard would the audience with great reluctance gradually stop clapping, thus bringing to an end another Horowitz event.

His pianistic wizardry lingered vividly in one's mind for days after the concert. It was not only the technical feats, however, that he seemed to conquer effortlessly, but also the electric magnetism he exuded that made one's spine vibrate and tingle from the neck down throughout the concert. Although he was not handsome, Horowitz always dressed impeccably, and had a gentle soft face with twinkling eyes that belied the devilish feats he was capable of hurling at his audience. No one could copy what went on behind those fabulous ten fingers that often sounded like twenty. This was Horowitz—god of the impossible!

Once, when he was featured on television, Madame Rosina Lhévinne remarked that no student should watch him too closely or try to copy his finger positions. He did everything contrary to the usual teaching methods professed for so many years. For instance, he sat very low at the piano, quite a distance from the keyboard, and played with flat fingers, embracing an entire segment of the keyboard.

Horowitz not only introduced a tremendous range of colors from the smallest ***ppp*** to earthshaking ***fff***, but he also introduced a new repertoire that had previously been deemed almost unplayable, such as Mussorgsky's *Pictures at an Exhibition* and the Rachmaninoff Third Concerto and Second Piano Sonata. And while he was labelled the last of the Romantic tradition, Horowitz introduced and premiered such diverse works as the Barber Sonata and the Prokofiev sonatas. He also programmed pieces almost unknown at the time, such as the Clementi and Scarlatti sonatas, which he played deliciously and delicately with great finesse and pearly filigreed scales.

I will reveal a secret that I have kept for forty-four years. I played a Town Hall recital in New York on Horowitz's concert grand. It occurred on April 4, 1949. I was 16. At the time, all available concert grands were assembled in the basement of the Steinway building on Fifty-Seventh Street, affectionately known as the "Steinway dungeon." All pianos were and are numbered, and some artists always returned to their favorite numbers. Two days before my concert, I went to the dungeon with my mother, who had studied with Dohnányi, and Bill Hupfer (former chief technician of Steinway & Sons) to choose a piano for my recital. Mr. Hupfer was a trusted and beloved expert who dealt with the idiosyncrasies of concert artists, and he had a fond heart for young pianists. He was also Horowitz's personal piano tuner.

Way back of the basement, I noticed a piano locked in brackets. My curiosity was immediately aroused, and I queried Bill Hupfer. He whispered to me, as if the ghosts could hear and carry the news to the outside world, "That is Horowitz's piano. It is in for some repairs." I gingerly asked if I could have the privilege of playing on that exalted instrument. I remember being enraptured by the silvery and yet sinewy sound of the piano. It required almost no effort; so light was its action that it almost played by itself.

Hesitantly I asked Mr. Hupfer if there was any possibility for me to play on the piano for my recital. He turned around to check for any spy lurking underneath other pianos. Although hesitant at first, he quickly made his decision, "If you promise *never* to breathe about it. Nobody, but nobody must know about this."

The experience turned out to be an unforgettable one. The piano was extraordinarily live and fast—so much so that it required tremendous control to restrain its fantastic velocity. It felt like a young colt ready to spring at any opportunity. The piano was so responsive that it almost felt as if it knew in advance what was expected of it. The magic of its sound will never leave me and will never be duplicated.

Josef Raieff

Josef Raieff was born in Kharkov, Russia. In Chicago he graduated from the American Conservatory. Later he studied with Josef Lhévinne and Alexander Siloti at the Juilliard Graduate School. In Europe he worked with Artur Schnabel.

Raieff performed throughout the United States and Europe. A well-known teacher, he has conducted many master-classes and piano seminars. He also collaborated with Rosina Lhévinne in four-hand recitals. Josef Raieff has been on the piano faculty of the Juilliard School for nearly half a century.

I am old enough now to have a long déja vu, and when I look down the time tunnel and muster my memories I see a long caravan of the great pianists of the past. There appears before my mind's eyes Paderewski, Lhévinne, Hofmann, Rachmaninoff, Moseiewitch, Levitzki, Horowitz, Rosenthal, Sauer, Bauer, Cortot, Gabrilowitsch, Schnabel, Backhaus, and Rubinstein; regrettably, and for some unknown reason, I never heard Godowsky or de Pachman except on recordings. There are also all the great living pianists whom I have heard many times, such as Ashkenazy, Richter, Tureck, to name a few.

I mention all these great pianists to form a parameter and frame around the super pianists of the twentieth century, namely Hofmann, Rachmaninoff, and Horowitz. Through all my years, I have felt and thought that Hofmann was the greatest natural pianist of them all. Rachmaninoff must have thought so, too, as he often said, and dedicated his Third Piano Concerto to him. Each of these piano geniuses had his own incomparable style, sound, technique, personality, and eccentricities, and it became a matter of taste and preference. Some thought Hofmann cold and detached. Everyone was in awe of Rachmaninoff as a composer and pianist, but I never saw anyone weep at one of his concerts. Horowitz, when he matured after his long "illness," became both the macrocosm and the microcosm of pianistic virtuosity. His pianistic genius had everything it was humanly possible to possess in the art. An awesome technique, a gorgeous sound—promethean power, an atavistically warm Jewish-Russian soul, an electric temperament, and super control. Also, he could make people weep at concerts.

I have other memories of Horowitz. The first time I ever heard his name was at a master class at the home of the pianist Ernest Hutcheson. Someone that evening announced that a young Russian pianist by the name of Vladimir Horowitz was coming to New York the following year to play and said, "Wait till you hear him." His prediction proved true. Horowitz came, played, and conquered.

Even Siloti, with whom I was then studying at the Juilliard and who rarely went to concerts except to the Rachmaninoff and Stokowski concerts, raved about Horowitz's playing of the *Carmen* Fantasy and his technique. This puzzled me very much, as technique per se was anathema to Siloti. He was mainly interested in tone production and making the piano sing. A short time after, he received a copy of the Moszkowski transcription of the *Carmen* Fantasy which was out of print, and asked me to learn it. It was the first indication I had from him that he was aware of my technical ability.

Siloti was a true pupil of Liszt and totally immersed in the late nineteenth-century style of subjective performance and interpretation. Even Harold Bauer, with whom I also worked, told me that audiences came to hear the performer. The composer was merely the canvas, the vehicle upon which the performer expressed himself. The public was more interested in the personality and projection of the artist than in the composition. Considering his generation of peers, Josef Lhévinne was an exception. In my work with him he was always sedulously careful and reverent of the composer's indications and wishes.

This all began to change in the 1920s and for the rest of the century, with the steller appearances of greats like Toscanini, Bruno Walter, Schnabel, and Serkin. Toscanini would scream at the man in his orchestra that it was not he but Beethoven who wanted that crescendo. Schnabel, with whom I studied in Berlin, always emphasized the fact that he was merely a servant of the great masters, trying in his performances to fulfill their wishes. In this he was truly humble, reverent and modest; otherwise, he cut a promethean swath with his worldly presence. Horowitz, like the Colossus of Rhodes, bestrode both centuries of interpretive feeling and concept.

As a child of the twentieth century, he was able to assimilate, fuse, and synthesize his own personality with the composer's wishes, and with puissant force propel and project whatever he played into an orbital atmosphere. It used to be said that there were many great pianists, such as Tausig, Rubinstein, Moscheles, Thalberg, etc., and then there was Liszt. It would be egregious of me to assume today that this one or that one was the greatest, but of this I'm sure. Horowitz is up there with the angels and either on the left or right side of God, who gave him his talent to begin with.

Norman Krieger

Norman Krieger began his musical training in Los Angeles, California. At 15 he went to New York, where he studied at the Juilliard School, later working with Alfred Brendel, Russell Sherman, and Maria Curcio. In 1987 he won the gold medal at the First Palm Beach Invitational Piano Competition, the Bruce Hungerford Memorial Prize, and the Victor Herbert Memorial Prize.

Krieger's orchestral appearances have included performances with the New York Philharmonic, the Milwaukee Symphony, the Boston Pops, the Los Angeles Philharmonic, and many others. A champion of contemporary music, Krieger has performed works by John Adams, Judith St. Croix, Lukas Foss, John Corigliano, and Lowell Liebermann. He has recorded the two Brahms concertos and an all-Gershwin disc.

When I think of Vladimir Horowitz, I am reminded of the great revolutionary artists and performers who uphold, uplift, and carry the standard of their art and craft to new heights and possibilities. Though human in his everyday life, Horowitz turned superhuman when he sat at the piano and brought life to scores.

I recall being guilty of trying to imitate him as a youngster, only to reach a series of dead ends. Ultimately, I realized there are no quick solutions to artistic development; it takes a lifetime to understand oneself, to find out what repertoire one has an affinity for, and for which not. It takes time to absorb, analyze, and re-create the music of the great composers. Horowitz understood this, and I believe he took a number of retirements for this very purpose. Each time he returned to the stage from one of these periods, it was clear he had gone on a passionate search for deeper knowledge of music and himself. He proved there are no shortcuts. I recall Adele Marcus, my teacher at Juilliard, telling me that Horowitz told her that he would rehearse the octaves in the Sixth Hungarian Rhapsody by Liszt in increments for six months before he played it in public, and spent five to six hours on two measures of a Chopin mazurka.

In an age of instant gratification, Horowitz, like a force of nature, allowed himself to develop as an artist at a pace where all his senses and faculties were at harmony. This is very much the opposite of what so many of his virtuoso performances sounded like; they sounded like they were made up on the spot, improvised. Today, we know he spent years of his life focusing on his weaknesses. Perhaps more than any other pianist, Horowitz's infinite dynamic range was always supported by and stemmed from an emotional reaction and conviction. His sound, larger than life, went through me like an X-ray. No two notes were ever played the same way, and that is the way he felt it. I recall attending the same recital program on two separate occasions. The contrast between the two was so enormous, yet each one as convincing and valid.

In my own search and discovery, I am inspired, driven, and humbled by Horowitz. He makes the piece seem that it could not be played any other way. His personality is so strong that I tend not to listen to his recording of a piece I am learning, though I will listen to a performance of his by the same composer.

In concerts, I was always astounded by one of the most important aspects of Horowitz's playing. He listened to himself with such intensity and concentration that, at times, it was truly hypnotic. Rachmaninoff had this, and I know Rubinstein did as well. In a sense, this is part of the mystical letting go of the self, or total quiet necessary to allow the inside of oneself to be heard and expressed.

It is said that musicians learn from each other, that each generation hands down its legacy. For me, Horowitz displayed living proof that human beings can overcome any obstacle he or she makes up one's mind to overcome. This is true in one's personal life as well as music. I carry within me every note I ever heard Horowitz play, and though his influence was enormous, I try to continue the example he always stressed: "Be yourself."

Maria Curcio

Maria Curcio was born in Italy. At 15 she studied with Artur Schnabel and began a performing career. During World War II she contracted tuberculosis and it became clear that her performing would be curtailed. Soon after, she started teaching, and in 1965 she moved to London, where her teaching career flourished. Hundreds of pianists, such as Martha Argerich, Barry Douglas, Jose Feghali, and Radu Lupu have come to study with her. In 1993 she will have made her first appearance in the United States, teaching master-classes. She has been on the juries of leading competitions; recently, her life has been the subject of the BBC 2 series Music in Camera.

As one of the great pianists of the twentieth century, Vladimir Horowitz marked a turning point in the development of the art of the keyboard. He was a forerunner in the mastery of technical proficiency; his unique style set him apart from other pianists and gave him a musical personality that was easily recognizable.

The style that Horowitz developed was revolutionary in many respects. The sounds that he created were unusually clear, due to the accuracy and precision of his playing; the dynamic range that he achieved went from thunderous and explosive yet resonant, to distant and almost inaudible yet always singing and communicative. His crescendos could be terrifying, while his cantabile passages were always rich. In order to create these many shades of color and sound, Horowitz utilized the pedal in ways that had never previously been perfected. He himself claimed to be able to apply dozens of precisely differing degrees of pressure on the right pedal.

Horowitz was often criticized for inappropriate pedalling (in

Baroque works), for exaggerating dynamic markings, and for extreme tempi, a statement with which I do not agree. Nevertheless, it was his adventurous and experimental qualities that allowed Horowitz to play such a wide variety of musical styles with such beauty and conviction.

David Wilde

David Wilde was born in Lancashire, England. He studied piano with Solomon and composition with Franz Reizenstein and Nadia Boulanger. In 1961 he won first prize at the Liszt-Bartok Competition at Budapest. In 1962 he was awarded the Queen's Prize.

Wilde has appeared frequently in recital and concerto. He has made recordings of the Wilson Piano Concerto for Chandos and of the Liszt Sonata and Schumann Fantasy for Saga. He has performed at the Henry Wood Promenade Concerts and has been soloist with Barbirolli, Leppard, Boulez, and others. He has given master-classes, and has appeared on and written radio and television programs for the BBC. In 1989 he performed the Tippett Concerto with the composer conducting at the BBC Tippett Festival.

Horowitz's brilliance was legendary: in scintillating performances of etudes by Moszkowski, Chopin, and Liszt; in the double octaves of the first and last movements of Tchaikovsky's B-flat minor Concerto and the dazzling prestissimo in the second movement; in the cadenzas of the Rachmaninoff D minor; in Scarlatti sonatas. His octaves could sound like the rattling of machine-gun fire; Liszt's Sixth Rhapsody seems perilously like a trick record. But there was no trick.

For Horowitz, there seemed to be no technical limits. Many years ago, in a BBC music quiz, the English virtuoso Cyril Smith was asked of a recording, "Is this one pianist, two pianists, or three pianists?" "Three," said Mr. Smith. "Or perhaps two unusually good ones." It was Horowitz playing the *Stars and Stripes Forever*. Indeed, Horowitz often thrilled and astounded us, but are these words of praise and meretricious medals awarded for mere titillation? Should we not search elsewhere for the Horowitz treasure: in the Merlinesque magic of the slower Scarlatti sonatas for instance, and in his Chopin waltzes and mazurkas?

Not long ago, busy with everyday practicalities and with the radio on in the next room, I stopped dead in my tracks, riveted by the beauty of a live recording made at a Horowitz performance of a Chopin mazurka. Lovely, too, is his recording of Schumann's *Kinderscenen*—even though the Knight of the Rocking-Horse does seem to be galloping over sheet metal. Horowitz's range of timbre, though always orientated toward brightness rather than toward sonority, was kaleidoscopic: in his hands, Scriabin's Fifth Sonata turns the piano into a color organ. His *Pictures at an Exhibition* is creatively wrested from Ravel's orchestration. Horowitz was himself a composer in the style of the late-Romantic virtuosi, and Mussorgsky would surely have applauded. And would not Bizet have lived longer if Horowitz had hurled his *Carmen* Fantasy at those murderous critics?

Horowitz played with superlative cantilena, bewitching rubato, and irresistible rhythm. The clarity of his articulation was grounded in a masterly staccato technique that placed agility before strength, lightness before sonority. Yet his beautiful pianissimo never lacked intensity, and his electric energy generated a charge of such high voltage that it might easily have carried a "danger" warning. His pedalling, like everything else about his playing, was uniquely personal: starkly sparing in big passages, where others would use it to increase the body of sound; swathed luxuriously around lyrical melodies like a mink stole. Though his clarity matched that of his father-in-law, Toscanini, his Romantic style imbued it with a capricious fervor that Toscanini would never have permitted himself. This quality sounded superb in nineteenth-century Slavic or Hungarian music, but it bordered on the willful and, together with his brilliance, could prove destructive to music of other traditions, especially music by some German composers—as in his recording with Toscanini of Brahms's Second Concerto. Brilliance out of place sounds merely brash.

And what of his piano? Horowitz attained to that rare category of artist who could command where others hope: like the great violinists, he always played on his own instrument, a Steinway; and that instrument was voiced, tuned, regulated, and molded to suit his ear, his fingers, and his exacting taste. He preferred to play on an action with half the normal weight, with hammers so toned that the bass was gigantic: the descant always sang bel canto, and the extreme treble sparkled like *Feux d'artifice*. All this enabled him to hold his marvelously supple wrists so low that, when he wished, he could comfortably lay his whole finger-length along the key without loss of power, and a mere flick of those astonishingly agile fingers could produce whatever sound he wished.

His recordings are already immortal; criticize them as one will, they represent the legacy of an instantly recognizable primal force which has changed the face of the pianistic globe.

Malcolm Binns

Born in Nottingham, Malcolm Binns studied at the Royal College of Music, where he received numerous prizes. He has played with important conductors such as Colin Davis, Antal Dorati, and Pierre Boulez, and in 1977 he performed the five Beethoven concertos with the City of Birmingham Symphony Orchestra to commemorate the one hundred fiftieth anniversary of Beethoven's death. He has recorded the complete Beethoven sonatas on original instruments for Decca, and has delved deeply into a great deal of neglected and worthy music.

Binns has recorded for Lyrita the four piano concertos by Sterndale Bennett. In 1992 he recorded concertos by Balakirev and Rimsky-Korsakov. He has had a close association with BBC radio and television spanning over a quarter of a century.

The sleeve-note of one of Horowitz's last recordings contains an interview by Joachim Kaiser, in which Horowitz complains about German performances of Beethoven being too slow and mentions some interpreters of Beethoven, including the British pianist Solomon, whom he apparently found "boring."

Many British musicians especially found that in later years, Horowitz went to the other extreme (for me, a good fault), and that he went right over the top. I remember that my professor at the Royal College in London, a Matthay pupil called Arthur Alexander, raved about the Horowitz concerts he had attended in the thirties. I have only the gramophone recordings of that time to base my reactions on, and they are for me some of the finest he ever made. Arthur Alexander talked to me about Horowitz's finger technique (it is always supposed, wrongly, that the Matthay school was only interested in weight techniques), and it wasn't until years later that I actually saw this stunning and, for me, somewhat perplexing phenomenon. One hears of potential young virtuosos the world over studying videos of Horowitz and attempting to analyze and copy his finger action. Good luck to them, but I don't think it is possible.

In fact, it is never possible to imitate a great artist, but we all absorb something, consciously or otherwise. A recent letter in the *London Times*, concerning the early retirement from the concert platform of the violinist Nigel Kennedy, discussed the problems in later life of child prodigies. It referred to Menuhin, Rachmaninoff, and Horowitz, whom the writer described as remaining infantile. "Child-like" would have been a kinder and more apt description, as there was always a feeling of youthful discovery in his performances, even in his last years.

I would have loved to have heard Horowitz play some of the music of his teacher, Felix Blumenfeld, who dedicated a late work to him. It would have been interesting to hear him in the famous left-hand study, which that other Blumenfeld pupil, Simon Barère, used to dazzle his audiences with, both aurally and visually. The record companies archives are turning up some unusual and fascinating previously unpublished material, and one hopes there are more delights there to supplement the classic performances one returns to again and again.

James Dick

James Dick studied with Dalies Frantz at the University of Texas. Later, in London, he became a pupil of Sir Clifford Curzon. He was awarded two Fulbright fellowships and, at the Royal Academy of Music, he won the Beethoven Prize. Within eight months he won top prizes at the Busoni, Tchaikovsky, and Leventritt competitions.

Since that time, Dick has been elected an honorary associate of the Royal Academy of Music, where he regularly gives master-classes. In 1979 he received the Presidential Citation of the National Federation of Music Clubs. He serves on the juries of international competitions, teaches, and performs regularly in the United States and Europe. He has performed with numerous symphony orchestras and has appeared with Kondrashin, Barbirolli, Comissiona, Semkow, and Ormandy. Dick is the creator of the Round Top Festival in Round Top, Texas.

Although music, interpretation, and performance are in constant evolution, our "recreative" world essentially refers to a traditional past, as required by the written score. Performing artists have the difficult task of working to find spontaneity of expression, genuine inspiration as well as the fulfillment of traditional expectations. To be original, illuminating, and still remain true to a score is a challenge worthy of the greatest artists.

Only rarely there may appear one who seems to transcend all rules and boundaries and achieve what is recognized as "genius," transforming the tradition and establishing new standards of performance and interpretation. Vladimir Horowitz was such an original. He was surrounded by other musicians of great brilliance, but he captivated the imagination of the public and history in a unique way. He brought a temperament to the concert stage that many characterize as "Russian." In the minds of many, Vladimir Horowitz represents the archetypal pianist of the so-called Russian school. That said, his career is proof that a truly masterful musical personality can, at most, be affected by a so-called school, but will always transcend it. He performed with an inner fire that was the fire of a gem, crystalline and brilliant, completely original unto himself. Brilliance and polished technique in Art, are, indeed, what is often associated with the Russia of Horowitz's youth, where those qualities were prized and highly honored. We need only think of Fabergé, Syevov, Repin, Nijinsky, Chaliapin, Kandinsky, and a host of others who were the legends of the early twentieth century.

But where is the balance to brilliance? There is a demanding aspect to performance that emphasizes a continuing study of the score and of the inner self, guided by an uncompromising integrity. It is a tradition that insists that the more one studies and perceives, the truer the Art. In that context I think foremost of Artur Schnabel, illuminating musical thought and performance for this century and beyond. These two stimulating and sensitive minds, Vladimir Horowitz and Artur Schnabel, influenced my life in a way that I could hardly have anticipated as a boy growing up on a Kansas farm and from a Russian-German family. It would not necessarily follow that I would ever know the slightest contact with Vladimir Horowitz or Artur Schnabel. My father was a farmer and an automobile mechanic in central Kansas. Our family circumstances were happy, yet extremely modest, and we loved great music. My father enjoyed singing and my mother played the piano. They saw to it that I began taking piano lessons before going to school. We made our own music at home and listened to recordings as well, which we regarded as treasures. I came especially to love performances of both piano and violin. Iturbi, Francescatti, Kreisler, and, yes, Horowitz, stand out in my memory. My life was to take me far from the Kansas farm and I would build a life as a musician and concert pianist. Those early recordings and lessons set me on a course and gave me those dreams. Though I never heard Vladimir Horowitz in a concert hall performance, I feel that I know something of him for deeper and more sustained reasons.

Upon graduation from high school in Hutchinson, Kansas, my parents, after much thought, decided to send me to study with the American-born concert pianist Dalies Frantz, at the University of Texas in Austin, rather than at a conservatory, which they could not have afforded under any circumstances. Mr. Frantz accepted me as a special student without fees. I did not know then that Dalies Frantz had studied with Vladimir Horowitz in Switzerland and Artur Schnabel in Berlin, and brought together in his incisive intellect the teachings of both of these great musicians. In fact, Mr. Frantz had been introduced to Vladimir Horowitz at Artur Schnabel's home in Berlin when Horowitz was there to play the Schumann Fantasy Op. 17 to Schnabel. The occasion was captured on film by Dalies Frantz on the terrace of Schnabel's Berlin apartment, and I include that photograph here for you. I must be frank to relate that the session, as I have been told, was stormy, but why should great spirits be timid? One of the results of that session was that Dalies Frantz was to study with Vladimir Horowitz and thereby bring together the influences of both of these unique men in his own person. Dalies Frantz passed this on to his students, and I had the good fortune to be one of them. Musicianship and intellect, fired with poetry and pianistic accomplishment, are the double gift of Horowitz and Schnabel.

In the Horowitz legacy of poetry of sound and scale of pianistic accomplishment, Horowitz can never be equated with definitions of mere virtuosity, which find "the empty too-much that comes from the pure too-little." To an excellent and astounding technique he added a rare perception and an extraordinary broadness of musical vision. No one in the world could question his greatness . . . he was a true Artist. He brought passion, poetry, and knowledge intensely to life through his art, and transformed all that he performed.

Grant Johannesen

Born in Salt Lake City, Utah, Grant Johannesen marked the fortieth anniversary of his New York debut in 1984 with a recital at Lincoln Center in New York. His dozens of recordings present a large range of repertoire, and his service to French music has been honored by the French government. Besides recording many works by French composers he was the first pianist to record the complete piano music of Fauré. He has also championed many modern works by North and South American composers.

Johannesen is heard throughout the United States in recital and orchestral appearances with major orchestras. He has served as a panelist with the National Endowment for the Arts in Washington, D.C., and has judged numerous international competitions. Johannesen served for ten years as president of the Cleveland Institute of Music.

My earliest memory of Horowitz was of an astonishing performance of the Tchaikovsky B-flat minor Concerto via radio with his father-in-law, Toscanini, and the NBC Symphony Orchestra. Barely a season later, Horowitz was booked into my home town, Salt Lake City, for a recital. This, as it turned out, was a singularly significant occasion. It appears that, since Horowitz was giving the American premiere of Prokofiev's Seventh Sonata a few days hence in Washington, D.C., he instructed the stage manager to announce a change in the program: instead of the "Waldstein" Sonata of Beethoven he decided to preview the Prokofiev Seventh for our public. Whoever delivered the news to the audience, it came out thus: "Mr. Horowitz will play a new work by Prokofiev instead of the Sonata in Waltz-time."

My studies in New York came shortly after, in 1941, when Robert Casadesus invited me to work with him at his home in Princeton, New Jersey. During the following years, Horowitz toured the United

States, and although he seldom played in New York they were always memorable performances. These were the years when his legend took shape. Horowitz and his wife had found country living in Connecticut most congenial, and it was in New England that circumstances drew us together. Our mutual friend David Rubin, director of artist relations at Steinway & Sons, worked very closely with Horowitz. I had purchased a wonderful old farm in Sandsfield, Massachusetts, in the mid-sixties, not far from the Horowitz home. With David Rubin and his wife and daughter close by, I was able to meet with the Horowitzes to try out piano scores with him in this tranquility, away from the hurly-burly of New York life.

Horowitz had a tremendous capacity to delve into the study of a composer such as Fauré. Over a long period, I had prepared to record the entire output of Fauré's piano music. My teacher, Casadesus, who was actually at the Paris Conservatoire when Fauré was the director, had encouraged my effort, and it seemed the right time to do it, since long-playing records were just coming in. I wanted very much to introduce this important piano literature to a larger audience. Few artists at the time had looked carefully into the richness of Fauré's piano music, so when Horowitz told me he had "fallen in love" with the French master's music, "particularly the great works beginning with Op. 63," the Sixth Nocturne, his encouragement gave weight to my project. He himself performed and recorded for RCA the Thirteenth Nocturne and Fifth Impromptu, but his enthusiasm and knowledge covered the complete Fauré spectrum. He found several of the early works "too much in the salon style of Tante Mathilde."

Horowitz was a deep student of the piano literature. Witness his discography, so filled with music off the beaten track. Once Horowitz asked me to play the Op. 4 Intermezzi of Schumann, a work I have championed since I was a young man, and still look upon as a significant piece in my repertory (even if it has yet to be anyone else's). Horowitz loved the composition and he deeply admired Schumann's music.

On that evening, he talked about the "rarely-heard" Rondo Op. 16, which he had been practicing. He told me that Rachmaninoff once ended a program in Milan with the work. He said, "It was a revelation to me, and Sergei brought down the house with this wonderful rondo. Grant, why don't you play it next season? I know you play a recital every year in New York. I think you will find it a real *trouvaille*, a brilliant unknown Chopin." He then sat down at his Steinway and delivered a stunning reading of the rondo. After Horowitz finished, all I could say was that I would rather he brought such a performance to "his" audience. (During this particular period, Horowitz had taken one of his long absences from public playing.) I could see he was pleased to hear the excitement he generated, not only from myself, but from everyone at the party. The rondo was indeed a "find," and we all begged him to use it as part of a program. As we left, he drew me aside and quietly said, "About the rondo, Grant. Maybe you will think about playing it the season *after* next?"

Horowitz evolved into a musical personality of singular splendor, finding his own specialities, performing when and where he pleased, and at the same time brilliantly understanding the psychology of the public market place. Although he did not give much notice to the greatest twentieth-century composers, I have fantasized that if he had lived even longer, he might have come around to composing, not another Sousa march, but a vehicle to hoist a new pianistic genius into the twenty-first century. Perhaps a sizzling meditation on . . . the "demon barber of Fleet Street," this from the beloved demon Pianist of East Ninety-Fourth Street.

Coleman Blumfield

Coleman Blumfield began his training in Chicago, later studying at the Curtis Institute of Music with Isabelle Vengerova. For two years he worked with Horowitz.

His career has taken him on international tours on behalf of the United States Department of State. He accepted an appointment as the first artist-in-residence to an American city (Flint, Michigan), and, during this period, he gave performances in all the Flint public and parochial institutions for the disabled. Under the Ford Motor Company's sponsorship he performed for over one million young people in 130 cities. Blumfield's new CD, dedicated to the memory of Horowitz, is on the Sonoris label.

Vladimir Horowitz was a profound pianist, perhaps unequalled in the twentieth century, and has influenced more pianists, for good or for bad, than any other. Comments such as "Horowitz is only a technician," "Horowitz doesn't understand certain styles," "His playing is too mannered," in my opinion were the result of jealousy and perhaps bias. His sound was unmistakable and I could identify it immediately.

I remember one of my acquaintances, just having heard a Horowitz recital a few years ago, went on and on about how much he disliked this and that about his playing, and then stopped complaining and said: "I can't believe that I'm still talking about a recital I didn't like, two weeks later."

For one of my birthdays, my parents presented me with a recording of the Tchaikovsky Piano Concerto No. 1, with Toscanini and Horowitz. This performance started my love affair with his playing and was the spark that set off my own concepts and approach to music. Almost every child has an idol or hero; mine was a celebrated pianist. Even on the less than ideal shellac recording, after being initially stunned by the brilliant octave playing, the articulation, the subtlety of nuance, I realized that although I was not yet fully comprehending everything, I was taken with the musical concept, the sweep of the opening chords, the delicacy of the opening theme of the second movement, the Slavic bite of the third, holding back at certain points and then letting the music have its own head.

From that time on I would save up a few weeks allowance and buy another record album, and so began to become acquainted with his then existing discography. I became familiar with his recordings of the Brahms Second Piano Concerto with Toscanini, the incredible Rachmaninoff Third with Coates, and, of course, the solo albums of Chopin, Liszt, Mendelssohn, Prokofiev, Barber, Mozart, Beethoven, and others.

At one point I was dating the daughter of a marvelous pianist, Gitta Gradova, a very close friend of Horowitz. Her daughter, Judy, and I were planning to go out, and were speaking on the phone. I could hear a passage from the Brahms Second Concerto being played very, very slowly, and I asked Judy, "Is Mom practicing?" "No," she replied. "It's Volodya." This was followed by complete silence from me. Judy asked "Are you okay?" I explained that I couldn't believe that my idol was practicing at her home and she was being very nonchalant about it.

After one of Horowitz's performances, Gitta took me backstage to meet him, and all I could do was simply stand and stare. Horowitz must have sensed my nervousness and asked me, "Would you like the signature?" All I could do was stare and nod weakly. The performance that night of his transcription of Mussorgsky's *Picture's at an Exhibition* elicited a comment the next day from one of the leading reviewers: "You had to be there to believe it."

During my formative years, I had the good fortune to study with Sergei Tarnowsky, who had been Horowitz's teacher in Russia. When he left for California I was accepted as a student by a wonderful pianist and teacher, Katja Andy, who subsequently, with Gitta Gradova, arranged for me to play for Isabelle Vengerova, who then accepted me as a pupil and enrolled me in the Curtis Institute of Music. Vengerova knew of my love for Horowitz's playing, and in her marvelous way helped me very much to grow and mature, to the point where I would be ready to be accepted as a student by him. When Vengerova died, I was told to call Horowitz to set up an audition. I played the *Variations sérieuses* by Mendelssohn, the G minor Ballade of Chopin, and the Seventh Sonata of Prokofiev. After each work he said "Bravo," and when I was finished he said to me, "You have the whip," meaning that the fire and temperament were there, and then went on to elaborate that we would concentrate on works requiring the singing tone, color, and above all the essence of the music. I was so excited that I remember running from his home on East Ninety-Fourth Street to Times Square before I could calm down enough to call my parents.

The second time (for my first lesson) that I entered the Horowitz's home, I was very taken with his devotion to art. From the Picasso *Acrobat at Repose* to the Degas to small objets d'art, I began to slowly realize that in order to play the way Horowitz did, practicing was only one of the building blocks. The absorption in painting, literature, sculpture, among others, was necessary in the growth of an artist. At one of my early lessons, he said, "You will be a pianist, but you must work to become a complete person—go to museums, theatre, read. An artist is like a sponge—you must try to absorb everything in order to recreate works of art on the piano." Quite an intimidating directive for a young person.

And then began two grueling years of hard work with Mr. Horowitz. The five-finger exercises for the strength and independence of the fingers; the chordal exercises for controlling a singing line surrounded by harmonic texture; the balance of accompaniment to melody; pedalling, sound production, musical color; the differences between full voice (on the piano), mezza voce, sotto voce; the difference (in sound) of staccato, legato, portamento. One of the first works studied was indeed the Mendelssohn *Variations sérieuses.* Where once the theme had sounded like an exercise in four-part harmony, now began to form different lines of color, texture, and essence, so that what I heard in my head began to emerge in sound from the piano. Of course, coming to the lesson meant walking around the block one extra time to try to settle my nerves before pushing the buzzer. I discovered that Horowitz was a very formal man. At home he always dressed impeccably in suit and bow tie. This was true even when I went to his summer home in East Hampton, New York, for lessons during the sweltering months of July and August.

For me, there was great excitement when Horowitz would assign new repertoire, or alternatively I would request to study a particular work and spend two or three weeks preparing. Some of the works included, in addition to the Chopin etudes and nocturnes, were Beethoven's "Waldstein," the Sonata in D major Op. 10, No. 3, Schumann's *Fantasiestücke.* For example, his comments about various instrumental timbres in the "Waldstein" were particularly helpful for me in realizing the orchestral potential of the piano. In the Chopin B-flat minor Sonata, his suggestions on the architectural design as well as the aesthetic of the work were extremely beneficial.

Another extremely important aspect of my studies with Horowitz concerned the approach to different registers of the piano. When I listen to some of his remarkable transcriptions, such as the Liszt rhapsodies, *Carmen*, Saint-Saëns, and others, I am aware that he has chosen the most correct registers of the instrument to project the musical ideas, and his color palette is dazzling. He demonstrated that I should not play a staccato in the middle register of the piano as one does in the upper extreme or lower. In playing chords, he taught that the chord is a unified sound, but is comprised of several voices and should be treated as such.

In the beginning of my studies, Horowitz, in addition to speaking, would demonstrate on the piano. But as time went on, the examples at the piano diminished, and rightly so. Studying with such a major musical personality could lead to imitation, which of course, was bound to happen. I worked very hard to avoid this but could not help being influenced by him as well as my other teachers. In music there is a continuity, such as the link between Haydn, Mozart, Clementi, Beethoven, and others, and in the piano from Liszt through Rachmaninoff and Horowitz. That, in my opinion, is very healthy and provides a tradition which is important and to which I very much adhere.

Horowitz, as a mature artist in the concert hall and in recordings, evolved, in my opinion, from a virtuoso firebrand into a very deep-thinking, multifaceted, and profound artist. From his performances of the small-scale works of Scarlatti to his last recording, there was always something very individual to be said by him—even in his programming, many times the unusual: a rondo of Clementi, whose works he championed; the fabulous performances of Scriabin sonatas—the Third, Ninth, and Tenth. In these works the tonal palette was extraordinary, as in the nervous twittering at the end of the Tenth Sonata, the biting dissonant chords at the climax of the Ninth. His artistic finesse in Schumann's *Kreisleriana* and *Humoreske* was unforgettable. Even when the performances were less than ideal—Liszt's *Mephisto* Waltz or the last Rachmaninoff Third, with Ormandy, these could be forgiven when you heard the Liszt Consolation or the Rachmaninoff Prelude in G major, in which there was magic in the wisps of sound floating ephemerally. I cannot forget the attention he would lavish on a Chopin mazurka or nocturne, or the elegance he brought to the Schubert-Liszt *Soirée de Vienne* No. 6. I am of the opinion that certain works that he recorded have become the standard by which all others are compared. The early recording of the Liszt B minor Sonata for me is the ultimate performance aesthetically, musically, and architecturally. Although there are a few technical errors, the sweep of the performance is irresistible, from the towering fortissimos to the most exquisite bel canto. It is true that other recordings are almost note-perfect, but that is exactly what they are, note-perfect recordings that hold my attention for perhaps one or two pages. The same can be said for the various recordings of others of the Rachmaninoff Third. I have a private recording of the concerto, performed in Carnegie Hall with Barbirolli in 1941, that contains some of the most incredible piano playing ever.

Looking back now to the time I was studying with him, when he would listen to a work I had prepared and he would say, "Is better"—that for me was enough to go back and work even harder. In addition to the artistry of Horowitz as a performer, he helped me as a teacher reach into my own musical personality, develop it, and ultimately stand on my own. I could not ask more than that from anyone.

In retrospect, I am convinced that I was extraordinarily privileged to work with and be influenced by one of the most brilliant and important musicians of the twentieth century. We are fortunate that the discography exists, but I for one miss that incredible sound live in the concert hall.

Veronica Jochum

Veronica Jochum began her piano studies in her native Munich. She attended the master-classes of Edwin Fischer, and later studied in America with Rudolf Serkin.

She has performed in more than fifty countries and with many major orchestras. Her repertoire includes over thirty-five piano concertos. Besides her interpretation of the classical masters, Jochum has explored a great deal of Schoenberg, Stravinsky, Bartok, and Hindemith, and has made pioneering recordings of Busoni and Clara Schumann. She has recorded for Deutsche Grammophon, Philips, and Pro Arte, and has collaborated with Bernard Haitink, Schmidt-Isserstedt, Raymond Leppard, Gunther Schuller, and Eugen Jochum.

I first heard Horowitz live in Boston after Martin Luther King's assassination. He came on stage with a black minister and played Chopin's Funeral March. From the first note, there was an electric excitement in the air such as I never had heard or felt produced by any other pianist. The whole recital left me almost frozen with breathlessness, and I was literally unable to sleep for two nights!

I now understood what Rudolf Serkin meant when he told me, when I first came to study with him in 1959, "You young artists *must* sign a petition and ask Horowitz to play again in public, for *everything* is there and he plays better than ever." (Serkin told me that when Horowitz was to perform the Tchaikovsky Concerto, he would practice octaves six hours a day, three slow and three fast. When I followed this strategy, I was kicked out of my apartment in New York.) He also told me about Horowitz's depressions, and that he thought that his fingers were made out of glass.

As a child, I used to look at Horowitz's signature, which I found second in my parent's guest-book (the first one being that of composer Gunther Raphael). His writing seemed to me to have a sense of beauty and a great deal of poise and confidence in the way it was placed on the page.

Horowitz was about a year younger than my father, the conductor Eugen Jochum. They performed together only once, and I never knew what they performed. Growing up, I heard his recordings, reflecting the power of a demon: the incredible Barber Sonata, the Prokofiev Seventh, Liszt's Petrarch *Sonetto 104, Au bord d'une source, Funérailles*, to mention a few—these became the standards for every pianist tackling those pieces. And when I heard him live, I felt a magical white-hot glow somewhere in each performance. I could not understand why so many pianists were impelled to imitate. It seemed that there was nothing one could "imitate," nothing more could follow in trying to do something "similar." There could never be a Horowitz school, his identification with the piano was more than just extremely personal. It was totally idiosyncratic.

I sometimes wonder if his extreme expressiveness and the extraordinary insight of certain aspects of the music were possible only through his superhuman mastery of the instrument. He was so different from his contemporary Rudolf Serkin, for whom the search for the meaning of the music was first, and giving shape to the inner image of each piece dictated the technical approach, which was often conquered by the hardest labor. Horowitz seemed to discover the *music* through his almost magically endowed pianistic talent. Occasionally, I was quite irritated with Horowitz, where his ability to master each and every detail of sound or touch seemed to hide the music itself. I remember that I could barely endure his *Arabeske* or *Traumerei*. I felt Schumann slip away from me altogether.

During his later years, I continued to be intrigued with the Horowitz mystique. At one concert, he played Beethoven's Sonata Op. 101, one of the most challenging pieces in the literature. I was deeply moved by this Beethoven playing. The first movement was like a dialogue not only with Beethoven but with God, like an intimate and loving encounter with his Creator. It seemed Horowitz had achieved simplicity at last? Later, in 1986, when he played in Moscow, I loved every bit of his Mozart, anachronistic as it may have been. It was like a child come home; the demon in him had been exorcised, and now there was this warm and unpretentious music making by a very human being, who seemed loving, happy, and grateful to be where he was.

This was almost paradoxical after experiencing the artistry of this inimitable, unique, and eccentric personality. As a postscriptum, I started to understand more of this through David Dubal's *Evenings with Horowitz*. The book is more than a mere biography, as it paints a picture of many encounters with a man who, although or because he was in his eighties, was without guards or shields, and reveals to an amazing degree his worries, his delights, his knowledge, his ignorance, and, most of all, the humbleness of a long life striving for perfection with an insatiable love for the piano and music.

Emanuel Krasovsky

Emanuel Krasovsky was born in Vilnius, Lithuania. In Israel he studied with Mindru Katz at the Rubin Academy, and in New York at the Juilliard School, where his teachers were Guido Agosti, Ania Dorfmann, and Ilona Kabos. Krasovsky takes an active part in Israel's cultural life and is a professor of piano and deputy director at the Tel Aviv University's music academy. He has appeared with many distinguished conductors, including Leonard Bernstein conducting the Israel Philharmonic. In the United States he has given solo recitals in New York, Boston, Washington, Chicago, and other cities.

Emanuel Krasovsky finds time to give lecture-recitals and master-classes, and is often heard in chamber music with violinist Vera Vaidman. He is the artistic director of the semi-annual chamber music festival in Zichron Ya'acov.

One day in November 1989, as the brutally sudden news of Vladimir Horowitz's death worked its way into our consciousness, an acquaintance music critic approached me after a memorial lecture I gave at the Tel Aviv music academy. "Let us see now that the living legend is no longer, if the 'magnetism,' 'uniqueness,' 'electricity' hold. I bet Horowitz's records *sans* the mystery of his persona will sit on shelves collecting dust just like those of hundreds of other pianists."

Admittedly, our man should not be counted among the fervent admirers of Horowitz's art. His question, however, seems an intriguing one to consider.

For the halo of awe—indeed, near deification—as well as unpredictability and quirky confusion around Horowitz seemed all but unreal in the second half of our century—a wild throwback to other times, another world. Paganini, Liszt, Anton Rubinstein might conceivably have enjoyed such treatment at the apex of the hero-worshiping Romanticism a century or so ago. But in our hard-nosed, cynical psychological environment . . . ?

I happened to witness this phenomenon closely—and actively. A Juilliard student at the time, I, too, experienced the shudder of excitement grasping New York's musical community as the *New York Times* on page 1 announced Horowitz's intention to give a recital at the Metropolitan Opera house—the largest classical music venue in the city, never before utilized for a solo performance.

With a few friends, I joined the ticket line outside the Met on a sleety afternoon (the tickets were to go on sale at ten next day). The police barriers were put up already, and the line grew incessantly; by dark, several hundred people cuddled against the cold rain.

Sometime past midnight, a commotion broke the frosty routine: as if by a miracle, Mr. and Mrs. Horowitz materialized, shaking hands, joking. An aide brought boxes of hot coffee and donuts from a nearby all-night shop. The spirits soared.

To this day, I recall the expression of bewilderment on the faces of late-night Manhattan passersby—not a group to be surprised easily—at the sight of an elderly, fur-clad couple followed to a car by a huge, cheerful mob.

I remember how on Sunday, November 17, 1974, the New York concert schedules were unceremoniously reshuffled to enable the audiences and the artists not to miss Horowitz at the Met. (Vladimir Ashkenazy, for one, advanced his recital at the 92nd Street Y by two hours.) And the intensity of anticipation at the Met; one could feel it physically.

I remember, too, Horowitz's remarkable appearance in the Carnegie Hall "Concert of the Century" when, upon his entering the stage with Isaac Stern and Mstislav Rostropovich for the Tchaikovsky Trio, an ovation broke out—longer and more excited than the one following the preceding item of the star-studded program.

What was it that drove the Horowitz admirers to such a frenzy? Was it his stupendous, fire-eating virtuosity?

It surely had a part—just listen to his thundering Lisztian octaves, his breathtaking filigree fingerwork (Moszkowski's *Etincelles*), his often gravity-defeating tempi. But there have been pianists able to play with no lesser brilliance and aplomb (I think of Josef Lhévinne or Simon Barère among others).

Was it Horowitz's uncanny sensitivity to, and control of, the piano textures, assuring the constant shimmer of vitality—sometimes fragile, other times bold and imposing—in his tone? A much rarer and more precious quality this, yet even here Horowitz is not quite alone; Gyorgy Cziffra's pianism, for instance, is most remarkable in this very respect.

In my piano literature class, I like to introduce the students to Horowitz's art through his renditions of two short, demonstratively non-virtuosic (in a routine sense of this term) pieces: the Scriabin C-sharp minor Etude Op. 2, No. 1, and the Schubert-Liszt *Ständchen.* Their first reactions to the performances deal unfailingly with the innate, direct *musicality* of the playing. The spirit of the music seems here liberated from its external shell. It may be ethereal, unpredictable, fickle—but it is as *real* as must have been the brain impulses which brought the music to being in the first place.

This, to me, is the point of departure in contemplating Horowitz's art. Sometimes—as when performing Schumann and Scriabin—the pianist's grasp of the music's spirit is shattering in its conviction. At other times, you take the Horowitz vision on faith. The technique, articulation, sonority—all these combine to deliver his vision with white-hot intensity.

One may find Horowitz's forays into the Classical repertoire controversial. One may love or hate his version of Mussorgsky's *Pictures* (personally, I admire it). One can judge his Liszt Sonata short on depth or nobility. And perhaps, during his long, often tortuous career, Horowitz did succumb occasionally to power for power's sake. Yet most of the time, he transmitted his inimitable musical outlook with unfailing courage.

He was fated to receive and develop a spectacular equipment for that purpose. Let us not confuse, though, the means with the message. For it was the message, I believe, that brought hundreds of music-lovers to the ticket line on a wintry night. It is this potent message which should retain its artistic meaning for the generations to come—not the least, for their own sake.

Lorin Hollander

Lorin Hollander is in the thirty-seventh season of a career that began with a Carnegie Hall debut at the age of eleven. He has performed with virtually every major orchestra and has given recitals in most of the world's principal music centers. He began piano at the age of four with lessons from his father. He also worked with Leon Fleisher and Olga Stroumillo.

Hollander has taken part in dozens of special musical projects and has been adviser to many organizations. He has often appeared on television and has had his own national recital series on PBS. He has regularly taken part in leading music festivals. In 1990 at Carnegie Hall, Hollander and Leon Fleisher gave the world premiere of the Concerto for Piano Three Hands, written especially for them by Gunther Schuller.

My earliest recollections of Vladimir Horowitz were as a very young child. My father was the associate concertmaster of the NBC Symphony with Toscanini. He used to return from rehearsals exhausted, but very often on the level of quiet reflection and enthusiasm. He would attempt to explain to his four-year-old prodigy son what the essence was that the Maestro attempted to get across to his musicians at rehearsal. It usually focused around the soul of the music, the heart, the humanity, the depth of emotional expression that Toscanini would in some way always find in every phrase and gesture of the music.

It was this that struck me first about the playing of Vladimir Horowitz. Every line was imbued with its own emotional content. His greatness lay not only in his remarkable variety of technique, which allowed for passagework of the lightest texture to the mightiest octave passages, but in the way in which each line of music had its own independence. Horowitz was like a small chamber ensemble. If one only listened to the bass line, one would get the impression that this was a very great cellist or bassist playing. The notes were connected by a variety of color, timbre, and a total cohesion. The middle voices were not only clear, but within that clarity there was content, and everything was played with an inner pulse, a flowing energy.

Horowitz at times was at the mercy of his own amazing resources. I think there was a kind of demonic element in him that he could not always control. I hear young students practicing Horowitz tempi, but it should be understood that this may not have been what Horowitz himself actually intended. I am not saying that when Horowitz was wanton, it was because of a lack of integrity or purpose, but because of a kind of volatility that took over the man's body and spirit.

I would guess, from hearing his recordings from around the time of his retirement at 49, that here is a man and artist being ripped limb from limb. If one listens to the B minor Scherzo from that period, it is almost painful as Horowitz attempts to hold back what seems to be another spirit driving him forward. It probably reached a point that it became too frustrating, too difficult, and too puzzling. Even too frightening to walk on the stage and have what one had worked for in terms of a warm, expressive interpretation be rendered almost a testimony to the fast and the technical, rather than the human and humane.

For me, Horowitz at his finest is the recording of the D minor Rachmaninoff Concerto around 1950. This is the most carefully laid-out, poetic, touching document that we have of this concerto. Here one hears the calm heart, the heart unpossessed, as it were. He sings every note with compassion. One hears a great soul in much of his Schumann, Scarlatti, Scriabin, and Clementi.

It was impossible not to feel the essence of the man as he played on stage. At times he was almost tragically vulnerable: so clearly a part of suffering humanity, tortured by his own inner world. The wonderful thing was that after all those years of retirement, he came out of the black morass not disgruntled, frustrated, or unable to communicate. Quite the contrary, he now seemed to have his own personal awareness of what it took for him simply to get through the day, let alone to perform the feats of miraculous musical utterances with which he lived his life. Horowitz had a human heart filled with light, and filled with darkness. In his case, it was through personal struggle that came his greatest music making.

Horowitz will not be remembered merely as a monumental technician, but as an artist with a unique personality. He fought to attain his own deeply personal expression. In an age that sorely lacks individuality, he shone like a beacon for those who also need to be themselves. Horowitz through his recordings left us a major human document. In these recordings, we experience his essence and his empathy for the human condition.

Peter Orth

Peter Orth is a native of Philadelphia. He studied with Adele Marcus at the Juilliard School and later with Rudolf Serkin. In 1979 he won first prize in the Naumburg Piano Competition, and in 1986 he was the recipient of the Fanny Peabody Mason Award. He received the second Shura Cherkassky Recital Award.

Orth has been guest soloist with many orchestras, including the Chicago, Detroit, Montreal, Pittsburgh, Utah, Saint Louis, and Philadelphia orchestras, and the New York Philharmonic. He has appeared in dozens of chamber music concerts, and has made two United States tours with Music from Marlboro. In 1988 he was invited to perform at Steinway's celebration of its five hundred thousandth piano at Carnegie Hall. During the 1990–91 season, Orth made a twelve-city tour with the Franciscan String Quartet, premiering the piano quintet by Lowell Libermann.

Musically, Vladimir Horowitz is an enigma for me. I cannot come to terms with many conflicting feelings. Upon listening to his recordings, I feel excitement and fulfillment for one minute, and the next moment I disagree profoundly with what he is doing. Yet I never find that what he does is tepid or indifferent.

I was never merely attracted to his superhuman power at the keyboard. Rather, it was his individual vision, with an illumination in one way or another of practically every conceivable aspect of the score. Horowitz was the great orchestrator on the piano. It was always a revelation to hear how he makes the piano into a hundred orchestral sounds.

I only heard him live twice, once in a performance of the Rachmaninoff D minor Concerto with Eugene Ormandy and the New York Philharmonic, and the other his last recital at the Metropolitan

Opera. The Rachmaninoff was spectacular, but the recital was even more memorable.

Apart from the legendary speed of his octaves and his utter command of sound, Horowitz possessed a unique primal electricity that was always present, whether playing Scarlatti or John Phillip Sousa. In the final analysis, my respect for Horowitz is boundless. This great artist came along and captured people's imagination in such a way that they were compelled to fall in love not only with him, but more important, with the piano itself and the piano recital. This fact has ennobled all pianists, and we must be endlessly grateful.

Horacio Gutiérrez

Born In Havana, Cuba, Horacio Gutiérrez appeared as soloist with the Havana Symphony when he was 11. In 1967 he became an American citizen; he graduated from the Juilliard School in 1970. That same year he won the silver medal at the Moscow Tchaikovsky Competition. Since then he has made regular appearances with the world's major orchestras. In 1982 he received the Avery Fisher Prize.

Gutiérrez won an Emmy Award for his appearance with the Chamber Music Society of Lincoln Center. His many recordings include both Brahms concertos, the Tchaikovsky First Concerto, the Prokofiev Second and Third concertos and recently, for the Telarc label, the Second and Third Rachmaninoff concertos. With the Y Chamber Orchestra he performed the William Schuman Piano Concerto in honor of the composer's seventy-fifth birthday.

I was born in Cuba. By age ten I had heard the names of Serkin, Van Cliburn, Rubinstein, but somehow not the name of Vladimir Horowitz. I was born in 1948, and I did not know that in 1950 Horowitz had given the world premiere of Samuel Barber's Sonata in my own Havana.

My family and I came to the United States when I was 13. We lived in Miami for about six months before moving to Los Angeles. In Miami, I met a man who had studied in Chicago with Sergei Tarnowsky. In Kiev, Mr. Tarnowsky had been the young Vladimir Horowitz's teacher from about the age of eleven until seventeen. I was told that Tarnowsky was living in Los Angeles in semi-retirement, and was advised to call and play for him when I arrived there.

In Los Angeles, I promptly bought some Horowitz records to see how good this former student of Tarnowsky was. Those were the days still of sheer innocence. I listened to the recordings and was overwhelmed. Soon I played for Tarnowsky and worked with him from the age of thirteen to eighteen.

Mr. Tarnowsky never charged me a penny. He was a wonderful man and teacher—proud, old-fashioned, and aristocratic. He had studied with Annette Essipova, a wonderful pianist who had been the second wife of Leschetizky. She was the teacher of many eminent pianists, and taught Prokofiev, who was Tarnowsky's classmate. I felt fortunate to be studying with a man who had such a tradition behind him.

Unfortunately, there had long been dissension between Horowitz and Tarnowsky. Horowitz had resented that Tarnowsky would come backstage after his concerts and criticize him, still acting the role of teacher even after he was famous. Horowitz generally credited Felix Blumenfeld, who was his teacher after Tarnowsky.

In 1966, I performed on a Bernstein–New York Philharmonic Young People's Concert. I had won an audition the year before. Tarnowsky decided to write to Horowitz about me, saying, "I believe in this young man. His admiration for you reminds me of yours for Rachmaninoff." He gave him the address where I would be staying in New York, and asked if he would see me.

Since I stayed at the YMCA on West Sixty-Third Street, I worried that I would not receive a message from him. But I did. His secretary asked me to come visit the Maestro at 9:30 P.M. on February 24, 1966. My first thought was that he wants to see me this late to get rid of me by 10:00 P.M.. Horowitz had been a celebrated recluse for years. He had only played again in May of 1965 after twelve years of silence.

I was only seventeen years old, and more than a quarter century has passed since that winter night, but I remember my excitement to this day. Mrs. Horowitz opened the door, and I went upstairs to the living room. Soon, Horowitz came in, greeted me, and proceeded to lie down on his couch. I smiled to myself, and remembered that Tarnowsky had told me that even in the thirties Horowitz had liked to stretch out on a couch. He asked me a lot of questions and seemed to like the fact that I knew a great deal about him.

Soon he asked me the inevitable question, "Why not play for me?" I had absolutely no desire to do this, but I knew I would have to. I played the Mendelssohn *Variations sérieuses* and the first movement of the Schumann Concerto. After I played, he was very complimentary. In the Mendelssohn, he showed me where to bring out the fifth finger for coloristic purposes. During the Schumann Concerto, he sang the orchestral part. He told me that he liked my pedalling in the Schumann, and said, "You are very talented." However I did not feel at all good about my performances.

I remember the complete feeling of unreality about those few days in New York. I was on stage with the New York Philharmonic with Bernstein, and now I was at Horowitz's home playing for him and Wanda Toscanini. The sense of unreality was heightened by the fact that it had been snowing in New York and I had never seen snow before. Sitting there somewhat dazed, I did not quite believe that Mr. Horowitz could really mean that I was very talented. But Mrs. Horowitz, who had been very quiet and was listening to every word, said, "If Mr. Horowitz says 'very talented,' he means 'very talented.' " I was pleased by this remark because she gave me assurance that it was not merely a random comment. They were both very gracious, and soon Coca-Cola and a large piece of cake appeared.

Mr. Horowitz continued to question me. He asked which performance of his Rachmaninoff Third I preferred. I told him that I liked the one with Reiner over the Albert Coates performance. He said, "I think so, too." I remember thinking it was curious that Horowitz was asking me this question. At 17 I was very young in both a musical sense and in worldly sophistication.

I told him that I wished that he would come to Los Angeles to play. He said, "Do you think people like me in Los Angeles as much as you do?" Here was the legend of the piano world asking me such a thing. At that tender age, I knew very little about human psychology.

Then he asked me about Tarnowsky. I told him he was well. Horowitz said twice, "I'm glad to hear that. I'm glad to hear that." Then he paused, and stared out into space. Finally he looked at me and said, "Of course, I don't need Tarnowsky now." It all was strange to me. Just before I left, he gave me his recording of Scarlatti sonatas. He signed it with the inscription: "To Horacio Gutiérrez, with my very best wishes for great success."

Later Horowitz did play in Los Angeles. Earlier, Tarnowsky had heard a recording of a Schumann work Horowitz was planning to play on his program. He told me that he did not like the interpretation, and wondered, "What shall I say to him afterward?" I replied, "Do you *have* to say you didn't like it?" He thought for a while, and reluctantly said, "I suppose not." The miracle to me was that one was still able to play, and the other was still alive to hear him. When Mr. Tarnowsky went backstage to see Horowitz, it proved to be a very happy and emotional reunion. It was their last. Mr. Tarnowsky passed away shortly after that concert.

When I came to Juilliard, Horowitz was toying with the idea of doing some teaching. He had remembered me, and Peter Mennin, the president of Juilliard, told me that he had expressed interest in teaching me. Of course, Horowitz could teach me many things, but I was already overly influenced by his recordings. Something in me shied away from such an immense force. I was diplomatic, and said I did not feel that I was ready. In 1974 I wrote him a note asking him to attend my New York debut, but he never replied.

I admire many pianists. The piano literature is so rich and so many pianists have contributed so much. But in the case of Horowitz, he is the only musician I can think of where there is an extramusical feeling. For instance, when one listens to records of Rachmaninoff, there is a warmth, a natural mastery, a freedom. And when you hear Artur Schnabel, one listens in awe to the magnificent insight into the music, its sense of inevitability. But when I think of Horowitz, there is something inexplicable about his playing, and his very personality at the piano. His face looks part devil, part clown. His very hand position at the instrument was a mockery of the classic hand position. Then there is his sound, which was different from any other pianist's sound. There seemed to be something outside the realm of music in his playing. He was a true, inimitable individual.

Musically, I never knew what to expect from Horowitz. The unexpected was the norm. For example, when he played Chopin's famous A-flat major Polonaise, I couldn't understood why, in a piece so apparently suited to him, he could not project its nobility and grandeur. Yet, in other Chopin works, he gave wonderfully idiomatic performances. This very aspect of the unexpected was always fascinating. At every concert, I was on the edge of my seat. And in terms of expressivity, Horowitz taught us more than anyone else. I think Issac Stern said, "Very few instrumentalists are given the gift of setting new standards." Horowitz showed us new avenues of emotion and dynamic colors. I will always miss him.

Tzimon Barto

Born in Florida, Tzimon Barto began piano studies at 5 and wrote an opera at 8. He went on to the Juilliard School, where he studied with Adele Marcus. He also trained as a conductor and operatic coach.

In 1986 Barto made his United States debut with the Boston Symphony conducted by Christoph Eschenbach. Since then he has appeared with such renowned conductors as Maazel, Conlon, Slatkin, and von Karajan, and with the Houston Symphony, National Symphony, Czech Philharmonic, and others. Barto is an exclusive EMI recording artist, and has recently released the Chopin preludes and Schumann's Kreisleriana *and* Symphonic Etudes. *He has also recorded a Liszt recital, the Rachmaninoff Third Concerto, Bartok's Second Concerto, the Ravel G major Concerto, and the Prokofiev Third Concerto.*

Dear Vladimir Horowitz,

Your colors still paint the world, you have given us freedom to risk all and to compromise nothing. Is it not wonderful to hear your sound drumming past time and right into our ears, forcing us to either abandon our own endeavor or jealously try to pursue you. Enjoy, love, adore . . . no sound nor world can compare with the eroticism which you pour upon a hundred musical fields. May you live forever, vase cracked, vase smattered, vase full, it does not matter, for the porcelain is the same. In the meantime, we weave our dreams hoping to entertain the gods as well as you did on your fine night here below.

Orpheus was so jealous when you came to play. In Kiev, swans are dancing.

Jeffrey Swann

A native of Arizona, Jeffrey Swann studied with Alexander Uninsky at Southern Methodist University in Dallas, Texas. Later, at the Juilliard School, he worked with Beveridge Webster. Shortly after, he went on to win the Dino Ciani Competition in Milan, and became a prize winner at the Queen Elisabeth Competition and the Warsaw Chopin Competition.

A prolific recording artist, Swann has recorded for RCA-Italy, Ars Polona, Deutsch-Grammophon, and others. His compact disc on the Music and Arts label, The Virtuoso Liszt, *won the Liszt Society's Grand Prix. Among his recent CDs are the complete Debussy etudes and preludes as well as the complete* Années de pelerinage *by Liszt.*

Even though I consider myself neither stylistically nor pianistically influenced by Horowitz, I nevertheless remain under the spell of this giant. Indeed, for musicians of my generation Horowitz had a mythical, magical quality. For me the most important aspect of the unique power of Horowitz was in his ability to transform a piano recital into an event of unique electric power. In our day we often see concerts that are labeled "events" of great importance: there is in these almost inevitably a sense of artificiality. One has the feeling that the event has been manufactured by the press, a powerful record company, or political forces. A Horowitz concert, on the other hand, was orchestrated only by the artist himself, by his unique ability to understand and communicate with the public. One obvious difference between today's "events" and a Horowitz concert: whereas today only the lay public seems excited (indeed, most musicians have cynically stayed away), for Horowitz it was the musicians themselves who were most agog. The special quality of a Horowitz recital is probably inimitable.

Other great artists of the past had their own quality. A Rubinstein concert was a universal love feast; a Horowitz concert was a magical display of mastery by a mysterious and powerful High Priest of music and the piano.

Another special aspect of Horowitz I personally greatly appreciate was his ability to take a special repertoire and make it entirely his own. Today there is a general tendency for all pianists to play a standard repertoire with a more or less middle-of-the-road point of view. Horowitz would disappear from public view only to return with some new discovery, be it Clementi, Bach-Busoni, some unusual piece of Schumann, or some bit of spectacular virtuosity. In all cases, these pieces would have such an impact on the public that pianists would scurry to their libraries and music stores to find copies and imitate the master. Even if one is not always in agreement with how each piece was played, how each stylistic decision was conceived, one remains reverent before the sheer power of imagination and commitment that was able to give each work—however insignificant in itself—such an indelible personal imprint.

John Perry

John Perry was educated at the Eastman School of Music, where he studied piano with Cecil Genhart. In Europe he worked with Carlo Zecchi. Perry has won numerous awards, including the highest prizes at the Busoni and Viotti competitions. He has performed throughout Europe and North America and has recorded on Telefunken, Musical Heritage Society, and CBC. As a chamber musician he has collaborated with some of the most renowned instrumentalists in the world.

Perry is professor of music at the University of Southern California and visiting artist-faculty member at Houston's Shepard School of Music of Rice University. During the summer he is an artist-faculty member of the Aspen Music Festival. He has held master-classes throughout the world, and sits on the juries of leading international competitions.

I grew up in a small, lovable town in northern Minnesota called Virginia. It was a town of 14,000 people, most of whom seemed to have come from eastern and northern Europe, or were at least first- or second-generation descendants of these musically nourished European families. I had no idea then how lucky I was to grow up in a small town that had a ninety-piece civic symphony orchestra that played monthly, a civic concert band that played several times a week all summer, a high school orchestra, and a high school concert band. Because of this musical environment, Vladimir Horowitz was a very familiar name to me at a very early age. Since I started playing publicly in recitals, musicals, for PTA meetings, and so on, when I was 7, I became somewhat of a curiosity in the town, and I was befriended by townsfolk, many of whom had fine record collections. It is still easy to recall the flush of excitement at first hearing such legendary performances as the Liszt Sixth Hungarian Rhapsody, the B minor Sonata, the Mussorgsky *Pictures at an Exhibition*, the Tchaikovsky Concerto in B-flat minor, with Toscanini, and many others.

Upon leaving home I attended the Eastman School of Music, where I studied with Cecile Genhart. There I was able to avail myself of the superlative collection at the Sibley Library, which gave me access to everything that Horowitz had recorded. During these invaluable years at the music school, when one learns so much, but not as much as one thinks, my previously unconditioned acceptance of all that Horowitz did began to be tempered by serious doubts. The vast knowledge I thought I had acquired did not seem to allow for the "liberties" and "distortions" I perceived in his performances. How could he dare do so many things against the composer's wishes?

The passing years, thirty-five of them since leaving Eastman in 1957, have peeled away layers and layers of assumptions. It is very difficult to distinguish truth from assumption, especially since you don't realize it's an assumption until you also realize that it isn't necessarily true. How can one assume that one knows the composer's intentions? Are all of the composer's intentions visually recognizable in the score? Is the score, therefore, the total sum of the composer's intention, or is it the point from which an artist begins to build his interpretation? Personally, I think many people overestimate the wrath the composer would feel toward an artist "personalizing" his composition. At least, it has been my experience in working with living composers that rather than being offended, they are usually excited by other possibilities concerning the realization of their scores. What seems to be always true, however, is that the composer is consumed by the desire to communicate.

If that is an important criterion, Horowitz is an exemplary case. That he communicated, and communicated strongly, we can all agree. I believe that this ability is the most important aspect of an artist's worth. Horowitz succeeded in doing this with the greatest of consistency, at the highest degree of intensity. One cannot conclusively say one knows whether or not what he did was always right. Fortunately, I no longer need to know whether it was right or not. To be able to indulge in the magic and to be thankful for its existence is quite enough for me.

Robert Taub

The American pianist Robert Taub won the 1981 Peabody Mason Award in Boston. He has performed a wide repertoire in concert and recording and has been guest soloist with the major orchestras. In 1992 he performed the Persichetti Piano Concerto.

Taub often performs twentieth-century piano music, and has frequently recorded and performed in recital the piano music of Milton Babbitt. He has recorded music of Schumann, Beethoven, and Liszt and he has recently recorded for Harmonia Mundi the complete cycle of Scriabins' sonatas.

I have vivid memories of attending my first Horowitz recital as a young boy; a performance at Rutgers University shortly after his 1966 recital in Carnegie Hall. His program included works of Scarlatti, Beethoven, Mozart, Scriabin, and Chopin. I remember an exuberant Horowitz, bowing graciously, carrying his white handkerchief in his left hand. I went backstage afterward, saw him briefly, and left my copy of the concert program with a member of his entourage so that he could autograph it and send it back to me later. He did so, I immediately framed it, and I still have it.

Around this time, even though I was really too young, I began to play two etudes of Scriabin: the hauntingly melancholic C-sharp minor Etude Op. 2, No. 1, and the bold, dashing D-sharp minor Etude Op. 8, No. 12. Was I influenced by Horowitz? Of course I was. He was the only pianist I had heard play these fabulous pieces live, in concert. He had also recorded them. He also played other works of Scriabin at Rutgers which, at first, seemed unusual: the Fifth Sonata, the Ninth Sonata, and the Tenth Sonata.

Soon I discovered another dimension of Horowitz, namely the recordings he had made in London in the 1930s of the Liszt Sonata, the last Haydn sonata, several Chopin etudes, and the Schumann Toccata and *Arabeske*. These performances seemed so fresh, so compelling, and natural. Gradually, as I began to form my own musical conscience, I realized that Horowitz, the sum total of Horowitz, was really more than just a fabulist pianist—more than the layers of mannerisms, more than the eccentricities. There was a great deal of adventurous spirit. Why else would he have dared to play, for example, so many works of Scriabin at a time when almost no one else did so? I found this adventurous spirit to be the single most influential aspect of Horowitz as an artist.

Boaz Sharon

The Israeli pianist Boaz Sharon studied in Tel Aviv. He won several first prizes in piano competitions, and has given recitals throughout Israel, England, and the United States. Sharon has earned special recognition for his performance of French music, making recordings of piano music by Koechlin and Debussy. Throughout his career he has championed the cause of neglected composers.

Sharon has given master-classes at the Rubin Academy in Jerusalem, in Sao Paulo, and in Ecuador. He is on the board of the American Liszt Society, and has given lecture-recitals at the Juilliard School and at Stanford, Cambridge, and Oxford. He is professor of piano at the University of Florida.

Everyone studying the piano comes across the name of Horowitz sooner or later. I was eleven years old and studying piano in Tel Aviv, Israel, when I first encountered the name Horowitz. The episode left a lasting impression on me. The year was 1960 and I was just assigned Chopin's Scherzo No. 1 in B minor by my teacher, Emma Gorochov. Madame Gorochov was an Odessa Conservatory–trained musician who later pursued her piano studies with Alfred Cortot in Paris. She was an intimidating and strict disciplinarian whose piano lessons were models in emotional crisis. Madame Gorochov often claimed that her piano students, particularly me, left her no choice but to take tranquilizers, and often she would interrupt her lessons to do so. She was also someone who reputedly did not hesitate to interrupt a piano concert given by her students if she was dissatisfied by the playing, audience or no audience. Now I know that she was also one of the best piano teachers for the formative years I know.

As I was laboriously studying the B minor Scherzo using Cortot's suggested technical exercises, Madame Gorochov suggested that I listen to Horowitz's early recording of that piece. At that time life in Tel Aviv was a lot simpler than it is now; people lived rather modestly and not many possessed a record player or records. One day she announced that the great moment had arrived. She had a friend who possessed both a turntable (an old beaten up Garrard, as it turned out (*and* a record of the Scherzo. Both prized possessions were located in a modest Tel Aviv apartment, and the guardian turned out to be, if memory serves correctly, a little old man who seemed to have turntable, record, and little else. The record was played once and then twice in an atmosphere of hushed silence. I could see increasing consternation forming on Madame Gorochov's face. Finally she spoke. "I am afraid it wasn't such a good idea to bring you here after all. Horowitz plays this piece much too fast. This might be a bad influence on you."

Months later I played the scherzo as part of a student concert in a packed house in Tel Aviv. As I played I kept glancing nervously toward the aisles, anticipating Madame Gorochov's imminent and dramatic interruption. But somehow I was allowed to finish the work. "Too fast," Madame Gorochov said afterward. "I knew that Horowitz's recording would lead you to this. "Too fast," she said again shaking her head sadly. I still play the B minor Scherzo from time to time, and I still think it is too fast.

Besides this little vignette, I have to add: Whenever I think that a piano composition has been exhausted technically and musically, that the phrases in that work have been played beautifully by a number of performers, and that nothing new of value or beauty can be discovered in that work, then comes Horowitz to prove me wrong.

Tamás Vásáry

Tamás Vásásry was born in Hungary and gave his first concert at the age of eight. Among his teachers was Dohnányi, and after his graduation from Budapest's Franz Liszt Academy he became assistant professor there to Kodaly. In 1956 he left Hungary, making his London and New York debuts in 1961. Since then Vásáry has played on the concert stages of most of the major music centers. His dozens of recordings have received critical acclaim.

In the last decade Tamás Vásáry has added conducting to his schedule, and he is frequently on the podium directing symphonic concerts as well as opera. He often directs from the keyboard in concerto performances. In 1991 he recorded a Liszt disc with the London Symphony Orchestra that included the newly discovered De profundis *for piano and orchestra. Recently he has been appointed principal conductor and artistic director of the Bournemouth Sinfonietta.*

In my youth, Wilhelm Backhaus and Vladimir Horowitz were my idols in the kingdom of piano technique. It was Annie Fischer who evoked for me the poetry of music. As with so many aspiring pianists, I was obsessed by the fascination of piano technique in its most physical sense. I was interested in breakneck speeds, volume of sound, technical fluency, and accuracy. I was held spellbound by these attributes. I felt, at the time, that the essence of musical poetry and artistic expression appeared instinctive and natural as the soul itself. As with the soul, I did not feel the need to be concerned, confident that once the technique was there, the soul would speak for itself. Few novice pianists avoid this illusion, only to learn much later how mistaken they have been.

During the time I was struggling to acquire mastery over my instrument, my hero was the unattainable star against whom all others were measured. That was, of course, Franz Liszt, whose playing lived in my imagination as if I had heard him in the flesh. I was age eleven studying at the Franz Liszt Academy in Budapest. My teacher, Lajos Hernádi, set before me the conscious examples of the virtuosity of Horowitz and Backhaus. He said, "Listen to the Chopin Etudes Op. 10 played by Backhaus. He plays them faster than anyone alive, but Horowitz makes each note shine."

When Horowitz played the Tchaikovsky Concerto in Budapest, the orchestra led to the notorious double octaves of the first movement at breathtaking speed. We wondered, How will the soloist match that? But Horowitz merely added an even greater speed. I heard this famous performance on the radio, and it was, for me, a peak pianistic achievement. Horowitz came to my imagination as a square, tall, dark man with powerful hands and a piano that was not wood but carved in stone.

Hernádi said, "learn the Sixth Hungarian Rhapsody of Liszt." Naturally I turned to Horowitz's performance for guidance. I was riveted by the tensions he created in that piece. At first, Horowitz toys with the famous staccato octaves, giving just a teasing glimpse of the tension and force that follows with each repetition—the full power still not unleashed, although one hardly knows where that power will come from. But that was one of Horowitz's secret powers: somehow, somewhere, there would always be more.

There were so many Horowitz performances that one can speak of. The mischievous grin of some dark demon in a bottomless pit is conjured up in his Rachmaninoff G minor Prelude. The Pagnini-Liszt E-flat major Caprice's scales roll out as silver pearls. In 1955, after wining a prize at the Marguerite Long Competition, I spent some of the money on my first long-playing records. Among them were Horowitz's recordings of the Schubert B-flat major Sonata, which sounds engraved in noble metal, and the Brahmns B-flat major Concerto, played with the purity of a fine silver blade.

The Horowitz recording that was the most special to me was the Liszt Sonata in B minor. He brought out all the mephistophelean power of the piece. Was this perhaps how Liszt himself played it? Maybe not, for Liszt's compositions suggest a mastery of moods, feelings, and colors above and beyond the materiality of the keyboard itself, whereas with Horowitz matter is central, and the main element of his music making, the piano itself, is always center stage. In every note, I felt an electrifying pulsation. Behind it all was the artist's aristocratic profile, his spine taut and controlled—his mind in powerful concentration. My auditive imagination no longer betrayed me, and the meticulously elegant, perfectly groomed bow-tied silhouette and sharp profile now fitted perfectly my vision of the artist behind the playing.

By the time I reached the West in 1956, I was groping toward my own artistic expression. I had given up teachers and masters, allowing myself to just listen to fellow artists, letting their individuality enrich me. I became acquainted with Marguerite Long's school in Paris, the school of Nikita Magalov in Geneva, I met my old idol Wilhelm Backhaus and the ethereal, poetic Clara Haskil, among many others. In 1961 I was to meet Horowitz himself.

Just before my Carnegie Hall debut, Fritz Steinway took me to Horowitz for an evening. Instead of an electrified homunculus, we were greeted by a genial, friendly, smiling host in an elegant dressing gown and the usual bow tie. Following introductory niceties, we talked about my Hungarian origins. Horowitz recounted that the greatest of all his success had been in Budapest, where the public kept applauding right through the intervals, forcing him to resume the second half with no break between the bows. It was said that when he first played in Budapest, only half a house greeted the yet unknown Russian virtuoso. But by the time the concert ended, he had a full house! Members of the audience kept calling friends to run over to the hall, telling them of the sensation going on.

Horowitz told me he originally wanted to be a composer, but realized he could only hope to become a Greenwich Village composer and decided to become a professional pianist instead. Fishing out a photo of himself at age twenty, in which he looked a little like Chopin, he said, "See, I still had lots of hair. I identified myself more with Liszt than with Chopin. That is why I wear this medallion with his picture," showing me a pendant. I mentioned to him my admiration for his records, and he put on a few of his records for us to listen to, the Saint-Saëns *Danse macabre*, which he thought was his best, some Clementi, and his own transcription of *Stars and Stripes Forever*.

His wife, Wanda, came in at one point and sat in a corner knitting. Horowitz asked me to play something for him, to which I complied reluctantly. I played a Bach prelude and fugue and a Beethoven sonata, but he steered me in a different direction. "Now play something pianistic." So I moved on to Liszt's *Saint Francis Legend*, which he found too slow for his taste, but my *Rigoletto* Paraphrase won his approval. On my "Winter Wind" Etude he commented, "Ashkenazy plays too little left hand and you play too much."

My Carnegie Hall debut contained but two works, the "Hammerklavier" sonata and the "Goldberg" Variations. These, too, were not pianistic for him.

Finally he went to the piano and started practicing. "I like to play scales and finger exercises like these which are musical, so that it never sounds like dry technique." He continued improvising and modulating, working in all sorts of arpeggios, double thirds, double sixths, and so on, creating an etude sounding vaguely like Rachmaninoff in style. Here was the idol of my youth sitting so near I could touch his elbow. His hands were beautiful, like a pair of purebred stallions. The fingers were long, slender, yet athletic, his fingertips slightly curving upward with exceptionally fine muscles such as I have never seen. This was my only time with Horowitz, but I shall never forget it.

During the last years of his life, Horowitz's humanity came through his playing more than ever. There was now a feeling of immateriality. He had reached toward the simplicity of Scarlatti and Mozart, whom he had touched little before. He had once said, "Mozart does not let the left hand work enough." In his last years, his complete supremacy over matter is still there, but the man in him comes forward, one who no longer played for the world. I saw his Moscow recital. It was as if he was playing in a magic circle all alone, playing only for himself.

Joseph Kalichstein

Born in Tel Aviv, Joseph Kalichstein studied in Israel before coming to New York's Juilliard School, where he worked with Edward Steuermann and Ilona Kabos. Early in his career he won the Young Artists Auditions. At the invitation of Leonard Bernstein he appeared in a nationally televised concert of Beethoven's Fourth Piano Concerto, and in 1969 he was the winner of the Leventritt International Competition.

Kalichstein has appeared with all the world's major orchestras. As a member of the well-known Kalichstein-Laredo-Robinson Trio, he appears in chamber concerts in all the major halls and music festivals. The trio has recorded extensively. Kalichstein has also recorded many solo albums, and his Schubert and Schumann albums are available on the Audiofon label.

The phenomenon called "Horowitz," incredible as it was, had yet an extra dimension for my generation of pianists: after all, here was a legend, one of the last survivors from that short list of piano immortals, a man we all knew from his classic recordings, a wizard of color and sonority, Superwrists himself, who all of a sudden came back to life and was going to play concerts right in our midst, like Zeus coming down from Mount Olympus, performing miracles on Fifty-Seventh Street. It was a remarkable confrontation between past and present, the past overtaking the present, challenging it, and yet trying to fit in. It inspired both awe and doubt.

In my case, the awe turned to fear; I had the great fortune of being offered an audition with Horowitz when he was considering joining the Juilliard faculty. My first reaction, that of pride and elation, turned quickly to panic. I could live with his rejection. But what if he liked me? Could I coexist with a legend—would he so overpower me that I wouldn't learn anything from him—and risk losing the little

I knew in the bargain? After much sleeplessness, I decided not to audition; I could not believe my own audacity!

Then, of course, he decided not to teach after all.

The doubt I remember feeling had to do with the unknown: how can any mortal match those earlier feats? Maybe he wasn't that great after all, and who wanted to find *that* out? I was extraordinarily nervous, for him and for us.

Needless to say, the awe grew, the doubt disappeared with the first concert. The mighty control; the haunting touch; the endless variety of color; the incredible chords, sonorities, and the equally incredible ability to voice and to have a melodic line pierce through, Heifetz-like, without ever banging or forcing the piano—it was *all* there, for us to marvel at for many years to come.

Tedd Joselson

Tedd Joselson was born in Belgium. At the Juilliard School he studied with Adele Marcus and had frequent coaching from Rudolf Serkin and Sir Clifford Curzon, as well as having a long association with Horowitz. He made his debut at the age of sixteen in 1967, at a recital in Kansas City. In 1992, at Munich's Herkulesaal, he gave the two thousandth concert of his career.

Joselson has made recordings of the Ravel, Prokofiev, and Tchaikovsky concertos with Ormandy and Mehta, Mozart concertos with the Norwegian Chamber Orchestra, and the Barber Concerto with the London Symphony. Between 1988 and 1991 he gave complete cycles in Europe of all the Mozart concertos. He has given the American and European premieres of Julian Orbon's Fourth Partite for Piano and Orchestra, which he, together with the Dallas Symphony, commissioned. It was recorded on the Olympia label with Falla's Nights in the Gardens of Spain. *From 1986 to 1988, Tedd Joselson held the chair in piano at Southern Methodist University in Dallas.*

"Green," Horowitz said—and I am still wondering: Was it my green shirt, the green cover of the Mozart score in the control room, or the green light in the studio? I never thought to ask. Why is it still on my mind?

During the mid-seventies, I played the Eighth, Ninth, and Tenth sonatas of Scriabin on my recitals at different times. Of course, Scriabin was closely identified with Horowitz, with whom I had become friends. One day during my recording session, Mr. Horowitz quietly came in. As we were listening to a playback, Horowitz went over to the piano (which Rachmaninoff had used for recording) and played an individualistic account of Scriabin's Tenth Sonata. The producer delayed our session, and Mr. Horowitz and I worked together on some complicated inner harmonic voicings. He talked of freedom, the control of the fingers, and the necessary spiritual abandon that such music needed.

I felt Horowitz to be rather shy and modest, even. In fact, he seemed to question his won staggering abilities. I heard him often admit that he was not able to do something or other at the keyboard. However, contrary to what has been a general misunderstanding, he did not need constant approval but, instead, sought honest, unbiased ears which might clarify and intensify his own interpretive views of the music.

I remember one night we were going through the Prokofiev Eighth Sonata. We could not determine the right feel for the opening of the third movement. He said, "Mozart's music can sound good at nearly any speed. But in most other music, tempo must be very exact. It has to be right." So on and on we experimented with the Prokofiev. At first, he was happier with his approach than mine, then we switched roles. Finally, he was still happier with his.

Horowitz was the great colorist of the piano. He heard music in colors. Which colors they were, only he knew. They were part of an inner vision of music. We are told that Scriabin also heard vivid colors, each key and chord being a different color. Perhaps on that day when Horowitz came into the recording studio and took over my Scriabin sonata, maybe that's what Mr. Horowitz meant when he said, "Green"—or was it? I will never know.

Shura Cherkassky

Shura Cherkassky was born in Odessa. In 1923 his family immigrated to America, where the child prodigy appeared at the White House for President Harding. He studied with Josef Hofmann, and in 1928 toured Australia and New Zealand, followed by three years of performances throughout Europe. In 1931 he returned to America and for the next six decades has continued a worldwide career.

The 1991–92 season presented birthday celebrations in Rome, Berlin, Tokyo, London, Geneva, Paris, and Amsterdam, and his eightieth birthday recital at Carnegie Hall was recorded. The Nimbus label issued an eight-CD birthday tribute. In 1986 New York's 92nd Street Y established the Shura Cherkassky Recital Award. In June 1988 he was one of twenty-five Steinway Artists invited to participate in the historic Carnegie Hall concert and telecast celebrating the one hundred thirty-fifth anniversary of Steinway & Sons. Last season, he toured the Far East and India, as well as performing once again in Russia.

It was in 1928 that I first heard Vladimir Horowitz. I was a teenager and I went with my mother, a pianist and teacher. The opening piece was the *Pastourelle* of Scarlatti-Tausig. From the very first note, a B, I was at once hypnotized. I repeat, *at once*. I cannot explain that feeling, but I have never forgotten that moment. I was glued to my seat. I had never had that feeling with anyone, and it has stayed with me throughout my life.

At the time I barely knew who Horowitz was; he was a newcomer on the American scene, and I went to hear him because his debut in the Tchaikovsky Concerto caused a sensation that was the talk of the town. If I thought the first group of his recital was extraordinary, I was soon to be even more astonished during his performance of Liszt's B minor Sonata. My mother and I looked at each other dazed.

I cannot exaggerate what Horowitz meant to me. He became my idol, a symbol in my life. Some people said to me during those years that I had Horowitz on the brain, and it was true. He was a standard. He was a personal revelation. From the first instant, I had understood that he was a phenomenon, and I was happy that such a pianist existed. I could not discuss or analyze why Horowitz was a titan. I am a purely instinctive person in everything, especially in music. My feeling about Horowitz was that he had been born of the gods. Nor were these feelings influenced by anyone.

I had just started studying with the great Josef Hofmann, and my adoration for Horowitz was not blind, as Hofmann was certainly one of the great virtuosi of all time. Hofmann at the period didn't know Horowitz's playing and said nothing to me about him. If Hofmann spoke about any pianist, it was Rachmaninoff.

I shall never forget the first time I heard Horowitz, in the Rachmaninoff Third. I believe it was 1930, on New Year's Eve at Carnegie Hall. As I was listening, I actually thought I was going to faint. I had to take a long walk afterward to clear my head; I was absolutely crazy. It was *his* concerto. He owned it. Horowitz loved Rachmaninoff, the man and the pianist. I remember he was inconsolable when Rachmaninoff was dying in California. He and Wanda were at the hospital often. Rachmaninoff passed away in 1943.

In 1986 I played the Rachmaninoff Third Concerto in London, at the Royal Festival Hall. After the concert, I was told Horowitz was there. Thank goodness I didn't know he was coming. Imagine playing the Rachmaninoff Third before Horowitz. I would have been embarrassed. Fortunately, I played it very well that evening, but nobody ever reached the heights Horowitz did in that concerto. Nobody had such terrific technique. Many people speak of Horowitz's sound in the bass, but I found his sound in the high registers unique. At the end of the cadenza of the Rachmaninoff Third, the treble is fantastic.

Once I did hear a performance that nearly reached the Horowitz pinnacle,; it was by Martha Argerich, who simply adores Horowitz. Several times she tried to play for him, but somehow it never happened. And it is terrible that she did not meet him. She was terribly unhappy that she never got to know him.

I first met Horowitz backstage at Carnegie Hall, a couple of seasons after his New York debut, and later in California. Naturally I heard him as often as possible, in the United Sates as well as in Paris and Berlin. It was in Berlin that he was playing the Chopin Barcarolle, and in the middle of the work a string broke. I think it was fixed, but I remember him asking the audience in German if he should start the Barcarolle again. They screamed and applauded, "Ja, Ja,"—and he began again. This may have been in 1933.

Horowitz told me when he had played in Hamburg, he received a tremendous ovation. After the recital, he walked outside and saw crowds of people. Horowitz asked, "Are all these people waiting for me?" He was told, "No, they are waiting for Hitler, who just made a speech in the next building."

I remember, I think it was in 1936, an interesting incident occurred. I played for Horowitz a Chopin ballade. He said, "It is very good, but I don't think you are entirely free in your playing. There seems to be someone standing over your shoulder. Perhaps it is your mother." He then said, "Maybe you should go to a psychologist. It may help you to be freer." He even gave me a phone number of somebody to see. I felt I didn't want to go, and, somehow, I never did. But I thought about it. Many people give advice, but I took this more seriously. After all, it was Horowitz who suggested it.

The last time I saw him was at his home. He was 82, and was interested that Arrau and Serkin were still going strong, and said he too wanted to keep playing. He said, "But these days, I don't play anything too virtuosic, the most difficult thing I play is Chopin's B minor Scherzo." I heard him do this work in London soon after. There were many false notes and he missed some skips, but it hardly mattered. The essence was Horowitz.

He was always highly conscious of the repertoire he was playing. I remember at the time I was gong to play the Pabst Paraphrase on Tchaikovsky's *Eugene Onegin*. Horowitz told me it was a bad piece. Perhaps so, but I like it, and have continued to play it. I was also at the moment playing the Chopin Variations Op. 2, a very elegant work but by no means the greater Chopin. I had heard it ages ago played by Robert Goldsand. I played a few of the variations for Horowitz. He told me to be even more rhythmic in the final variation. He was right.

Horowitz was modest. Once I said to him, "You know, you are certainly the world's greatest pianist." He waved his hand and muttered, "No, no. Don't say such things."

I have often been asked who was the greater artist, Horowitz or Hofmann. As a youngster, I used to imitate Hofmann a great deal. I still listen to Hofmann's few records in awe. He was possibly a greater musical mind. However, I think Horowitz was a greater virtuoso, a greater pianist. He somehow appealed to the whole world. Hofmann could not communicate on that level.

Horowitz's Liszt playing alone was incomprehensible. One cannot estimate the playing of the Sonata, *Funérailles*, the rhapsodies, the virtuoso works like the *Danse macabre* or the *Carmen* Variations. Then there is his Scarlatti, and his Schumann is beyond words. I am thinking of his sound in Schumann, the inner longing. In so many works, nobody has reached Horowitz's level, and most likely no one ever will.

Index of Contributors

General Index

Page numbers in bold type reference essays by contributors to this book.